MEDINA

BY THE BAY

MEDINA

BY THE BAY

Scenes *of* Muslim Study
and Survival

MARYAM KASHANI

DUKE UNIVERSITY PRESS *Durham and London* 2023

© 2023 DUKE UNIVERSITY PRESS
All rights reserved
Printed in the United States of America on acid-free paper ∞
Project Editor: Bird Williams
Designed by Matthew Tauch
Typeset in Garamond Premier Pro by Westchester
Publishing Services

Library of Congress Cataloging-in-Publication Data
Names: Kashani, Maryam, [date] author.
Title: Medina by the bay : scenes of Muslim study and
survival / Maryam Kashani.
Description: Durham : Duke University Press, 2023. |
Includes bibliographical references and index.
Identifiers: LCCN 2023011534 (print)
LCCN 2023011535 (ebook)
ISBN 9781478025177 (paperback)
ISBN 9781478020219 (hardcover)
ISBN 9781478027232 (ebook)
Subjects: LCSH: Muslims—California—San Francisco Bay Area. |
Muslims—California—San Francisco Bay Area—Social conditions. |
Cultural pluralism—California—San Francisco Bay Area. |
Minorities—California—San Francisco Bay Area. | Intercultural
communication—California—San Francisco Bay Area. | Community
life—California—San Francisco Bay Area. | San Francisco Bay Area
(Calif.)—Ethnic relations.
Classification: LCC F870. M88 K374 2023 (print)
LCC F870. M88 (ebook)
DDC 305.6/97097946—dc23/eng/20230403
LC record available at https://lccn.loc.gov/2023011534
LC ebook record available at https://lccn.loc.gov/2023011535

Cover art: Kameelah Janan Rasheed,
composition from video stills. Courtesy of the artist.

Publication of this book is supported by Duke University Press's
Scholars of Color First Book Award.

To all the seekers

and

Hajjah Dhameera Ahmad (1950–2017)

For the truths are obscure, the ends hidden, the doubts manifold, the minds turbid, the reasonings various; the premises are gleaned from the senses, and the senses (which are our tools) are not immune from error. The path of investigation is therefore obliterated and the inquirer, however diligent, is not infallible. Consequently, when inquiry concerns subtle matters, perplexity grows, views diverge, opinions vary, conclusions differ and certainty becomes difficult to obtain.

ABU ʿALI AL-HASAN IBN AL-HASAN IBN AL-HAYTHAM
(d. 1040), *The Optics of Ibn Al-Haytham*

In my writing and filmmaking, it has always been important for me to carry out critical work in such a way that there is room for people to reflect on their own struggle and to use the tools offered so as to further it on their own terms. Such a work is radically incapable of prescription. Hence, these tools are sometimes also appropriated and turned against the very filmmaker or writer, which is a risk I am willing to take. I have, indeed, put myself in a situation where I cannot criticize without taking away the secure ground on which I stand.

TRINH T. MINH-HA, "'Speaking Nearby': A Conversation with Trinh T. Minh-ha" Nancy N. Chen and Trinh T. Minh-Ha

CONTENTS

A NOTE ON
TRANSCRIPTION,
TRANSLATION, AND
BLESSINGS

I use a modified version of the transcription system outlined in the *International Journal of Middle Eastern Studies* (IJMES) for transcribing words and phrases from the Arabic language into English. For ease of reading, I have omitted the use of diacritical marks, with the exception of the Arabic letters 'ayn (') and hamza ('). Most translations from Arabic to English are mine with references made to Hans Wehr's *A Dictionary of Modern Written Arabic*, Edward William Lane and Stanley Lane-Poole's *An Arabic-English Lexicon*, and other cited texts. For Qur'anic translations, I predominantly referred to Abdullah Yusuf Ali's *The Meaning of the Holy Qur'an*, Sahih International (www.tanzil.net), Muhammad Asad's *Message of the Qur'an*, and Marmaduke William Pickthall's *The Meaning of the Glorious Qur'an*, relying upon a particular translation in each instance, but substituting another translation or phrasing as necessary.

In quoted text, I convey the spoken transliteration and the live translation from English to Arabic of my interlocutors as this translation is what is heard by their audiences or students. I italicize the first time (and sometimes the second if it has been awhile) that an Arabic word or phrase makes an appearance in the text. I discontinue italicization to convey how it operates with/as English as part of a global Muslim lexicon. Similarly, for proper names and Islamic concepts and phrases commonly used with/as English, I often use spellings that are common in the English language, rather than following the IJMES system (e.g., "El-Hajj Malik El-Shabazz" instead of "al-Hajj Malik al-Shabazz," "Kameelah" instead of "Kamila," "deen" instead of "din," or "Alhamdulillah" instead of "al-hamdu li-llah").

In Medina by the Bay as elsewhere, many Muslims follow the mention of the Prophet Muhammad with *salla Allahu ʿalayhi wa-sallam,* "blessings of God be upon him and grant him peace." I do not include the greeting in the text (unless it is spoken in a direct quote), but feel free to take a breath and extend this blessing with every reference to him, as some Muslims do. One may also extend these blessings to his family, *salla Allahu ʿalayhi wa-alihi wa-sallam. Radi Allahu ʿanhum,* "may Allah be pleased with them," as this blessing is similarly uttered after mention of the *Sahaba* (Companions of the Prophet) and other prophets, and appropriate conjugations are used for an individual man (*ʿanhu*), woman (*ʿanha*), two people (*ʿanhuma*), or a group of women (*ʿanhunna*). Similarly, one may say "may Allah have mercy on her/him/them" for ancestors. Such verbal expressions and gestures invoke an ethical and embodied crafting of Muslim consciousness, pace, and discipline toward cosmic recognition and spiritual genealogies. Respect.

ACKNOWLEDGMENTS

Bismillah al-Rahman al-Rahim. In the name of Allah, the Most Gracious, the Most Merciful. Poet and Zaytuna College graduate Rasheeda Plenty writes in her poem "Book" about the seeds of knowledge that are planted and cultivated within us, how we become "bewildered when a soft rain begins to fall inside of us . . . we stand gazing at our chests to see what will come from our bodies/this strange planting, here." As I write these acknowledgments in the midst of a decades-long inquiry into questions of knowledge, I find it impossible to account for all the "strange plantings" that contributed in one way or another to "the ink and bark with all the green pressed out" of this book. And yet. . . .

I first express eternal gratitude to and seek forgiveness and mercy from Allah, the all-knowing. I am also grateful to and seek grace and forgiveness from the ancestors and the students (and their families), scholars, and staff, past, present, and future of Zaytuna College and the Muslim communities of the San Francisco Bay Area. Your generosity and patience have been a great gift and lesson. Most of you are not named directly in this book, but you know who you are, jazakum Allah khayran. I thank the Zaytuna founders Shaykh Hamza Yusuf, Imam Zaid Shakir, and Dr. Hatem Bazian and its board of trustees, Advisory Committee, Academic Affairs Committee, and the Executive team and staff who approved and enabled my initial research, especially Farid Senzai. Teachers, imams, shaykhs, and shaykhas Souhad Zendah, Dawood Yasin, Abdulkarim Yahya, Adnan (Adrian) Wood-Smith, Khalid Waajid, Muhammad Shareef, Saliha Shakir, Rasheed Shabazz, Rania Shah, Athar Siddiqee, Irfan Rydhan, Yahya Rhodus, Sundiata Rashid, Aïdah Aliyah Rasheed, Ebadur Rahman, Khadijah O'Connell, Rami Nsour, Randy Nasson, Abdul Rauf Nasir, Yusuf Mullick, Feraidoon Mojadedi, Aaminah Norris, Amir Abdel Malik, Mahan Mirza, Radia and Shakir Massoud, Shirin Maskatia, Ali Malik, Mariam Lovejoy, Rusha Latif, Ayesha

Khan, Colleen Keyes, Munir Jiwa, Amina Jandali, Sulaiman Hyatt, Ali Hassan, Liliana Hanson, Abdul Latif Finch, Zain Elmarouk, Rania Awad, Tahir Anwar, Bilal Ansari, Abdullah bin Hamid Ali, Sumaya Albgal, Hisham Al-Alusi, Sumaira Akhtar, Mohammad Abdurrazzaq, and Siddique Abdullah taught me much in the most explicit and subtle of ways. Ustadh Haroon Sellars (the force is strong with this one and his family) consistently served as a reminder and teacher in this seeking and wayfaring along the Prophetic path; the best parts of my writing and films are due to his and others' guidance. Jazakum Allah khayran. The failings are my nafs and other whispers.

May Allah have mercy on and be pleased with Hajjah Dhameera Ahmad to whom this book is dedicated; I flourished in the gardens she planted and continue to learn from her today. Thank you to Brothers and Sisters Saadat, Nisa, Azizah, Yusuf, Ismail, Timothy, and the rest of the Ahmad and Simon families for being her joy and light and for the innumerable sacrifices. I pray that this text honors her legacy.

This research was significantly supported at critical moments by the Spencer Foundation and the National Academy of Education Dissertation and Postdoctoral Fellowships. Additional material support was provided by the California Council for the Humanities—California Documentary Project and the Austin Film Society; the Humanities Research Institute, Unit of Criticism and Interpretive Theory, and Campus Research Board at the University of Illinois at Urbana-Champaign; the PEO Foundation Scholar Award; the College of Liberal Arts, the Graduate School, the Department of Anthropology, the Center for Middle East Studies, and the Center for Asian American Studies at the University of Texas at Austin. I thank everyone at the John C. Danforth Center on Religion and Politics at Washington University in Saint Louis (especially Marie, Leigh, Laurie, Rachel, Debra, and Sheri) where I landed during the Ferguson uprisings. Co-teaching and thinking with Lerone Martin, the ancestors—Malcolm, Martin, and James—and our students continues to inform how I approach the work we do in the classrooms and on the streets; Ronit Stahl was the most brilliant of co-fellows and companions.

In the early stages of this work, Kamala Visweswaran, Sofian Merabet, Craig Campbell, Hina Azam, Charles Hirschkind, and Lok Siu were great champions, mentors, and interlocutors, as were Kamran Ali, James Brow, Kristen Brustad, and Mahmoud al-Batal (and all my Arabic teachers from Los Angeles and Austin to Beirut, Cairo, and Damascus, and most especially my beloved Skeiker family), Tarek El-Ariss, Maria Franklin, Kaushik Ghosh, Ted Gordon, S. Akbar Hyder, Denise Spellberg, Katie Stewart, Eric Tang, and everyone at the UT Center for Asian American Studies. I especially want to acknowledge Sofian, who lifted me up and nudged me forward, and Kamala, who took a chance on a struggling filmmaker, reminding me that I "think visually." I hope that I honor the intellectual genealogy and ethical-political praxis she has bestowed upon me as I further the transmission.

While at UT Anthro, I was blessed to be among faculty and student co-horts of African diaspora, activist, and borderlands anthropology who pro-duced scholarship as part of decolonizing, Third World, and Black feminist traditions and politics. May we carry and plant those seeds wherever we go. Thank you to my companions in Austin and beyond, Can Aciksoz, Mohan Ambikaipaker, Alix Chapman, Claudia Chávez Argüelles, Chris Cuellar, Pablo Gonzalez, Sam Gosling, Juli Grigsby, Zeina Halabi, Abdul Haqq, Celeste Hardy, Sarah Ihmoud, Hafeez Jamali, Mathangi Krishnamurthy, Nedra Lee, Elizabeth Lewis, Chris Loperena, Emily Lynch, Ken MacLeish and Rachel Pomerantz, Courtney Morris, Siyar Ozsoy, Mubbashir Rizvi and Alia Khan, Saikat Mitra, Solange Munoz, Alisa Perkins, Indulata Prasad, Ed Radtke, Luciane Rocha, Deana Saukam, Ruken Sengul, Leyla Shams, Bjørn Sletto, Raja Swamy, Elizabeth Velazquez Estrada, Halide Velioglu, Tane Ward, Chelsi West Ohueri, Mark Westmoreland, Ahmed Yusuf, and so many others who provided dancing, dining, and deep conversations.

Thank you to Amu Nasser, Seemi Chaudry, Amina Waheed, Petrina Chi, Dharini Rasiah, and the Zaytuna ladies for providing places to lay my head. Sara Ludin and Farah El-Sharif, I cannot express how blessed I feel to have benefited from your intellectual and spiritual companionship especially so early in the process. I have been blessed that so many more cared to usher this work into existence or to usher me personally through it, from the Bay to Chicago. Su'ad Abdul Khabeer, Tahir Abdullah, Kalia Abiade, Sabahat Adil, Arshad Ali, Bita Amani, Abdurrahman Benavidez, Louise Cainker, Sohail Daulatzai, Alireza Doostdar, Hannah El-Amin, Ubaydullah Evans, Ronak Kapadia, Sadaf Khan, Darryl Li, Damon Locks, Nura Maznavi, Elham Mireshgi, Nermeen Mouftah, Hadiyah Muhammad, Nadine Naber, Atef Said, Saadia Shah, Shalini Shankar, Lan Tuazon, Shirin Vossoughi, Walter, and Azadeh, Jessica Winegar, and Emrah Yildiz provided love and laughter. Rabab Abdulhadi, Maytha Alhassen, Kecia Ali, Zaheer Ali, Evelyn Alsultany, Donna Auston, Joanne Barker, Roger Begrich, Aisha Beliso-De Jesús, Sylvia Chan-Malik, Anila Daulatzai, Garrett Felber, Zareena Grewal, Sarah Gualtieri, Keith Feldman, Jenny Kelly, Marisol LeBrón, Shabana Mir, Jawad Qureishi, Mariam Sheibani, Musa Syed, and Pauline Vinson, aided in critical ways at critical points. Russell Rickford, the Brothers Johnson

Khalil and W. Chris (twin), Samiha Rahman, and by worthy extension, Rasul Miller were Spencer's greatest gifts. Ruthie Gilmore, Trinh T. Minh-ha, and Vijay Prashad graciously offered questions, answers, and models for continuing with this difficult and destabilizing work.

Gender and women's studies and Asian American studies at the University of Illinois at Urbana-Champaign have been exceptional spaces of collegiality, mentorship, and safe harbor in the larger oceans of academia. I especially thank my former and current chairs and mentors, Siobhan Somerville, Mimi Nguyen, Martin Manalansan, Soo Ah Kwon, Samantha Frost, Augusto Espiritu; our amazing administrative gurus, Christine Lyke, Virginia Swisher, Felix Fuenty, Tasha Robles, and Jacque Kahn; undergraduate assistant Julia Son; and my current and former colleagues Teresa Barnes, Toby Beauchamp, Ruth Nicole Brown, Antoinette Burton, Jody Byrd, CL Cole, Karen Flynn, Behrooz Ghamari-Tabrizi, Cindy Ingold, Mahruq Khan, Susan Koshy, Natalie Lira, Vicki Mahaffey, Ghassan Moussawi, Chantal Nadeau, Fiona Ngo, Naomi Paik, Yoon Kyung Pak, Amy Powell, Ricky Rodriguez, Sandra Ruiz, Lila Sharif, Blair Ebony Smith, Krystal Strong (for all the things), Emma Velez (Lugones!), and Damian Vergara Bracamontes. Additional thanks to Umrao, Brett, Alison, and Natalie and my NCFDD crew for being a consistent grounding. And major gratitude to John Jackson Jr. and Lara Deeb for ongoing guidance, support, travel, and pushing me to commit.

My research benefited greatly from workshops and presentations at UC Berkeley's Anthropology as Transgression and Translation Working Group (thank you Sultan!); the Islam In/Of America Workshop and Sensory Cultures Working Group at Yale University; the Department of Anthropology at the University of Zurich, Switzerland; the Migrations of Islam Symposium at Michigan State University; the Islamic Studies Workshop and the MSA at the University of Chicago; Shifting Borders: American and the Middle East/North Africa at the American University of Beirut; Leiden University Centre for the Study of Islam and Society; Department of the History of Art, UC Riverside; Washington University in Saint Louis; Harvard University; Northwestern University; American Islamic College, West Chester University; and everyone I benefited from at multiple Screening Scholarship Media Festivals at the University of Pennsylvania (especially Deborah Thomas, Mariam Durrani, Arjun Shankar, E. Gabriel Dattatreyan, Tali Ziv, Jo Siegel, and Harjant Gill). Thank you to Salah Brown for facilitating my video installation, *When They Give Their Word, Their Word Is Bond*, at Siete Potencias Africanas and to the entire Ethnographic Terminalia team for your ongoing vision and labor in expanding the possibilities of ethnographic theory and practice.

Ken Wissoker guided me through a crossroads of where this book and I could and would go. Thank you for the long commitment, conversation, and guidance. Thank you to the Duke crew, Ryan Kendall, Chad Royal, Bird Williams, Matthew Tauch, and others for the careful ushering of this strange planting. So much gratitude for my research assistants, Hana Jaber, Muna Jaber, and Noor Doukmak. Noor provided critical attention, queries, and conversation that got me through the final stages; the book is better for her care and labor, and I look forward to seeing her scholarship and relations bloom.

A special thank you to Sandie Christenson and Eungie Joo for being my first touchstones for pursuing a PhD. Eungie, thank you for modeling brilliance and relation as a curator, scholar, and sister and for inviting me to Sharjah. Thank you to Sheikha Hoor Al-Qasimi, Ryan Higa, Sataan Al-Hassan, and the rest of the Sharjah Biennial staff for engaging so beautifully with my work. To my Underground Railroad sisters, Tina, Petrina, Omana, Jade, Elena, and Adia, thank you for always being home. Gratitude to Marty Aranaydo for being kin, teacher, and companion, but especially in this case for your keen artistry, eye, memories, and faith. Thank you to Jeff Chang for thinking with me and writing our histories; Joseph Monish Patel for the education, friendship and kinship. To my BBO family, especially Kameelah, Nabihah, Hoda, Iesa, Hazel, Alaa, Nouha, Brother Khalid, Shannon, and Ali, building a better world with you has been one of the great privileges, joys, and challenges of my life #FreeThemAll.

The creative work and generosity of Kameelah Janan Rasheed graces the cover of this text. Thinking, learning, and creating with her has been humbling and profoundly pleasurable. Working with the talented and visionary Sarah Elawad has likewise been a beautiful endeavor.

The Kashani family across the North, West, East, and South Bays made coming home sweet and time too short. My parents Kimiko and Mansour, my sister Marjon, my Rana family (in Texas, the Bay, and Pakistan), and Junaid have endured this process as much as I have, if not more so. Thank you all for everything you make possible. The poets best express what it means to have Junaid Rana as my companion in spiritual, intellectual, and political life and struggle: as Mahmoud Darwish says, "I am who I am, as/ you are who you are: you live in me/ and I live in you, to and for you/I love the necessary clarity of our mutual puzzle."

CAST OF CHARACTERS

(those who appear in more than one chapter, in order of appearance)

BROTHER MASOUD calls the blues adhan and is a convert to Islam who was raised in the Pacific Northwest and relocated to the Bay Area during his time working on ships. His family migrated north during the Great Migration from Mississippi and Louisiana.

SABA is a white Muslim woman originally from the Midwest who lives in Oakland who participates in hearings to prevent the expansion of surveillance in Oakland.

FATEMEH is a Zaytuna College student raised in Southern California by her North African and white parents.

NUR is my DSLR (digital single lens reflex) camera; *Nur* means light in Arabic.

THE UMMA is the community of believers.

ZAHRAH is a Zaytuna College student born to Black Caribbean parents and raised in Brooklyn.

IMAM ZAID SHAKIR is an African American Islamic scholar, co founder of Zaytuna College and founder of Al-Ansar Mosque (pseudonym) in Oakland.

THE PROPHET MUHAMMAD (d. 632) Muhammad ibn Abdullah was born in the year 570 in Mecca and was orphaned at the age of six. Raised by his uncle to become a merchant-trader, he received revelation from Allah at the age of forty, becoming the Messenger of Allah, the final prophet in a monotheistic lineage that includes Abraham (Ibrahim), Moses (Musa), and Jesus (Isa). He would go on to spiritually and politically lead a diverse religious community that would eventually become the world's second-largest and fastest-growing religion.

SHAYKH HAMZA YUSUF HANSON is a white American Muslim scholar, co-founder of Zaytuna Institute and Zaytuna College.

DR. HATEM BAZIAN is a Palestinian activist and scholar, co founder of Zaytuna College and advanced lecturer in Asian American Studies, UC Berkeley.

MALCOLM X, EL-HAJJ MALIK EL-SHABAZZ (1925–1965) is a Black Muslim scholar, community organizer, and ancestor.

ABU HAMED AL-GHAZALI (d. 1111) is an Islamic scholar born in Tus, Khorasan, (now Iran) whose contemporarily read work, including *Ihya' 'Ulum al-Din* (*Revival of the Islamic Sciences*), focuses on the spiritual or inward dimensions of Islamic thought and practice.

HAJAR is a Black Muslim woman raised in the Bay Area who was a part of the As-Sabiqun movement at Masjid Al-Islam in East Oakland. She is currently a university professor in Northern California.

IMAM ABDUL ALEEM MUSA AND AS-SABIQUN MOVEMENT Oakland-raised Imam Abdul Alim Musa converted to Islam while in prison and established Masjid Al-Islam in East Oakland in 1981. The As-Sabiqun movement was established as a national movement in 1995 by Imam Musa.

HAJJA RASHEEDA (ROSA) was born in San Francisco in 1950 to a Black Catholic family with roots in Louisiana and Oklahoma. She became a member of the Black Panther Party for Self-Defense in 1967 and participated in the Third World Strike at San Francisco State University. She converted to Islam in the 1970s and was an educator and principal in Oakland public schools, while also raising four children (and grandchildren) with her husband in Oakland.

OSCAR was born and raised in Oakland in the 1970s–1980s. Having been a student activist and a Black nationalist in high school, he converted to Islam in the 1990s.

SHAYKH MUHAMMAD SHAREEF is a Black US-born Muslim who returned to the United States in 1990 after studying Islam in East and West Africa as a representative of the Jama'at of Shehu Dan Fodio. He established the Sankora Institute (SIIASI) in 1986 to further learning and to preserve African Islamic manuscripts and texts. He lived and taught in Northern California for many years and currently lives in exile from the United States after experiencing FBI surveillance and infiltration in his communities.

HAROON is the audiovisual technician and coordinator at Zaytuna College. He moved to the Bay Area from the East Coast in the 1990s to be a part of spreading the message of Islam at Zaytuna Institute. He is an African American convert to Islam, husband, and father in his forties.

AMINAH is an Arab student at Zaytuna College from the Midwest.

STEVE is a Black student at Zaytuna College in his mid-twenties who had converted to Islam shortly before joining Zaytuna. He is originally from the South and graduated from a prestigious university on the East Coast. He commuted to Zaytuna from San Francisco where he lived and worked full time in addition to being a student.

IMAM BENJAMIN PEREZ (1933–2009) was a Latino and Indigenous (Seminole/Yaqui) man from Central California who moved to Oakland in 1955 where he joined the Nation of Islam. He was dedicated to connecting Latinx and Native peoples to Islam through *da'wa* and served as a prison chaplain from the 1960s onward.

MARIO was born to a white mother and an African American father in Berkeley. He converted to Islam and attended Masjid Al-Islam in East Oakland as a teenager. He moved to Syria in his early twenties and later migrated to Tarim, Yemen, to study and teach at Dar al-Mustafa Seminary.

HABIB 'UMAR BIN HAFIZ is a descendant of the Prophet Muhammad and highly influential Yemeni scholar of the Hadrami diaspora. He established Dar al-Mustafa Seminary in Yemen in 1996 and Dar al-Zahraa Seminary for women a year later. He is consistently ranked highly on a list of the "500 Most Influential Muslims" in the world.

MATTHEW is a white convert to Islam who served as one of the first student life coordinators at Zaytuna College.

MARY is a Latina Muslim from the East Bay who converted to Islam as a teenager. She is married to Michael, a Filipino convert.

RUQAYYA is a third-generation Black Muslim student at Zaytuna who was born and raised on the East Coast.

INTRODUCTION

SCENE 1—HEAR THE CALL OF THE BLUES ADHAN

OVER BLACK

We hear shuffling steps, distant birds chirping, a rumbling hum of traffic from the freeway, murmurs, and whispers as PEOPLE enter a large room. Above the hushed sounds, a voice sails; it wails; it twangs; it rides.

BROTHER MASOUD

> Allahu akbar, Allahu akbar, Allahu akbar, Allahu akbar. Ashhadu an la ilaha illa Allah. Ashhadu an la ilaha illa Allah. Ashhadu anna Muhammadan rasul Allah. Ashhadu anna Muhammadan rasul Allah. . . .

FADE IN

INTERIOR. STOREFRONT MOSQUE, NORTH OAKLAND, MIDDAY.

We see the anthropologist's POV (point of view) from the women's section. Sunlight streams in through an open door. Bookshelves full of shoes line the far wall. A few elder MUSLIM MEN and WOMEN sit on metal folding chairs, MEN toward "the front" of the room, WOMEN arranged in loose rows behind them. CHILDREN bounce around receiving hugs and joyful exclamations. Some MEN and WOMEN stand in prayer or are seated in their respective sections. Pitched and pitchy, BROTHER MASOUD continues to call the *adhan* (the Muslim call to prayer), holding his hands to his ears as he rotates back and forth to his right and left sides.[1]

The camera PANS to a back wall with a Chinese calligraphic print of Arabic text hanging above three preteen and teenage BROTHERS sitting on the floor below it.

... Hayya ʿala as-salah, hayya ʿala as-salah. Hayya ʿala al-falah, hayya ʿala al-falah. Allahu akbar Allahu akbar. La ilaha illa Allah.[2]

FADE OUT

The adhan is always called in Arabic and though the words are always the same, this call is particular to this place. Brother Masoud was a sailor living in the Bay Area after growing up in the Pacific Northwest. His family migrated there from Mississippi and Louisiana after World War II during the Great Migration north and west by African Americans. Brother Masoud's adhan, in its modal tonality and timing, calls Muslims in harmony with the blues rhythms and inflections carried by African Americans, predominantly from Texas, Oklahoma, and Louisiana, to the Bay Area in the Great Migration throughout the twentieth century (Murch 2010; Self 2003; Woods 2017). Those blues rhythms and modalities convey inheritances from West African Islam carried by captive Muslims shipped to the Americas throughout the sixteenth to nineteenth centuries (Diouf 1998; El Shibli 2007). Masoud's blues adhan also carries a refugee rhythm from Southeast Asia, as Masoud learned how to call the adhan from a Cham imam in Seattle.[3] This call traveled across Southeast Asia, the Pacific, and the Atlantic, and through the South and up to the North, down the West Coast, to a storefront mosque in Oakland. I heard Masoud and others call blues adhans in mosques and industrial park community centers in Oakland, Fremont, and San Francisco, California. As it emerges from western lands and histories, via eastern lands and refugee migrations, this Arabic, its tonality and cadence, is uncanny to Arabic speakers who come from where these words were revealed. Nevertheless, this blues adhan signifies and beckons: *What do you hear?*[4]

CUT TO:

INTERIOR. BOARD OF SUPERVISORS MEETING, DOWNTOWN
OAKLAND, EVENING.

We see the young woman approach the podium, taking a deep breath before
beginning her statement. A subtle tremor in her breath accompanies a firm
stance as she folds her arms behind her back and begins to speak.

SABA

You can pave over the blood of the martyrs, but you can't fossilize the
spirit of resistance. Terrorist, gang member, provocateur—these are
all codewords for a person that's in the way of profit and power, both in
Oakland and internationally. (*Pause.*) As a Muslim I demand that you
cancel plans for your monitoring center. We are not stupid. We know
that the purpose is to monitor Muslims, Black and brown communities, and protestors. This will have a deep impact on our Muslim communities. These communities are all monitored in different ways, but
all of these ways overlap in our Muslim community.

CUT TO BLACK

Saba was one of many Muslims who attended and spoke at hours-long
city council meetings in Oakland's City Hall in the winter of 2013–2014.[5]
Given a minute and a half, with an additional two minutes ceded by other
speakers, Saba proceeded to explain why she was opposed to the council's potential approval of Phase II of the Domain Awareness Center, a
city and portwide surveillance system that would integrate visual surveillance data into a centralized network connecting private and public systems, the Oakland Police and Fire Departments, and the Coast Guard.
Saba connects how the figuring of "terrorist, gang member, provocateur"
within languages of securitization, policing, and governance racialize and
mark "Muslims, black and brown communities, and protestors" as problem
populations that "get in the way" of capital. Her concern for monitoring
and the threat of her obscurity inhered in the camera's inability to register
her facial features (she wore a veil on her head and across her lower face)
except for her light skin and eyes. The camera registers her nervousness,
though—the tremble in her voice and the way she held the cuffs of her
sweater sleeves, her preparation to speak—indexed by the notes she made

in her notebook and the names of others who ceded their time; and her historical ties to the Bay Area in recognition of all the times the port was used by demonstrators to protest war, capitalist extraction, colonial dispossession, and extrajudicial police violence. *What do you see?*

CUT TO:

SCENE 3—REFUSALS AND OFFERINGS

EXTERIOR. COURTYARD OF SMALL COLLEGE CAMPUS, BERKELEY, NIGHT.

We PAN ACROSS a large green hedge with red blooms lit by a single flood light. FATEMEH standing still, reads from OFF SCREEN and slowly comes into view.

> FATEMEH
>
> O well for him who lives at ease/ With garnered gold in wide domain/ Nor heeds the splashing of the rain / The crashing down of forest trees/ O well for him who ne'er hath known/ The travail of the hungry years/ A father gray with grief and tears/ A mother weeping all alone.

CLOSE UP of FATEMEH'S hands holding a book. Camera PANS UP to FATEMEH'S face.

> FATEMEH (CONT'D)
>
> But well for him whose foot hath trod/ The weary road of toil and strife/ Yet from the sorrows of his life/ Builds ladders to be nearer God.

FADE OUT

Fatemeh's disposition was quiet and thoughtful, both in the classroom and in social settings.[6] A first-year student at Zaytuna College, an emergent Muslim liberal arts college in Berkeley, California, she was cautious with her words and conscious of the spaces she occupied. She had declined to participate in one-on-one interviews for my ethnographic research, but when I approached her about doing a film portrait, she surprised me with her willingness and enthusiasm. I had previously associated her disinterest in interviews as a shyness and reticence about her own self-representation.[7] Yet, she also had a playfulness that emerged in her everyday self-expression and performance, as in class projects. Fatemeh chose the terms of her self-representation, distinguishing between conducting an interview and performing a recitation of someone else's words. An expansive self-image emerges in her choice to perform "Tristitiae" by Oscar Wilde (1854–1900), a particularly witty and flamboyant nineteenth-century Irish writer and poet, in a garden in the middle of the night. There was aspiration and pleasure, a thrill and playfulness. *What is being refused, what is being offered?*

The above scenes introduce a worlding, an attunement and a tuning in, that I, as ethnographer, filmmaker, so-called expert, have coproduced and assembled to address the struggles and strategies of everyday (Muslim and non-Muslim) life in the San Francisco Bay Area in the twentieth and twenty-first centuries. Throughout *Medina by the Bay,* ethnographic, historical, and anecdotal scenes, written in the screenplay genre, perform multiple tasks. Within the scenes are audiovisual cues—landscapes, words, gestures, and characters—that inform the substance of this ethnography. The three scenes above reference the hailing of "Muslims," from being called to pray and hear the blues to being marked as populations, whether by the "terror industrial complex" (Rana 2017b), which includes the prison and military industrial complexes, or by the ethnographer/filmmaker. While the first scene is a documentary recording of something that happened in real "ethnographic time and place" at a mosque in North Oakland in 2011, the second is "found footage" culled together from public recordings on the internet. The third scene is an edit of a staged performance that I (and my camera Nur) produced in collaboration with Fatemeh and her classmates in the Zaytuna College courtyard on a winter night.[8]

To hear the blues adhan, to see connections and refuse to be seen, to make an offering of ethnographic truth through a staging, these *ethnocinematic* gestures have different aesthetic qualities and functions, yet all constitute something of the dynamics of the "Medina by the Bay" as a geography and project. They are brought together in montage to introduce the form and content of this text: the ethical, spiritual, and political stakes of knowledge practices—how we narrate, represent, transmit, dispute, and enact collective survival in this life and the next. The stakes, of course, are high—flourishing life and premature death; salvation and the next-life geography of souls; mobility and displacement; and accumulation, dispossession, and exploitation of social, cultural, and material resources. This is much-examined academic and movement-based terrain, but what this study offers, humbly, is an analysis of such stakes from the perspective of the lives and deaths, refusals and offerings of a multiracial and multiethnic *umma* (community of believers), in order to make a more comprehensive argument about how knowledge, power, and ethics happen under specific sociocultural and material conditions and how an attention to such conditions may enable us to make different choices with and for one another.

By looking at one diverse religious community as a microcosm for the Bay Area, *Medina by the Bay* thinks through these issues on a microscale in ways that have relevance to a larger geography of relations of power and constellations of belief and accountability. It is a call to balance ethics and politics on more than a telos of individual—and at times communal— liberation, survival, and "happiness" (Sara Ahmed 2010); it is a reminder to ask, "in what way do I contribute to the subjugation of any part of those who I define as my people?" (Lorde 1984, 139). It is about how we are implicated in one another's lives and deaths (from other human beings to the natural world and the objects we create) and how we must call ourselves to account.

Medina by the Bay is an argument for taking Islam and Muslim ways of knowing and being seriously. While Muslims are often absorbed into sociopolitical struggles as victims (e.g., Muslim Ban, refugees, victims of war, colonial occupation, and heteropatriarchy), they are actively ignored or willfully neglected by scholars and activists as sources of knowledge and models of practice, largely due to overriding (Islamophobic) concerns about patriarchy, jihadism, homophobia, being spread by the sword aka colonization, and not being fun/free (lots of rules about food, drink, clothes, prayer, sex, etc.). Following the lead of Muslims themselves, I show another moral and ethical vision and embodied framework that offers one way out of a liberal humanist hegemony built upon centuries of racial capitalist and imperialist exploitation, destruction, and disavowal. Muslims are a billion strong; emerge fiercely from the carceral geographies of prisons, jails, and camps (Malcolm X 1965; Bukhari 2010; Daulatzai 2012; Slahi 2017; Felber 2020); endure under the most stringent and dehumanizing of sanctions and occupation (Iran, Iraq, Palestine, Black Muslims); and continue to produce thousands if not millions of people who have memorized and embodied the entire Qur'an across fourteen centuries (Ware 2014).[9]

Medina by the Bay runs with multiple projects of study and struggle toward getting at what is at stake, "no less than the truth about the world," while acknowledging "that something about the perspective, experience, and knowledge of the oppressed is not making its way into existing dis-

courses" (Alcoff 2011, 71; Kelley 2016). I invite my readers into "complex
communication," which "thrives on recognition of opacity and on reading
opacity, not through assimilating the text of others to our own" (Lugones
2006, 84) but rather, engaging in creative and transformative processes in
which we decipher our respective "resistant codes" and logics (Lugones
2006, 79; see also Glissant 1997).[10] To readers who know little of Islam,
you will pick up and get lost at times, and I ask you to be my accomplices
toward taking seriously the possibility that Muslim ways of knowing and
being have something to offer you. For those who know something of
Islam, whether through study or practice, I likewise ask for you to be my
companions (as in the *Sahaba*) as I bring other ways of knowing and being
to bear on what it means for Islam and Muslims to survive on Turtle Island,
in what we call North America.[11]

FROM MECCA TO MEDINA

"This is like, kind of, our Medina, you know?" Zahrah was sitting with her
classmates in a wide circle on the green grass of their campus courtyard,
a shared space that held a UC Berkeley extension program, the American
Baptist Seminary of the West (now Berkeley College of Theology), and the
nascent Zaytuna College (est. 2009). It was the last day of their first year,
and their professor Imam Zaid Shakir was asking them to relate what they
had studied over a yearlong Islamic history course to their contemporary
context. For Zahrah, the daughter of Caribbean immigrants who had
grown up in Brooklyn, coming to Zaytuna College was like the earliest
Muslims migrating to Medina. Having grown up Muslim in a post-9/11
New York, Zahrah had been featured in a published collection of writings by Muslim youth, and by the time she graduated from Zaytuna, she
would receive multiple invitations to the Obama White House and be
interviewed for many articles and news stories. At Zaytuna, she and her
classmates reenacted the migration toward freedom that the original
seventh-century *hijra* (migration) to Medina entailed: they could (as her
classmates said) "be free" as Muslims, to explore what that meant to them
on their own terms. She recounted, "We can be more at home here and
really make something of our own and really establish ourselves, and then
go back out, you know, when we've decided who we are."

In the Islamic tradition, Medina as a place and idea is connected to the
622 CE/1 AH hijra of the Prophet Muhammad and the first community of

Muslims in the Hejaz (modern-day Saudi Arabia).[12] The Prophet Muhammad was forty years old and living in the city of his birth, Mecca, which
was a center of religious pilgrimage and trade when he began to receive the
revelations of the Qur'an in 610 CE. Many of the first to hear the message
of Islam and convert to this new way were women, youth, the enslaved, and
tribeless people. As more and more people converted to Islam, traditional
relations of power, lineage, and hierarchy were disrupted; the agitated
leaders of Mecca started targeting the new Muslims. In order to preserve
their safety and survival, the community migrated physically and spiritually, leaving their beloved Mecca.

The Prophet Muhammad initially sent a small group of Muslims to Abyssinia (Ethiopia), where the Negus, a Christian king, offered them asylum.
A few years later, the rest of the community left Mecca for Yathrib, a northern oasis populated by Jewish and pagan tribes, where many were converting to Islam and where the Prophet was invited to mediate between these
conflicted tribes (the Prophet Muhammad's grandfather Abd al-Muttalib
was also born in Yathrib to Salmá, who had been an influential woman in
the matriarchal traditions there) (Lings 1983). As he left Mecca, the Prophet
Muhammad turned back to it and stated, "You are the most beloved of the
cities of Allah to me, if the *mushrikeen* (polytheists, those who acted against
the Muslims and Islam) did not force me out, I would have never left you"
(*Zaytuna College* 2020; Ibn Kathir 2003, 9:96).

The small, beleaguered community was welcomed by the *Ansar* (the
Helpers) into Yathrib, which would be called Medina al-Nabi, "city of
the Prophet," and they entered into protective covenants with the different
tribes.[13] Free to practice Islam openly, the Prophet took on a new role as political leader and arbiter within this diverse community of new Muslims, Jews,
and pagans, and a new society came into being. The documented sayings and
practices of the Prophet Muhammad, or *hadith,* are understood as the "tradition" or *Sunna* (way or practice) of the Prophet. The root letters, h-d-th,
refer to something happening, yet "hadith" is also translated as "modern" and
"new," connoting the transformative impact and newness of the revolutionary social, economic, and political changes the Prophet implemented.[14]

The multiple meanings of "hadith" speak to how we understand the
"generative rather than prefigurative" characters of traditions (Kelley
2021). With the emergence of new forms of relations and social structures
came the frictions of letting former customs, beliefs, and hierarchies go.
The conflicts that arose and were resolved in Medina—betrayal and expulsion, war and peace, hypocrisy and forgiveness, property relations and

mutual aid—continue to inform contemporary Muslims in terms of what it means to live in relation at multiple scales: as a servant of Allah (God) and as a member of a socioeconomic, spiritual, and political community.

In one of our first conversations, Zahrah spoke to me about why she came to the not-yet-accredited Zaytuna College when she was offered scholarships to prestigious universities: "I need to develop myself spiritually. And . . . it's my responsibility to gain Islamic knowledge because it's the most important knowledge that you can have. . . . I remember my sister said, 'It's poor *adab* (manners) to not walk through a door when Allah has opened it for you, especially if it's something that will only bring you benefit.'[15] And so, that's one reason why I wanted to come. You know, I felt like if I didn't come, then it was possibly a poor reflection on my character, as in why would I choose not to come here, and postpone my Islamic knowledge or potentially not do it at all?" Zahrah also had a secondary reason for choosing Zaytuna, and this was the influence of her father, who had converted to Islam as a teenager: "I kind of always felt like, 'Well, what am I going to do . . . that is as comparable to what he did?' And so, I thought this was the best way to carry on that transition in his life, you know, because becoming Muslim is the biggest blessing that Allah can give to your family, and so I felt like this was a continuation of that for me and for my family." At eighteen years old, Zahrah already carried a sense of spiritual, ethical, and political responsibility that she associated with being and becoming Muslim. Moving to Berkeley and attending Zaytuna was a commitment to personal development, which would benefit herself, her family, and her communities.

Zaytuna College, like the larger Bay Area, is a unique site of Islamic knowledge production and Muslim encounter, where racial, ethnic, gender, sexual, class, and sectarian differences come into contact. It seemed like the ideal site to consider what epistemological and ontological alternatives, ways of knowing and being, Muslims in the United States could offer in a highly contentious landscape of Muslim representation and politics post-9/11. Part of the college's uniqueness was that it was cofounded by three "American Muslims," Shaykh Hamza Yusuf (Mark Hanson), who is white; Imam Zaid Shakir (Ricky Mitchell), who is Black; and Hatem Bazian, who is Palestinian.[16] While their racial and ethnic differences were significant, within the context of Muslim institution-building, what was more striking was the diversity of their intellectual genealogies, spiritual dispositions, and political commitments. Yusuf studied with individual teachers for decades, most notably in Mauritania, Saudi Arabia, and the United Arab Emirates, and later received his doctorate in Islamic Studies from the Graduate Theological Union in California in 2020; Shakir studied Islam at Abu Nour University and privately in Damascus, Syria, and has a master's degree in political science from Rutgers University; and Bazian earned his doctorate in Near Eastern Studies at UC Berkeley in 2002. Bazian is also a senior lecturer in Ethnic Studies at UC Berkeley and runs an Islamophobia research center.[17]

While Zahrah and the other students at Zaytuna had grown up watching YouTube videos and listening to audio recordings of the college's Muslim scholars, I had first heard of Zaytuna in 2006 when it was still an institute based in Hayward, a small East Bay city south of Oakland where the San Mateo Bridge connects the West and East Bays. In a *New York Times* article, Zahrah's and Fatemeh's future teacher, Imam Zaid Shakir, was described by students as "the next Malcolm X," and Zaytuna Institute was described as a thriving center of Islamic learning (Goodstein 2006). The institute became Zaytuna College in 2009 and welcomed its inaugural class of students in fall 2010.[18] At the time they were supported by a fluctuating staff of about ten people, who were mostly Pakistani, although there were also Afghan, Latinx, African American, (east) Asian American, and white Americans (not everyone was Muslim). Zaytuna's inaugural cohorts consisted of recently converted Black, Asian, Latinx, and white Muslims; second- and third-generation Black Muslims; Muslim students from African, Arab, Asian, Caribbean, Latinx, and South Asian families; and Indigenous converts.[19] A few were from the Bay Area, but most of the students came from other regions of the country—Southern California, the Pacific Northwest, the South, the Midwest, and the East Coast—and grew up in other cities and suburbs. Like the historical Medina, Muslims migrated to the Bay Area to participate in the envisioning of a new or renewed society, another Medina, by the Bay. In this encounter with other tribes, beliefs, and peoples—both Muslim and non-Muslim—they would be called upon to respond and submit to a revelation that invited them to reevaluate the world and their place in it.

Zahrah's classmates and teachers believe that Islam and Muslims have something to offer the world, that Islam as a way of being and knowing can address the ills of society at local, national, and global scales. In their lineages, they cite Muslim figures ranging from scholar al-Ghazali (d. 1111) to the founder of the world's oldest university, al-Qarawiyyin (in contemporary Morocco), Fatima al-Fihri (d. 880); more locally, they reference figures like El-Hajj Malik El-Shabazz, also known as Malcolm X (d. 1965) and sports icon al-Hajj Muhammad Ali (d. 2016).[20] This text subsists with El-Shabazz as Muslim ancestor and *wali* (one with a standing with Allah);

his interpretive work with the Islamic tradition; his assessment of global racial systems, U.S. empire, and colonization; his commitment to Black people, the Third World, and our collective liberation; and his capacity to learn, admit mistakes, and *change his mind.*

Do Zaytuna College and Muslim communities carry forward the anti-imperialist, anti-racist, internationalist, and faith-centered social justice legacy of El-Shabazz? Or do they offer pathways to cultural citizenship that buttress a settler colonial United States, establishing themselves as authoritative voices and representatives amid a "crisis of authority" (Z. A. Grewal 2013)? These questions are complicated in these pages, but to jump scales from the school to the national and international does not account for Zaytuna's emergence within the specific local and regional political economy and cultural geography of the San Francisco Bay Area in the late twentieth and early twenty-first centuries (1400s AH). Specifically, I needed to account for the Medina by the Bay's emergence on Indigenous land and through the Black radical tradition and how a multiracial umma is inducted into "grounded relationalities" (Byrd et al. 2018) and struggles for liberation and autonomy as a matter of faith, while also articulating what Islam has contributed and continues to contribute to such traditions of study and struggle, however unthought or unnamed.

While the establishment of the historical Medina was a significant endeavor toward living justly in intercommunal relation, it was not without contention, conflict, and betrayal as individual and communal trusts and covenants were sealed and broken. I consider and invoke these early histories and their attendant theologies in order to think about how contemporary Muslims of the Bay Area have practiced and can practice Medinan relations, forms of mutual refuge and responsibility with Indigenous and other populations of the Bay Area, without reinforcing a settler colonial structure and its attendant logics of race and religion. I expand my frame temporally and spatially, zooming out from Zaytuna College to consider the ebbs and flows of Muslim communities throughout the Bay Area from the 1950s to the present to demonstrate the contingencies of how forms of Islamic belief and practice emerge from a specific time and place and how socioeconomic forces and geopolitical agendas impact which Muslim ways of knowing and being flourish and which are subject to precarity.

How Muslims move through and mark time in these interlocking and overlapping spaces complicates the ways that Muslims and urban geographies are typically studied.[21] The ethnographic study of Muslims in the United States, informed by theories of race and racialization, has been at the forefront of developing analyses of anti-Muslim and intra-Muslim racisms in relation to anti-Blackness and US empire.[22] I expand the stakes of this work toward questions of Muslim epistemic and material survival and the implications of being in grounded relationality. As Karl Marx wrote, "*religious* suffering is at the same time, an *expression* of real suffering and a *protest* against real suffering. Religion is the sigh of the oppressed creature, the sentiment of a heartless world, and the soul of soulless conditions" (Marx, 54). It is also something more. With my discussion of material conditions, sociopolitical categories, and critical analyses, I do not want to suggest that Muslim faith is simply "the opium of the people" (54) or "a mystifying thing that we need to look past in order to understand what is 'really' going on"; rather, as Lara Deeb has argued, "faith *is* what is going on, it is a very real thing in and of itself, located in practices, discourses, inner and outer states, relationships, and effects in the world" (Deeb 2006, 40). Similarly, Sylvia Wynter suggests that religion provides an alternate structure of belief that "has served as a humanizing and revolutionary ideology for great movements of the people" (Wynter n.d., 57). While Marx focuses on the individual "oppressed creature," Muslim ways of knowing and being expand beyond the individual toward how Muslims are situated in relation to a "heartless world" and "soulless conditions," regardless of and in relation to their own individual suffering.

In consideration of such ethical-political and salvational requirements, I am interested in how Islam is mobilized as a force—and how Islamic forces themselves mobilize—to reorder selves, logics, spaces, and relations of power. While some anthropologists think that the anthropology of Islam is too concerned with Islam, given Muslims themselves can be rather ambivalent about it in their everyday lives, I conjecture that Muslims and others harbor noncommittal and contradictory feelings about the settler colonial state, racial capitalism, war, traffic, the internet, multicultural liberalism, and patriarchy, but that doesn't make them any less constitutive of everyday lives and relations.[23] I draw from what I observed, participated in, and missed in Muslim communities in the San Francisco Bay Area in my visits between 2010 and 2022 but also on a longer history of growing up in and being in relation to the Bay and its lapsed and devoted Muslims, lapsed and devoted Catholics, Jews, Christians, and Buddhists, atheists and agnostics, Maoists and Marxists, red-diaper babies, activists, artists, queers, straights, studs, dykes, preppies, hippies, trannies and trans people, transplants, criminals and the criminal-minded, the haves, the have-nots, Indians and Native Americans, Mexicans, hella Filipinos, Black folk, Chinese folk, mixed kids,

racists, living legends and legacies, hip-hop heads and punks, family, everyone Allah has willed and created.[24]

In the context of *Medina by the Bay*—the project, my "cast of characters"
are both practicing and nonpracticing Muslims, those who go to mosques
and those who are "unmosqued." They are Black; North, West, East, and
South African; Arab; West, South, Southeast, and East Asian and Pacific
Islanders; Latinx; Native American; European; and white American Muslims. They are Sunni, Shi'i, and other sectarian and nonsectarian formations. They are refugees of war, empire, and colonization (especially from
Afghanistan, Yemen, and Palestine); they are Indigenous; they are descendants of enslaved Africans; they are recent immigrants and second-, third-,
fourth-generation United States citizens; they are documented and undocumented; they arrived as students, as working-class laborers and farmworkers, as technicians, doctors, and university professors; they are unemployed
and underemployed; they are cisgender men and women; they are transgender; they are straight; they queer gender; and they are the displaced, the
displacing, and the stuck in place. Yet, because they are Muslim in that they
are oriented or disoriented, identifying or disidentifying toward Islam and
the umma in one way or another, this casting, this unruly aggregate, offers
one lens through which to understand the particularity of Muslimness in
the Bay Area for a collective body that is anything but particular.

While this text emerges from this unruly aggregate, it is neither an examination of Muslim identitarian politics nor a reductive transparency of
who Bay Area Muslims are and what they believe. Neither is it an exposé
nor hagiography of particular figures or institutions.[25] Rather, I propose
that through the (micro) lens of one diverse "community," *Medina by the
Bay* provides an alternate view of the (macro) socioeconomic and cultural
dynamics of the Bay Area in the late twentieth and early twenty-first centuries and poses a question more broadly about how we think and act ethically and politically about knowledge and survival.[26]

In my cutting from history to the present day, I chart the vectors of possible futures. I take responsibility for this particular place and time and
work toward resonance "to explore and develop the ability to speak to very
different groups of people without having to name them all" (Trinh 1999,
37). This means that while I invite the umma to approach matters of our
collective survival anew, I likewise extend that invitation to all others who
consider Muslim survival as part of theirs or sense the resonances in our
respective struggles. Nominative processes have been a critical component
of a power/knowledge nexus that orders the world and the people within it

toward the maintenance of material and discursive power and the political orders they work with and through. I approach this work as a form of extension, "reaching for you/whoever you are/and/are you ready?" (Jordan 1977, ix), as an invitation toward hearing the call *without* naming you in advance.

KNOWLEDGE AND SURVIVAL

From the seventh century onward, becoming Muslim meant subsuming (though not necessarily breaking) traditional ties of kin, tribe, and geography for the reordering of life in Islam and with the Prophet Muhammad. Knowledge practices were a critical part of conceptualizing the self as a Muslim within a myriad of affiliations—a homeland, an occupation, a school of law, or a bloodline. Conversion to Islam became a strategy for material and spiritual survival in which Muslim converts and reverts engage in a "life-long study of Islamic history and Muslim scholarship," incorporating knowledge into everyday life (McCloud 1995, 3).[27] This includes making the testimony of faith in the Arabic language, learning how to ritually cleanse one's body, memorizing the words and bodily motions of daily prayers, changing one's diet, and reorienting one's self to Allah and all that Allah created.

Students, teachers, and community members often referenced the following Qur'anic verse when discussing differences within the Muslim community as both a challenge and instruction: "O mankind! We created you from a single (pair) of male and female, and made you into nations and tribes that ye may know each other. Verily the most honored of you in the sight of Allah is the most righteous of you. And Allah is Knower, Aware" (Qur'an 49:13). This verse is understood to describe the ontological condition of difference as an epistemological and ethical challenge. To "know each other" is put in relation with righteousness, being God-conscious, imbuing the relations of difference with an ethical imperative for survival and salvation.

The fundamentals of Islamic tradition based in the Qur'an and Sunna (the sayings and actions of the Prophet Muhammad documented in hadith and the *Sira*, the Prophet's biography) and the corpus of Islamic law and scholarship have "survived" fourteen hundred years via oral transmission, textual transcription, mimetic practice, knowledge-based genealogies, and state-based support and sponsorship.[28] While many scholars, laypeople, pundits, and politicians operate as if Islamic knowledge is not disavowed in Muslim-majority societies and that Islamic knowledge and practice continue to govern everyday life, others contend that the shifts that occurred in

Muslim societies from the eighteenth century onward, if not sooner, have subsumed and splintered Islamic epistemologies, apportioning which aspects of Islamic tradition belong in the modern nation-state and its governing apparatus and which have become privatized or relegated to religious authorities like the 'ulama' and mullahs (T. Asad 2003; Agrama 2012).[29]

At the same time, a full accounting of the theological and material consequences of coloniality and the colorline and how they have infused the historical Muslim world since the Portuguese kidnapping and enslavement of West Africans in 1441 has not taken place (Du Bois 1990; Wynter 2003).[30] While states, scholars, and laypeople may claim to be Islamic, they often make such claims while holding fast to a colonial (and secularizing) order of knowledge, difference, authority, and being (Devji and Kazmi 2017; Hallaq 2013; Mamdani 2001; Najmabadi 2005; S. A. Jackson n.d.; Wadud 1999).[31] The race-concept, liberal humanism, and the global transformation wrought by colonial racial capitalism all introduced modalities of thought, belief, and power that reorganized how social and spiritual life were governed and what role Islam and Muslim actors played in that governance (Robinson 2000; Melamed 2015; Koshy et al. 2022). *Medina by the Bay* brings forward some of this accounting and examines the material conditions that shape how Islamic politics and ethics are articulated and practiced in efforts to ensure the survival of Islam and Muslims.

While survival is neither "an academic skill" nor "a theory" (Lorde 1984, 112, 139), both formal and informal knowledge practices and consciousness-raising have been essential to what it means to survive—materially, spiritually, and as a people. Toward that end, religious, racial, and ethnic minority communities have long created their own schools and colleges as a "way to redeem the process of formal learning and as a way to pursue, indeed prefigure black [and Muslim] cultural and political sovereignty" (Rickford 2016, 4). Started in Oakland in 1966, the Black Panther Party's survival programs attended to the sustenance and survival of hearts and souls as they taught children and community members to celebrate their Blackness, their bodies, their histories, and their cultures. They also addressed survival through an ethics of care: feeding children breakfast, distributing clothing and shoes, driving and escorting elders, providing medical and dental care and ambulance services, and community defense and political advocacy.

I do not think of survival as "subsistence or 'mere' survival" (Gumbs and Wallace 2016, 383). Rather, "survival" conjures legacies of Muslim and "black feminist poetics and practice" that require us "to remember our existence always in the context of our guardian dead, those ancestors that survive

16   through us and our community, which has suffered differential unjust death" (2016, 383).[32] Within the tradition of Islam, ancestral work and the ties that bind believers to revelation and its transmitters take multiple forms—from the constant remembrance and reference to the Prophet Muhammad, his Companions (the Sahaba), and the early scholars and figures to remembrance of the Muslims who lived and died in these waters and on this soil, especially the millions of African Muslims who were kidnapped from their indigenous homelands and enslaved in the Americas from the sixteenth to nineteenth centuries (Diouf 1998; GhaneaBassiri 2010; Gomez 2005).[33]

For Muslims, material survival is subservient to spiritual survival; we can have housing, clothing, food, health, education, and employment, but if our hearts have hardened toward Allah and one another, we are already dead. The Islamic tradition offers important lessons for how we understand the material and spiritual as part of a unity, *wahda* (oneness), and *tawhid* (oneness of Allah), in which our everyday acts and attitudes work within and reflect a metaphysics of oneness. Everything is thus related, and it is through this relationality that the ethics of knowledge and survival emerge. While ethics shape individual practice, such practices mean little without the context of community through which one develops their *deen/din* (faith, religion) and earns personal and collective salvation.

Survival is thus not only a matter of preserving one's own safety and subsistence; it is also a matter of accountability in which one bears "responsibility for the violence of the nation of which you are a subject" (Edwards 2016, xxv). Regardless of how we may identify or disidentify with the United States as a nation-state formation, we bear responsibility for its violence both "here" and abroad. If we fail to recognize this responsibility, "there is no future that any of us will share" (Lorde 1988, 440). This is quite literal as we come to terms with our responsibilities to the earth as our material extinction now has a timeline. Allah expects us to do wrong: "By the One in Whose Hand my soul is, were you not to commit sins, Allah would replace you with a people who would commit sins and then seek forgiveness from Allah; and Allah would forgive them" (an-Nawawi 199 #, no. 422).[34] And these culpabilities repeat throughout millennia—countless times the Qur'an gives accounts of entire peoples who go astray and are then destroyed. Inevitably, we will get lost, sin, cause harm, suffer, repent, and be guided back to the path by Allah's grace or be tried in the afterlife. The tradition of Islamic renewal and resurgence speaks to the circular and eternal nature of study and struggle (*jihad*) and an abolitionist possibility for transformative justice at the scales of ethical relations with self, other, and God.

In her lecture for the "Malcolm X Weekend" at Harvard University in February 1982, Audre Lorde discusses how she "didn't really hear Malcolm's voice until it was amplified by death"; in the last year of his life, she understood him to be moving toward an "inevitable confrontation with the question of difference as a creative and necessary force for change" (Lorde 1984, 134–35). As he established both the Muslim Mosque, Incorporated, and the Organization of Afro-American Unity, El-Shabazz signaled the need to strive for justice in coalition with other groups, while also continuing the moral and spiritual development that being in Muslim community yielded. Like El-Shabazz, Lorde argues "we must move against not only those forces which dehumanize us from the outside, but also against those oppressive values which we have been forced to take into ourselves" (Lorde 1984, 135). She asks us to recognize "some piece of humanness that knows we are not being served by the machine which orchestrates crisis after crisis and is grinding all our futures into dust"; we are then called to recognize "that any attack against Blacks, any attack against women, is an attack against all of us who recognize that our interests are not being served by the systems we support" (Lorde 1984, 139). Lorde speaks here to survival as a matter of souls—sustaining one's heart (humanness) when the world and its prevailing ideologies and structures harden hearts and encourage human beings to forget their metaphysical and relational contexts.

In the Qur'anic telling of the story of Adam's sons, Cain (Qabil) and Abel (Habil), a decree is made to the children of Israel, "if any one slew a person—unless it be for murder or for spreading corruption in the land—it would be as if he slew the whole people: and if any one saved a life, it would be as if he saved the life of the whole people" (Qur'an 5:32). This verse seems to contradict itself by giving instances in which killing another is just at the same time that it states that killing one person is like killing all of humanity. Read in the context of the entire Qur'an and Sunna, it is the tension between these conditional statements and how this may or may not happen in practice that shapes the struggles of Muslim ethical and political life. This terrain opened for El-Shabazz and others a possibility for self-defense and protection that distinguished itself from the Christian doctrine of "turning the other cheek," while at the same time compelling the conversation of what it means to use force and the heavy toll that it potentially brings upon the soul and humanity at large.

Similarly, in the narrative of conquest and deliverance exemplified by the Old Testament story of the Israelites and Canaanites, God commands the Israelites to "drive out all the inhabitants of the land before you" (Numbers 33:52). Understanding the role that this story has played in liberation theologies, Osage scholar Robert Warrior suggests centering the Canaanite experience and paying attention to how such "conquest narratives have made their way into Americans' consciousness and ideology" (2005, 7). Shadaab Rahemtulla considers how the Qur'anic version does not include a promise of land, but rather, Allah "makes a preferential option for the oppressed simply by virtue of being oppressed, irrespective of their faith" (2020, 215). This reorientation of how we understand land, the oppressed, and the interpretation and mobilization of sacred texts demonstrates how the materiality of where, how, and with whom we live is intimately tied to what we believe and know at a spiritual and metaphysical level.[35] As I consider Islamic and Muslim survival in the Bay Area, I hold in view how theories and theologies of race and religion have been wielded throughout a settler colonial continuum from Spanish conquistadors and missionaries to contemporary statecraft and (liberation) theologies that have mobilized Exodus and the "promised land" for its tropes of freedom, deliverance, and redemption at the expense of the Indigenous peoples and lifeways of the "promised land."

GEOGRAPHY AND INFRASTRUCTURE

"Medina by the Bay" as a conceptual frame, social geography, and "infrastructure of feeling" (Gilmore 2017, 237) draws from where we are grounded, the land of the Bay Area itself, its waters, its earthquakes, the blood and bones in its soil, its flora and fauna, and the cultures that have emerged through time in relation to this place.[36] These cultures manifest as mosques, Islamic schools, bookstores, restaurants, and grocery stores, which constitute private infrastructures that are connected to and enabled by private and public infrastructures like the internet, media, freeways, trains and buses, shipping lines, banks, and school systems, as well as Islamic infrastructures or pillars like *zakat* (alms tax), *salaat* (prayer), *hajj* (pilgrimage), *sawm* (fasting), *shahada* (witnessing and the testimony of faith), and Islamic laws and customs regarding food, education, morality, place-making, and congregational prayer. By bringing forward the interrelatedness of these natural, material, and affective infrastructures, I demonstrate the contingencies of Islamic belief and practice, how geography, cultural and socioeconomic forces, and geopolitical agendas impact which Muslim ways of knowing and being become normative and dominant or marginalized and diminished.

The Qur'an states that all of creation (from thunder and winds to bees, spiders, stars, light, darkness, and figs) are signs "for those who use their minds" (2:164), guides toward understanding ourselves as part of that creation, in relation to Allah, one another, and the natural world. These Qur'anic injunctions resonate with (Muslim and non-Muslim) Indigenous theories and cosmologies that understand "land as pedagogy" (Coulthard and Simpson 2016; L. B. Simpson 2017) and "water as relative" (Yazzie and Baldy 2018), that teach "us to think about knowledge in continuous movement, transition, and change" (Barker 2017) and "knowledge as always already a place" connected to other spaces and times (Goeman 2013, 163).

Knowledge as place and in continuous movement is enacted at multiple scales as Muslims travel throughout the Bay Area to attend lectures or communal prayers, crossing the Bay over and under its seven bridges, listening to Qur'anic recitations or Islamic lectures initially on audiocassettes, then CDs, MP3s, and other digital files. Knowledge as place also exists in the space between shoulders and feet as Muslims line themselves up for prayer, whether in mosques, living rooms, prison yards, parks, or plazas, and in the shadows students' bodies cast as they calculate midday and afternoon prayer times (Kashani 2014).[37] The Medina by the Bay is also a contested geography in which forms of epistemic and material violence have shaped the distributions and dispossessions of people and resources across its lands and waters, at the same time that the Bay Area has been an epicenter of social and political reimagining and struggle with significant local and global reverberations. Beat and Black Power, free speech and free love, gentrification and gay pride, hip hop and hyphy, Silicon Valley and slow food, multiple movements and modes narrate the Bay Area as vanguard and anomaly in relation to the rest of the United States.

Descendants of the region's original human inhabitants, the Indigenous peoples collectively (and anthropologically) referred to as the Ohlone (Ramaytush, Chochenyo, Tamien, Awaswas, Karkin), Patwin, Yokuts, and the Coast and Bay Miwok, continue to seek visibility, recognition, land, and sovereignty in struggles with the nation, state, counties, and private entities (Field, Leventhal, and Cambra 2013; Nelson 2021; Sogorea Te' Land Trust 2021). The destruction of their ancestral "native economies, polities, and cosmologies" for the sake of productivity "in the European sense" was also a "wholesale transformation of the coastal ecology of California" committed in the names of Christianity and empire, and then for the state of California (Field and Leventhal 2003, 99).[38] The Bay Area also continues to be home to a large urban Native population, composed of members of many Indigenous nations who were forcibly encouraged to leave reservations from the 1950s onward in the Bureau of Indian Affairs' Urban Relocation program. This federal effort to assimilate Indigenous peoples toward their nonexistence failed to disappear Native peoples, who continue to maintain connections to their tribal lands, reservations, traditions, and to one another (Ramirez 2007). Muslims in the Medina by the Bay articulate multiple strategies for Islamic and Muslim survival, some that are articulated "*inside* First Peoples' sovereignty" and others through "settler rights" (S. Jackson 2019, 346). As places like Zaytuna College reorient Muslims to their reciprocal relations with the land, "to restore balance and order on earth in a manner consistent with a Qur'anic worldview and in conformity with our divinely mandated function as stewards of God on earth, *khalifatul Allah fil 'ard* (viceregents/stewards of God on earth)" (Zaytuna College 2018), they may likewise orient themselves beyond the "benevolent use of the land" (S. Jackson 2019, 346) toward grounded relations and solidarities (Coulthard and Simpson 2016; Coulthard 2014).[39]

Hajar is a Black Muslim woman whose parents migrated to the Bay Area from the East Coast and Texas in the 1960s.[40] Currently a university professor, she started teaching at a Muslim elementary school in East Oakland in the 1990s. The school was part of As-Sabiqun movement, established by Imam Abdul Aleem Musa in 1995 with a five-point plan aimed at creating "a community within a community, a city within a city, a nation within a nation—an Umma determining and directing its own affairs" (Al Rashid 2014, 44). Part of the vision for the movement was to create "New Medina," a Muslim community governed through the concept of "geographical integrity" in which Muslim communal life was centered around the mosque, schools, businesses, *da'wa* (calling/inviting to and within Islam), and social welfare institutions. Ultimately, this vision for New Medina faced numerous setbacks; despite attempts to be independent of the state, "we definitely had influences of the state all around us because they sanctioned violence on our communities, on ourselves; the police are running rampant around our community." For Hajar and others, the ideal of a local community was consistently challenged by a larger socioeconomic and geographic context where "you want to be in it, but not of it, but then you can't really—unless you have enough power in terms of money and resources to actually do something." So, while the community had their own forms of security, they could not contend with "the guns and the violence and all those things; we could not impact those things on the terms that we had."

At the same time, Hajar's community developed relationships with an
Indigenous community who invited them to visit and stay on their reservation south of the Bay Area, and it was there and during other retreat gatherings that Hajar gained a sense of what freedom and sovereignty could look like, "to actually have just your own land and your own everything, right? . . . I distinctly remember them saying, 'You have left the United States.' And that was such a profound moment for us and for our children to see that and stuff like that. It was beautiful. It was absolutely beautiful. And that to me is what it should be or could be."[41]

While Hajar refers to "your own land and your own everything," she is not emphasizing possession as property to be exploited for capital; rather, she invokes the idea of land as a communal means of reproduction and site of possibility removed from the violent effects of racial capitalism, organized abandonment, and colonial relations. In her account, a Black-led multiracial Muslim community sought the sovereignty of and sovereignty with Indigenous peoples through Islam and their own relationships to the lands and water of the Bay Area. These experiences emerged from a "grounded relationality" in proximity, that recognized the sociopolitical, material, and geographic tethering of our collective struggles in particular places (Byrd et al. 2018; Coulthard 2014; Nichols 2018). The groundedness of this relationality is "situated in relation to and from the land . . . and other elementary or material currents of water and air" without "precluding movement" (Byrd et al. 2018, 11). Rather than comparative frameworks of commensurability and disconnection, a relational analysis attends to "dynamics of co-constitution, interaction, and friction" (Byrd et al. 2018, 5). In grounding this work in the specificity of the San Francisco Bay Area, the land and water relatives of the Ohlone, Patwin, Yokuts, and Miwok and the home of so many other relocated peoples, I attend to our proximate relations at a regional scale, focusing on the inhabitants of Medina by the Bay in ways that are not limited to our Muslim kin. Imagining, recovering, and enacting survival and ways of living that are not "tethered to the death of the Other" are essential ethical and political commitments for Muslims who seek to follow a Prophetic path (King 2019, xi; Shange 2019b).

The Bay Area exemplifies how a particular region presents challenges to more nation-based hegemonic ideologies of race, sex, and politics while not being immune to them as people and ideas come and go (Ramirez 2007; Shange 2019b). "The accumulated history" of the region informs how people make sense of social relations, how they know one another across and through difference, and how they practice living in proximity

22 (Massey 1994, 156; Cheng 2013); yet these same accumulated histories also bear the weight of new histories, peoples, and ideas that simultaneously are made possible by the histories that they obscure and negate. The recent affluence in the region and in the Muslim community has dramatically transformed the progressive, creative, and working-class cultural landscape and with that affluence comes the high rates of turnover, exile, and exodus that take critical memories with them (Solnit 2000, 22; Banks et al. 2012; Maharawal and McElroy 2018; Menendian and Gambhir 2019).

The Bay Area, like much of the country, is resegregating. The unfinished work of the civil rights, Black freedom, and Third World movements reached a zenith in public schools, for example, in 1989, when they were at their most desegregated nationally (Chang 2016, 70). State governments have been at the forefront of dismantling those hard-fought achievements in schooling, housing, employment, and antiracism toward carceral geographies, geographies that are not limited to prisons and law enforcement, but that enable the inequality that "capitalism requires" and "racism enshrines" (Gilmore 2017, 240; see also Gilmore 2007; Shange 2019b, Sojoyner 2013). One cannot separate local and regional infrastructures and infrastructures of feeling from one another as the particular "implies entire historical geographies in constant churn . . . any category or system has many dimensions, necessitating analytical stretch in order to perceive the material world in a variety of overlapping and interlocking totalities" (Gilmore 2017, 229).

One of the earliest Muslim schools in the Bay Area was the Nation of Islam's University of Islam, which became the Clara Muhammad School in Oakland in the 1970s. Hajja Rasheeda, one of the first teachers at the school, had been a Black Panther and member of the Black Student Union at San Francisco State during the establishment of Black and Ethnic Studies in the Third World Strike of 1968. Other teachers and community members at Clara Muhammad and Masjid Al-Waritheen (of the Warith Deen community) embodied Black Power infrastructures of feeling as well. In the 1980s these Bay Area Black Muslims—many of whom were professionals and middle-class homeowners, with the leadership of Wallace (Warith Deen) Muhammad, the son of the Honorable Elijah Muhammad—were able to purchase and then maintain three buildings, including a former Catholic church that held the school and a mosque, in Oakland's Fruitvale District. In the 1990s, Oscar, a recent convert to Islam, began attending the mosque, where every spring, Imam Faheem Shuaibe named all the young people going to college the next year and asked them to stand up.[42]

Oscar grew up in West Oakland's Lower Bottoms, deeply informed by
its Black Panther histories; three generations in Oakland, his people migrated from Arkansas on his mother's side and Louisiana on his father's.

It was at Masjid Al-Waritheen where I first met young adults, young
people in my peer group who were going to places like Yale, MIT,
Georgetown, Howard University. This is the first time I met people in
my peer group who were actually going to college, Black folks. They were
producing young adults, Muslims like that. And I was blown away. I remember one sister, Tawhidah . . . she went to Yale. . . . I remember after
jumu'a (Friday congregational prayer) going up to her like, "Tawhidah,
you're going to Yale!?" She was like, "Yeah. But it's not that big of a deal,
you know." I was like, "What!?" And she was like . . . she was downplay-
ing it. I was like, "Man, you're going to Yale." She was like, "Yeah. And
they paying my way too. I got a free ride." "Wow," I was super impressed.

Over the next decade, the Warith Deen community faced multiple
demographic and socioeconomic challenges in what Oscar referred to as
a "bustling" and intergenerational community: "They had elder women,
elderly folks, young adults, teenagers" who began to age, move away from
Oakland, or migrate to other Muslim communities or away from Islam. During the subprime mortgage crisis of 2007–2010, the Warith Deen community lost the Clara Muhammad School and mosque building. The costs of
maintaining the large, old building, combined with the diminished financial
resources and geographic proximity of the community, bad and impossible
choices, and predatory banking structures, contributed to the loss of this
significant fixture in Bay Area Islam. Meanwhile, the Muslim Community
Association in Santa Clara County and the South Bay Islamic Association in
San Jose, both founded in the 1980s in Silicon Valley and which are predominantly upper- and middle-class Arab and South Asian, have built schools,
acquired additional real estate, and expanded multiple times both before
and after the subprime mortgage crisis. Similarly, Zaytuna College has purchased twenty million dollars of church, school, and residential properties
in North Berkeley within its first decade of existence (2009–2019).

These brief references to accumulation and abundance and dissolution
and dispossession are both particular to and emblematic of larger dynamics in the Bay Area. When Oscar says, "the Black Muslim community goes
the way of the Black community," he means that the socioeconomic and
cultural conditions of the larger Black population imply the conditions
of Black Muslim communities. African Americans suffered massive losses

in the subprime mortgage crisis and have been heavily impacted by urban redevelopment and gentrification in the metropolitan Bay Area. African American Muslim communities have seen their mosque attendees and members dispersed to the outer reaches of the Bay Area from their earlier communal foundations in San Francisco and Oakland. While they are in relation to a larger community of Muslims, they also live in proximate relations with their non-Muslim families and neighbors. What is happening to Muslims in the Bay Area, who are estimated to be about 250,000 people (one of the largest concentrations in the country), says a great deal about what is happening to the entire Bay Area (Bazian and Senzai 2013).

Despite such communal losses, a proliferation of US-based Islamic schools, institutes, programs, seminars, conferences, and distance-learning programs in the last three decades speaks to the structural conditions of *some* Muslims having more resources and (leisure/devotional) time (Deeb and Harb 2013); a (neoliberal) faith in the charismatic power of education, expertise, and certification (Starrett 1998; Z. A. Grewal 2013); a desire to produce institutions toward establishing generational continuity, security, and cohesion (Haddad, Senzai, and Smith 2009; Memon 2019); and the need to be conversant with a media and social landscape in which Muslims are (still) compelled to explain and defend themselves and their faith (Alsultany 2013; 2012; Jamal and Naber 2008).

Muslims are distributed across the socioeconomic spectrum, and a growing resegregation in the Bay Area puts specific demands on educational institutions like Zaytuna. How the Zaytuna administration recognizes its role in ameliorating or reinscribing historical and social injustices, especially regarding education, gender, race, and class, is a significant marker for the potential to reorder society in line with its historical legacies. An analysis of the logics at play at Zaytuna College and other Muslim spaces throughout the Medina by the Bay are important for bringing forward the contradictions, conflicts, and transformations that emerge when market-driven, neoliberal logics meet social-justice and faith-based logics, such as in "Islamic finance," "social justice capitalisms," "black neoliberalism," and "progressive conservatisms" (Dawson and Francis 2016; Riguer 2017).

Zaytuna College's proximity to and the fiscal patronage of Silicon Valley is present in the dot-com vocabulary often uttered at the school. Zaytuna was called a "start-up," currently in "Zaytuna 2.0," and many of its administrative and managerial leadership have been recruited from the tech industry. Such proximity and influence have impacted how the college is organized and managed. Following trends in education nationally, Zaytuna College initially hired (Muslim) business professionals, rather than those with educational experience, to manage the institution. This intentional form of management and bureaucracy surreptitiously impacts the dynamics of the social and intellectual atmosphere and student and administrative staff morale.

Zaytuna has made a significant commitment to let students graduate debt free (as part of a larger Islamic critique of debt and interest), and they have graduated many local students who would have not otherwise been able to access higher education. But the question remains both there and throughout the Medina by the Bay: Who is asked to sacrifice or work harder, and how are piety discourses mobilized to support austerity measures and achievement gaps? While maintaining the need to center Muslim agency and accountability (like when students break codes of conduct or do not keep up their grades), I wonder to what extent a Muslim school can intervene with transformative, rather than punitive, responses. Which Prophetic modalities are foregrounded at which moments and how? How does resegregation *within* the Muslim community occur in relation to a dynamic discourse of Muslim heterogeneity? I likewise bring these questions to the fields of education and the academy more broadly. How do we reorient our knowledge production and transmission toward the needs and knowledge of the most vulnerable in ways that foreground, rather than suspend, the grounded relationality of schools and their local communities (Shange 2019b)?

Toward addressing some of these questions, chapter 1, "Medina by the Bay," presents scenes of study and survival in Medina by the Bay (with a focus on Oakland and the East Bay) that evoke the contexts and processes through which formal and informal knowledge practices (*daʿwa, taʿlim,* and *taʾdib*) evolved from the 1950s to the present. These scenes are not an exhaustive rendering of Medina by the Bay's past and present; rather, they are demographic, geographic, and affective portals and structures for the following scenes and chapters to move through and against. Chapter 2, "Roots, Routes, and Rhythms of Devotional Time," expands space and time to consider the global effects and ethical and political implications of Medina by the Bay, how affinities are formed through an Islamic kinship of faith, spiritual and knowledge-based genealogies, and liberatory lineages that reorder how differences (racial, gender, class, sectarian) shape relations and responsibilities. In chapter 3, "Codewords and Counterinsurgent Continuities," I trace historical continuities that demonstrate how government surveillance and infiltration policies (the state's desire to know, control, and destroy), as well as Muslim alliances and solidarities, impact which forms of Muslim life and knowing survive and which do not.

The deep context of the global war on terror, the terror-industrial complex, and a related structure of white supremacy, settler colonialism, and racial capitalism "make writing [and filmmaking] and analysis a careful, complex instantiation of jurisdiction and authority" (A. Simpson 2014, 105). Through my ethnographic research, I asked Muslims to speak and be seen, surveyed/surveilled even. Not speaking when one is compelled to "answer for" Islam, not demonstrating that one is not an "oppressed" Muslim woman—Muslims are often denied these rights to "silence" and opacity. While much of my research came to have use-value for the college (my video footage was used in Zaytuna promotional videos and students and community members consistently spoke of their appreciation for opportunities to reflect), I was also acutely aware that I was contributing to an "incitement to discourse" about Muslims (Foucault 1978).

Trinh T. Minh-ha addresses the ethical and political relations of knowledge production by maintaining "a self-reflexively critical relationship toward the material, a relationship that defines both the subject written and the writing subject, undoing the I while asking 'what do I want wanting to know you or me?'" (1989, 76). Trinh's question about "wanting to know" orients my own production and transmission of knowledge. It remains important to produce counterknowledges that are useful for the communities to whom we are indebted and that reorder our epistemological assumptions, while also remaining attentive to how "our work is sometimes, even often, willfully misread, misinterpreted, and misused" (Fernando 2014, 27). To protect and anticipate future "concerns of the community" and to attend to the "asymmetrical power relations that inform the research and writing," I do not discuss "everything" that I saw and heard (A. Simpson 2014, 105).

I navigated a space in-between where I had a multiplicity of statuses at Zaytuna College and elsewhere: student, Muslim woman, audiovisual technician, community member, and researcher.[43] Despite the open doors, I was viewed with a weary acquiescence by those who are always being defined by others, as when one student introduced herself strategically and playfully as one of my "experiments" to a friend. Haroon, the audiovisual technician at Zaytuna, framed my being there another way: "Your being named Maryam is not an accident at all, so your involvement in this project is the writing of your personal story and your journey with and to knowing Allah, and you are in a very unique position that is unprecedented in this organization . . . it's like miraculous."[44] While acknowledging this great privilege and what he called "the scary aspect," Haroon urged me to remain "conscious of that sense of accountability, and to take it on in

the best way possible." Haroon made clear to me, as did others throughout
my time at Zaytuna, that I should not see my work and relationships as
"simply research." I should "seek benefit" and examine my own relationship
to Allah. This was not a unanimous position, however.

Others at Zaytuna believed that I should maintain a "critical distance"
so that I could maintain "objectivity" toward what was happening at the
college. If I became too close to people and the lines between "on the record" and "off the record" became blurred, I would become too biased to
see clearly, or worse, I would exploit and manipulate such relationships
and invade and betray privacies (Stacey 1988; Wolf 1996). Such fears were
not unwarranted as many individuals had already experienced the media
misrepresenting them, and they were sensitive to how Muslims were portrayed. There was also a heightened sense of ethics in terms of what was
private, what wasn't, and when it came to talking about events at the college, at what point it was unethical to speak about other people who were
not present in the room.[45] It is for this reason that I found moments of
refusal or resistance useful "diagnostics of power" (L. Abu-Lughod 1990).
My interlocutors' refusals informed my own refusals in the "ethnographic
calculus of what you need to know and what I refuse to write," film, or edit
for presentation (A. Simpson 2014, 105).

Toward that end, in chapter 4, "Out of Bounds," I consider the ethical-
political bounds and responsibilities of ethnographic relation and representation and how embodied forms of knowing from tears and gendered
geographies to forms of intimate distance and filmmaking offered ways to
navigate tensions between opacity and making visible toward an elaboration
of how power, knowledge, and ethics intersect. In chapter 5, "Epistemologies of the Oppressor and the Oppressed," I return to the Zaytuna classroom
where students and teachers discuss Frantz Fanon's *Wretched of the Earth*. I
bring theories and theologies together to consider how we reorder our ways
of knowing and being from the position of the wretched and oppressed.

REFUSALS AND OFFERINGS—THE ETHNOCINEMATIC
AS KNOWLEDGE AND ETHICS

In the opening three scenes and throughout, I emphasize the *cinematic*
and ethical implications of ethnographic participant-observation, analysis, and representation by presenting my research (observations, interviews,
archives, etc.) as ethnocinematic scenes, to get at the critical function of

INTRODUCTION

the (audio)visual in shaping our epistemological and experiential conditions and to demonstrate the intertextual limits and possibilities of engaging the ethical, (audio)visual, and textual together.[46] Film and digital technologies alter our perceptive and cognitive capacities; our knowledges of the world—how we sense, think, and make meaning—are mediated by images, and our sensory apparatuses are accustomed to receiving and forming images according to the parameters and expectations put in place by cinema (Keeling 2007, 5). So, when Muslims watch videos of Islamic scholars online or listen to Qur'anic recitation or lectures in their cars or on their mobile devices, they are being shaped by the cinematic effects and common-sense logics of media (Hirschkind 2006; Hirschkind and Larkin 2008; Moll 2010; Vries and Weber 2001). They are also impacted by how the figure of the Muslim is mobilized in state discourse and popular culture.[47] Additionally, visual and multimodal anthropologists consider how the camera itself and the process of making ethnographic films enable embodied forms of knowing and seeing that transmit knowledge and affect in ways that are distinct from text (Collins, Durington, and Gill 2017; J. Jackson 2004; D. MacDougall 2006).

By staging ethnographic performances (as in Scene 3 above) and offering ethnocinematic scenes throughout this text, I explore the possibilities of breaking from a "totalizing quest of meaning" (Trinh 1991, 29) and reformist "politics of visibility," toward getting free "from the world of the cinematic and the common senses that animate it" (Keeling 2007, 10).[48] My writing and filmmaking foreground the ethics, politics, and shape of ethnographic relationality through experimental form while also attending to a need for counterknowledge. This tension is present throughout as I struggle with what "speaking nearby" rather than about can look like, while also giving the reader (historical, theoretical, spiritual) tools to deploy (Trinh 1991).

Traditional ethnographic vignettes produce images for the reader that convey a sense of "being there," reinscribing the anthropologist's authority to describe and analyze what was witnessed. By writing ethnocinematically, I draw attention to the pressure that visual and discursive regimes put "on the ways images commonly present themselves as an index of what they appear to record" (Keeling 2011, 58). My ethnocinematic scenes combine multiple ethnographic and historical "events" in juxtaposition and also narrate scenes I did not observe but was told about. I arrived at this form because I struggled, and eventually refused, to tell the history of Islam in the Bay Area in a linear timeline and from a single point of view. There are infinite points of view, Muslim and non-Muslim, human and nonhuman;

my camera Nur had its own point of view that exceeded the possibilities
of what I could see or do, while prayers and supplications made centuries
before demanded presence. By exposing some of the cinematic apparatus
in this way, I draw attention to the incompleteness—whether by choice or
chance—of what is not included. In some cases, there are ample images; in
others, there are no images nor sufficient ways to image. For example, in
chapter 2, I describe a scene as it would appear in a film, and indeed this is
how my camera captured this event. In chapter 4, I return to that scene to
describe what the camera could not capture—years of history, centuries-
old prayers, and distant prophecies; I discuss the difference between describing a scene with text versus showing the scene as a set of moving images
in a particular political, ethical, and affective context.

I am also interested in what this ethnocinematic approach offers in
its ability to traverse, collapse, and expand space and time. Historical figures and alternate geographies are made present in devotional gatherings,
classrooms, and conversations. Thinking cinematically through montage
enables me to narrate a different metaphysics and radical relationality of
ethnographic space and time in much the same way that Muslim scholars
and their students localize and historicize Islam in their rhetorical leaps
and devotional bounds. "The camera introduces us to unconscious optics"
in which time and space can expand, contract, and otherwise defy our phenomenological expectations (Benjamin 1968, 239).

I also draw upon the cinematic and Fanon's feelings of lived experience
as Black: "I cannot go to a film without seeing myself. I wait for me. In
the interval, just before the film starts, I wait for me" (2008 [1967], 107).
This moment of anticipation, endurance, and potential exposure refers
to "the relationships of time made visible by cinema" and "the possibility
of *exploding* the lingering logics of colonial reality" that construct Blackness and Muslimness as distinct, however overlapping and co-constitutive,
problems (Keeling 2003, 107–8; Bayoumi 2008). The conceptual notions
of and affective feelings toward Islam and Muslimness, both Black and
non-Black, are entangled with colonial and secular logics and cartographies that in the United States situate both Islam and Muslims as foreign,
invasive, irrational, illiberal, ungrievable, and terrifying. Muslims themselves, (dis)identifying their own lived experiences with the cinematic images and logics that shape them, enact these same logics despite themselves.
I conjure the cinematic form and the intervals that mark time between past
and future as a space of possibility that breaks from commonsense logics
that animate our ways of knowing and being. My "editing" of past and

contemporary moments offers just one set of connections and ruptures with the hope that other possibilities and questions can emerge and "be perceived in the interval, gap, or break between them" (Keeling 2011, 73).

Twelfth-century Islamic scholar Abu Hamid Muhammad al-Ghazali (d. 1111) situates seeing and knowing as ethical practices that one must cultivate: "Were it not that He has placed an image (*mithal*) of the whole world within your very being you would have no knowledge of that which is apart from yourself" (al-Ghazali 2010, 59). For al-Ghazali, being able to "see" is contingent on the will of Allah and one's ethical becoming; one must protect one's (seeing) heart, so that access to images is not cut off, and at the same time nurture the heart's ability to see. Seeing and knowing are ethical relations that are characterized by a tension between the limits of an autonomous subject who experiences the world through her senses and that which is enabled by external forces. So, when a Muslim student surrounds herself with photographs of Muslim scholars, she also invites the images to "work" on her, enjoining her to be more like these spiritual models. At the same time, negative and racist images similarly work on us, corrupting and hardening our hearts, impacting our capacities to see and know ourselves and others. The epistemological and phenomenological implications, then, are that images "become forms of thought constituting a new kind of knowledge— one that is grounded in visual communication, and thereby dependent on perception, demanding the development of the optical mind" (Emmelhainz 2015, 2; see also Connolly 2002). The "development of the optical mind," the "seeing heart," and the cinematic go hand in hand in describing how our logics, beliefs, and behaviors are shaped by images of the world that we may or may not apprehend, understand, or know.

EPISTEMOLOGY FOR THE NEXT

Around 1998, more than a decade before I heard the blues adhan in the storefront mosque in North Oakland, that same space was called Masjid Al-Ihsan (Mosque of Excellence), and it was a Naqshbandi *zawiya* (lodge of the Naqshbandi Sufi order). In this small two-room storefront, Shaykh Muhammad Shareef, a Black US-born Muslim who had returned from decades of study in East and West Africa, drew "a cross section of the Muslim community in the Bay Area" to receive "something that many of us had never gotten, which was one-to-one transmission of a religious text from a shaykh to the students in a traditional manner where you read the text and the shaykh comments. You read, he comments. You read, he comments. And everybody has to participate."

Shareef was raised in the Nation of Islam in Connecticut and followed the son of the Honorable Elijah Muhammad, Imam Warith Deen Muhammad, in the "Transition" of many in the Nation toward Sunni Islam in 1975. Shareef then traveled to Africa to recover, as Oscar puts it, "that chain of transmission, that scholarship, that Islamic, that sacred tradition" that was disrupted when African Muslims were enslaved in the Americas. "So, he was about trying to connect us to . . . connecting us to Prophet Muhammad *salla Allahu 'alayhi wa-sallam* (may God honor him and grant him peace) through our African ancestors, through that spiritual lineage."

Oscar described this class to me as "the highlight of many of our week," where young and old students would gather for two hours every Sunday evening to study *Tariq al-Janna,* the *Path to Paradise,* written by Shehu Uthman Dan Fodio (d. 1817), a Fulani scholar of Maliki *fiqh* (jurisprudence) and founder of the Sokoto Caliphate (established in 1804 in present-day Cameroon, Burkina Faso, Niger, and Nigeria). Oscar described *Tariq al-Janna* as "a manual that outlines the fifteen traits of uprightness that Imam al-Ghazali talked about in his *Ihya' 'Ulum al-Din* (*The Revival of the Religious Sciences*); Sheikh Uthman Dan Fodio condensed it into a small treatise that a person could read and begin to implement immediately." Shareef taught this class before any other, inverting the traditional order of Islamic study. Rather than beginning with the fiqh of *ibadat* (worship), like the requirements of ablution and prayer, Shareef told students like Oscar, Rasheeda, and others you will meet in these pages that "'We want to *begin* with *tasawwuf* (Sufism) because it's important that we not become arrogant with knowledge.' And he mentioned that the last, the most difficult blameworthy characteristic for a student to rid themselves of, after having learned a little bit, is arrogance. 'And so, we want to enter the study of knowledge, of sacred knowledge, religious knowledge, with some humility. So, we're going to study this book first.'"

Similarly, over a decade later at Zaytuna College, one of the first lessons that Imam Zaid Shakir imparts upon his students at Zaytuna College is the lesson conveyed by Imam Ibn Rajab (d. 1393): "Jubayr ibn Nufayr said: 'I met 'Ubada ibn al-Samit and said to him, "Will you not listen to what Abu Darda' is saying?" I then informed him of what he said concerning the loss of knowledge. He said, "Abu Darda' has spoken truthfully. If you wish I will inform you of the first knowledge to be removed from people. It is humility (*khushu'*). You will enter the central masjid and hardly find a single humble person! """ (al-Hanbali 2001, 10). Shakir repeatedly reminds his students that "knowledge arrogates." Knowledge makes one make claims (often in proprietary ways), such that cultivating humility becomes a foundational ethic of Islamic knowledge seeking. This humility does not prevent or limit critique, but instead enables one to reflect on one's practice of critique or intellectual inquiry with the ethics of knowledge, power, and mutual survival and salvation at the forefront.[49]

In Linda Alcoff's call for an "Epistemology for the Next Revolution," she urges scholars to move beyond description and critique toward a reconstruction of "how to make truth claims both responsible to political realities as well as reliable and adequate to the complexity of reality" (Alcoff 2011, 70). As Alcoff argues, it has become necessary not only to decolonize, but also to reconstruct epistemology, especially in the face of a political conservatism that uses "postmodern" critiques of scientific positivism to disprove theories of climate change, public health, and socioeconomic theories of the widening gaps between rich and poor. Indeed, (Bay Area) Muslim critiques of and apprehensions about critical theory, including those I witnessed, stem from its deconstructive quality, which seems to run counter to a theologically informed metaphysics of space and time. This common aversion to deconstruction and Allahless visions of (individual) liberation form the grounds upon which Muslims, like those at Zaytuna College, sometimes ally themselves with conservative Catholics, Christians, Jews, and nonmonotheistic conservatives. An epistemology for the next "requires us to uncover and reassess disavowed knowledges and to clarify the grounds of our own claims of adequacy or epistemic progress" while also disinvesting a reconstructed epistemology "of a mastery that would ignore the identity and situatedness of knowers while maintaining its normative capacity" (Alcoff 2011, 70).

Alcoff and liberation theologist Enrique Dussel's *political epistemology* is founded on a specific truth claim, "that currently existing social theories do not meaningfully engage with some of the most critical difficulties faced by the global poor" (Alcoff 2011, 71). Anthropological works that situate the global poor, disenfranchised, and dispossessed at the center of analysis and likewise as sources of social description and theory are moves toward a political epistemology when they also question and consider the categories and relations of power that inhere in the anthropological project (Harrison 1997; Smith 2012; Jesús and Pierre 2020; Visweswaran 1998; Jobson 2020). This means taking seriously "the work of thinking through the ontological implications of our truth claims" and the claims to truth our interlocutors articulate (Alcoff 2011, 71). While Alcoff directs her call to contemporary scholars, I recognize how political epistemologies, which are grounded in the knowledge and experiences of the most vulnerable, have been reconstructed time and time again by those same communities as matters of survival. The blues adhan functions in this text as a way to remember and be called by these political epistemologies of our liberatory lineages.

In his analysis of the blues and plantation power in the Mississippi Delta, Clyde Woods attempts to "bridge the gap between the blues as a widely recognized aesthetic tradition and the blues as a theory of social and economic development and change" (Woods 2017, 20). For Woods, a "blues epistemology rests on two foundations. The first involves the constant reestablishment of collective sensibility in the face of constant attacks by the plantation bloc and its allies, and in the face also of a daily community life that is often chaotic and deadly" (Woods 2017, 29–30). The second attends to "social relations in the plantation South as one of the foundational pillars of African American culture" (Woods 2017, 30). Woods understands the South, and the Mississippi Delta more specifically, "as a Mecca," which suggests that the movement from the South to the North marks the establishment of multiple Medinas like the one by the Bay (Woods 2017, 290). The blues as a form of communication, analysis, and mode of being emerged from the South post-Reconstruction. As a foundational infrastructure of feeling, it shapes the contours of places like the Bay Area where African Americans migrated and continued the "constant reestablishment of collective sensibility," faced with a plantation epistemology that extended to white supremacist and racial capitalist structures in Northern cities. In a world largely ordered by such plantation epistemologies, a blues orientation cohered in African American theories and praxes directed toward collective survival and "nothing less than a new life" (Rosemont 1975, 8).[50]

Throughout the sixteenth through the nineteenth centuries, West African Islamic epistemologies and ontologies contributed a Muslim poetics to the blues challenge to plantation ethics and logics (Diouf 2019; El Shibli 2007).[51] Sylviane Diouf (1998) demonstrates how Islamic notions of the self and community continued to persevere under the conditions of slavery as Muslims sustained practices such as fasting, charity, remembrance of Allah with prayer beads, and prayer. Muslims actively led and participated in slave revolts and maroon communities, contributing to the eventual emergence of the blues as a "theory of social and economic development and change" and the Black Radical tradition (Woods 2017, 20; Gomez 2005; Austin 2012; Robinson 2000; Lovejoy 1994; Reis and Brakel 1993).[52]

When Brother Masoud calls the adhan in Scene 1, we (ideally) hear the whole world—the spread of Islam, forced and willful migrations across the Atlantic and Pacific, and migrations from the South to the North—and a circular history of 1,400 years.[53] The adhan called by Brother Masoud was first called by Bilal ibn Rabah (al-Habashi, the Abyssinian, 580–640 CE), the most well-known among many African-descended Companions of the Prophet Muhammad. While in Medina, Bilal became the first *muezzin,* caller of the adhan, after the Prophet designated him to do so because of his "penetrating voice" (Ibn Hisham, Ibn Ishaq, and Guillaume 2001, 236). From that moment, he would climb onto the roof of the tallest house in Medina (and later in Mecca) and call out the adhan until the day the Prophet passed away.[54]

In 1975, Imam Warith Deen Muhammad referred to himself and the community of Muslims whom he led in the Transition as Bilalians, "because of the great dissatisfaction and confusion among our people concerning a proper and dignified name for themselves" (Muhammad and Aleem 2014). A year later, Imam Muhammad further elaborated: "We are here with a new consciousness that is not a black consciousness or a white consciousness but a divine consciousness" (Muhammad and Aleem 2014). As Precious Rasheedah Muhammad and Mahasin Abuwi Aleem state, Imam Muhammad's use of "Bilalian" "was designed to free the minds of a people; to move beyond the trappings and limitations of colorism and racism; to enable them to see themselves as slave servants of Allah alone; to follow the moral arc of Bilal ibn Rabah; to be truly free" (2014). This *spiritual* political epistemology marked the particular experience and history of Bilalians as a "new" ethnic group "of this land" (W. D. Muhammad as quoted in Abdul Khabeer 2017a, 36), which drew upon African descent but specifically emerged in the "context and process" (L. B. Simpson 2017; Barker 2018) of struggle and freedom-seeking in the United States and the Americas. The worlding, collective sense-making, and freedom-seeking of the "Bilalians" is part of what it means to both call and respond to the blues adhan.

The combination of the blues with the adhan speaks to the specific call of Islam in these lands and what it requires of Muslims in their ethical relations to this place, themselves, one another, and Allah.[55] The blues adhan demands a listening to history and its lessons, to what Black experience and epistemologies offer Black people, those who were here before, and those who have arrived more recently. To listen to the blues is to hear the lessons of enslavement, Emancipation, Reconstruction, Jim Crow, the Great Migration, redlining and racism, COINTELPRO, and mass incarceration. It is to hear the broken promises and the harmonies and "cacophonies" of histories of dispossession, struggle, and survival (Byrd 2011). The blues adhan also requires us to attend to visions for economic, social, and cultural justice that arrived with other migrations to the San Francisco Bay Area. Land-based, anticolonial struggles and exile from Palestine to India to Fiji to Afghanistan offer their own blues epistemologies as well; while their rhythms and tonalities may differ, they also cry "a new society being born" (Woods 2017, 39). The blues adhan connects all Muslims to a Qur'anic injunction to assist orphans, those in bondage, the indigent/wretched/damned, travelers, and the poor. Through its ethical and political focus on the most vulnerable in our society, Islam provides the resources for a counter humanism and epistemology for the next, should Muslims see, listen, and reflect.

A significant element of Islamic and Muslim survival, "one of the most astounding features of our own tradition," is a commitment to *ikhtilaf* (difference) and its coexistence with *ijmaa'* (consensus), meaning that for centuries, Muslims have coexisted with one another with an understanding that different Muslims followed different schools of law and practiced certain elements of their faith differently, while also agreeing on certain fundamentals (S. A. Jackson 2011). Throughout the text I discuss how difference *between* Muslims and as Muslims was articulated and experienced in classes, *khutbas* (sermons), geographies, conversations, and everyday life. This challenge of difference and multiplicity is an essential quality that Muslims must remember, as we consider "how can one re-create without re-circulating domination" (Trinh 1991, 15)?

From the ethnocinematic to an epistemology for the next, *Medina by the Bay* is a practice of research/filmmaking/writing as creative event—"A creative event does not grasp, it does not take possession, it is an excursion. More often than not, it requires that one leaves the realms of the known, and takes oneself there where one does not expect, is not expected to be" (Trinh 1991, 26).[56] I write as a form of invitation for you to engage without the expectation that you are receiving a translation of "a reality outside itself," but rather "the emergence of a new reality" (Trinh 1989, 22). It is an invitation to wander and travel within Medina by the Bay.

For those who inhabit Medina by the Bay, it is an invitation to reflect upon it attuned to other frequencies and rhythms. It is an around the way approach from "an around the way girl" to interrogate the produced and fixed meanings around race and religion that provide some explanation for how the United States continues to be at war with, dictates to, sanctions, incarcerates, kills, and starves Muslims around the world, while Muslims are simultaneously signifiers for, actors in, and resistors of the multicultural and multidenominational possibility of the colonial racial capitalist state.[57] As I bring theories and theologies together, I expect you to feel some discomfort, but that for me makes space for a new reality, for an essential, however difficult, conversation toward our mutual survival, the unveiling of hearts, and all that entails.

CHAPTER 1

MEDINA BY THE BAY

———————

SCENE 1

FADE IN

EXTERIOR. BAPTIST SEMINARY COURTYARD, BERKELEY, 2011,
SUNNY, MID-AFTERNOON..

WIDE—We see a group of STUDENTS sit in a wide circle on green grass facing
their teacher, IMAM ZAID SHAKIR.

CUT TO:
MEDIUM CLOSE UP—ANTHROPOLOGIST sits in the circle, watching and taking
notes.

ANTHROPOLOGIST (VOICE-OVER [VO])

It was neither the first nor the last time we sat in a circle on the green
grass of the Zaytuna College courtyard (CUT BACK TO WIDE SHOT of
class from above). It was the last day of Islamic History class, and PRO-
FESSOR SHAKIR indulged the STUDENTS' requests to sit outside in the
sun for the second half of class.

CUT TO:
MEDIUM TRACKING—Ten minutes before. The ANTHROPOLOGIST exits a classroom where students are excitedly gathering their books. She runs down a long
hallway to a room with cubicles set up. She arrives slightly out of breath and
addresses the bearded Black man, HAROON, sitting at his desk.

ANTHROPOLOGIST

As-salaam alaykum, Brother Haroon. Imam Zaid is taking his class out to the courtyard for their last class. It might be a nice thing to film.

HAROON

Wa alaykum as salaam, Sister Maryam! Thank you for letting me know. *Insha'Allah* (Allah willing) I can get out there after I finish a few things.

ANTHROPOLOGIST

Insha'Allah!

CUT TO:

WIDE—We see the grassy courtyard where SHAKIR and the STUDENTS reflect on the year and the specific texts they read that semester like Ali Allawi's *The Crisis of Islamic Civilization* and Sylviane Diouf's *Servants of Allah: African Muslims Enslaved in the Americas.* HAROON approaches the circle with both his recently acquired HD (high definition) video camera on a tripod and his smaller DSLR (digital single-lens reflex camera). As SHAKIR and the students go around in a circle, HAROON, robust yet unobtrusive, maneuvers around the student-teacher circle, filming and photographing "learning at Zaytuna College." Making quick eye contact, the ANTHROPOLOGIST silently reaches for HAROON's DSLR, yearning to participate in the image-making from her eye-level vantage point in the circle.

AMINAH (ARAB STUDENT
IN HER LATE TEENS)

I guess because there are so many Muslims from different backgrounds that are in America, they have that as a strength, like our diversity is a strength.

CUT between wider shots from HAROON's camera outside the circle and close-up shots of students' notebooks and hands, as well as medium shots of single students as they speak or listen to their classmates and teacher, shot from the ANTHROPOLOGIST's POV.

At the core of all these problems that we have been discussing, at least at some level, is the myth of the autonomous individual as a possibility, and so, rather than going for this political power grab and just inverting authority and as Allawi mentions, giving it a Muslim veneer, I think we have an opportunity to actually build the kind of net that held Muslim societies together, through building our inner spirituality and building a community that is interdependent, rather than everyone going their own separate way, which is kind of the drumbeat of dominant society.[1]

RASMEA (NORTH AFRICAN STUDENT IN HER EARLY TWENTIES)

Kind of going back to what Aminah mentioned about Muslims from different countries, and with different types of Muslims, I think that just reflects what Islamic civilization was before: that it wasn't really just this one country . . . and I feel like that creates an opportunity for us to get beyond just like focusing on nationalistic and ethnic markers and really thinking about creating, focusing on the Islamic framework, and how can we move forward in this kind of project of recreating Islamic civilization.[2]

IMAM ZAID SHAKIR

And recreating through creativity, because our situation is new. It's unprecedented. Especially here in this country, for Muslims. So, no one should see their horizons limited by anything that's out there. Either in the sense that "oh we can't measure up to that." Like "this is the ISLAMIC and we can't measure up," or in the sense that, well, "it's never been done that way," but as long as we adhere to the fundamental principles, then we can do whatever we want and dare to envision different types of institutions, different sets of parameters to guide our action, different visions of what a community should be, and not necessarily a community where we're all living in one enclave, but a community that's united by common principles, by common struggles, by common ideals, and then moving through history toward a common destiny. That, that's what a community is. . . .

CUT TO:

PHOTO AND VIDEO MONTAGE of Muslim individuals, families, groups standing and sitting, staring at the camera in moving portraits. IMAM ZAID SHAKIR and ZAHRAH continue over the montage.

IMAM ZAID SHAKIR (VO)

... Creating a space where you can have real intellectual freedom, but where you can use that toward fulfilling a higher spiritual mission, and that is to make a contribution from a different space to a world that's increasingly being overwhelmed by just a hegemonic oneness ... and that you can have this plurality, diversity of thoughts, of ideas, orientations, and it can all be pushed and moved toward a common goal and a common direction, insha'Allah.

ZAHRAH (VO)

I think I would agree with Aminah and the others, who said that our diversity could very well be our strength, whether that's ethnic or class, or in terms of religious interpretation, and it reminds me of very, very early Islam—the Prophet *salla Allahu 'alayhi wa-sallam* (May God honor him and grant him peace), people leaving their tribal affiliations to become a part of something that transcends the tribe. . . .

I remember in the very beginning [of the academic year], Shaykh Hamza was talking about the so-called outlaws in that time in Arab society who were so fed up with all the tribal divisions and with what was thought to be, what was thought to make someone honorable, and all those things that went with belonging to a tribe. And so, they kind of outlawed themselves into their own tribe, and to me, I found similarities with early Islam, where people were also fed up with what it meant to belong to a tribe. And once they saw the truth of Islam, they could kind of put the two next to each other and see what was truth and what was falsehood.[3]

CUT back to MEDIUM CLOSE-UP of ZAHRAH.

And so, I think in some ways, we are like them, where we've been broken apart and split from our tribal associations, and we have this opportunity to, I don't know, this is like kind of our Medina, you know? Like we can be more at home here and really make something of our own and really establish ourselves, and then go back out, you know, when we've decided who we are. And we can go back out and, insha'Allah, spread our message of truth and goodness to all the people.

FADE OUT

In an expanded director's cut of a scene from the introduction, we see and hear Zahrah and her classmates conclude two semesters of studying fourteen hundred years of global Islamic history. The scene conveys the ethnographic and ethnocinematic relation we practiced at Zaytuna College while also evoking the dialogic process of the class. Throughout this first academic year, Shakir guided his students through an expansive history of Muslim figures, events, and thought, presenting Islamic history as a global history to understand our collective present and imagine possible futures. Shakir and his students emphasize Islamic history's generative, rather than prescriptive qualities; it yields lessons that require creative thinking and praxis oriented to the specificity of their time and place, that draws from their diversity and locates itself outside of the logics, myths, and boundaries that govern the "individualistic" society in which they live.

That the students can imagine Zaytuna as "their Medina" speaks to the freedom and possibility they experience and how connected these are to their aspirations and plans for establishing society anew. Steve speaks about "building our inner spirituality and building a community that is interdependent," envisioning and rethinking Islamic frameworks toward new social formations. This impulse to turn to Islamic knowledge—its histories, theories, and theologies—and its ethics—how humans relate to and structure their lives with one another, and with Allah—has been an ongoing practice that shaped Medina by the Bay. In this chapter, I reduce the geographic and historical scale of Islamic history to less than a century of Muslim life in the Bay Area to consider how Islamic knowledge practices informed and transformed selves and social relations. I put *da'wa* (socioreligious activism and invitation) and *ta'lim* (teaching/ instruction of *'ilm,* knowledge, and *'ulum,* sciences of Islam), and to a lesser degree *ta'dib* (cultivation of *adab*), in relation here to demonstrate how the ethics and politics of knowledge and survival are intertwined.[4] I show how formal and informal knowledge practices are related in ways that emphasize the transmission of knowledge as a set of relations and Islamic ways of being, ordered by the seeking itself rather than the pursuit of a degree. Personal, communal, and institutional histories evoke a sense of how diverse Muslim ways of knowing and being emerge and how knowledge-practices are often at the center of ensuring the survival of Muslims and Islam.

When Imam Zaid considers the difference between community as "enclave" (whether geographic or ethnic) and a community "united by common principles, by common struggles, by common ideals, and then moving through history towards a common destiny," he raises the importance of understanding the pursuit of Islamic knowledge as a communal responsibility and experience not bound by a specific geography or national belonging.[5] While formal schooling has been an important communal project throughout Muslim history and geographies, the history of Medina by the Bay demonstrates how informal sites of learning were equally significant and necessary for communal autonomy, reproduction, and survival. As Muslims fulfilled their communal and individual obligations of transmitting and learning Islamic knowledge, they reordered the logics and structures of their social relations at multiple levels. One reason was that many of the earliest Muslims in the Bay converted to Islam, so unlearning and relearning, to "select and reselect liberatory lineages" (Gilmore 2017, 237), was an essential part of becoming Muslim.

Classes at Nation of Islam temples, rented storefronts, mosques, and community centers were critical parts of shaping infrastructures of feeling that transformed social relations and political practice both within and beyond Muslim communities often in tandem with Muslim organizing at colleges and universities. From rallies on Sproul Plaza at UC Berkeley and Friday prayers at city halls to securing street corners, campaigning against liquor stores, teaching chess and martial arts, and organizing camping trips, mentoring, and programming for Muslim and non-Muslim youth, Muslims were inviting others to Islam through their practices of critique, community, multiracial solidarity, and activism (da'wa). Elementary schools were essential sites for organizing young families in Muslim communities that likewise served non-Muslim neighbors. Parents were teachers, caregivers, and maintenance workers, both during school and after school, recognizing that raising children together sustained them materially and spiritually. The Bay Area began to resegregate in the 1990s after becoming its most socioeconomically and racially integrated around 1989. As communities were pressured by external and internal forces like police surveillance and infiltration, doctrinal and political differences, interpersonal strife, gentrification, gun violence, and economics, the personal and material infrastructures they built became more difficult to sustain.

The following scenes move through three overlapping geographies and histories through which da'wa and ta'lim shape the contours of Medina by the Bay. This is not an exhaustive history that names and dates every movement, location, nor emergent strategy, "strategy for building complex patterns and systems of change through relatively small interactions" (A. M. Brown 2017). Rather, these different histories and geographies are offered as openings and portals through which we get a sense of the heterogeneities of Muslim study and struggle. These lineages provide geographic, demographic, and affective infrastructure for the following scenes and chapters to move through and against.

SCENE 2 cinematically juxtaposes the experiences of three individuals who joined the the Nation of Islam (NOI) in the 1950s, 1960s, and 1970s, respectively. In the 1950–1960s, the NOI was the predominant form of Islam in Medina by the Bay, concentrated in Oakland and San Francisco, while Arab, Iranian, South Asian, and other Muslims also began to establish communities in San Francisco and beyond. In LIBERATORY LINEAGES, I trace multiple movements—*Up from the South, Across the Pacific,* and *Through the Counterculture*—to chart some of the ways of knowing and being that constitute Medina by the Bay. The 1970s–1990s are a period of growth and multiple transitions and migrations as Medina by the Bay expands north and south on both the East and West sides of the Bay; the 1990s–2000s mark another wave of conversion, migration, and movement as new formal and informal schools and institutions emerge. SCENES 3–5 consider this later time period from multiple points of view that conclude this chapter where I began—at Zaytuna College.

MONTAGE

EXTERIOR. FARMLAND IN THE CENTRAL VALLEY
OF CALIFORNIA, 1950S, DAY.

We see a young couple, BENJAMIN, a Latino and Native (Seminole/Yaqui) man, and CECILIA, a Latina woman, say goodbye to their families, leaving the Central Valley. They drive west and then north along the coast and across the Bay Bridge into Oakland.

BENJAMIN (VO, NOW IN HIS SEVENTIES)

My parents lived in Tulare County, small town near Fresno, Califor-nia . . . *Alhamdulillah* (Praise be to God), I was blessed to get married in 1955, went on my honeymoon to the West Coast, and I migrated to Oakland, California.

INTERIOR. CANNERY. EAST OAKLAND, 1950S, DAY.
We see BENJAMIN working (on an assembly line canning cat and dog food) and talking with a middle-aged Black man.

BENJAMIN (VO, CONT'D)

I was able to get a job with CALO Pet Food. One of the brothers work-ing here (at the cannery) was a captain (in the NOI), and I had a chance to work with him and talk with him, become friendly with him, so he invited me to hear about Islam, and I liked it the minute I heard it.

INTERIOR. SECOND-FLOOR ROOM ON SEVENTH STREET AND
HENRY IN WEST OAKLAND, 1955–1957, EVENING.
We see BENJAMIN sitting at a NOI meeting in Oakland. He is the only non-Black person. He listens intently to speeches of multiple speakers over a few hours. After the meeting, he happily eats bean soup, whiting fish with fresh vegetables, and bean pie.[6]

BENJAMIN (VO, CONT'D)

I saw there was a lot of knowledge in their teachings to Black people. Their food was delicious. They were friendly. I liked it there, and I stayed. Our source of information was the ministers that were traveling between here and Chicago, and we, for a time, helped disseminate the *Herald Dispatch* out of Los Angeles, the *Amsterdam News*. And any other news that would carry our thoughts and inspirations.[7]

ANTHROPOLOGIST (VO)

It took two years for Benjamin to get his "X" because the Nation of Islam had not yet made official "concessions" to enroll non-African Americans. The Honorable Elijah Muhammad "finally made the decision, well, if he's Indian, we can take him in as an Indian" (Waajid 2021a).

EXTERIOR. BERKELEY HIGH SCHOOL, BASKETBALL COURT. EARLY-1960S, DAY.
We see a sixteen-year-old LOUIS (African American) practicing basketball with his classmates. He stops and notices the JANITOR who walks and works with a sense of dignity.

INTERIOR. LIVING ROOM, SAN FRANCISCO, 1967, NIGHT.
We see KATHLEEN CLEAVER, ELDRIDGE CLEAVER, and ROSA, an African American seventeen-year-old young woman, sitting together assembling *The Black Panther* newspaper. KATHLEEN and ELDRIDGE tell stories, ROSA listens, while assembling the papers.

RASHEEDA (ROSA IN HER SIXTIES, VO)

So, here I am, sixteen-, seventeen-year-old Catholic schoolgirl. . . . I would finish my day at school and then go check in down at the Panther office. . . . I either worked down at the office or go out selling papers, serving breakfast that morning, working on food distribution. . . . You know, all the work that was involved in the early movement days of taking care of the people. Sometimes I would be on security, and I would have my book here, have my little gun here (she laughs) 'cause I was supposed to be keeping the place safe. Now, was I the biggest critical player? No. Strictly a foot soldier. . . . Eldridge and Kathleen, you know becoming acquainted with them, listening to them, their humorous stories. . . . There were some rich tales being told as we were taking our little razors and cutting articles. . . . She (Kathleen) would type the articles, and we would cut the articles out, and we would lay them out.

INTERIOR. STUDENT LOUNGE, UC BERKELEY, 1968–1969, EVENING.

We see LOUIS (a few years older) and other young African American men gambling, dollars and coins strewn across the table. Another young man approaches them, holding a stack of *Muhammad Speaks* newspapers. The young men are annoyed but accommodating.

NOI BROTHER

You gotta buy a paper!

LOUIS

Alright man, sure, we'll buy a paper, just leave us alone.

INTERIOR. DORM ROOM, NIGHT.

We see LOUIS sitting on his bed, reading the *Muhammad Speaks* paper—studiously reading articles, taking notes, and laughing at cartoons.

ABDUL-MALIK (LOUIS IN HIS SEVENTIES, VO)

That was probably my most studious contact with Islam at the time, reading that newspaper. . . . I began to hear some people from our neighborhood embrace this organization and join this organization called the Nation of Islam. They became Muslims as we were saying then. In my evolution into the kinda Black consciousness that was rising at the time, that newspaper was somewhat of an integral part because I remember taking the cartoons out of the paper. They had some fantastic cartoons in the paper. And I was using that for at least one class that I wrote something concerning the cartoons in that paper.[8]

INTERIOR. MEETING/CLASSROOM, NATION OF ISLAM TEMPLE 26, WESTERN ADDITION, SAN FRANCISCO, DAY.

We see a blackboard. On the board is a drawing of the Nation of Islam flag, a star and crescent in the center with the letters F, J, E, and I in each corner. A young man points to the flag, teaching about each symbol. Women sit on one side of the room, while men sit on the other.

I was a college student at the university looking for a way to help
the movements that were going on to bring more dignity to African
Americans, the civil rights movement. Malcolm had just been killed
four years before that. An intense debate was going on between the
members of the Nation and those who were influenced by Malcolm's
leaving the Nation and so on and so forth, and I found the arguments
of the people who, . . . most of my classmates were persuaded that
the Nation of Islam was a path to the betterment of the condition of
African Americans, of Black people, and I joined that group.

NOI MINISTER

The "F" stands for freedom, "J" stands for justice, "E" stands for equality, and "I" stands for Islam . . . we don't turn cheeks—that is only going
to get you two broken jaws.[9]

CUT TO:

We see BENJAMIN and other brothers study martial arts with a Chinese instructor in Alameda and then teaching at the temples to larger groups as part of the
Fruit of Islam training.[10]

ABDUL-MALIK (VO)

. . . The Nation of Islam, you know, they had a moral component that I
think that's what separated them for me . . . they seemed to be better
organized. Freedom, justice, and equality is what they were, what the
cry was, what the goal was. And so that captured me to the degree that
I wanted to work for this cause. So, I joined the cause in San Francisco.
Didn't know at the time when I first joined that there was a temple
in Oakland. . . . I never really liked San Francisco: the distance, the
weather, the streets, the narrow streets, left and down and all that. . . .
So, I was really happy when I found a place in Oakland. So, I became
a member of the mosque in 1969 in Oakland that eventually earned a
number.

Imam Benjamin Perez (1933–2009) is recognized in both the NOI and in the Bay Area Muslim community as a "pioneer" dedicated to connecting Latinx and Native peoples to Islam through da'wa.[11] He was active in the farmworkers' movement and coordinated an interview with Cesar Chavez for the *Muhammad Speaks* newspaper. He passed away in 2009; scenes of his life are drawn from interviews he conducted with journalists, researchers, and fellow Muslims, and the memories of those he impacted. He was a significant role model for younger Latinx and Native Muslims, and he started numerous organizations and initiatives to increase the conversion/reversion of Latinx and Native Muslims throughout California and beyond while also increasing the understanding of other Muslims through his lectures and writings. He served as a prison chaplain from the 1960s onward.

Hajja Rasheeda was born in San Francisco in 1950 to a Black Catholic family. I first met her at Masjid Al-Ansar in North Oakland, and we quickly became sister-friends, as she enjoyed discussing and strategizing the future of the community and its role in changing the conditions of Black and brown people.[12] She had retired from her work as a principal at an Oakland elementary school, but she continued to be an active advocate for the young people of Oakland through her work with charter schools, Muslim schools, and her mentorship of Muslim women. Hajja Rasheeda was a pillar in the community, a critical part of its infrastructure of feeling, as she coordinated and participated in multiple feeding programs, organized mosque fundraisers, attended board meetings, and embodied a long history of Bay Area activism that continued into her final days. She encouraged me to consider these longer histories, and we spent much time discussing the internal and external challenges that lead to the flourishing or diminishing of Muslim communities, especially in relation to the community's spiritual development and transformative effect on the larger Bay Area. As I discuss in chapter 3, she continued to be active in the movement, which she entered first through reading groups and events in San Francisco and then with her participation in the Black Panther Party for Self-Defense (BPP). Black students at San Francisco State University (College at the time), recruited her to enroll in the fall of 1968, where she immediately joined campus movements.

I first met Abdul-Malik at Hajja Rasheeda's home in Oakland. While Rasheeda initially joined the BPP in 1967 and later joined the NOI around 1972–1973, Abdul-Malik joined the Nation of Islam in 1969 while a student athlete at UC Berkeley; though he had many friends in the BPP, he was unsure about the organization because "they were doing some stuff under the name of revolution that didn't interest me." He was drawn to the "moral component" and organizational structure and vision of the Nation. Like Perez, he became a prison chaplain, serving incarcerated Muslim communities throughout Northern California both before and after "the Transition," the 1975 communal transition of many in the NOI to Sunni Islam. In the 1980s he studied Islam in Sudan (where he met Shaykh Muhammad Shareef); in the 1990s he was a fixture throughout the many classes and organizations of Medina by the Bay; and in the 2000s he returned to his studies, receiving his master's degree from a US-based Islamic seminary program. While Oscar, whom we met in the introduction, had many informal and formal teachers, he learned from Abdul-Malik

> what a Muslim should be doing when they're not praying . . . working
> with people who are in need. Every Thursday night we at juvenile hall
> doing Islamic studies. On the weekends, we study the Qur'an, learn-
> ing Arabic. When you have free time on a Friday, you volunteer in the
> prisons with the incarcerated Muslim population . . . between *dhuhr*
> and *maghrib* (midday and sunset prayers), hanging out with Abdul-
> Malik . . . we would go to three or four different *masajid* (mosques)
> between Berkeley and Oakland . . . he would just drive around, and he
> knew everybody. We would go there, pray, and eat, and then meet some-
> body, pray, and eat, and do the thing. So, it was really Abdul-Malik who
> introduced me to everything.

Hajjis Benjamin, Rasheeda, and Abdul-Malik were all drawn to the NOI for its commitment to Black (and other) people and the infrastructure it provided for material, spiritual, and moral/ethical becoming. Its anti-white supremacist cosmology and projects of self-determination and vision for Black liberation drew thousands of people into their temples and influenced a wider discourse among African Americans about material and spiritual survival in the urban North, especially after World War II (Curtis 2006; Curtis 2002; Lincoln 1961; S. A. Jackson 2005; Gibson and Karim 2014; Taylor 2017). In the *Fatiha* (the opening chapter of the Qur'an), Muslims beseech Allah to guide them so that they will be among those guided on the Straight Path. Who and how Allah guides is a mystery (Mittermaier 2011). Several people close to Elijah Muhammad have said that when he guided African Americans, Latinx, and Native peoples to the Nation of Islam via a racialist theology, he meant it as a necessary step before they could fully accept Al-Islam, the global religion. Abdul-Malik says, "We believe there was a strategy in how he brought what he brought . . . Fard Muhammad to a great degree and Elijah Muhammad to a lesser degree maybe . . . but he was the one to expose his sons and some of that generation of Muslims to . . . if you want to call it 'classical Islam.' . . . My point is that Elijah Muhammad exposed his population to these knowledges that later became manifest."

Islamic history is marked in cycles through which renewers (*mujaddidin*), like al-Ghazali (d. 1111), Ibn Taymiyyah (d. 1328), and Shehu Usman Dan Fodio (d. 1817), revive the faith, preserving and propagating Islam as it circulates within and across different populations, worldviews, and geographies.[13] In the 1920s and 1930s, the Ahmadiyya movement from British India targeted African American populations for da'wa primarily on the East Coast and in the Midwest (El-Hajj Malik El-Shabazz and his friend Shorty Jarvis studied Islam in Boston in the 1940s with an Ahmadi brother) (Turner 2021); it was both a pedagogic effort to encourage greater piety and Islamic conduct and a proselytizing movement targeted at potential converts. Rasheeda's husband converted to Islam through the Ahmadiyya movement in St. Louis, and when he joined the Nation in the 1970s in Oakland, he taught many of its members the Fatiha of the Qur'an. Prior to and continuous with the NOI and the Ahmadiyya were informal exchanges of da'wa that Muslim migrants engaged in as a form of everyday life, whether they were Syrian peddlers selling their wares to non-Muslims or South Asian sailors settling in Harlem or New Orleans (Howell 2014; Bald 2013; O. Safi and Hammer 2013; GhaneaBassiri 2010).

I suggest that in the United States, the Honorable Elijah Muhammad and El-Hajj Malik El-Shabazz (Malcolm X) were perhaps the most influential revivers through their da'wa in African American communities.[14] While both were initially exposed to "orthodox" Islam and converted to Islam in prison, neither was well-educated in the formal sense of high school diplomas, college degrees, or Islamic certifications like *ijaza* (authority to teach a particular text or subject) and *isnad* (a chain of transmission from scholar to student). In El-Shabazz's own words, "I am not educated, nor am I an expert in any particular field—but I am sincere, and my sincerity is my credentials" (Malcolm X 1990, 20). El-Shabazz's life experiences and diligent forms of study shaped his approach to da'wa, ta'lim, and ta'dib. El-Shabazz was a *da'i,* one engaged in da'wa as the primary spokesperson for the Nation. What the NOI referred to as "fishing"—recruiting members through street corner preaching, selling newspapers, and providing services, jobs, and education—in Islamic terms was a form of da'wa, what is translated as "invitation," but can include forms of proselytizing, socio-religious activism, and moral/spiritual rectification. El-Shabazz's efforts to procure scholarships for Black Muslims abroad and his own teaching of history and sociocultural analysis in the NOI and the Organization of Afro-American Unity are good examples of ta'lim, while ta'dib, the restoring of just relations, was a driving force for his life's work, exemplified through his evolving approaches to the Fruit of Islam, self-discipline and comportment; gender relations; his critiques of power and its abuse; and his work for social justice: the restoration of Allah's cosmic order from the racism that corrupted it.

After his passing in 1975, the majority of Honorable Elijah Muhammad's community transitioned with his son, Imam Warith Deen Muhammad (whom Elijah Muhammad had sent to Egypt for Islamic studies), toward "orthodox" Sunni Islam, while thousands of other African Americans reverted or converted to Islam directly throughout the twentieth century. While the dominant narrative of African American Islam is that of the Nation of Islam, Sundiata Al Rashid reminds us "that before the invention of the personal computer, the Internet or the mobile phone, Blackamericans, who may have been the most disenfranchised group ever in this nation, were able to find Islam and form Muslim communities almost entirely independent of any outside missionary work" (Al Rashid 2014, 9). While the "missionary work" often made initial introductions, Al Rashid emphasizes the myriad and creative ways that Black people incorporated Islam into their liberatory lineages and infrastructures of feeling. From the proto-Islamic Moorish Science Temple (est. 1917) and the Nation of Islam to the "orthodox" Islamic Mission of America/Darul Islam movement (est. 1924), these movements aimed to break free of white supremacist common sense and colonial modes "in a ritual of purification" that reoriented them toward a global majority of the emergent Third World and anticolonial movements across the Atlantic (Al Rashid 2014, 12).

In contemporary usage, da'wa continues to take on multiple forms in the United States and throughout the Americas, drawing from the dynamic interchange between these geographies and a global Islamic revival that moved through Africa and Asia throughout the twentieth century and gained traction with the 1979 Islamic Revolution in Iran. Da'wa as "the sensibility of modern socioreligious activism and the spirit of doctrinal innovation," as well as an institutional and "individual obligation" is perhaps the driving impulse of many of the Muslim formations I discuss

(Mahmood 2005, 56–62). In the next section, I zoom out from the personal histories that **SCENE 2** introduces and present public and personal histories that constitute geographic, demographic, epistemic, and affective infrastructures that inform the dynamics of what comes later.

LIBERATORY LINEAGES

UP FROM THE SOUTH · When one listens to Muslims in the Bay Area, one hears multiple accents and traces in speech. Growing up in the Bay, my ears were full of multiple Black vernaculars and English as a second language.[15] There is a Bay Area drawl, an ease that reflects the Southern inflections that came northwest in the Great Migration, and a unique syncopation in words and phrasing that reflects the ways different language systems come to live in English. One can still hear Southern traces in Bay Area mosques, whether in the blues adhan or in the way someone will say "See you at the MASjid," stressing the first syllable and giving it a long, flat "A."[16]

Following an initial wave in the early twentieth century, the majority of African Americans in the Bay Area migrated during and immediately following World War II. They followed defense jobs—the Bay Area was the "largest shipbuilding center in the world" (Broussard 2001, 190)—and fled agricultural mechanization and Jim Crow in the South (Murch 2010). The National Association for the Advancement of Colored People (NAACP) and the West Coast branch of the Brotherhood of Sleeping Car Porters were highly influential in assisting Black migrants' "access to highly paid wartime employment" that diminished in the years following the war (Murch 2010, 17). Political culture, metropolitan space, and migration were closely interlinked in the East Bay. According to Murch, "The influx of southern migrants profoundly altered the social organization of northern California's African American communities, ultimately laying the groundwork for their political mobilization in subsequent decades. Migrants, initially branded as unwelcome 'newcomers,' quickly subsumed the small pre-war population into their quest for political access, a higher living standard, and in the case of the fortunate few, upward mobility. . . . New social cleavages emerged based on the timing of arrival, as well as between the groups able to realize the opportunity the San Francisco Bay Area afforded and those excluded from decent jobs, housing, and education" (Murch 2010, 16).

Rasheeda's father was from Lake Charles, Louisiana: "He came to California via the navy. He had been in Port Chicago actually, right around the bombing there.[17] And my mom was from Tulsa, Oklahoma; her mother knew a young man who was arrested and threatened to be hung by the Klu Klux Klan" during the Tulsa Massacre of 1921. "So, they both came from significant backgrounds and came to California for a better life. I believe they really wanted out of the South. I don't think they ever looked back. They went back to bury relatives because, you know, we were poor. So, we bury relatives and maybe try to visit when people were sick, but they looked to the North and headed to the North." While Rasheeda's family settled in San Francisco, where her father eventually became a supervisor at the post office and a well-known entrepreneur and her mother became a saleswoman at the Emporium Department Store, most African Americans, like the families of Abdul-Malik and others, migrated to the East Bay. Oakland's Black population went from 8,462 (3 percent of the population) in 1940 to 47,562 (12 percent) in 1950, and by 1980 Oakland was 51 percent African American (151,484 people), with the majority hailing from Texas, Louisiana, and Oklahoma, and to a lesser degree Arkansas and Mississippi.[18] The influx of Black people and the Southern culture, music, and faith they brought with them solidified an emergent Black middle class and force for political transformation.

Seventh Street in West Oakland was the center of Black life in the East Bay, from homes, churches, and union offices to blues clubs, bars, and smoke shops. Marcus Garvey's Universal Negro Improvement Association's West Coast headquarters was nearby on Eighth and Chester; the same building, Liberty Hall, was then occupied by Father Divine's Peace Mission. The NOI's Temple 26 was first established on Seventh Street down the road from the Brotherhood of Sleeping Car Porters, Slim Jenkins' Place (a blues and jazz club), and the West Oakland Church of God, to name a few. After Brother Malcolm's first visits to California in the mid- to late 1950s, Nation of Islam temples became more established, first in West Oakland and then in San Francisco's "Harlem of the West," the Western Addition (in the Fillmore).[19] Richmond and Sacramento also had temple numbers, while NOI communities in East Palo Alto and San Jose did not receive temple numbers. What is clear is that the Nation was a significant presence in much of the Bay Area, an active participant in a dynamic field of Black consciousness-raising and organizing.

El-Shabazz's 1957 travel in Los Angeles is well-documented as he responded to the murder of two Muslims by police officers there, but his Bay Area trips are less documented.[20] In Abdul-Malik's own historical research, he learned from an elder sister that El-Shabazz taught in the two-story building on Seventh and Henry around 1956–1957. Benjamin Perez met Minister Malcolm around this time in the late 1950s, and they "took a personal interest in each other, and we did good work together" increasing da'wa to Black, Latinx, and Indigenous communities throughout Oakland and nationally (Waajid 2021a). Their initial meeting was motivated by Minister Malcolm's interest in learning Spanish (Galvan 2017, 6). In 1961, students at UC Berkeley and members of the NAACP youth section organized to bring Minister Malcolm X to campus; they moved his talk to the YMCA's Stiles Hall off campus after he was banned by university administrators. Minister Malcolm "joked playfully with the audience that UC Berkeley had prevented him from speaking because he *was* a religious figure, while San Quentin had done so because he *was not*" (Murch 2010, 71). The minister astutely connected the university and the prison as relational structures of power and sites for collective study and struggle toward transformative change. Muslims had been organizing in San Quentin and other prisons throughout California for their rights on the grounds of religion, while prison officials and state entities consistently designated the NOI as a political organization rather than a religious community (Felber 2020).

Within a year of Malcolm's talk, "Elijah Muhammad: Messenger to the American Negro," the students (including Donald Warden, who would become Muslim thinker/writer Khalid Al-Mansour) who organized his visit would go on to form the Afro-American Association, which went from a campus study group to an "important force in Bay Area black politics" (Murch 2010, 71). This association, as well as the Nation of Islam, were instrumental precursors to the development of the Black Power movement and the Black Panther Party for Self-Defense in 1966.

Young people from throughout the Bay Area became deeply engaged in these study groups in which they read and discussed an assortment of critical texts from cultural anthropology, sociology, and literature, and later religious texts like the Bible and the Qur'an.[21] Students applied their studies to social action and community engagement; they began "street speaking," holding events like film screenings and conferences, and engaging in early forms of social media (newspapers, campaigns to engage Black celebrities in producing music, and radio and television programming). "All of these innovative methods of outreach focused on a single goal—encouraging local black youth to value education itself, independently from the legalistic framework of racial integration" (Murch 2010, 93).

Merritt College students Bobby Seale and Huey Newton began the Black Panther Party for Self-Defense in Oakland in 1966, after attending

events at the NOI temple, studying with the Afro-American Association,
and being exposed to the politics of decolonization throughout Africa and
Asia through international students, movement organizing, and antiwar
and anti-imperialist activism. Black and brown people and places were
being segregated, criminalized, and targeted by city, regional, and federal
officials for "urban renewal." The bustling Seventh Street corridor, increasingly overcrowded due to redlining and disenfranchised by deindustrial-
ization, was struck multiple times: the Cypress Freeway was built in the
1950s, splitting the neighborhood in half and separating it from downtown; a USPS distribution center was constructed in 1959–1960, wiping
out twelve blocks of housing and businesses; and BART's (Bay Area Rapid
Transit) West Oakland line was built as an overpass, towering over Seventh
Street's remaining businesses and homes (1960s–1970s). The Nation of
Islam offices were likewise displaced, and the community eventually made
its way east to Fruitvale while also waxing and waning in San Francisco and
throughout the Bay.

ACROSS THE PACIFIC · From at least 1900, Muslims, as well as Sikhs
and Hindus from the Punjab Province of British India, arrived in and settled throughout the West Coast from Washington to California (Leonard
1992, 32, 35). Muslims made up about 10 percent of the British Indians
who came to the Americas. In the early twentieth century, Karen Leonard
describes how Muslims sold tamales and popcorn in San Francisco, while
most of their counterparts were working in agriculture in the rural interior
of California, where the Sacramento and Imperial Valleys were "'just like the
Punjab'" (1992, 35). These farmworkers and their descendants established a
mosque in Sacramento in 1947. Other Punjabi Muslims worked with Sikhs,
Hindus, and leftist anticolonialists from the Indian subcontinent in the
Gadar Party (established in 1913 near Mission Dolores Park), an anticolonial and internationalist political movement based in San Francisco in the
early twentieth century (Ramnath 2011; Bald 2013; Sohi 2014).[22]

Muslims from the historical "Muslim world" continued to arrive at an
accelerated pace throughout the twentieth century, some as students, others
looking for work or joining family members. Most of the earliest Arab migrants to the Bay Area, dating from the early 1800s, were Christian Arabs
from the Levant. Muslim and Christian Arabs continued to immigrate to
the San Francisco Bay Area from the 1950s to the 1970s, often arriving in the
Bay Area through family and village networks and working in factories and
menial jobs (Naber 2012). Beginning in the 1950s, Muslim Yemenis worked

as farmworkers in the San Joaquin Valley. Many Arabs who may not have intended to stay in the United States were later unable or less inclined to return to their country either due to war, occupation, or lack of socioeconomic opportunity. Through familial and social networks and investment, both Christian and Muslim Arabs were able to invest in small businesses and in this period tended to identify with one another through pan-Arab nationalism rather than along sectarian lines of religion. Similar flows occurred for other Muslim populations from Iran, Turkey, Afghanistan, Pakistan, Nigeria, India, China, and other Muslim-populated countries.

Contrary to contemporary attitudes regarding "immigrant" Muslims and their upper- and professional class statuses, the population has been and continues to be socioeconomically diverse. In Nadine Naber's ethnography of Arab Americans in the Bay Area, one of her elder interlocutors discusses this 1960s and 1970s population wave and its diversity in class, religion, political ideology, and country of origin: "'More Arabs from Gulf States came to the Bay Area and more and more from Palestine, Lebanon, Syria, Jordan, and we also saw more and more North Africans and more Muslims. Some were already educated and economically sufficient. They became professionals who came directly into banking, real estate, and engineering. Others were not—they became farmers, taxi drivers, janitors, dish-washers'" (Naber 2012, 41).

African, Arab, and South and West Asian students, workers, and refugees established ethnic enclaves, prayer and community spaces, and businesses that became an essential part of the cultural fabric of the Bay Area, informing the ways *all* Bay Area residents imagined their situatedness in the world. For almost two decades, the Islamic Center of San Francisco and the Moslem Mosque in Sacramento (about 100 miles away) served the majority of Muslims and new coverts to the faith until the transition of NOI communities into Sunni Islam in 1975.

The Islamic Center of San Francisco, also known as "Crescent Street" or the "Markaz" (Center), was established in 1959 by Pakistani, Indian, and a few Arab immigrants in Bernal Heights, a multiracial working-class neighborhood that has become increasingly gentrified.[23] It is the oldest continuously operating mosque in the Bay Area. Beginning as a place where Muslims could host weddings and funerals, Crescent Street also became the base for the Tablighi Jama'at, an Islamic revival da'wa movement, especially from the 1970s onward until members purchased a building in Richmond across the Bay. Amir Sahb, of the Richmond Masjid Ar-Rahman, states that "the Jamaats would travel to many areas that had no mosque and set up in a local brother's garage and do the work from there. This was the impetus of many of the Bay Area mosques that grew out of these community visits" (Al Rashid 2014, 47).

At the same time, the Islamic center hosted a Sunday school for Muslim children. In Sunnyvale in the South Bay, Athar, a prominent community leader in the South Bay, and his siblings begrudgingly got out of bed at 7 A.M. every Sunday to make the drive to San Francisco for his 9 A.M. to noon Islamic classes (10 A.M.–1 P.M. in the winter). "It was mainly our parents who were teaching. My father . . . he taught I believe it was history. My mom also taught, you know, another course in '*ibadat* (acts of worship), so there was no, you know, there's no training, there's no, 'Let's make sure these folks have their credentials.' This was, 'If you want your kids to get an Islamic education, then come on over, but be prepared to teach.'" When Athar's family arrived from Hyderbad, India, via Minnesota where his father Waheed finished his PhD in electrical engineering in the mid-1960s, they joined a handful of families who had arrived in the 1950s–1960s to work primarily as engineers in an emergent Silicon Valley.

Knowing the difficulty of arriving in and acclimating to a new country and having received hospitality from one of the first South Asian families in the South Bay when he arrived, Waheed went over to the Stanford Student Center and put up a small poster. As Athar recounts, it said, "'If any Muslim is here from India or Pakistan, give us a call,' and he put his number there and that's how many, many people in the late sixties, early seventies got to know the community, because we would invite them over and have them over for dinner . . . and my dad would print out a photocopy of all the contacts and the phone numbers of other Muslims and say, 'Here. Here are other people that you might want to get to know.'"

The largest and most diverse Muslim population surges came in the years following the 1965 Immigration and Nationality Act that changed immigration quotas and enabled greater immigration from the Global East and South. Other critical factors include the 1967 Arab-Israeli War, the Soviet-Afghan War (1979–1989), the Islamic Revolution in Iran (1979), the Iran-Iraq War (1980–1988), civil wars in Yemen (1962–1970, 1986, 1994), Fijian independence and the military coups of 1987 (1970–1980s), and the Bosnian War (1992–1995), as well as more recent events like the first Gulf War (1990–1991) and the wars in Iraq and Afghanistan (2003–2021), focal points of the US "forever war," its "colonial expansion and war-making in the Greater Middle East across the long-twentieth century" (Kapadia 2019, 8). That most of these events were heavily influenced, enabled, or caused by American imperialism speaks to how migration to the United States is hardly a matter of individual choices and American dreams. Displacement from land; religious, ethnic, and political persecution; and war shaped the experiences of people pushed out of or fleeing their homelands. How one arrived and under what conditions, as well as who and what was left behind, further demonstrates the resonance of *hijra* (migration) to Medina (and the concomitant longing for Mecca) as an ongoing thematic in Muslim life.[24]

These experiences impacted how Muslims approached their material, cultural, and spiritual survival in Medina by the Bay. Working immigrants throughout these periods tended to focus more on securing immediate material needs—maintaining employment, housing, security, or establishing businesses; they were also sending remittances to families and communities abroad. Entrepreneurs who invested in real estate or otherwise accumulated or pooled sufficient wealth often moved out of the cities and into the suburbs, thereby further expanding migratory networks and patterns. The Bay Area became a destination because, as Athar says, people were "looking for a place where they feel safe, they can raise our families . . . where there's ample economic opportunities and jobs . . . a place that's affordable—believe it or not, there was a time at which the Bay Area was actually affordable—and, you know, they're looking for good schools."

California has been the top destination for immigrants to the United States since the mid-1970s, and in 2000, "California became a 'majority minority' state, with people of color constituting more than 50 percent of the population" (Pellow and Park 2002, 19). People were more likely to move to a place if they had a contact or family member there or if they knew there was a community with which they could share food, language, customs, and news of home. When a community reached a threshold of families, community members pooled resources to build a mosque and then a school. Crescent Street Mosque was often one of the first starting points for new Muslims, whether they were new to the Bay Area or to Islam, yet within a few decades, the Bay Area would have hundreds of mosques, schools, and cultural centers.

THROUGH THE COUNTERCULTURE · Post–World War II, the Bay Area was also attractive to young white Americans who traveled to Berkeley and San Francisco to participate in the burgeoning counterculture with its foundations in the Beat movement and the region's progressive and union-based politics. While Murshida Rabia Martin (1871–1947), a follower of Inayat Khan (d. 1927), established a *khanqah* (a gathering place for a Sufi order) in Marin County in the North Bay in the 1920s, the most visible traces of Islam among white Americans emerge out of the 1960s and 1970s when according to Gisela Webb, "large numbers of (mostly) young middle-class Americans located the cause of racism, the Vietnam War, and the evils of technocracy in a spiritual sickness that establishment religions in America had not only failed to solve but had fostered" (Hermansen 2000, 159; Bazzano and Hermansen 2020).

At the "wisdom traditions" Shambhala Books in Berkeley or the beatnik City Lights Bookstore in North Beach, one could find books on Islam and Sufism. In Berkeley, where some of the books were published, there were small collectives of (soon-to-be) white Muslims living together, in tune with the psychedelic and Eastern religion–seeking attributes of the time. As poet Daniel Abdul Hayy Moore reminisces, "we had a light spiritual schedule, getting up in the morning, doing some Yoga and Zen meditation out on the top floor deck in the sunshine, and reading sections from the Nicholson translation of Rumi's *Mathnawi*, which I had just purchased from Shambhala, down on Telegraph Avenue. It was for us a mysterious book full of surreal tales, fabulously imaginative, whose purpose was to know Allah, but we didn't yet connect it with Islam and living Sufism, which had a very limited presence amid the Hinduism and Buddhism that prevailed then."[25]

Ties were made to Muslim communities in England and Morocco through travel, writing, and particular individuals; while a few blocks away Hamid Algar began teaching courses on Islam and Middle Eastern Studies at UC Berkeley in 1965, where he influenced generations of Muslim students. Algar's Shi'i-informed Islam based on his studies in Iran came together with the internationalist and social justice politics of students in the area. The "transformative power of education" (Murch 2010, 91) and a connected ethical self-making was a significant mobilizing force, and students organized across campuses to defend free speech, establish women's studies and ethnic studies, and oppose the Vietnam War, apartheid, and US imperialism in Iran and later Central and Latin America. College campuses, junior colleges, and universities were critical nodes in social movement building and protest; they were also sites of multiracial interaction and dialogue and often drew minority elites from around the country and the emergent postcolonial Third World.

The Muslim population in the Bay Area swelled in the political and countercultural hotbed of the 1960s and 1970s. Numerous political agendas came together as international students became involved in local civil rights struggles and antiwar protests, while also drawing attention to international struggles in their own countries. The 1980s and 1990s witnessed both continuity and resurgence in solidarity politics with Palestine and antiwar activism—this time the first Gulf War—and numerous local issues and state-based ballot initiatives concerning juvenile justice, immigrant rights, affirmative action, police brutality, and other issues that consolidated progressive and radical interests.

SCENE 3—FIVE SHAHADAS A WEEK, AN ISLAMIC MOVEMENT, PART 1

INTERIOR. AFRICAN AMERICAN HISTORY CLASS, BERKELEY HIGH SCHOOL, LATE 1980S, DAY.

We see a classroom with walls covered with Black history posters—the West African Islamic kingdoms of Mansa Musa and Askia Muhammad Touré. Berkeley High School is the only high school that has an ongoing African American Studies program post–civil rights in the United States. The students are reading *The Autobiography of Malcolm X.* MARIO, an African American young man, is at full attention as HIS TEACHER leads discussion.[26]

MARIO (NOW IN HIS FORTIES) (VO)

At that time around '88 in Berkeley High, all I would do was wake up late, go to lunch, meet my friends, cut school all afternoon and do other stuff. Except my Black Studies classes, I would go to, and I would pass. I was in upper-track English, and it was called "World Literature" and all of the books were written by Europeans, so there was an element of just kind of wanting to party and another, feeling disillusioned with the system that I was in. So, at that point, when I was beginning to get exposed to Islam, something about Malcolm's life probably was the first inspiration and then the fact that there were those Muslim kingdoms that were African, just gave me, like, kind of a feeling of respect or some sort of an allegiance with Islam and the Muslims, and it was very much associated with, you know, being an African American in this context.

Mario was born and raised in Berkeley, the son of a white mother and an African American father. After his parents' divorce, his mother put him in the care of an African American woman, who had moved to Berkeley from the South, in order to "know my father's culture." He was reared by this "church-going religious woman" and "revolutionaries that were Left, very far to the Left, like we had friends that were Sandinistas that came and lived with us, and we went and visited in Nicaragua and friends that went to El Salvador and all kinds of Central American activists and people associated with that, and so I was around agnostics and atheists on my mother's side." Mario's upbringing represents both the stereotypes and the realities of the Bay Area in the 1970s and 1980s. Berkeley and Oakland had been at the forefront of civil rights activism in the 1960s as exemplified by the Free Speech, Black Power, and antiwar movements, and the Third World Liberation Front struggles at San Francisco State (1968) and UC Berkeley (1969), and Bay Area progressive activists were also deeply involved in anti-imperialist struggles in Central America and the Middle East (Hobson 2016; Naber 2012; Nasrabadi and Matin-Asgari 2018).

Hajja Rasheeda introduced me to Mario on one of his return visits to the Bay from Tarim, Yemen, where he had made hijra. After converting to Islam, Mario married Nurideen, who was born into the Brooklyn-based Dar Ul-Islam movement and raised in the East Bay.[27] Shortly after his graduation from Berkeley High, Mario and Nurideen moved to East Oakland, a block away from Masjid Al-Islam, in order to live near a mosque where he could attend the five daily prayers. Begun by Oakland-raised Imam Abdul Alim Musa (who had converted to Islam in prison where he had been serving time for drug-related crimes) in 1981, the mosque eventually started a school, owned properties, and started businesses in the area surrounding the mosque. Prior to opening Masjid Al-Islam, "Imam Musa traveled around the country by car to raise funds . . . he would drive to college towns and visit with members of the Muslim Student Associations. He drove from Oakland to Michigan on two separate occasions and raised $80,000, which he used to purchase a building in East Oakland" (Al Rashid 2014, 28). Imam Musa and a core group that included the young Mario, Nurideen and her family, Hajar, and others fostered a dynamic Muslim community that included African American Muslims in the area; university students; South Asian, Arab, and West Asian Muslim immigrants and their families; and a growing convert population. "People were taking shahada, *yani,* three, four, five shahadas a week. And at the *jama'aat* (Friday congregational prayers), it was literally spilling out of the mosque. We opened a school, Alhamdulillah. And that was like, they were trying to be an Islamic movement."[28]

When Imam Musa launched the As-Sabiqun movement ("as-sabiqun" means the foremost) in 1995 at Masjid Al-Islam, he developed a five-point program that included the needs for and roles of the mosque, school, businesses, daʿwa and social welfare institutions, and geographical integrity. The mosque "serves first and foremost as a regular place to worship Allah (swt) in congregation, but also as a haven of security and fortress for the preservation of Islam. It is a center of spiritual and moral training" (Musa in Al Rashid 2014, 41). In terms of the school, "all knowledge must be accompanied by *taqwa* [God-consciousness]. Correct education, adab, and discipline can only come from Islamic schools. Islamic schools can raise children with a strong Islamic identity so that they can effectively meet and deal with the challenges of growing up in the West, and so they could be the ones to mold society (inshaʾAllah) instead of having society mold them" (Musa in Al Rashid 2014, 41–42).

Following the example of the NOI, establishing businesses was seen as a way to "make the movement financially stable and independent," while they also aimed to "respond to the need for spiritual and material assistance among themselves as well as those of the general society" by starting social welfare organizations (Al Rashid 2014, 42–43). Finally, Imam Musa encouraged his congregation to live close to the masjid. As stated in one of their early newsletters:

> In a non-Islamic society, there is a need for a model community where people can see Islam in action. This is achieved by the believers living together, working together, praying together, and building a true picture of a functional Islamic society. With this developed society also comes solidarity and physical safety as well as psychological security in numbers and likeness. As we move closer to the locale of the masjid, we become a concentrated, single-minded people. In time, all of the healthy institutions needed to plan and sustain growth are manifested. As this process continues, we become a community within a community, a city within a city, a nation within a nation—an Umma determining and directing its own affairs. (Al Rashid 2014, 43–44)

Self-determination, autonomy, and communal security—psychological, economic, spiritual, and physical—were seen as necessary parts of developing an umma in the urban American landscape. Seen as an elder, Hajja Rasheeda and her family moved between the Masjidul Waritheen in Fruitvale and Masjid Al-Islam in East Oakland (her husband worked in San Francisco, so he often attended congregational prayers there). While having entered Islam in the Masjidul Waritheen community, she often preferred the internationalist, lumpen-proletariat, and politically engaged congregation of Masjid Al-Islam. Similarly, young people like Oscar moved between the different spaces, creating a networked infrastructure that connected disparate communities.

Masjid Al-Islam was in a section of East Oakland that was also a locus of drug activity, prostitution, and gun violence. According to Mario, "we were safe in that environment, because of the respect that they had for Muslims and because . . . probably Imam Musa still knew people in Oakland that if you messed with him and his community you would just be . . . it was just understood. We were fine; we were comfortable; it wasn't no thang . . . Brothers would be racing down the strip and like honk and hold out a 'black power' [fist] as they rolled by the mosque." Mario was one of the young brothers who "lined the streets around the masjid" in black shalwar kameez (the long dress shirt and baggy pants worn in the Indian subcontinent) (Al Rashid 2014, 57). He remembers feeling "safe in that environment" and had gone abroad to study before the full extent of gun violence impacted the Masjid and As-Sabiqun movement.

Although Imam Musa established a security team at Masjid Al-Islam, he was vocal about his desire to not work with the police and not take on the neighborhood drug dealers. He regarded the drug dealer on the street as a "future Malcolm." This differs from the approach of his fellow imam, Imam Jamil Al-Amin (formerly H. Rap Brown) of Atlanta, Georgia. "Imam Jamil felt as though there should be a crime-free zone around the masjid so that families could feel safe and the community businesses could grow. Imam Musa did not agree with this outlook, not because he was for crime, [but] because he believed in each person's ability to change" (Al Rashid 2014, 44). Both imams recognized that involving law enforcement, with whom they both had negative experiences, was not a solution for communal safety and security. Yet Al Rashid asks whether "future Malcolm's" could be produced without prioritizing spaces "where children did not have to pass open-air drug markets on their way to school, or have to worry about being recruited by the local drug dealer" (44–45). This issue of how to sustain the community both materially and spiritually became important as these communities felt the pressure of leadership struggles, emerging Muslim movements, police infiltration and entrapment, and the further economic stratification and resegregation of the Bay Area.

There was a great deal of exchange between the East Oakland Muslim community and the university and college communities at the time. In the late 1980s, UC Berkeley had two *jumu'a* prayers. According to one brother, "the fourth floor held the 'wahabi' [*sic*] service and the fifth floor held the 'movement' service" (Al Rashid 2014, 55). Muslim students worked with the Black Student Union and other progressive groups on issues related to Palestine and South African apartheid and often incorporated the militant hip hop of the era in their work. They took Hamid Algar's Islam classes at Berkeley and listened to Imam Musa's khutbas (sermons) on the fifth floor of the student center, and then they left campus to attend Sunday ta'lim classes and Tuesday Brotherhood classes at Masjid Al-Islam; Hamid Algar would also give khutbas at jumu'a prayers at the YWCA across from campus. The "mixing of campus and community life gave the mosques a vibrancy not present in places where students generally stick to the Muslim Student Association while community members stick to the mosques" (Al Rashid 2014, 62). The campuses likewise became more vibrant as students and community members synthesized and challenged respective epistemologies and applied them in their everyday lives. Masjid Al-Islam, the Berkeley campus, junior colleges, and a diverse Muslim student body were also places where the sectarian divides between Sunni and Shia were less pronounced. Their anti-imperialist and internationalist support for the Iranian Islamic Revolution (1979) and Palestine, as well as other critiques of US empire, marked this vibrant period in its connections between what was happening locally and globally.

Amir Abdul Malik, a graduate student at San Francisco State University, took over at Masjid Al-Islam in 1988 when Imam Musa moved to Washington, DC. The amir traveled extensively as he was a much sought-after public speaker on college campuses due to his fiery speech style and his attention to social justice issues, especially Palestine. Black Muslims embodied a significant bridge between the internationalist support that the Black Panthers yielded to Palestine in the 1960s and 1970s and the current Black and Palestinian solidarity movements. While raising the political consciousness and activism of his congregation, the amir also encouraged young Muslims like Mario to read the books at the mosque's library, in particular the works of Muslim theologian and philosopher al-Ghazali. This was Mario's introduction to the *Ihya' 'Ulum al-Din (The Revival of the Religious Sciences)*. Meanwhile, Mario's sister-in-law, Nurideen's sister Naima, prepared to travel to Damascus, Syria, to study the Islamic sciences at Abu Nour University.[29] She traveled with a group of women who were part of the second wave of (Black) Muslims from the Bay Area to travel abroad as seekers of sacred knowledge; Abdul-Malik and members of the

Warith Deen community from both Oakland and San Francisco traveled
with their families to Sudan in the 1980s.[30] Naima and her sisters preceded scholars like Imam Zaid Shakir who later rose to prominence, and
she paved the way for Mario, who eventually traveled from Syria to Tarim,
Yemen. Naima, who was a teenager at this time, remembers a great sense of
community at Masjid Al-Islam; for her, the youth and energy of the community reflected the first community in Medina, and she lamented upon
her return to the Bay Area decades later in the 2010s that she no longer felt
that sense of community.

On a presunrise morning in 1996, Mario walked down the street to Masjid Al-Islam to pray *fajr*, the dawn prayer. He and his family then left for
Syria. He was twenty-four years old. After visiting Tarim, Yemen, in 1997
with an African American brother from Chicago and an African English
brother from Liverpool, England, he prepared to move there, where he enrolled in a "Ghazali bootcamp" at Dar al-Mustafa, the seminary begun by
Habib ʿUmar, a descendant of the Prophet Muhammad and highly influential scholar of the Hadrami diaspora (Knysh 2001). Mario eventually became
one of the primary translators for the program, and in 2011, Habib ʿUmar
traveled to the Bay Area to visit the places his students had come from.

While Mario's biography is unique, his life history crosses multiple
Muslim spaces in the Bay Area Muslim landscape and speaks to the way
Islam was perceived and experienced by African American populations in
the 1980s and early 1990s. The question of geographical integrity and how
to relate to one's non-Muslim neighbors exemplified an ongoing commitment to Black people and predominantly Black neighborhoods. In the
progressive Berkeley classroom, Islam was African dynasties, kings and
queens, and the revolutionary work of Malcolm X. On the city streets,
Islam was Malcolm X and Black Power, converted gang populations, the
Five-Percenters (1980s and 1990s hip hop was full of Islamic references),
the "bow-tie Muslims" (the Nation of Islam), and the "liquor store Muslims." Liquor store Muslims were often Arab immigrants (some of whom
were Christian) who had arrived with little formal education and English
language skills (thus fewer avenues for social mobility), predominantly Yemeni and Palestinian, who worked in and collectively purchased preexisting
grocery/liquor stores in predominantly African American neighborhoods.
They were often displaced from their own homelands by war, occupied
lands, and poverty, while they also participated in the further disenfranchisement of these neighborhoods. Their lack of formal education and
language neither explains nor excuses this harm; as a second-generation

Yemeni store-owner states, this "fast-money" comes with its own "moral deterioration and abysmal life" where one no longer battles "'with notions of good and bad deeds'" (Alhassen 2010). Shakir and others from Zaytuna Institute led a "Coalition of Concerned Bay Area Muslims" in a campaign to discourage Muslim store owners from selling liquor, and a number of store owners repented and have been seeking ways of "getting out" of the liquor store business or converting them to healthier alternatives that benefit the well-being (*maslaha*) of the larger community (Alhassen 2010).

For older African American Muslims who had been Black Panthers, in the Nation of Islam, Dar Ul-Islam, the Sabiqun, Shehadah Moors, the Jama'at of Shehu Dan Fodio, followers of Warith Deen Muhammad, Ahmadi, or otherwise, Islam was and continues to be many things, not only sociopolitical, but profoundly spiritual and internationalist as well. For Mario and others, becoming Muslim was an easy transition. There were several small mosques they could attend in the area where they received guidance from a wide array of Arab, South Asian, West Asian, and African American Muslims. While changes were already afoot, the Islamic landscape transformed dramatically in the years following Mario, Nurideen, and Naima's departures.

SCENE 4—"I WAS WORKING MY *** OFF FOR ISLAM" —AN ISLAMIC MOVEMENT, PART 2

INTERIOR. MASJID AL-ISLAM PRESCHOOL CLASSROOM, 1990S, DAY.

We see a classroom with storm damage—its roof collapsed, flooded and water stained, floating toys and books. About ten to fifteen COMMUNITY MEMBERS arrive with sandbags, cleaning and construction supplies, and school supplies. TIMELAPSE—the community members rebuild the space.

HAJAR (VO)

I believed, and they believed, and I think that everybody that I worked with, like, we really did love each other. We did really have a family. It was a beautiful experience. And we also thought like, even though we didn't have like—my God we did not have a lot—but it was okay because we had each other and that was more important. And we also could imagine that it would get better. So, like we had a situation where I think it was like an El Niño or something like that, and the school got flooded, the preschool classroom got completely flooded and gutted . . . everything was a wreck. We raised the money and like, it was rebuilt by us, you know? We went to Home Depot; we did all the painting; we put up the wallpaper; we redid the floors; *we* did it. It was me; it was my students; it was sisters, brothers, people taking shifts. And we rebuilt that entire classroom space, and it was beautiful. It was beautiful. It was beautiful. And we did it ourselves. You see?

In the 1980s and 1990s, Masjid Al-Islam and Masjidul Waritheen both had full-time elementary schools (Masjidul Waritheen's Clara Muhammad School was established in the mid-1970s and eventually expanded to include a high school), while being significant centers for national movements. Masjid Al-Islam School was established in 1988 in a building they purchased and converted near the mosque, starting with six children, and eventually growing to more than one hundred students from kindergarten through eighth grade, as well as preschool/daycare for many of the teachers' children. The schools served Muslim and neighborhood families who did not want to enroll their children in what were seen as "failing" public schools. At the same time, several Muslim teachers from these schools also worked in the Oakland Public School system. They often had to balance their commitments to all of Oakland's children, their Muslim communities, and their own families.

Hajar, whom we met in the introduction, was first a teacher and then an administrator at the Masjid Al-Islam School, which was the center of an extended family that developed around the mosque: "the masjid was our central place for everything . . . we had all our meals together; we had prayer together . . . we were in each other's lives every single day and supporting each other through that." Hajar also wrote plays for the children to perform: "This is during the time of the Iraq War and all this stuff was going on. So, we did a lot of fundraisers, like we would perform plays and then donate money to the Red Crescent and stuff like that." The Masjid Al-Islam School served "African-American students and then we had Palestinians, Sudanese, Somalians [sic], Egyptians, Indo-Pakistani, you know, folks. And the teachers were [of a] similar makeup. So, it was a very racially and ethnically diverse group," including Afghan and Iranian students as well.

The Masjid school went from kindergarten to eighth grade, and there were constant efforts to keep students both within the school and within the community. As Hajar described: "I had a lot of young women in middle school whose parents didn't necessarily think that they should go beyond . . . because their moms had only maybe a fifth-grade education. So, we went to their homes and advocated for them, with their moms and then eventually with their dads . . . we made a promise and a commitment to teach these girls, saying they're in the United States, so we wanted them to be able to continue to have opportunity at education . . . and it was based on a trust that we had built with them." Once students graduated from Masjid Al-Islam School, they often attended public high schools.

Educators like Hajar wanted to apply for public funding to start a Muslim high school, while the mosque leadership opposed "secular education" and working with the state, despite the fact that many young families were being supported financially by the state and despite the consistent presence of the state via policing in East Oakland. For Hajar, this contradiction put a "tax" on families who were struggling financially, which contributed to the disintegration of marriages, institutions, and the notion of geographical integrity as families who were able moved away. She raises some of the challenges and contradictions that arose in trying to maintain the Sabiqun philosophy of geographical integrity and independence from the state: "The bottom line is yes, you can have a vision, but you have to be very clear about what's the cost of it . . . we ended up with nothing and then we also ended up with our kids literally dead . . . it shouldn't have happened at all."[31]

Frustrated with the contradictions and a growing sense of disillusionment with leadership choices, as well as concern about raising her children amid gun violence, Hajar and her family eventually moved out of East Oakland, and she pursued a PhD in education. While the notion of geographic integrity held great promise, it came up short if New Medina did not provide children with safe places to play, learn, and grow. Hajar also demonstrates that individuals were key to infrastructures of feeling—from the passionate speeches of Amir Abdul Malik to the everyday showing up, (re)building, and maintenance of schools and community ties. Mario left the Bay Area, but what he learned in Medina by the Bay travels with him in his many migrations and practices of ta'lim, ta'dib, and da'wa as an Islamic scholar. Although Hajar left Masjid Al-Islam physically, she continues to build and sustain community by maintaining the bonds of kinship forged there.

REWIND—HISTORICAL INTERLUDE/MAKE YOUR OWN
MONTAGE: COLD WAR/DRUG WAR/WAR ON TERROR

In a document produced to reflect on his time in the United States prior
to exile, Muslim scholar Shaykh Muhammad Shareef connects American
neo-imperial covert actions in Nicaragua and Afghanistan to demonstrate how the CIA, and the US government more broadly, impacted what
forms of Islam would flourish throughout the 1980s, while also enabling
the flow of drugs into American cities. The influx of drugs decimated
already-struggling African American communities that were increasingly
underemployed because of the closing of factories that had long buttressed
working- and middle-class communities in the Bay and elsewhere (Shareef
2015; see also Webb 1998). Add to this the urban renewal and public infrastructure programs of the 1950s–1970s that often plowed through the
commercial centers of Bay Area African American communities like the
Geary Boulevard project in San Francisco's Fillmore and the demolition of
the Seventh Street business district and housing of West Oakland, respectively, where by 1950, 80 percent of the African American population lived
(Self 2003; Oakland Planning History 2013).

African American communities were collateral damage of the Cold
War, while at the same time the sociopolitical energies of African American Muslim communities were being "redirected" away from serving their
communities and building connections to African Islam toward imple-
menting US foreign policy in the Middle East, when in 1984, "the CIA
turned to the *sufis, salafist and tabligh* assets throughout the Muslim world
schooling them in anti-communism counter insurgency training. Magi-
cally a series of related *fatwas* came from all three camps declaring 'commu-
nism' the number one enemy of Muslims. Thus, the *Tablighee,* the developing *Salafist* and *Sufi* brotherhoods joined hands again recruiting African
American Muslims to fight in Afghanistan" (Shareef 2015, 155–56). Much
of what Shareef describes happened throughout the United States, especially on the East Coast, but there were also recruitment centers, by way
of Muslim charity organizations and mosque communities, in Los Angeles
and the Bay Area as well (Cooley 2002, 69).

While multiple sites of Medina by the Bay were in development, approaching what many Muslims referred to as "a golden age" at the end of the
millennium, the US proxy war in Afghanistan vastly shifted a global understanding of Islamic jihad, beginning the shift from an anti-Communist

Cold War to a hot one with "terror."[32] While American military resources were used to train and supply Muslims for this jihad in the 1980s, similar discourses of jihad are now criminalized as the US geopolitical relationships to these groups and discourses have shifted (Mamdani 2004, 128; Li 2020).

An epistemic transition occurred in the 1970s and 1980s as more foreign-born Muslims arrived in the United States and the United States' Cold War with the USSR turned to Afghanistan. Transnational networks like the Tablighi-Jamaat informed the kinds of Muslim teachings and practices that were taught in many Muslim spaces, while the Saudi government bankrolled the spread of Salafism and Wahabism via Saudi-trained imams. Muslims were recruited to become *mujahidin* (those who struggle or fight in the cause of Allah) for what was narrated as an Islamic struggle—albeit supported with finances, weapons, and training by a neocolonial American regime from Carter to Reagan—against the "godless evil empire" of the USSR, personified by the pro-Soviet People's Democratic Party of Afghanistan, which had begun instituting changes that the United States would rally around to support their invasion in 2001—women's education and gender equality, land reforms, and a separation of church and state. At the same time, Afghan emigrants and refugees from the American proxy war and the Communist state, the largest population of Afghans outside of Afghanistan, settled in the Bay Area, building the Little Kabul section of Fremont.

This brief interlude serves to situate what was happening globally in a parallel timeline to Medina by the Bay to demonstrate how state actors mobilized and reoriented religious discourses and networks in service to the Cold War. Drugs, guns, and the drug war all fulfilled needs of the state, expanding its reach and resources in ways that further extracted life, resources, social ties, and time from Black and brown communities.

SCENE 5—THE ORGANIZATION OF KNOWLEDGE AND POWER

INTERIOR. LIVING ROOM, FREMONT, 1990, DAY.

We see OMAR, a teenage Chicano sitting in his living room. *Donahue* is on the television. OMAR is not listening at first, but as Minister Louis Farrakhan of the reassembled Nation of Islam responds to audience comments, OMAR's attention is drawn to the television.

The young lady said she is afraid of violence. And isn't it sad, that
we who have been the victims of so much violence, now whites fear
violence from us! We do not have a history of killing white people.
White people have a history of killing us. See, and what you fear, it is
a deep guilt thing that white folks suffer. You are afraid that if we ever
come to power, we will do to you and your fathers, what you and your
people have done to us. And I think you are judging us by the state of
your own mind, and that is not necessarily the mind of black people
(reelblack 2020).

CUT TO:

INTERIOR. CHICANO STUDIES CLASSROOM, MID-1990S, DAY.

We see OMAR sitting at his desk where the class is reading and discussing
Carlos Fuentes' *The Buried Mirror: Reflections on Spain and the New World.*

CUT TO:

INTERIOR. CONCERT HALL, HAYWARD, MID-1990S, NIGHT.
We see a crowded hall full of Afghan families enjoying the music of musicians
onstage. We see a montage of concert fliers and posters and young Afghan students, including QASIM, a young Afghan man distributing fliers and hanging
posters. We hear Afghan music from the stage that carries through the entire
scene.

QASIM (NOW IN HIS FORTIES, VO)

I wasn't a practicing, so-called practicing, practicing [Muslim]. I was
never un-practicing, where I left the religion or didn't believe in it or
anything like that. I prayed, you know, being raised in a religious family
has those benefits, where you see your mom pray five times a day and
even if you don't pray five times a day, you pray a couple times a day
or one time a day or something, but at one point it has that effect on
you. . . . So, even though when we came to this country I kind of lost
track of the religion for the first few years, especially in high school
and then the first couple of years of college, and then you have that
awakening.

CUT TO:

EXTERIOR. OHLONE COLLEGE CAMPUS, FREMONT, DAY.

We see RAFIQ (Lonny), a young African American man wearing a white rim-
less cap on his head and calling the adhan in the middle of campus quad. OMAR
stops and listens, standing with other students from MEChA (Chicano Student
Movement of Aztlán). All students stop what they are doing, drawn to it or away
from it.

OMAR (IN HIS FORTIES, VO)

Lonny was all about knowledge, super active . . . he was the leader of all
the ethnic groups. There was so much activism to be done, we couldn't
really attend our classes! One summer he disappeared. . . . We come to
find out that he took the summer off; he stayed at home with his father
and started reading books about Islam and learned what his father went
through as a Muslim. His father was a Muslim from Malcolm X days . . .
when he came back, it wasn't Lonny the activist, it was Rafiq the Muslim
da'i, the one who calls people to Islam. All the people that he knew, he
was calling them to Islam; he stopped the ethnic emphasis activism, and
it was all about Islam. . . . When it came time for the afternoon prayer . . .
it was like time stopped. Everyone stopped in their tracks, like what was
going on? It was interesting because there were certain people who
would run to it, and a lot of them who ran away from it were the Afghans,
they would actually go into hiding. And then when the adhan stopped
and the people went to go pray, they would come out of hiding.

FADE OUT

I met Omar and Rafiq years apart at Zaytuna College when each was em-
ployed there; I first visited Qasim at his Islamic bookstore. Qasim's family
emigrated to the United States from Afghanistan in the early 1980s. He
was part of a large extended family that had settled in Fremont, a section
of which would soon be called Little Kabul. Qasim wanted to become
a professional musician, and it was the organizational skills he brought
from putting on concerts and events with the Afghan Club that he redirected toward what eventually became the Islamic Study School and then
Zaytuna Institute. As Qasim read more about Islam (Huston Smith's *The
World's Religions* [1991] and Ghulam Sarwar's *Islam, Beliefs and Teaching*
[1982]), his excitement at this new knowledge mobilized him to share it.

He began teaching his nephews and nieces and started the Masjidi Youth Center (MYC—there were enough Masjidi children to form a collective, design a logo, and print T-shirts).[33] As this group expanded beyond just the family, it moved from individual houses to the local mosque and became the Muslim Youth Center (they wanted to keep the logo).

Omar was a Chicano student activist at Ohlone College in Fremont in the 1990s. Because he initially thought of Islam as a good religion for Black people, but not something that he as a Latino was connected to, he viewed his affiliation with Islam and Muslims as solidarity in struggles for social justice. As Omar recounts, his student activist comrade Lonny was a major presence on campus, creating an umbrella organization of Black, Filipinx, and Mexican student organizers called the Organization of Knowledge and Power. Lonny was raised by his Christian mother on the East Coast and joined his Muslim father in Fremont after graduating high school. Encouraged to engage in street preaching by his Christian maternal grandfather, Lonny/Rafiq was a charismatic speaker and organizer. He gave talks after football scrimmages and though he was still an undergraduate, he also guest-lectured in ethnic studies courses. He became a guest teacher at the MYC, and his knowledge and *akhlaq* (character) impacted not only Qasim and Omar, but also many in the community.

Omar's interest in Islam had already been piqued by listening to Farrakhan, reading Malcolm X, and learning how a quarter of words in Spanish were of Arabic origin. He waited for Rafiq to approach him about Islam since he had been doing the rounds among their activist friends: "I was a little shy; I was too embarrassed. Actually, there was an element of pride, too, to be honest. Like 'whoa, what is this you are doing?' I had to wait for him to come to me. . . . I actually kind of regret that, not being more humble about it." Around 1993, Rafiq invited Omar to his house for dinner and showed him a book about Islam in America. They had known each other for years through campus organizing, but now Rafiq was leading him toward Islam. He showed Omar a picture of his father in the front row of an audience listening to Malcolm X on a street corner in Harlem. "He's basically just telling me hadith and Prophetic stories. I'm listening and listening and that was it. I remember the feeling distinctly, 'I believe in this. I didn't believe in it before. But this is what I am now.' I walked in a regular person, and I walked out and I had *iman* (faith). It was very strange."

Eventually, Rafiq started leading a *halaqa* (a study circle) on Friday evenings at a mosque in Fremont. For Omar, this was a significant development: "This is when my circle of friends changed dramatically. I stopped hanging out with the Mexicans and Filipinos and everyone else and all my new friends are now Afghans and Rafiq. And these are the kids who were all born in Afghanistan, this is how new they are to America. Their parents come over as refugees, and they want their kids to go to the mosque, and they do, but it's because of this young Black kid. . . . We just sit in a circle, and we are just talking about the deen, you know. Stories about the early community and that's all it really is. It's really, really basic. We're not really learning how to pray; we're not learning all of the obligations of being a Muslim. We're just learning about stories."

Rafiq eventually transferred to a university in San Diego, leaving Omar, Qasim, and others to consider what came next. The MYC and the gatherings at the mosque continued to grow from Fremont to Hayward. A Pashtun brother, Qari Amin, was teaching a Qur'an class for children whose families were mostly low income or welfare recipients in a small storefront on Mission Boulevard in Hayward. With little money and surrounded by car dealerships and repair shops (the original location is now a parking lot), he and Qasim foolhardily and faithfully decided to expand and move into the larger storefront next door. A couple months earlier, Amin had flown to Pakistan and met a Pakistani electronics store owner from New York on his plane. Amin told the man about his Qur'an school, and when this store owner returned to New York, he sent Amin a check in time to pay rent. The *zakat* or *sadaqa* of $1,000 sent across the country demonstrates the level of trust developed on a plane to Pakistan and an intention to materially support and thereby spiritually benefit from the nobleness of transmitting knowledge.[34]

In addition to receiving a check at the right time, Omar and Qasim traveled to mosques like Masjid Al-Islam every Friday, asking for donations for their school after *jumu'a,* much like Imam Musa had done a decade earlier. While Masjid Al-Islam did not serve a wealthy congregation and, like all mosques in Medina by the Bay, fundraised to support its own institutional needs, Omar and Qasim knew that their request to fundraise would be accepted and supported by the community, even if it was a few dollars at a time.

Within a month and a half, the Islamic study school "grew like fire" to three hundred people with a hundred-person waiting list. Qasim was initially surprised by the attendance because he was neither a scholar nor was he teaching anything "special." "What I was teaching was so basic that now that I think about it, it's funny. Like I was teaching how to make *wudu'* (sacral ablution), but I knew like two or three hadith about the purification of the wudu'. 'Oooohhh!' 'When the water falls from your hand, all your sins are falling, the Prophet said.' And people were just amazed at that, because nobody had ever explained it to us that way."

Eventually, there was a desire to go deeper into the Islamic tradition. And this is when Omar, Qasim, and their friends heard about a new imam in Santa Clara, down the 880 in the South Bay. Over the course of a few weeks, they drove down for jumu'a and listened to this young scholar.

FADE IN

INTERIOR. A SMALL STOREFRONT CLASSROOM ON MISSION
BOULEVARD IN HAYWARD, 1995, DAY.
We see a young white man with a short goatee and dark brown hair sitting before an intergenerational group of MUSLIM MEN and WOMEN in a large room with homemade curtains. There are four TV screens displaying images of audiences in other cities, and large Super VHS cameras pointed at THE TEACHER and the two hundred STUDENTS. Many of the TWO HUNDRED STUDENTS in the room are AFGHANI, but there are also SOUTH ASIANS, ARABS, LATINX, AFRICAN AMERICANS, CAUCASIANS, and FILIPINX. THE TEACHER is discussing the Sira, the biography of the PROPHET MUHAMMAD to his one thousand students.

FADE OUT

Hamza Yusuf Hanson, a white Muslim convert, had recently moved back to the United States with his family to study nursing and be the imam at the MCA (Muslim Community Association) in Santa Clara. He had spent more than a decade living abroad, studying Islam in England, Spain, Mauritania, and the United Arab Emirates. His original plan had been to become a nurse and to return to Mauritania and serve people there. Yet, as he began teaching, he learned that there were dedicated students who desired the knowledge he had gained abroad.

The first time Qasim heard one of Yusuf's khutbas, he was turned off by the turbaned, bearded, and robe-wearing "Arab" who was speaking too much Arabic to a largely non-Arabic speaking audience. Qasim became upset with his cousin for "ruining his jumu'a" when his cousin replied, "That was Hamza Yusuf, man! That was the white guy!" Stunned, Qasim lamented that he hadn't really listened to the khutba, and he decided to return the next week. In the following week's khutba, Yusuf addressed the issue of debt, interest, and poverty that had been festering in Qasim's mind for the past week. Embarrassed, he felt as though Yusuf was addressing him directly. After the prayer a crowd of people gathered around Yusuf, and Qasim snapped a mental photograph of the moment:

That day I said to myself,

> I want to serve this man. . . . I heard the truth; I heard that there's no way someone can say something and can affect you, affect your heart, unless it's from the heart. Not only it's from the heart, but it's based on a solid foundation of this religion . . . and then what happened? That effect didn't leave me. That same feeling I had that day, is the same today, increased, daily. And not only the love increased, but the desire to serve, because [back] then . . . I didn't know what I was doing, but I just did it. But later on, I realized, "Oh, that was a great thing we did."

Qasim, Omar, and their friends invited Hamza Yusuf to teach an introductory course at the Islamic Study School; he eventually offered multiple twelve-week courses on Islam, the Arabic language, the Sira, *Purification of the Heart* (a translation and commentary of Imam Muhammad al-Mawlud's [1844–1905] *Mathara al-Qulub*), and *Prohibitions of the Tongue* (al-Mawlud's *Maharim al-Lisan*). These courses were broadcast to student gatherings in New York, Philadelphia, and Toronto. Qasim used S-VHS recording equipment from the local public access television station (where he had a program) to record these lectures, which were eventually distributed as cassette tapes, CDs, and videos, popularizing Shaykh Hamza Yusuf and the burgeoning movement in the Bay Area.

What started as the Islamic Study School was incorporated into a nonprofit called the Zaytuna Institute in 1996. When the property on Mission Boulevard was sold around 1998–1999, Hesham Al-Alusi, an Iraqi civil engineer and contractor, assisted Yusuf and his growing supporters and community in purchasing a property on Jackson Street in another part of Hayward. Two women donated stocks in Google to Zaytuna Institute, totaling more than $200,000, which helped cover the costs of the purchase. The predominantly Afghan community in Fremont came in to beautify the property that contained a small house and an overgrown yard that was bordered on one side by the BART line. Commuter trains zipped by all day, connecting Hayward and Fremont to Oakland and San Francisco. The neighborhood was low income and working class, and the particular cul-de-sac in which the institute was located was popular for drug transactions and other illicit activity. While this environment was similar to Masjid Al-Islam's, this part of Hayward was not as densely populated, and few members of the congregation lived in geographic proximity to the institute.

From 1998 to the early 2000s, the Zaytuna Institute experienced rapid growth—hiring employees, coproducing "Deen Intensive" and "Rihla" retreats, providing classes and shelter, doing outreach, and for many, providing a space of community. From 2004 to 2008, a pilot seminary program took place, eventually graduating three men and two women who went on to further studies, teaching, and leadership positions. Several scholars from overseas or who had returned from study overseas, including Shaykh Salek bin Siddina from Mauritania and two African Americans from the East Coast, Zaid Shakir and Abdullah bin Hamid Ali (by way of Syria and Morocco, respectively), became scholars in residence at Zaytuna and throughout the Bay Area. In 2007, Zaytuna Institute moved to Berkeley, and in 2009 it became Zaytuna College, a Muslim liberal arts college for undergraduates. Zaytuna's outreach program became the independent nonprofit the Ta'leef Collective (est. 2005) based in Fremont, California, under the direction of two converts to Islam, Mustafa Davis and the late Whitney Usama Canon.[35] Much of Zaytuna's work with prison inmates continued under the direction of Rami Nsour and Nabil Afifi as the Tayba Foundation (est. 2008), which was briefly based at the Jackson Street property in Hayward. Other active members of the Zaytuna community participated in the development of Islamic elementary, middle, and high schools and an active homeschooling movement. Zaytuna began an intensive summer Arabic program in Berkeley in 2008 and the college opened its doors in 2010.

The hunger for knowledge that the Islamic Study School and Zaytuna Institute grew out of was shaped by the need to understand the meaning behind particular Islamic practices and laws, as well as a desire to reshape one's relationship to and knowledge of oneself, others, and the world. While Afghan parents wanted their children to attend the local mosque, the fact that they were led there by a young Black man often made them uncomfortable, while Rafiq's interpretation of Islam, his Blackness, his "Muslim cool" (Abdul Khabeer 2016) gave the young people a way to make sense of how to be Muslim and Afghan within their particular experiences of racial capitalism, American empire, and global discourses of Islam. Much like Mario's experience when he first began reading al-Ghazali, the students who gathered at these classes experienced an "awakening" to this world that many had been born into but of which they only had a ritualized understanding.

In the early years of Zaytuna Institute, there was a great deal of exchange between teachers and students throughout the Bay Area. Yusuf even taught at the Qur'anic Arabic Conference during Ramadan that Masjidul Waritheen held annually. Multiple Muslim Student Associations were activated, and numerous community and advocacy organizations and publications were established.[36] People like Haroon, the Zaytuna audiovisual coordinator who had heard an audio recording or watched a video, moved to the Bay Area to be a part of this Islamic movement. Yusuf encouraged Muslim converts he had met through his travels and study to return to the United States or to US cities from the enclave communities they had built in places like New Mexico to be a part of this emergent Medina.

While most Muslims weren't particularly aligned with one group or another, there were also Muslims who were dedicated to specific scholars, leaders, or movements emerging throughout the Bay, including the Sabiqun, Zaytuna Institute, the Tablighi-Jamaat, teachers such as Shaykh Muhammad Shareef or Shaykh Nuh Keller, and the Warith Deen Muhammad communities in San Francisco, Oakland, and the South Bay. There was also overlap between different communities. In 1991, Muhammad Shareef asked Hamza Yusuf to be on the board of advisers for the Sankora Institute (SIIASI). Shareef established the Institute in 1985 in Sudan "with the permission and support of the Sultan of Maiurno" and was commissioned by his teachers to return to the United States as a da'i "to call people to Allah and to the *minhaj* [way or path] of *Shehu* Uthman ibn Fuduye" (Shareef 2015, 158). Shareef returned to the United States in 1990 after ten years abroad studying Islam in Africa. After initially teaching in Houston, he moved to California and did da'wa in mosques, Islamic centers, universities, and in the California prison system as both a volunteer and paid Muslim chaplain. By 1993 he felt that "the call of African Islamic traditions should be made in the place where African Americans were largely becoming Muslim, and that was in the U.S. Penitentiaries" (Shareef 2015, 158).

While most of these movements coexisted, especially at the leadership level, charismatic leadership with devoted followings produced schisms over doctrinal issues like whether one needed to follow a particular school of law (*madhhab*), what direction to pray in, how Muslims should dress and what they should eat, how to engage American citizenship and imperialism, and what role "politics" should play in Muslim communities (and this was all before September 11, 2001). In the aftermath of September 11, 2001, these philosophical differences came to a head, especially after Hamza Yusuf's televised appearances. Shareef and Yusuf especially disagreed, based on their different understandings and experiences of US history, citizenship, and politics, on how Muslims should govern themselves and be governed on the bases of civil versus human rights and what specific Islamic legal categories and levels of authority applied to different Muslims.

Scholars like Imam Warith Deen Muhammad and Hamza Yusuf were critical of US foreign and domestic policies and mainstream culture, while they also paved a theoretical road to America's redemption through a reclaiming of its founding principles and ideals infused with the ethical ideals of Islam and additionally in Muhammad's case, the cultural traditions and liberatory struggles of Black people. For immigrants who disrupted their families, cultural continuities, and senses of belonging and home, finding redemption and purpose in the American context made meaning of their hardships and sacrifices. For Shareef and others, Muslims who left Muslim majority countries for the United States where they were in the minority lost their religious authority and should not dictate or shape Islamic practice nor relations with the state on these lands and in these contexts. Also appealing to ideals of the American Revolution, Shareef articulated the work of Muslims as continuing an unfinished revolution for liberty and justice for all, beginning with prisons and the urban disenfranchised and potentially gaining protected status and sovereignty as a minority nation under the auspices of the United Nations along the lines of Indigenous nations (Shareef 2015).

For young converts and first-, second-, and third-generation Muslims in the United States, Yusuf articulated the dissonance between the American dream and American realities as a charismatic role model, offering an alternative, meaningful, dignified, and, at times, exotic way to be in the world. Some critiqued Zaytuna and other "schools" as clique-ish and cultish, while others found belonging, purpose, and spiritual kinship. The force of this multiracial movement oriented around the purification of the heart pulled young people and elders—their presence, their time, their material support—away from places like Masjid Al-Islam, Crescent Street, and the Warith Deen Muhammad communities.

A few families lived within walking distance from the Jackson Street location. Even though the BART train practically went through Zaytuna's backyard, there was limited public transportation access. As a "commuting community," everyone else had to drive there. Some people came from as far away as Santa Barbara or San Diego on a weekly basis (about a six- or eight-hour drive, respectively) to attend Yusuf's classes, while others came from all over the Bay Area. Many material realities of everyday life were shed upon entering the sanctuary of the Zaytuna Institute with its trees, flowers, yurt, and archery targets, assuming one had the means to get there.

80　　　The disjuncture between the idealistic Muslim community within Zaytuna's classes and retreats and the material conditions outside were apparent to both the "Zaytunies" and those looking in. As Zaytuna and Yusuf's international profile grew, the ripple effect of Zaytuna's classes—the translation to everyday life—wasn't happening at the level many hoped. There was a tension between what was being expressed in the classroom and how such knowledge could have greater social impact.[37] People's expectations were lifted, and it is in the unfulfilled expectations, recognition, and loss of community that much of the tension lingers. The move from Zaytuna Institute to Zaytuna College in 2009–2010 was informed by this thinking about its role in Muslim communities and a need to shift from consuming Islamic knowledge as a feel-good experience to activating it through serious engagement and praxis. Zaytuna had filled a need, whether intentional or unintentional, that mobilized people around these classes and the space in Hayward. For some, it was a safe haven where people could just "be Muslim"—no awkward gazes, questions, or judgments about their difference; for others it was alienating and disengaged from the world. There was an overreliance on this sanctified space and particular personalities, rather than the extension of this space and teaching into one's home, school, mosque, neighborhood, or workplace. As one former student mentioned, "In Hayward, you could be in a bubble, and I think that was part of the move from Zaytuna Institute to what it's trying to be . . . not to be in a bubble." Another student saw the transition and its contemporary traces more critically:

> Community is a group of people who are able to withstand the vicissitudes of time. Like they are going through life together dealing with the problems that they have. From what I've seen is that "our community" is a pretentious kind of paradigm that is supposed to weed out any problems and create the perfect Islam, based in tradition that is intellectually stimulated and spiritually motivated and all these kinds of things. . . . I think that part of it is fantasy, is imagination. It works well within walls; it works well in a speech, but as soon as we hit the streets it doesn't work like that anymore. . . . I also don't think that an institution is a place where community should be born. I think that's false; that's where education should happen, not where community should be born.

Indeed, it is unlikely that all the work that Yusuf and others put into the institute was about only a few hundred people being better Muslims and having a "community." When Hesham Al-Alusi encouraged Yusuf to formalize the classes that he was teaching in the 1990s, Yusuf initially called

the institute "Al-Qarawiyyin" after al-Qarawiyyin University in Morocco, 81
which is considered the oldest university in the world. When Alaloosi advised that this name was too difficult for Americans to say, Yusuf came up with "Zaytuna," after Jami'at (University) al-Zaytuna in Tunisia (*zaytun* is also the Arabic word for olive). In the naming of the institute, it appears that Yusuf had high aspirations for these weekly classes of a hundred people in a Hayward storefront.

Zaytuna's move from public classes in Hayward toward projects like the seminary and college in Berkeley caused a great deal of communal trauma, in part because of how it was communicated and approached in a way that discounted that the community (and not individual personalities) had built the institute. Zaytuna's move to Berkeley and then the farther move north to the Berkeley Hills geographically reflects the distance from communities in the Bay Area flatlands, yet also brings Imam Zaid's and Imam Musa's contrasting notions of "community" and "geographic integrity" to the fore.

"Community" is an incomplete and perhaps impossible term for what Zaytuna scholars are trying to accomplish. The *umma* as word-concept more fluidly speaks to both the local and global scopes of thinking in terms of collectivities. As one former Zaytuna staffer put it, "They [Yusuf and Shakir] have the weight of the umma on their shoulders." It was the entire community of Muslim believers (through the expanses of time and place), the future of not only Islam in the United States but also Islam worldwide with which they were spiritually, intellectually, and politically linked. In the minds of its founders, much of the work of Zaytuna is preparing a ground. The work in Hayward was a toiling of the soil, the college a planting of seeds—the fruits of Zaytuna's olive trees, yet to come. As Sherman Jackson stated at Zaytuna College's second convocation ceremony in the fall of 2011, "Zaytuna as an institution is not only a life-long project, its success is something that cannot be achieved in any one lifetime. None of us will likely live long enough to see Zaytuna come to its full and complete success" (S. A. Jackson 2011).

⊚ ⊚ ⊚

While throughout the 1960s–1980s, the Transbay corridor between San Francisco and the East Bay's Berkeley and Oakland marked the primary spaces of a Bay Area Muslim landscape, by the 1990s and into the 2000s much of the most vibrant activity and interaction shifted farther south and east. While San Francisco, the North Bay, and the East Bay continue to be significant sources of Islamic knowledge and institutionalization, the

MEDINA BY THE BAY

South Bay and the farther reaches of the East Bay are now home to the majority of the Bay Area's Muslim populations, schools, and places of worship. This area around the counties of San Jose and Santa Clara, which is also known as Silicon Valley, is one of the wealthiest areas of the nation due to the high-tech industry. Yet within the same geographic space in which "enormous wealth, scientific innovation, and prosperity" flow, there likewise exists "relentless attacks on public and environmental health, the oppression and immiseration of thousands of workers and residents" who undergird and endure long commutes within the shiny façade of dot-coms and high-tech gadgets (Pellow and Park 2002, 3). Muslims make up a good proportion of those who have "made it" in Silicon Valley, and it is the combination of that wealth plus monetary and physical efforts by the poor, working, and middle-class Muslims who line the East Bay, from Vallejo to Richmond to Oakland to San Leandro to Hayward and Fremont, who have enabled the physical expansion of suburban mosques and the purchase of multiple properties for Zaytuna College in a time of economic depression.[38]

Buildings mark passages of time and movements of populations, ideas, and economies, while remaining constant to how spiritual communities organize themselves spatially. Reflecting the layers of engravings, paintings, windows, and walls of the many mosques, churches, temples, and synagogues around the world that have witnessed religious wars, expulsions, conversions, extinctions, and migrations, the Masjidul Waritheen and Clara Muhammad School were formerly in a Catholic school and church and are now condos; the Islamic Study School started in a Jewish-owned building and is now a parking lot; the Islamic Cultural Center of North America in Oakland was started by Iranian Shi'i Muslims in a Masonic Temple for the Oakland Scottish Rite; the Jackson Street property had been owned by a Christian group that included a Christian Iraqi; and Zaytuna College began in a rented space of a Baptist seminary. In 2012, Zaytuna College started purchasing property on "Holy Hill," north of the UC Berkeley campus, next to the Graduate Theological Union. The first property they purchased is a former Christian church and school; most of the additional properties have also had Christian institutional histories.

In this chapter I opened portals to Muslim movements by the Bay—the way Muslims interpreted Islam as a strategy of material and spiritual survival and the different ways they approached the survival of Islam as a way of knowing and being for the future. A critical question remains about the roles of institutions like schools and colleges in relation to the communities they serve and from which they emerge.

Zaytuna College is a critical node in the recentering of the Bay Area Muslim landscape, if not the global Muslim landscape. While access to social and economic capital has contributed to Zaytuna's ability to sustain and reproduce itself, what are the political implications of its epistemological and ethical approaches? While Muslim study at Zaytuna College now takes place in a bucolic setting set apart from much Bay Area life, this does not necessarily disconnect it from what happens below, as Hajar and others demonstrate that buildings are not the only infrastructures of community. It becomes important to think about how Zaytuna or other Muslim spaces are implicated in the resegregation of the Bay Area, its ongoing socioeconomic and housing insecurities, and the continued siege on Black ways of knowing and being that have dramatically diminished once-thriving communities. The traces of multiple migrations are quickly becoming illegible as knowledge and modes of Islam give way to the powerful influences of a hegemonic and monolithic American capitalist culture in succeeding generations. Being priced out of San Francisco and increasingly Berkeley and Oakland, many Muslims are moving to the outer reaches of the East Bay. In choosing to locate Zaytuna College in Berkeley, the school's founders and students take advantage of not only its academic resources and cache, but a complex cultural landscape in which affluence and poverty, indigeneity and migration commingle in close proximity, imbuing the region with great political urgency.

I allude to communal losses, while holding onto their bloom. At Masjidul Waritheen in Oakland, the next generations of teachers and students continue their practices of Muslim study and struggle. Haneefah Shuaibe-Peters, a graduate of the Sister Clara Muhammad School who holds a Doctorate in Education, directs the An Nas Children's Islamic Institute, which teaches five- to thirteen-year-olds Qur'anic Arabic and Islamic social studies and operates a youth business loan program that uplifts and empowers young Muslims (ages nine to eighteen) to apply for a free business loan toward being "business leaders in their communities" (Masjidul Waritheen 2021). During their most recent graduation, Shuaibe-Peters invoked the Bantu concept of Ubuntu, often translated as "I am because we are," to conjure the memories of a community that raised her, her liberatory lineages, and the infrastructures of feeling that sustained her Muslim becoming and that move her to keep building:

> I am because of Sister Clara Muhammad's commitment to her children. I am because Sister Da'iya Taha wrote the CMS song. . . . I am because Brother Saddiq taught me how to play football and called me "no hands

Haneefah." I am because Brother Ra'uf told us to keep it simple in Arabic class. He know the rest. I am because Sister Vivian introduced me to computers, and I still to this day would play Oregon Trail. I am because I ate hot lunch every day. I am because I never wanted to miss the *shabooya, sha-sha-shabooya* roll call. I am because Brother Emmett was a stone-cold janitor, and you best not step on his wet floors. I am because Sister Anisa taught me to be patient with babies in the nursery, and it's why Sister Aisha trusted me with Q and Z. I am because Sister Cora taught me the colors with Fat the Cat. "My name is Fat the Cat. I'm happy, and I'm fat. And I can change my colors just like that . . . " (Waajid 2021b)

CHAPTER 2

ROOTS, ROUTES, AND RHYTHMS OF DEVOTIONAL TIME

SCENE 1—COMPANIONS

FADE IN

INTERIOR. THE TA'LEEF COLLECTIVE, FREMONT, SPRING 2011,
NIGHT.

We see a large room with light green carpeting; a Kufic calligraphy painting
on the wall says, "Baraka MUHAMMAD, Blessings of MUHAMMAD." WOMEN are
seated together on the right side of the room, MEN on the left side; all are facing
an elevated platform with cushions and a small table with floral arrangements.
Sitting at the edge of the platform is IMAM ZAID SHAKIR, holding a microphone
and speaking to the congregation.

IMAM ZAID SHAKIR

So who are we? Who is this community? This community is . . . is dis-
played here. This community of the descendants of Bilal al-Habashi,
radi Allahu 'anhu (may God be pleased with him). So, we see in this
community Africans, both those who have come here voluntarily and
those whose ancestors came here involuntarily. We see the descendants of Salman al-Farsi; we see many Asians in our ranks—from
South Asia, from Central Asia, from Southeast Asia, and they are the
descendants of Salman. . . . We have here the descendants of Suhaib
al-Roumi; we have many Europeans—Muslims who have converted to

Islam; Muslims who have emigrated here from Bosnia or Albania or
other parts of Europe. We have here the grandsons and the granddaughters of the Arabs, the grandsons and granddaughters of Abu
Bakr and 'Umar, 'Uthman, and 'Ali *radi Allahu 'anhum ajma'in* (may
God be pleased with them all), that's who we are.

Shakir traces genealogical lines from the seventh-century first genera-
tion of Muslims who gathered around the Prophet Muhammad to the
Black, African, (South, West, Central, East and Southeast) Asians, white,
European, and Arab Muslims who have assembled in a suburban business
park in Fremont just off Interstate 680. In Shakir's invocation the Sahaba
(Companions) of the Prophet Muhammad are distributed across modern racial, ethnic, and continental categories—Bilal al-Habashi (African),
Salman al-Farsi (Asian), Suhayb al-Rumi (European), Abu Bakr, 'Umar,
'Uthman, and 'Ali (Arab). This first generation of Muslims exemplify how
Islam transformed social relations in its earliest days, and they are referenced
as ancestors in faith, geography, and tribe. These are grounded relationships
of proximity and intimacy across distance—an Afghan Muslim is bound to
a Black Muslim, seated shoulder to shoulder on a green carpet in Fremont.
Their being in common space and faith embodies an echo, promise, and
prophecy enacted by Salman and Bilal (both of whom had entered Islam
enslaved and were then liberated by the interventions of Prophet Muhammad and Abu Bakr, respectively), Companions not only to the Prophet, but
also to each other, fourteen hundred years ago. Shakir's efforts to bind his
audience through a common lineage and legacy of the first Companions
generates connections and possibilities, as well as limits and omissions,
that demonstrate how Islamic ways of being and knowing reorder relations
as forms of kinship and companionship toward liberatory praxes.

Shakir's address to his diverse audience was an introduction for Yemeni
scholar and descendant of the Prophet Muhammad, Habib 'Umar bin Muhammad bin Salim bin Hafiz of Yemen.[1] Habib 'Umar was in the Bay Area
at the invitation of his students, who include Mario from chapter 1 and many
of the students of the Islamic Study School and the former Zaytuna Institute. In spring 2011, Habib 'Umar's "Tranquility amidst Turbulence" tour
traveled to cities across North America, the locations of the tour based on
where Habib 'Umar's Arab, Black, Filipinx, South Asian, North African,
white, and Latinx students came from. He wanted to learn about the places
and people who produced them and further the work of da'wa, ta'lim, and
ta'dib that his students had started upon their returns.[2] They were now his

translators and hosts in Toronto, Atlanta, Detroit, Chicago, Washington, DC, New York, San Diego, Los Angeles, and the San Francisco Bay Area. The tour settled for its final week in the Bay Area, presenting events at places like the Ta'leef Collective in Fremont, Zaytuna College in Berkeley, Fiji Jam'atul Islam of America (a small mosque established by predominantly South Asian Fijians thirty years ago) in South San Francisco, the Muslim Community Center (a large suburban mosque) in Pleasanton, San Jose State University, University of San Francisco (a private Jesuit university), the Graduate Theological Seminary in Berkeley, and Castlemont High School (a public, predominantly Black high school in 2011) in East Oakland.

While the previous chapter covers multiple historical and geographic points of Medina by the Bay, this chapter expands space and time to show the transformative process and effect of Medina by the Bay at a global scale. When young Black and brown Muslims from North American cities travel to Tarim, Yemen, they bring their knowledges and experiences with them, influencing the Habib's Islamic consciousness and geography. He comes to North America to witness his students and their collective ancestors on these lands and waters.

When Shakir articulates a spiritual genealogy that produces a "kinship by faith" (Izutsu 2002), he conjures a liberatory lineage that crosses oceans, borders, and fourteen hundred years. He suggests that through the Sahaba, and later through El-Hajj Malik El-Shabazz and the enslaved African Muslims in the Americas, today's umma inherits an anti-racist and abolitionist legacy that moves Islamic ethics and politics toward liberation grounded in Islamic visions of justice. Moving between the tour and Zaytuna College, this chapter considers the limits and possibilities of these legacies and lineages, while also asking how hierarchies and relations of power in the umma—how the social capital of Islamic knowledge intersects with race and gender—order and disorder our aims for a more just world.

In SCENE 2, we encounter the Habib's first stop in the United States at the grave of El-Hajj Malik El-Shabazz, Malcolm X, eighteen miles north of Harlem, New York. Reenacting practices of grave visitation in Yemen, Habib and his students articulate a localized history and geography of Islam, as well as the cure that El-Shabazz offers Muslims in turbulent times (Ho 2006). In the section EMBODIED RELATIONS I discuss how female students at Zaytuna College move through and constitute the gendered infrastructure of Muslim spaces. They respect and desire gendered differentiation and distinction, while they also mobilize their knowledges and desires for proximity to Muhammadaic dispositions by testing practiced limits and expanding relational possibilities.[3] I return here to thinking about grounded relationality in proximity, how the geography of bodies—being shoulder to shoulder, among known and unknown graves, or "in the women's section"—carries lessons, legacies, and different forms of accountability and responsibility. Particular individuals and their ethical and political dispositions become parts of infrastructure; they connect and enable; they may also restrict and disable. The ways Muslims embody, move within, and transit through infrastructures of feeling demonstrate the possibilities and limits of this liberatory lineage and its ethical and political implications. In the final four scenes, I expand ethnographic space and time to demonstrate how Shakir, Habib 'Umar, and others invoke the Sahaba, El-Shabazz, and the African Muslims who were transported to and enslaved in the Americas throughout the sixteenth to nineteenth centuries.

Before moving to the next scenes in our narrative, there is more to say about our opening scene. Shakir invokes infrastructures of feeling of the seventh-century Sahaba to "renovate" the consciousnesses of the twenty-first-century multiracial and multiethnic Muslims seated before him (Gilmore 2017, 240). Grounded relationality, like kinship, must be cultivated. Shakir recalls past infrastructures to provide the affective and spiritual foundations and possibilities for recognizing and responding to grounded relationalities in common faith, space, and proximity today and tomorrow. This is significant in many ways.

Conversion to Islam has been a consistent occurrence throughout history, such that developing ways to articulate identification with and induction into the umma became a necessary part of transmitting this new way of knowing and being. It was precisely the possibilities of a new sociopolitical order, and a belief in Muhammad's message, that attracted people to Islam (Izutsu 2002, 58). According to Izutsu, "Muhammad made a daring attempt to abolish the principle of tribal solidarity and to replace it by that of monotheistic faith which would make possible a new organization of society with a wholly ritualized way of life as a manifestation of the eternal order here on earth. It is clear that this revolution—for 'revolution' it certainly was—was prompted at first by a purely religious motive, though as time went on the principle of *kinship by faith* began to assume more and more a rich political coloring" (2002, 59, emphasis added).

It was this political coloring that set the stage for a crystallization of knowledge practices. The concept of a kinship by faith is important for understanding the revolutionary and ethical nature of Islam from the seventh century to the twenty-first century. Muslim conversion often disrupted relations of power that stressed tribal and familial affiliations and statuses, while gendered forms of relationality were likewise brought into relief in the Qur'an and Sunna. At the same time, ethnic, tribal, political, and gendered notions and traditions often endured or returned in practice despite the revolutionary tenets of the Prophetic tradition.

In a kinship by faith, individuals are bound not by genealogies of blood, tribe, or race but by a specific attachment to Islam as a tradition of beliefs, practices, and knowledges. This form of spiritual or sacred kinship is often articulated through a notion of the umma, or what Jamillah Karim calls "ummah ideals," a "double commitment to both brotherhood and sisterhood and justice . . . to both harmony and equality at the same time" (2009, 7).[4] Umma ideals are great mobilizers, though their practical applications are entangled in many other structures of identity and attachment. The umma concept ideally encourages Muslims "to know each other" (see Qur'an 49:13) across forms of difference, yet as Karim and others have shown, notions of the umma do not automatically enjoin Muslims to be anti-racist or to question and resist the white supremacist logics of anti-Blackness, settler colonialism, and assimilation in the United States and elsewhere (J. A. Karim 2009; McCloud 1995; S. A. Jackson 2005; Abdullah 2010; Chan-Malik 2011; O. Safi and Hammer 2013; Abdul Khabeer 2016; Auston 2017).

Throughout the twentieth century, African Americans were particularly attracted to Islam for its anti-racist and liberatory potential and for its ties to the African continent (Abdul Khabeer 2017a; McCloud 1995; Curtis 2002; Taylor 2017). Globally, Islam was likewise mobilized for its sociopolitical and spiritual potential, yet for Muslims who immigrated from Muslim-majority countries to the United States, Islam increasingly— though not always—became tied to the maintenance of ethnic identities and traditions in both antagonistic and complicit relation to the hegemony of racial capitalist American cultures and pressures to assimilate and become model minorities. This "ethnic particularism" often manifests as an "ethnoreligious hegemony" that identifies Blackness as un-Islamic and furthers white supremacist logics of anti-Black and anti-immigrant racisms within Muslim communities.[5]

While "Blackness is central to the histories, engagements, entanglements, and experiences of U.S. American Islam" (Abdul Khabeer 2016, 5), racism and ethnoreligious hegemony within Muslim communities and the larger sociopolitical worlds in which they are embedded have (dis) regarded Black Muslim authenticity, knowledge, experience, and leadership with skepticism or fetishism. Similarly, colorism that privileges lighter skin and particular ethnicities (for marriage partners in particular), white privilege for white converts, and Arab privilege in a global racial formation, in addition to other forms of national, ethnic, racial, and gendered forms of discrimination and exploitation, continues to contradict Qur'anic and Prophetic ethics of difference, knowledge, and righteousness (Z. A. Grewal 2009; M. M. Knight 2013; 2009; Rana 2011; Tourage 2013). Ongoing debates about "what Islam says" about justice and what Muslims should do about it exemplify the stakes of how we theorize difference and intersubjectivity toward enacting grounded relationalities (umma, kinship, solidarity, companionship, etc.) and social justice (Kashani 2018a).

Imam Zaid Shakir cultivates grounded relationalities and a kinship by faith through his introduction of Habib 'Umar by situating all Muslims on equal footing vis-à-vis their common ancestors, the Sahaba. The Sahaba were people who saw or spent time with the Prophet Muhammad, who as the ideal Muslim and Messenger of Islam is the embodiment of Islamic infrastructure.[6] Their stories about how he lived and what he said comprise a significant corpus of Islamic knowledge that informs how Muslims live their everyday lives and shape their relations—to themselves, Allah, and others. Shakir also suggests that the Sahaba themselves are models for Muslims in terms of how to relate with one another. They are companions, associates, comrades, fellows, or friends; fellow travelers (Wehr 1979). Shakir proposes that being in common space because they are in common faith—whether in the seventh century or today—demonstrates relations of proximity and companionship that engage, rather than subsume, difference.

Second, the first Muslim community transcended tribal lines and kinship networks and was initially constituted by and attuned to the concerns of women, the enslaved, and youth. The first Muslim community reflects Shakir's contemporary audience; their social relations are informed by both Islam and the *jahili* (ignorant/pre-Islamic) socioeconomic, gendered, and tribal/racialized structure of the societies in which they live. Therefore, the logics of racial capitalism push against the radical transformations that Islam proposed for the most vulnerable in society; ethnic particularism may manifest as ethnoreligious hegemony and racism; "cultural" gender and behavioral norms may be thought of as Islamic because they carry over from Muslim-majority countries, despite their contradictions with the Prophetic way and the capaciousness of Muslim ways of knowing and being. While Shakir mentions Sahaba who had been enslaved or were youth, he could have also mentioned any of the female Companions of the Prophet Muhammad, like his first wife Khadija, his daughter Fatima, and his later wife

Aisha, who were Arab; Baraka bint Tha'laba (Umm Ayman), who was Abyssinian; and Zunayra al-Rumiyya (the Roman), just to name a few.

Third, Shakir addresses Arabs in the room as the spiritual and regional descendants of Abu Bakr, 'Umar, 'Uthman, and 'Ali, the four Rightly Guided Caliphs in Sunni Islam who became leaders of the Muslim community after the death of the Prophet Muhammad. Although the Prophet was Arab and Shakir is introducing an Arab descendant of the Prophet to a room in which other descendants are also sitting, he pointedly demonstrates that everyone in the room is a descendant of the Prophet's Companions and is therefore connected to the Prophet through this first community of Muslims. This small rhetorical gesture forestalls any claim to racial/ethnic hierarchy or privilege in Islam, despite its historical foundations among Arabs in the Arabian Peninsula and in the Arabic language. According to Shakir, whether they were born into Muslim families or had converted to Islam, all in the room were on equal footing as companions in relation to the Prophet Muhammad.

While the oft-quoted verse of the Qur'an states that "the noblest of you, in the sight of Allah, is the best in conduct. Lo! Allah is Knower, Aware" (Qur'an 49:13), a Prophetic saying also refers to his family, Ahl al-Bayt (people of the house) as a means for Muslims.[7] Thus, a descendant's bloodline is only as good as their deeds, and an Arab or any other Muslim who comes from a historically Muslim territory is also judged on his or her conduct before his or her ethnic origin. The deference that Shakir showed Habib 'Umar—he rushed to him, lowered himself, and kissed his hand—made clear that Shakir believed Habib 'Umar to be of the knowledgeable and righteous descendants of the Prophet Muhammad. Habib 'Umar and others returned the deference, praising Shakir in his teachings that evening and ensuring that Shakir sat in a chair at the same level as 'Umar and his translator, who was a US-born white student of both the Yemeni Habib and African American Shakir, while the rest of the audience sat facing them on the floor.[8]

Finally, while Shakir's genealogical mapping does not seem to account for the Latinx and Indigenous converts in the room, the omission reveals how tribal and regional affinities, as well as geographies, were defined in the seventh century as compared to the contingencies of how geographies, bodies, and identities are defined today. While many Latinx Muslims have selected and reselected ancestors through connections to Africa and Muslim Spain, how did they understand their ties to the Sahaba in this moment (Abdul Khabeer 2017a; Galvan 2017)?

FIGURE 2.1 Community members arriving for the evening program at the Ta'leef
Collective in a business park in Fremont (author).

In the introduction, I mention the Prophet Muhammad's deep ties to
the city of his birth, Mecca, and the welcome his community received in
both Abyssinia and Medina. When the *Muhajirin* (Migrants) from Mecca
arrived in Medina, they were embraced and assisted by the *Ansar* (Helpers), who were of the two tribes that welcomed the Prophet to Medina in
order to bring peace and mend relations between them. While Shakir's
narration does not "name" everyone in the room, we can take its lessons to
think about how the first generation of Muslims sought refuge, provided
refuge, and became refugees; their narratives of vulnerability, mobility, and
exile, as well as possession and dispossession, extend the potentiality of
what this legacy of companionship offers. Similarly, the Sahaba's relationships to one another and the ways they reproduced life in particular places
may shift our understandings of what it means to belong to a people and to
a place outside of regimes of property and the nation-state.

What this scene, chapter, and book attempt to demonstrate is how Muslims have sought survival via Islamic (dare I say decolonial and abolitionist)
structures, ways of knowing, and being: that the lessons we learn from the
Sahaba extend beyond what they remembered of the Prophet Muhammad;
we also learn from the harm they caused one another—from their tribal-
ism and abuses of power to disavowal and death—and how they sought
culpability, repair, and accountability for themselves, one another, and their

Lord. There are stories, words, and practices in the Muslim past, as infrastructures of feeling, that "we can use" (N. Knight 2015; Kashani 2018b).

SCENE 2

FADE IN

EXTERIOR. FERNCLIFF CEMETERY, HARTSDALE,
WESTCHESTER, NEW YORK, SPRING 2011, DAY.

We see and move through a cemetery on a gloomy day of light rain. Green grass pokes up around flat tombstones, THE HABIB walks swathed by a crowd of men who struggle to maintain a place in the shuffling orbit around him. They hold umbrellas over him, while likewise enabling his way across the wet grass. A microphone and camera phones try to keep pace with his assertive gait. We are at the burial place of EL-HAJJ MALIK EL-SHABAZZ, popularly known as MALCOLM X, formerly known as MALCOLM LITTLE. Standing at his grave, this assembly makes supplications with a genealogical roll call and greetings of peace to THE ANCESTORS (may God's mercy be upon them) and THE PROPHET MUHAMMAD (peace be upon him).[9]

In Tarim, Yemen, where Habib ʿUmar is from, a tradition of touring graves and learning the genealogies of Sufi saints localizes and historicizes Islam in the region while also cultivating a sense of community: "The point was to get along, to have hearts that were clean" for all who engage in acts of pilgrimage (Ho 2006, 222). These visitations produce the region as an origin for its diaspora: "What is available is a cure for this world and the next, salve and salvation. One takes in the history with the cure" (Ho 2006, 205). Yemen, as an origin, as an "archive" for Islam, was what initially drew students there, as Tarim is imagined by Muslims as a place to learn and live an "authentic" Islam (Z. A. Grewal 2013, 82). In turn, students return home and bring their teachers with them, connecting people and practices in Tarim to people and places in North America. Engseng Ho discusses the "the cumulative results of . . . actions and movements" across the Indian Ocean of the ʿAlawi diaspora, of which Habib ʿUmar is a part, that "reshaped this space, the relative positions of places within it, and the distribution of diasporas around it" (Ho 2006, 122). I discuss here similar actions and movements tracing alternative genealogies that span the Oceans Atlantic and Pacific and the coasts East and West. The axis of

FIGURE 2.2 Habib 'Umar and his students at the grave of El-Hajj Malik El-Shabazz (Malcolm X), Westchester, New York, in spring 2011 (Ali Bhatti).

place is crossed by multiple axes of time as Imam Zaid Shakir and Habib 'Umar make present and relevant particular figures of historical time in the rhythms of devotional time.

In the United States, the tour begins at the grave of El-Hajj Malik El-Shabazz in Westchester County, New York. This is Habib 'Umar and his students' pilgrimage to another destination that becomes an origin, an archive of Islam that redirects aspirations for Islamic origins in the Arabian Peninsula toward Islamic origins in these lands and waters of the Americas, sites of conflict, suffering, and liberatory praxis. Through their acts of visitation, they historicize and localize Islam on Indigenous (Wappinger) Lenape land; El-Shabazz's life and death signify a connection to the land and an ethical and political model for how to be in relation to it and its inhabitants. El-Shabazz's life history, *The Autobiography of Malcolm X* (Malcolm X and Haley 1965), and teachings continue to revive Islam globally such that some Muslims consider him a *wali*, a person of standing with Allah. El-Shabazz becomes a "saint," a both historical and spiritual figure for Islam locally and an important node in the Prophetic line, tied not by genealogy of blood but by a tradition of faith and da'wa.[10] The remembrance of El-Shabazz, whether through grave visitation or rhetorical reference, facilitates a historical grounding and legacy of Islam in the Americas, proposing a way of being twenty-first-century Muslims in proximate relations on contested land.

The visitation to El-Shabazz's grave is a recognition and blessing of a status that Brother Malcolm already holds in the hearts and minds of many Muslims.[11] To reclaim the *spiritual* Malcolm, the Allah-conscious El-Hajj Malik El-Shabazz, is to situate his life's work and legacy toward rectifying just relations (ta'dib) within a genealogy that leads back to the prophets of Islam. By recognizing El-Shabazz as a global Muslim figure, this visitation likewise proposes an alternative directionality for and understanding of Islamic knowledge and practice.

This visitation also brings El-Shabazz's figurative body in relation to the Prophet Muhammad's because Habib 'Umar is a descendant of the Prophet who many believe embodies his teachings and example. The dispositions of the Prophet Muhammad, his Family, and his Companions continue to impact Muslims today, mediated through the stories that are told again and again in the tradition and through the "living proofs of Islam," an honorific appellation given to those whose actions or scholarly prowess are compelling examples of the possibilities of Islam and its ongoing traditions. The textual traditions of hadith and the Sira describe his, his

Family's, and his Companions' characters, whether explicitly or implicitly through their words and actions. Just as the Prophet Muhammad affected the people around him in the seventh century, the force of these ethical dispositions continues to affect the world and effect change in individual lives and in larger social contexts.

El-Shabazz was not extensively trained in the Islamic sciences, nor was he a college graduate or infallible, but the knowledge he had he communicated and acted upon, and for this he is inducted into a tradition of those who "summon" to, "revive," and "renew" the deen. That much of his work would be seen as political in nature is taken not as an aside, but as integral to his significance and legacy as a spiritual figure seeking a truth for which he was martyred. As one narration states, "There will always be a group from my people striving for the truth, unworried by those who frustrate them, until Allah's appointed hour, and even then they will still be at their task" (al-Haddad 2011).[12] Islam is likewise historicized and localized through other graves, marked and unmarked, of enslaved Muslims from Africa throughout the Americas. As Islam makes historical and spiritual time, it also extends through space, not only traveling from East to West but also emerging and radiating out from Harlem, Detroit, Chicago, Berkeley, and Oakland to other parts of the Islamic world.

El-Shabazz and his autobiography continue to inspire as examples of personal and political transformation (Marable and Aidi 2009; Njoroge 2013; Curtis and Johnson 2015; Aidi 2016). In the first two years at Zaytuna College, students who had yet to read El-Shabazz's autobiography, but who had most likely seen the Spike Lee joint (1992), put it on their reading lists as an "American Muslim must-read." Between the references to El-Shabazz their teachers and fellow students made and the stories they heard about conversions to Islam inspired by the book, most students were struck by the narrative, which gave them insights into an experience often much different from their own. The book was also used as part of the college's initial English curriculum.

Despite Manning Marable's query regarding the veracity of the autobiography, "How much isn't true, and how much hasn't been told?" (2011, 10), the text and the iconic man it represents continue to impact the Islamic landscape and can be counted among the mediated forms of da'wa like printed pamphlets, books, and recordings that seek to bring people into or strengthen their understanding and practice of Islam. Speaking truth to power, "making it plain," and being memorialized in narratives of praise, critique, and accomplishment, El-Hajj Malik El-Shabazz as an

Muslim wali or saint continues to bring converts to Islam and be an ethical-political model for Muslims, Black or otherwise. That his ethical work for Black liberation could also translate as an example of da'wa internationally speaks to the ways and directions in which Islamic knowledge and practice travel.[13] This is an important intervention that challenges the idea that Arabs or South Asians from historically Muslim lands are the only sources of authentic knowledge and practices of Islam (whether in the media or among Muslims themselves, rarely are regions like West and East Africa, East and Southeast Asia, China, and the Philippines referred to as historically Muslim lands, despite their centuries of history and greater populations of Muslims). By remembering El-Shabazz and being present with him, whether through grave visitation or rhetorical reference, Muslims cultivate bonds of kinship with both El-Shabazz as ancestor and with one another. His grave, alongside the continued force of his words, image, biography, complexity, and contradictions, facilitate a historical grounding and legacy of how to be Muslim in a multiracial, multiethnic, and still contested United States.

Notably, Marable's biography of Malcolm X was released during Habib 'Umar's "Tranquility amidst Turbulence" tour, and the ensuing controversy about the book (its veracity, ethics, and sources) was much talked about as people carpooled around the Bay Area to attend Habib 'Umar's events. Marable's consideration of Malcolm being "almost sacred" and "not a saint" (perhaps from a Christian perspective) does not account for his meaning within Islam (Marable and Aidi 2009, 300). El-Shabazz was "present" through the visitation to his grave, the build-up to and controversy of the new biography (which Imam Zaid Shakir had just received from one of his students), and the passing of its author Manning Marable a day before its release. In addition, the first of five congressional hearings on the "Radicalization of American Muslims in the U.S." had just been held. For many in the community, there was a convergence of forces at work in this time of attack, controversy, and blessings.

Claiming Malcolm spiritually means different things for different people, and accounting for different interpretations of the "archive" and its potential limits, contradictions, and omissions is an ongoing task.[14] His legacy can be read as an anti-racist and internationalist liberatory praxis grounded in deep belief, but it has also proven susceptible to reform narratives that incorporate Malcolm into a civil rights history of the United States's redemption (Kashani 2018b). Applying lessons he learned to his own iconicity, we remember his fallibility and refrain from exalting him beyond critique. Approaching Malcolm as an ancestor produces alternative understandings and praxes for how the family, religious authority, sexuality, and the public and the private are figured. Such an ancestral legacy and liberatory lineage may disrupt, rather than reinforce, the logics and structures of white supremacy, patriarchy, and the vulnerabilities to premature death they engender.[15]

Additionally, the enshrining of El-Shabazz and the "Tranquility amidst Turbulence" tour positions the 'hood as a critical space and *source* of Islamic consciousness, knowledge, practice, and renewal. In the Bay Area, Habib 'Umar's students walked him through increasingly gentrified, though still diverse (predominantly Black, Latinx, and Asian), multiracial neighborhoods, while also hosting events in suburban spaces largely populated by middle- and upper-class Arab, Afghan, and South Asian families. Imam Zaid Shakir dubbed Habib 'Umar's stop at Castlemont High School, down the road from Masjid Al-Islam, "Habib in the 'Hood," pointedly drawing attention to this particular tour stop in East Oakland, the predominantly Black (though increasingly less so) neighborhood where the Islams of his students were first cultivated. Habib 'Umar shared the high school stage with four Black imams primarily from the Warith Deen Muhammad communities of Oakland and San Francisco.

The da'wa of the tour, Habib 'Umar's summoning of diverse populations through the work of his students, reveals an important disjuncture largely experienced through race and class in the umma. When Habib 'Umar visits El-Shabazz and walks through and prays in the 'hoods of the Bay Area and elsewhere, he walks in the steps of ancestors recalling, for instance, El-Shabazz's great love for people suffering injustice and Allah-consciousness that fueled him for their defense. 'Umar's tour traversed universities, mosques, and these community spaces, drawing links between the formal and informal forms through which knowledge and belief are cultivated and transmitted, while also demonstrating what he learned from his students, that the 'hood and its peoples are where Islamic da'wa and the ideal community it seeks to cultivate come from and should be sustained.

If Afghan, Yemeni, African, and Iraqi War refugees, Arab and South Asian tech entrepreneurs, engineers, doctors, gas station and liquor store owners, janitors, taxi drivers, their US-born children, white and Latinx converts, and African American Muslims of diverse experiences come to see El-Shabazz as their saint and Black liberation and global solidarity as their legacy, what does this do to their (generally speaking) model minority narratives of assimilation and prosperity? How would this legacy shift their narratives of being "good" Muslims in an "exceptional" United States, and enable them to connect the processes of policing, extraction, and abandonment as well as strategies for survival and knowledge production that happen in the 'hood as intimately related to military occupation, militarization, bombings, authoritarianism, and corruption; religious, racial, and ethnic persecution; and the dispossession of farmers and workers elsewhere? In Medina by the Bay, these narrative shifts and social transformations have been occurring for decades and a new generation is inducted into this liberatory tradition with every introduction of El-Shabazz's life story and teachings. At the same time, there are alternative efforts that aim to reform El-Shabazz's message as one of American redemption, that undermine his global message of solidarity, anticolonialism, and calling the United States to account.

EMBODIED RELATIONS

As the "Tranquility amidst Turbulence" tour traveled to cities across Canada and the United States, many of Habib 'Umar's lectures, workshops, and congregational prayer events were streamed live and posted online for his international audience. The physical tour was preceded by a mediated buildup that included pictures on the walls of a student's room, videos posted online and shared on Facebook, stories exchanged, and his spiritual essence in the faces, beings, and teachings of his students who are spread throughout the country and concentrated in the Bay Area. In her room at Zaytuna College, Aminah, an Arab student from the Midwest, had framed pictures of Habib 'Umar that she had downloaded from the internet and one small picture that her brother had purchased and brought back for her from Tarim, Yemen.

Young Muslims who had returned home from study in Tarim dramatically reoriented Aminah's understanding of Islam, what it made possible in terms of the transformation of people's character that then impacted her own:

> Although I went to an Islamic school, I didn't necessarily feel like I loved what I was doing or what I was learning. I mean, some of it was exciting. We had some pretty good teachers and pretty good speakers, but it wasn't something that I necessarily wanted to devote my life to. It's kind of like I was born into this, you know what I mean? And then here comes the "angel of mercy" named Tarek, and he's just like beautiful in every way, inside and out.[16] His character is amazing, you know. And I was just like,

"Oh, this guy is something else," and I had seen the positive effect he had on my brother, and all this kind of stuff. And so, I just was like, "Whatever he is doing, I gotta be a part of that right now!" And so that's how it started for me. It's an immense blessing. And I feel like this is the reason that I am here, that I am with such amazing scholars, and that's how it started. [It] was, really, good character. And I feel like that's the entire point, you know, of this religion is good character. Good character with your Lord, good character with people, you know?

Aminah's reoriented relationship to Islam is shaped by her witnessing of particular individuals whose "good character" embody Islam, its potential meaning, and its significance for her. As I mention earlier, notions of adab, *akhlaq*, or "good character" are mediated within specific contexts and are likewise entangled with classed, gendered, and racialized notions of beauty, piety, dress, and comportment. That she is able to imagine and aspires to this ethical future for herself demonstrates the particular ways that "good character" can be recognized across gender, although the traits of "good character" are often marked as distinctly feminine or masculine.[17] This type of recognition relies on particular ethical dispositions "to see" and impact one another. Aminah's recognition of Tarek's "amazing character" is dependent on her recognizing his traits as those that she desires and seeks to emulate.

In describing her Midwestern adventures during Habib 'Umar's tour to her classmates and me, Aminah laughed as she explained how awkward it sometimes was because she and her friend Yuri, a Black woman in her twenties, were often the only women in particular spaces.[18] They thought that they probably "weren't supposed to be there," but they continued to occupy discrete spaces along the walls in these gatherings. They were excited, nonetheless, and following the tour to its innermost spaces transgressed norms of conduct in Tarim that were being replicated in the Midwest, but these sisters pushed through their awkward feelings, eager to participate in and witness this historic event. Their sincere desires to be close to this teacher, this descendant of their beloved Prophet, and their anticipating and expecting that these men of "good character" would recognize their intentions, desires, and "rights" outweighed their concerns of what was "proper" adab in those moments. Aminah, Yuri, and the men present pushed against the *normalizing effect* of adab in terms of "one's proper place" toward the *potential* of adab in restoring just relations and a fullness of humanity through seeking knowledge, transformative encounters, and ethical relations. Aminah and Yuri acknowledge their "breach of propriety" by situating themselves in door frames and discrete spaces, yet they maintain and perhaps reinvigorate the male students' attention on their common "object of love."

Back in a two-bedroom Berkeley apartment and crowded around a computer screen, the sisters and I prepared for the Habib's arrival by tracing his travels, watching him arrive at airports from Toronto to Los Angeles, his students rushing to kiss his hand in greeting and performing *nashid* accompanied by a daff player.[19] We watched videos posted to Facebook in which the Habib places his hands on children's heads, sits in the passenger seat of a rented SUV, converses with his former students both young and old, and makes a pilgrimage to the resting place of El Hajj Malik El-Shabazz. As the sisters pointed out people they knew in the videos, they pondered how they would greet the Habib:

> ZAHRAH: You know, we should develop some kind of greeting custom for women, with *shuyukh* (Arabic plural of shaykh), you know, something that's similar, but obviously not kissing his hand.
> ZEINAB: Yeah, we should have something, you know?
> RUQAYYA: Like touching his shawl?
> ZAHRAH: Kissing his shawl! Maybe?

In this brief interchange and in Aminah's Midwestern adventures above, the female students acknowledge the gendered etiquettes that delimit their physical contact and proximity to the Habib. While male acolytes rush to kneel before the Habib and kiss his hand, there did not seem to be a corresponding greeting for women. Women were on the peripheries of these welcome scenes, if they were there at all. As the video proceeded, one of the girls pointed out a sister in a black *niqab* (face veil) and *'abaya* (a flowing garment) standing off to the side. Zeinab points at the screen, "Oh, there's like one woman." Aminah replies soberly, "Yeah." Zeinab laughs.

At the "women's event" at a mosque in Pleasanton, I was sitting in the front row. After a riveting introduction by one of his female students, a well-known (in particular circles) women's teacher based in California, I too felt compelled to veil my face out of respect for the traditions of Tarim. Place and geography mattered in terms of how we carry and dress ourselves and how we relate to one another. In the Pleasanton mosque, the women were asked to scoot further back to leave about fifteen to twenty feet between them and the Habib and his translators. At Zaytuna College the relationship between the Habib and his female audience shifted. In the Zaytuna library, the female students were seated in chairs quite close to the Habib. In this

FIGURE 2.3 Watching Habib ʿUmar arrive at the airport in Southern California. There is "one woman" on the right side in the background (author).

coed audience, Habib ʿUmar seemed to direct his lecture to them, looking directly at them as he told stories about Fatima, the Prophet Muhammad's daughter. His stories were spoken with such intimacy that the *Ahl al-Bayt* (the People of the House, the Prophet's Family) drew close and immediate in this smaller gathering. Both male and female students were brought into this genealogy of knowledge conveyed from the Prophet Muhammad to his daughter Fatima to her descendants and community. Habib ʿUmar brought meaning into this relationship as a foundational tenet of what being Muslim was all about, regardless of one's bloodline.

When I filmed the Habib in these closer quarters at Zaytuna College without a veil, he looked directly at me and my camera, Nur. Was Nur a veil through which it was appropriate to exchange intense eye contact? To answer this question, I return to al-Attas's notion of adab: the "recognition and acknowledgement of the reality that knowledge and being are ordered hierarchically according to their various grades and degrees of rank, and of one's proper place in relation to that reality and to one's physical, intellectual and spiritual capacities and potentials" (al-Attas 1980, 17). The events at the mosque and at Zaytuna College showed how event organizers, Habib ʿUmar, his students, and his audiences may or may not recognize and acknowledge the order of their knowledge and being, distinguishing between female students of knowledge at Zaytuna and what was perceived to be more of a female lay audience at the mosque.

I emphasize that this ordered distinction is not one of value in the vein 103

of white supremacy, heteropatriarchy, and capitalism; the Zaytuna students are not more important or valuable than the Muslim women at the mosque, nor vice versa. Rather, the labor they are all engaged in, whether asking questions about their families or their studies, is necessary to fulfill communal and individual obligations to Allah, themselves, and one another. The means through which they relate to one another (space, dress, comportment) are to be shaped according to these communal and individual needs for reproducing a just community. This just community does not necessarily reflect commonly held "feminist" or liberal notions (even among Muslim women) in that women did not have "equal" access to a male scholar nor were female scholars featured for male audiences; they upheld norms regarding dress that seem to "oppress" women, and oriented the Pleasanton conversation around domestic issues of child-rearing and husbands; some women did indeed bristle and raise objections to how the tour was organized and the Yemeni forms of gendered adab it encouraged. Indeed, notions of hierarchy and degree are often mobilized to provide justifications for sexism, misogyny, exclusion, enclosure, and punishment, where power is exercised outward as a form of discipline, rather than inward as ethical praxis.

The tour attempts to present a different order of valuation. For his students and fellow scholars, Habib ʿUmar is set apart because he brings *nur* (light), and one's distance from him does not dictate the amount of light one will receive but rather is a function of one's specific role, capacity, and needs. *Taqwa* (God-consciousness) is the primary characteristic by which human beings will be judged, and only Allah can make that judgment. When human beings attempt to create essential or eternal hierarchies, based on man-made characteristics like race, sex/gender, nation, or class, they are attempting to be God-like, engaging in *shirk* (associating partners with God, a form of polytheistic idolatry, the greatest sin in Islam). While human beings may be put into social, economic, or cultural positions of privilege, power, or access as a matter of Allah's will, these are ethical and moral tests with particular responsibilities. The female audiences and students respect the elevated social status of Habib ʿUmar and their own teachers as people of knowledge and, in the Habib's case, as a knowledgeable descendant of the Prophet Muhammad. The female students are privileged in that they have a particular access to scholars most women do not, in that many avenues for sacred knowledge have increasingly excluded women. In looking to find a way to greet him or engage with him as students, they did not want to disrupt particular understandings of knowledge hierarchies or Islamic gender relations, per se, but they also recognized how there are different ways to enact and interpret prescriptions for gender difference and separation. In the case of my camera, Habib 'Umar was transmitting to whomever would receive his teachings via our recordings; at the same time, the intensity of his gaze was also a reminder that his image and lessons were now entrusted to me and that I needed to attend to myself, my own adab, as well.

These distinctions are significant in a place like Zaytuna College, which is attempting to create a space where women have the same access to and benefits of their teachers and their teaching. While the classroom imparts a space of egalitarian opportunity and thriving, it is in the extracurricular spaces of Zaytuna and the wider Muslim landscape that Islamic ideals are set against the complexities of everyday practice. As Zaytuna College attempts to produce male and female scholars and global citizens, defining and nurturing that scholarship will involve counteracting many of the institutionalized forms of sexism and heteropatriarchy that shape not only multiple Muslim landscapes, but American ones as well.

At the former Zaytuna Institute, students were separated horizontally by gender with wooden arabesque lattice dividers standing between them. During the first student orientation at Zaytuna College, the students were assembled in three long rows in which the male students sat in the first row, while the female students took up the second and third rows. Within the first week of classes this mosque-like seating arrangement was quickly subverted. Male students intentionally took the rear rows, while the female students sat in the front. Hamza Yusuf later had the students rearrange the desks into more of a semicircle in which students sat in pairs. While they initially sat in same-sex sets of two, they later sat in mixed pairs at times, depending on what seats were available when particular students arrived in class. After one pair of students became engaged, they always sat together. Female and male students sat in both the front and back rows, on the left and on the right of the classroom, providing students with their desired proximities to their teachers and to one another.

By not replicating more typical North American mosque formations (men in front, women in the back or in a separate room), the scholars and students at Zaytuna suggest that there are other ways to enact gender-specific spaces and, consequently, attitudes about and practices of gender. Yet, cultural norms maintain their hegemony, and gender separation has often been interpreted by both Muslims and non-Muslims as a matter of female devaluation and exclusion, rather than a way to uphold valued forms of gendered sociality, (female) authority, and knowledge. Matthew, the former student life coordinator at Zaytuna College, was quite aware of how exclusionary norms entered Muslim space, and he often wondered about how to be proactive in creating egalitarian experiences for the students.[20]

> We need to understand as a community, the default is that Sisters are not welcome; they don't have much access to scholars and to knowledge, and so we need to think a bit more almost like affirmative action, doing a bit more to balance it out, by involving the Sisters a bit more. I think when I say these things, I say it more in terms of dynamics and some feelings that can develop, but in terms of the day-to-day things, many of the Sisters here are leaders, just as much if not more so than the Brothers . . . but still there's a potential for dynamics to develop, especially when we have some classes in the prayer room, or around prayer times, when the Brothers are just right up front next to the scholars, and the Sisters are ten feet back. We have to be proactive in terms of balancing out the effect that that can have on the dynamic.

Matthew expressed that part of his understanding came from being in conversation with his Muslim wife. By listening to her and by thinking about her experiences as a woman in the same spaces, he came to have greater understanding and consideration for the female students' experiences. Following an oft-quoted hadith, many Muslims speak of marriage as "half of one's *deen* (religion)."[21] If one marries, understanding and relating to one's spouse and their gendered experience may enhance one's ethical capacities in terms of social relations outside the home as well.[22] Being married or having children also impacts to what degree and in what ways one can pursue Islamic knowledge.

For example, Aminah's classmate Mary is a Latina convert originally from the Bay Area. Her older brother had first converted to Islam, and she followed a few years later at the age of fourteen. She married Michael, a Filipino convert right before she started at Zaytuna, having already attained a previous bachelor's degree in English elsewhere.[23] When I first started talking to Mary, I recognized her frustration and exhaustion with the balance of school and family life. In addition, she was also commuting every day from Hayward and had to move her car every two hours so that she did not get a parking ticket. While she tried taking public transportation, the distance, expense, and indirect route proved difficult. Mary excelled in her academics, yet she lamented the limits of her participation in extracurricular events and student life and in forging relationships with the other female students.

American society taught Mary as a young woman of color that she had to assert her rights and "go for hers." At the same time, her teachers taught her that though pursuing knowledge was one of the most important things a Muslim could and should do, one should not do so at the expense of someone else who had a right over her time and attention. This was not a topic covered in al-Zarnuji's *Instruction of the Student: The Method of Learning* (a thirteenth-century manual for students of sacred knowledge), and so she asked Imam Zaid Shakir about it during their student orientation while they were reviewing the text. In al-Zarnuji's (d. 1223) time it was unlikely that a wife and mother of young children would have been a student of knowledge full-time (though if she had come from a scholarly family, she may have already received *ijaza* [permission] to teach multiple texts). Mary asked Shakir how her time should be prioritized and managed. He said that her husband and stepchild had rights over her and that her responsibilities as a wife and mother should come before her studies. But what such rights looked like was another terrain of negotiation, and it was only through Mary and Michael's conscious efforts, communication, and knowledge that such exchanges could happen.

My conversations with Mary evolved over time as she and Michael worked together and learned how to manage their mutual rights and expectations. With each semester she was more at ease as they each made sacrifices (he had to discontinue his own Islamic studies graduate education to continue working full-time in the tech industry, while she delayed graduation to care for her newborn), gained benefits, and negotiated how to be in Islam, marriage, and community together within the social and geopolitical contexts of racial capitalism and an increasingly gentrified Bay Area (this especially affected commute times and rent prices). She stated that it was not only particular aspects of Islamic knowledge that shaped the contours of their relationship, but also time and a holistic approach of being in touch with their individual and communal capacities. It was the mutual understanding and (continuing) work that made such ethical relations and transformation possible.

A few years after Mary's graduation from Zaytuna, she and Michael decided to leave the Bay Area. While Medina by the Bay had nurtured their Muslim becomings, they joined other Bay Area Muslims in creating an intentional Muslim community in rural Pennsylvania. Like their non-Muslim counterparts, they joined thousands of other people from the Bay who increasingly found the struggle to live and work there in conflict with the ethical lives they wanted to live. Their hijra (migration) signifies the further impact of what emerges from the urban and suburban landscapes of Medina by the Bay, its continuation and evolution as it encounters other peoples and geographies.

I draw on Mary and Michael's relationship, as well as what Matthew, Aminah, and her classmates observed and experienced, to extend Shakir's articulation of the Sahaba's companionship and kinship by faith. The work that scholars and students do in terms of drawing attention to liberatory lineages of racial and ethnic difference also apply to how companionship and kinship must be felt across and through other forms of difference, including gender and sexuality (Wadud 1999; 2006; K. Ali 2016; Taylor 2017). While egalitarian seating arrangements and coeducation at Zaytuna or Ta'leef mark them as non-mosque spaces, they also participate in the reinscribing of value and meaning to differences of gender and sexuality that contribute to the harm of vulnerable Muslims.

Even at Zaytuna, despite the changes in seating arrangements and the modest dress of female students, the male students still considered the female students "distracting." The female students commiserated in private with me, exasperated by the brothers' inability to discipline themselves and their gazes ("How much more do we need to cover?"), blaming the sisters' and their attire for their own lapses in concentration and piety. As Abdul Khabeer states, this approach results in the "infantilization, emasculation, and dehumanization of Muslim men. . . . Men are incapacitated by patriarchal regimes that establish a singular frame through which they are allowed to imagine and interact with women, children, other men, and themselves" (2018, 288). The struggles of what this has meant for the community emerge when people are privately and publicly called to account for the harm that they cause or participate in.

A few years after the "Tranquility amidst Turbulence" tour, one of the host organizations sent out an email announcing the severing of relations between the organization and one of its founders because of a betrayal of trust and an abuse of power. This was part of a damaging trend of "spiritual abuse," in which imams, teachers, and community leaders abuse their social and spiritual capital and standing as scholars, spiritual leaders, or "celebrity shaykhs" to coerce, manipulate, and abuse their students, followers, and employees, and it evoked a range of contested and complex issues in the Islamic tradition regarding authority and ethical cultivation and multiple and temporary marriages, for example (Ansari 2015). Rather than address causes, communal culpabilities, and rippling traumas, many conversations often focused on the ways that spiritual abuses were disclosed and when and how Muslims should conceal, reveal, and otherwise attend to one another's harmful behaviors and practices. I allude to this event not to hash out what happened but to think about what kinship by faith means when harm occurs within the umma, especially by those who engage in daʿwa, taʿlim, and taʾdib. I also write as a way to hold myself accountable to my multiple communities; I struggled about whether to write about this event and how, asking myself what my ethical and Islamic obligations were to my interlocutors and to my greater community. In thinking about those who had been harmed or felt betrayed, I could not describe and think about the spiritual presences and transformative forces that flowed through Medina by the Bay during Habib's tour without also addressing how those same spaces directly or indirectly enabled forms of harm and betrayal. I also had to contend with my own feelings of culpability as I had participated in and invited individuals I cared about to programs in these spaces, while I was also compelled to rethink all my interactions with particular individuals, questioning my own memories and analyses, while also holding onto the knowledge and lessons I had received.

The discourses of policing and Homeland Security often present danger and insecurity in the form of a stranger, the foreign Muslim, the masked criminal. Yet, we often experience harm in our most intimate spaces and relations; we harm and are harmed by those closest to us in relation to larger structures of harm like the state and structures of belief like white supremacy and heteropatriarchy (INCITE! 2006; Kaba 2021). Casting one out of the community is something Western law performs (Razack 2008); Islamic law's orientation is toward the well-being of the community in which religion, life, intellect, lineage, and property are preserved, following the Prophetic hadith, "No harm, nor harming" (J. A. C. Brown 2009b).[24] This is why repair—of our relations, hearts, faith, and trust—and transformation—of the conditions, beliefs, structures of power, and institutions that made harm possible—must take precedence in how we relate to one another. Otherwise, our hearts grow hard, our faith diminishes, our knowledge is less certain, and the institutions we have struggled to build falter.

The dissonance between the intellectual, spiritual, and affective influence that a daʿi or an ʿalim, a caller to or scholar of Islam, engenders and then the sense of harm, betrayal, disbelief, and anger their private acts may cause animate the critical work that Muslims must attend to. What could have led to an opportunity for conversations about gender dynamics, power and authority, and charismatic leadership of the greater community instead tended to focus on the individual himself rather than the context within which he hurt himself and others. As in many cases of gendered harm and abuses of power, victims and survivors were decentered and the character, reputation, and memory of the one who harmed was deemed more valuable and vulnerable. At the same time, punishments are external limits, and the Prophet Muhammad and early jurors went out of their way to avoid the strictest of punishments, offering doubt whenever possible, knowing that the harshest of individual punishments had communal and intergenerational reverberations (Rabb 2014). Muslim communities have been under attack for so long that we cling to charismatic figures in ways that Brother Malcolm taught us to avoid, while also being quick to cast out our imperfect relations ("bad" Muslims) as a misguided strategy of preservation and survival.

The umma is neither exceptional nor an anomaly; it is a microcosm for society at large in which relations of power manifest in complex ways. One cannot disentangle how what happens in Medina by the Bay is also enabled by norms and logics that permeate a larger North American society in which women continue to be seen as the public and private property of men, rather than as companions with whom one shares reciprocal rights and responsibilities of relation and where carcerality and punishment are seen as the only possibilities for safety and justice. Again, our ethical relations with our selves, Allah, and one another must be cultivated, and seeking forgiveness, repair, and transformation become our pathways toward justice and salvation in this world and the next.

SCENE 3

CUT TO:
INTERIOR. ISLAMIC HISTORY CLASS, ZAYTUNA COLLEGE, BERKELEY, SPRING 2011, DAY.

We see two-person tables arranged in a semicircle around a large teacher's desk at the front of the room. Male and female students sit alone or in pairs in no particular order or arrangement. Books and notebooks are spread out on their desks, and every student holds a paperback copy of Sylviane Diouf's *Servants of Allah: African Muslims Enslaved in the Americas* (1998). The instructor ZAID SHAKIR sits off to the side in a black chair as MARY sits at the teacher's desk, facing HER CLASSMATES and leading them in discussion. HER CLASSMATES include a recent AFRICAN AMERICAN CONVERT to Islam, a WHITE AMERICAN CONVERT to Islam, two SECOND-GENERATION AFRICAN AMERICAN MUSLIMS, ONE SECOND-GENERATION BLACK CARIBBEAN AMERICAN MUSLIM, two PAKISTANI AMERICAN MUSLIMS, two ARAB AMERICAN MUSLIMS born to parents from Syria, and a NORTH AFRICAN AMERICAN MUSLIM born to a father from Algeria and white American mother. Also sitting to the side by the window with a copy of the book, a notebook, and camera is the ASIAN AMERICAN MUSLIM ANTHROPOLOGIST/FILMMAKER born to parents from Iran and Japan.[25]

MARY

In the examples that [Diouf] is giving, what is the thing that African Muslims really linked to their faith?

ZAHRAH raises her hand. MARY nods to her to speak.

ZAHRAH

Their last possession, I know she mentions one slave, and I think this is probably . . . indicative of other slaves that were Muslim . . . they actually carried the Qur'ans with them through the Middle Passage, so it . . . shows if they had anything, they had their faith.

Knowing she is a diligent student and prepared for class, Shakir has asked Mary to lead the discussion. Pursuing a second bachelor's degree, Mary was one of a few students who had grown up in the Bay, while Zahrah came to Berkeley and Zaytuna straight out of high school in Brooklyn, New York.

The students learn about the first Muslims in the Americas, the estimated two to three million Muslims who were shipped against their will to the Americas during the transatlantic slave trade, and their efforts to maintain their Islamic practices despite the harsh realities of enslavement. According to Diouf, these Muslims attempted to maintain their Indigenous traditions, values, and customs and were often at the forefront of rebellions and revolts. She follows traces in artifacts, stories, languages, and customs to articulate some of the ways that Muslims maintained their identities. For homework, the students had read through "Chapter 2: Upholding the Five Pillars of Islam in a Hostile World."

The study of enslaved Muslims within the context of an Islamic history class serves multiple purposes toward imagining an Islamic future in the Americas through an understanding of its past. As Islam is attacked

for being a foreign threat, incommensurable with American ideals, under-

standing its long history in the Americas becomes an important articulation for its foundational presence in the establishment of the United States.
Diouf states that within the violence of slavery itself, a lack of educational
structures was one of the reasons that Islam—though it left traces—did
not survive generations of enslavement. The linguistic, geographic, social,
and kinship ruptures caused by systems of slavery made it difficult for Muslims to pass on their knowledge, belief, and practices.

The presence of these peoples and the force of their devotional practices centuries earlier yield a spiritual and metaphysical force that Shakir
recognizes and mobilizes later that evening. Interred in these lands in both
marked and unmarked graves, these Muslim saints, forefathers, and fore-
mothers are part of a spiritual genealogy of Muslim suffering and resistance.
El-Hajj Malik El-Shabazz is another node in this genealogy, and Shakir attempts to induct a multiracial constituency into this line through raising a
collective historical consciousness. Organizing around suffering, resistance,
and turbulence, Shakir's course and Habib 'Umar's tour work in tandem
to articulate multiple histories and ancestors through which contemporary
Muslims can understand their communal and individual roles. These histories do not mobilize narratives of Black labor to have a "seat at the table";
rather, they articulate liberatory lineages, recognizing the ways of knowing
and being that Africans brought with them and the ongoing work of their
prayers, practices, and spiritual forces. When Zahrah recalls that these Muslims carried their Qur'ans (as embodied knowledge) through the Middle
Passage, she states that "if they had anything, they had their faith." According to Shakir and his students, when Muslims come under attack and when
they feel challenged by the obligations of their faith, it is to their faith that
they must hold steadfast, and it is their Muslim ancestors in the Americas
that they must remember. They are seen as ethical-political models through
which to understand suffering and striving, steadfastness and resistance.

At the end of the semester, Shakir has the students recollect the lessons of the semester and consider their present circumstances as Muslims
in the United States through the lens of Islamic history. Zeinab, a student
of North African and white descent remembers Diouf's book, and recalls,
"The struggles that the slaves went through in upholding their religion.
A lot of Muslims in America, they have this kind of opinion, you know,
where it's really a struggle upholding your faith, wearing hijab, eating halal
food, and just to read these stories and seeing how . . . the slaves were able
to hold onto their Islam, it's really something." She struggles to find the

words to complete these thoughts, but the other students nod in understanding. While recontextualizing their own everyday struggles within this history is significant, Zeinab's struggle to find words also conveys that learning these histories requires something more.

SCENE 4

CUT BACK TO:

INTERIOR. TA'LEEF COLLECTIVE, HAYWARD, LATER THAT EVENING, NIGHT.

We see IMAM ZAID SHAKIR continue his introduction of HABIB 'UMAR.

IMAM ZAID SHAKIR

There is not a place on the face of this earth where people are converting to Islam like they are converting to Islam in America. We should never lose sight of that fact, because sometimes we forget, sometimes we forget. Our community are rich Muslims, [and] there are poor Muslims, and we should never forget the poor Muslims, because that's why Habib 'Umar is here, it's the poor Muslims. We said he was called by people—they weren't even poor! They were slaves! A poor person owns something, they didn't even own themselves, but they owned their faith, and they fought to hold onto their faith.

We're studying right now in a class I'm teaching, Islamic History, those African Muslims, those poor Muslims who were brought here, who prayed here—under the conditions of slavery—who fasted here, even though they were half starving . . . and could barely eat, but despite that they fasted Ramadan. We have written documentation. They fasted Ramadan. Despite that they put food aside from their meager rations so they could give others *sadaqa,* charity. There's written documentation of that. And some of them were *'ulama'* (scholars), like Ayuba bin Suleiman (aka Job Ben Solomon, 1701–1773), 'Umar bin Said (Omar ibn Said, 1770–1864); these were scholars, and some of them were *awliya'* (saints, plural of *wali*), some of them had a standing with Allah *subhanahu wa-ta'ala* (Glory be to God, the Most High).

Shakir continues to articulate a litany of ancestors, ranging from the Companions to the Muslim scholars forcibly moved across the Atlantic in the Middle Passage. That Shakir refers to the Companions of the Prophet Muhammad instead of a history of civil rights sets the terms for Muslim unity beyond American multiculturalism toward a more expansive geography and temporality. As the voluntary movement from Tarim, Yemen, across the Indian Ocean shaped particular diasporas—their distribution and their relations—so did the involuntary movement across the Atlantic and movements driven by war, occupation, poverty, and hope across the Pacific. The living and the dead come together through historical texts and remembrance, in person and as ancestral traces, as cure and history (Ho 2006). If the history is taken as part of the cure, then Shakir is administering a dose.

In Shakir's narrative, it is the devotional force of enslaved Muslims in the Americas centuries earlier whose prayers have been answered. These prayers called for Habib ʿUmar and the Prophetic presence he embodies to be made manifest on American soil at a critical and particularly dark and pivotal moment for Islam in the United States. Habib ʿUmar's tour in North America began days after the first congressional hearings on the "Radicalization of American Muslims" led by Representative Peter King of Long Island, New York, which followed a decade of ongoing American wars in Iraq and Afghanistan; profiling, policing, and imprisonment in the United States; and increased critiques of Islam in the media. Shakir situates this period as one prophesied and prayed toward, besieged and blessed:

> And some of them were awliyaʾ, some of them had a standing with Allah subhanahu wa-taʿala, and they prayed for this day, they prayed for one day, one day, they prayed one day there would be free men and free women in this land that say "la ilaha illa Allah, Muhammadun rasul Allah." They prayed that one day there would be people who would come here, and they would bring the light into this darkness, and they would touch the hearts of people, and they would do it at a time when Islam is besieged, when the Prophet of Islam is ridiculed, when the religion of Islam is defamed, and they would be living proof of the power that Allah subhanahu wa-taʿala says, when He says, "Yuriduna li-yutʾfiʾu nur Allahi bi-afwahihim wa-Allahu mutimmu nurihi wa-law kariha al-kafirun, wa-law kariha al-kafirun, wa-law kariha al-kafirun" [Qurʾan 61:8, Shakir repeats the last phrase three times for emphasis]. That Allah would complete His light even though those who reject this religion—who fight this religion, who hate this religion—even though they despise it. La ilaha illa Allah those are the people of rasulAllah, salla Allah ʿalayhi wa- sallam. Never forget them. Never forget them because if we forget them, we will forget our way.[26]

FIGURE 2.4 The evening prayer in the overflow room at the Ta'leef Collective in Fremont, California, with a mural by eL Seed, a Tunisian Canadian "calligraffist." There is a video projection on the right-hand wall that is simultaneously broadcasting Habib 'Umar's program in the main room (author).

Imam Zaid invokes centuries-long prayers as they break dawn on an entrenched history. There is a rupture, a break, an indescribable making present, not plain but complex, an upheaval and a sigh, a storm and then a calm, a summoning—more than emotion, something vast and contained, something expressed in the space of translation insurmountable. There is a recollection of a vision, a story told years ago in Damascus, Syria, where Shakir studied Islam.

SCENE 5

FADE IN
INTERIOR. DAMASCUS, SYRIA, 1990S,
TIME OF DAY UNKNOWN.

We see a younger ZAID SHAKIR sitting in a room with one of his teachers, SHAYKH MUSTAFA AL-TURKMANI. AL-TURKMANI is speaking to SHAKIR in Arabic, and SHAKIR attentively listens. AL-TURKMANI's voice gradually fades out as a WOMAN'S VOICE fades in, translating his words into English. The screen fades to BLACK as only the WOMAN'S VOICE is heard.

We begin with a vision transmitted to us over two hundred years ago, a mystical foreshadowing of a time becoming. Sayyid Muhammad Mehdi ar-Rawas, a Rifaʻi (Sufi order) scholar describes this vision:

"The stupefying illumination of that scene, whose light was revealed to me, and whose veils were drawn back for me, showed me that Allah would bring forth from depths of the unseen, from the overflowing unseen realities involved in that Muhammadaic state, men from whom the blinding luminosity of that [Muhammadaic] state would be removed from their hearts. Thereafter, springs of wisdom will burst forth from their hearts and will flow from the tongues of those men in unperceivable ways. Among them will be those who were the worst of disbelievers yesterday, transformed today into the purest of believers. Allah will surely complete His light.

"It is as if I see this being realized and divine forces are moving forth; unseen secrets are being manifested; tongues are speaking [with unprecedented wisdom] . . . the fragrances of Prophetic acceptance are diffusing all around. A large number of Christians in Western lands, when they are at the peak of their strength and power—a spirit from the proof of the Muhammadaic, Prophetic succor will be sent over them—Allah will guide the stray among them, and He will rectify their situation. They will be guided to faith in the pure Oneness of Allah and the message of His Noble, Chosen Prophet, peace upon him. Their numbers will grow.

"This is a sign of Allah that He has concealed in the depths of the unseen as a gift to the trustworthy Prophet, as a source of aid to the religion, and as a manifestation of divine care for the Muslims. I continued to see that divine aid extending itself outward, and the fresh water of that sea quenching the thirst of all attaining to it, extending its springs and rivulets to the people. Thus, does your Lord say, '[Bringing about such things] is easy for Me.' A glance from the eye of His care transforms a bitter enemy of Allah into a saint. Allah guides with His light whomsoever He pleases."[27]

Shakir references the events of this vision that night at Taʼleef Collective. The truth of the vision and the force of what he later refers to as "Muhammadaic breezes" come in the form of Habib ʻUmar and the multitudes of people embracing Islam. Shakir is reminded that when Islam and the

Prophet are under attack, Allah will "complete His light." Through a Prophetic presence embodied in Habib 'Umar as a knowledgeable descendant of the Prophet Muhammad, this tour binds the figures of El-Hajj Malik El-Shabazz (who identified himself as "Satan" in his autobiography), the "worst of disbelievers yesterday, transformed today into the purest of believers," enslaved Africans in the Americas, and the diverse Companions of the Prophet as spiritual and "tribal" or ethnic ancestors to contemporary Muslim communities. In traversing racial, ethnic, and class boundaries throughout the Bay Area, the tour reshapes the logics of "distinct yet densely interconnected political geographies," as well as the ways that particular populations are distributed and related to one another within them (Gilmore 2002, 261). These devotional exercises simultaneously reinforce and transgress modern boundaries of nation, race, and time toward an alternative understanding of ways to be in the world as Muslims, kin, and companions.

SCENE 6

FADE IN

INTERIOR. BACK IN ISLAMIC HISTORY CLASS, ZAYTUNA COLLEGE, BERKELEY, SPRING 2011, DAY.

We see the end of history class; Imam Zaid closes the book he is holding (*Servants of Allah*) and asks the students a question.

IMAM ZAID SHAKIR

How does this speak to us, as Muslims now, in America? How does this speak to you . . . now we're reading these, our history, our Muslim ancestors? It doesn't matter your race or ethnicity, if you're Muslim, that unites Muslims. *La ilaha illa Allah, Muhammadun rasul Allah,* not race and ethnicity. Those are [our] Muslim ancestors; they were in horrific circumstances. How does seeing how they strove to overcome their circumstances, how they strove to keep Islam as an integral recognizable religion that any Muslim from anywhere in the world would recognize, as opposed to some syncretic mishmash? What does that say to us?

It's really inspiring; it inspires me just to see the depth of struggle that they went to, to really practice their faith and being able to practice it in conditions that were really opposing, and that . . . how easy we have it comparatively and how much more we should be fighting and struggling to shape it in the cultural context and the times we live in.

Zahrah and her classmates were witness to a number of convergences those few weeks in April. While students tried to keep up with Habib 'Umar's tour, they also took turns leading discussions on *Servants of Allah*, meeting in the student lounge to discuss the different chapters they were responsible for reading. That same week the Latin American philosopher of liberation theology, Enrique Dussel, visited both UC Berkeley and Zaytuna College. That he and Habib 'Umar sat in the same library within days of each other speaks to the expansive possibilities of learning during the first years of Zaytuna College, and the potential alternative epistemologies that were being consolidated within its walls. Shakir invited Sylviane Diouf to give a talk a few weeks later, and she laid out several potential trajectories for future research. For Shakir it was important that the students have a sense of their collective history not only so they can recognize the "depth of struggle" (as Zahrah puts it) of their ancestors, but also so they can "rally the Muhammadaic forces" of today (Shakir 2010). "Now is not the time for Muslims in the West to hide or run away in the face of the abuses some elements in western societies are heaping on Islam and its adherents. Now is the time for us to stand up and become messengers and ambassadors of the truth we profess." Contrary to what one may expect, Shakir speaks not of "uprising during the day" "played out before flashing lights and cameras."[28] Rather, "those who cannot see beyond this physical world have in many instances bitten into the poisonous fruit of material power. As a result, Qur'anic truths, which alert us to sources of metaphysical strength, become marginalised in both our consciousness and in our strategic thinking" (Shakir 2010).

Shakir (2010) speaks about those waking up for prayer in the darkness of the night: "When they emerge into the light of day they themselves will be the light that a dark world is seeking." By harnessing or beseeching a metaphysical strength through worship and servitude, Muslims will find purpose in their lives: "This is the basis of the good life and the foundation of a community of virtue and service. This is the foundation of meaningful and lasting social reform" Shakir 2010. While for some this stance may seem quietist, passive, individualistic, and overly mystical, for Shakir this is an effort toward sustainability, both individual and communal, culled from years of experience watching people "burn out" or "lose their way" in sociopolitical movements. What also emerges in Shakir's comments are multiple "dialectics of discipline" (Felber 2020).

Shakir disciplines by admonishing Muslims who shape their lives, theories, and theologies according to sociopolitical and material realities at the expense of the unifying force of Islamic belief in tawhid (oneness of God). This can manifest in upholding white supremacy through racism and exploitation, but he seems to suggest that it also manifests in forms of cultural nationalism opposed to white supremacy. In Shakir's mention of "syncretic mishmash," he may be aiming a critique at the Nation of Islam and forms of Muslim activism (and scholarship) that seem to disregard or deny certain tenets of what he and others consider essential to Islamic orthodoxy and adab. Second, Shakir argues that Muslim ritual practices cultivate "metaphysical strength" as a form of discipline that Muslim communities, especially activists, need to "reform" society. Third, the state and capitalist respond to these multiple disciplinary impulses with their own forms of discipline, often as violence, but also in subtler ways that endorse and enable some forms of Islamic discipline over others.

These multiple disciplinary impulses and techniques demonstrate the entanglement of discipline and liberation; as we articulate our liberatory lineages and pathways, we must also contend with the contingent embodied and ideological differences we encounter along the way. The above six scenes attempt to convey a multiplicity of ways to narrate the meaning of Medina by the Bay, its contradictions and promises, and how knowledge, ethics, and politics are put in relation. Putting theories, theologies, and praxes in relation means being open to potential and mutual transformation, toward what M. Jacqui Alexander calls a "different metaphysics" of "living intersubjectivity premised in relationality and solidarity" (Alexander 2005, 8).

In the same Ta'leef Collective room two years later, Shakir speaks to his multiracial audience again, alluding to the differences between the experiences of the community sitting before him and those of El-Hajj Malik El-Shabazz and his family. "All praises due to Allah who has blessed us with this gathering. He's blessed us with two great blessings, with ample nourishment and with security. . . . 'So let them worship the Lord of this sacred house who has fed them and driven away from them hunger and has made them secure from fear' (Qur'an 106:3–4). So, we gather here with no fear by the grace of Allah subhanahu wa-taʿala." The community seated before him has wealth and "ample" nourishment, and despite attacks on Muslims in the media and through surveillance, they are in relative security.

Two days earlier, the body of El-Shabazz's grandson, Malcolm Latif Shabazz, was received in Oakland for a funeral at the Islamic Cultural Center of Northern California after his murder in Mexico City.[29] When a call went out to raise $40,000 to transport Shabazz's body back to the United States, money was quickly raised in the Bay Area, with many small gifts of five or ten dollars (Valrey 2013). After the funeral, his body was sent on to New York where he was laid to rest with his grandparents, El-Hajj Malik and El-Hajja Betty Shabazz. Shakir uses this account to demonstrate how the Bay Area community (both Muslim and non-Muslim) recognizes the significance, sacrifices, and spiritual kinship of the Shabazz family and likewise how the Bay Area, through a divine design, has a particularly significant Muslim infrastructure, producing many innovative and ample organizations and institutions.

This juxtaposition of security and fear with the two Shabazz deaths draws attention to how this gathering of Muslims, this kinship of faith, is situated within a prejudicial system of who lives and who dies where and for whom. Such ironies of chance and systemic violence are familiar to an immigrant population that crossed waters as refugees of wars in Afghanistan and Yemen and that witness relatives in South and West Asia and throughout the Arab world and Africa as victims of American drone strikes, proxies, intervention, exploitation, and war. Yet, making the connections between such explicit forms of violence and the everyday affective and impactful violence of structural racism, Islamophobia, targeted incarceration, poverty, and a media structured around white supremacy is more difficult, though it is a lesson both Malcolms clearly articulated and understood.

Much like many other young Black and brown youth in the criminal justice system, young Malcolm Latif Shabazz accepted a plea bargain for lesser jail time, pleading guilty to crimes he did not commit rather than taking a chance on a trial in an expensive and racially biased legal system. Once he was released and became politically active and spiritually motivated, speaking to groups around the country and abroad, making his hajj, studying Islam, traveling throughout the Arab world, and beginning to write his own autobiography, he may have been targeted by federal agencies, much like his grandfather and other family members. From elder Malcolm to younger Malcolm, we suture (Sunni/Shiʿi) sectarian divisions toward Muslim solidarities and coalitions. As I think about his grandfather's legacy, the lessons and legacy of his grandson's life and death remind us to take seriously and address the effects of white supremacist racial terror on generations of families, social movements, and neighborhoods and to look toward repairing and transforming ourselves and our spaces in ways that recognize and support our relative security and sustenance amid, and often enabled by, the most vulnerable and besieged among us.

The events I describe above plot a metaphysics of relationality that designates the figures of El-Hajj Malik El-Shabazz, enslaved African Muslims in the Americas, and the first generation of Muslim Companions as ancestors to all Muslims, whether they are Asian, African, or Arab, Latinx, or Indigenous. Such genealogies and geographies suggest that there are more potential liberatory lineages and radical relationalities that account for land, water, and others. El-Shabazz made such connections through his proximate relations with activists like Yuri Kochiyama, who introduced him to Japanese survivors of the American nuclear bombing of Hiroshima and Nagasaki, and the ways his travels in Egypt and Gaza connected him to the decolonial struggle of Palestinians (Fujino 2005; Curtis 2015). Such kinship and decolonial praxes offer an alternative orientation toward understanding how individuals and communities are bound to one another, with sets of rights and responsibilities not bestowed by and through the state, in their pursuits of justice. In closing this chapter on Muhammadaic breezes, I draw our attention to the first of the Companions, the Prophet Muhammad's first wife, Khadija, who held her husband and guided him toward realizing that he was indeed receiving revelation. She was the first Muslim, believing in the message of these revelations even before the Prophet himself. By recognizing her as ancestor and model for companionship, Muslims are called upon to guide one another to truth (an old/new epistemology for the next) and to accompany one another in transforming our worlds as we move in proximity to them.

CHAPTER 3

CODEWORDS AND COUNTERINSURGENT CONTINUITIES

SCENE 1

INTERIOR. A LARGE PUBLIC HALL IN DOWNTOWN OAKLAND, CALIFORNIA, 2012, EVENING.

We see Oakland City Council Hall filled with BAY AREA RESIDENTS; a YOUNG WHITE MAN approaches the podium and addresses the CITY COUNCIL MEMBERS seated before HIM in a raised semicircle.

ALEJANDRO

Madame President, distinguished council members, the Prophet Muhammad, peace and blessings be upon him said, "Whosoever sees evil, let him change it with his hand. If he is not able to do so, then let him change it with his tongue, and if he is not able to do so, then with his heart. And that is the weakest form of faith."[1] I stand before you today primarily as a concerned citizen. But more importantly, as a Muslim . . . shortly after I had converted to the beautiful religion of Islam, my mother, the woman who held my hand and sat next to me as I took the testimony of faith, the *Shahada,* sent me a handwritten letter in the post. In it, she said to her son,

Dear Alex,

Your recent life choice has forced me to write this letter. I'm warn-
ing you to be mindful of what you say on the phone, or what you
type in your emails, and what you do. Because there's a real possibility that the government will be watching you. You, a Muslim.[2]

I picked up the phone and called my mother immediately.

I said, "Mom. Don't worry. You don't have to write letters. I'm
a Muslim. I know my government is watching me."

CUT TO:

SCENE 2

FADE IN

TENS OF THOUSANDS OF PAGES IN AN ONGOING VERTICAL
SCROLL, 1950S–2000S.

Starting with the San Diego Police Training Bulletin "The Muslims!!!!!," we see re-
dacted FBI files of Bay Area Nation of Islam chapters, incarcerated Muslims, Black
Panther Party members who were or became Muslim, and Bay Area–based Muslim groups scroll up the screen in silence. The files transition from surveillance
files to Department of Corrections and court documents of multiple cases brought
by Muslims pertaining to religious rights in prison from the 1950s and 1960s.[3]

CUT TO:

SCENE 3

EXTERIOR. SOLANO PRISON, CALIFORNIA DEPARTMENT
OF CORRECTIONS, 1990S, DAY.

We see a group of INCARCERATED MUSLIMS put together a case demanding their
rights to better treatment as a religious group. They discuss how to gain the right
to have beards, eat halal food, and gather for congregational prayers, especially on
Friday afternoons. The INCARCERATED MUSLIMS pose questions to the MUSLIM
CHAPLAIN, who answers their questions about the requirements of the faith.

CUT TO:

INTERIOR. ZAYTUNA COLLEGE CLASSROOM, 2010, DAY.

We see STUDENTS sitting at their desks in a classroom with the blinds drawn. It does not get totally dark, so one can see students' faces. THEIR ECONOMICS PRO-FESSOR, HATEM BAZIAN, sits on the side of the classroom. They are all watching a congressional hearing on C-SPAN being projected on a pull-down screen at the front of the classroom. On the screen they watch as a SOMALI FATHER from Minneapolis talks about his son, as SHERIFF LEE BACA talks about partnerships with the Los Angeles Muslim community, as a "MUSLIM EXPERT" talks about how dangerous and radical his community is, and as CONGRESSMAN PETER KING presides over the American Muslim Anti-Radicalization Congressional Hearings. The STUDENTS and THEIR TEACHER are flabbergasted, frustrated, amused, angry, terrified, and sad.

FADE OUT

SCENE 5

INTERIOR. ALAMEDA COUNTY JAIL IN OAKLAND, CALIFORNIA, 2015–2019, NIGHT AND DAY.

We see a YOUNG ARAB MAN sitting in a local county jail cell. He gets up and paces; he stands in place; he lies down; he sleeps; he wakes; he eats; he uses the toilet; he gets angry; he writes; he reads; he cries; he prays; he makes his bed; JAIL GUARDS ransack his cell and take notes he wrote for his lawyer; he puts on cleaner socks; he walks out of his cell for an hour every two days; he looks at the sky. Repeat with some variation, time lapsing over three years and four months.

FADE OUT

In the ethnocinematic montage above, I weave together fragments of a past and present "terror-industrial complex" (Rana 2017b) and its toll on Medina by the Bay. The montage itself and the rest of this chapter attempt to render what has been conceptually difficult for non-Muslims, and often Muslims themselves, to understand, namely that this terror-industrial complex has had long-lasting, real, and harrowing effects on the social relations and life chances of Muslims in the United States, as well as their brethren abroad (Kapadia 2019; Maira 2016). "Surveillance effects," which Sunaina Maira describes as "the social and cultural registers through which surveillance is negotiated in daily life" (2014, 90), structure everyday Muslim life in the Bay Area and range from a fear that counterintelligence cases from the 1960s and 1970s never die to the insidiousness of suspicion and "the feeling of being watched" (Bendaoui 2018) that infiltrates the most intimate of Muslim spaces. The domestic battlefield of the war on terror has been waged both obliquely and directly, imprecisely and acutely, impacting kinship and survival from the individual to the institution. The challenge of conveying the durational and affective impact of counterintelligence and war on terror policies on social relations and how they dovetail with the carceral logics of the state (and society) edges against my ability to comprehend and express it; the scenes written above would take years, generations to watch in the linear space-time of the cinematic. But this writing as an ethnocinematic creative event, as an aesthetic gesture, solicits "new temporal alliances in the spaces of the event to unearth the deadly effects of oppressive time," while also evoking processes through which we learn and unlearn, "to disappear and then reappear as another being in the world" (Ruiz 2019, 13).

In the previous chapter, I discuss how liberatory lineages reorder logics of difference toward a kinship of faith and how legacies of Black struggle require Muslims of all backgrounds to wish for their brothers and sisters what they wish for themselves (a riff on a well-known hadith) as a form of ta'dib, a restoring of adab and just relations.[4] These legacies also teach us how Black and Muslim dissent, Black and brown life, and dissent for life (as in fair wages, open borders, anti-imperialism, anti-racism, and protecting water, for example) are related to one another via local and federal law enforcement, disciplinary regimes, and acts of solidarity, coalition, and companionship.

In this chapter, I relate the history of surveillance on Bay Area Muslim communities to contemporary events toward demonstrating how for some, COINTELPRO, the FBI's Counter-Intelligence Program (1956–1971) never ended, and that the war on terror merely expanded the net. I focus on these histories less to provide an analysis of the machinations of surveillance and counterintelligence regimes but rather to demonstrate how government infiltration and policies, as well as the alliances and solidarities that Muslims make, impact which forms of Islamic knowing and being survive and which do not. By looking at how Black Muslims bridge the surveillance regimes of the 1960s to the contemporary era of surveillance in which "the man" is still watching, listening, and intervening, I bring these histories together not as comparative phenomena, but as *continuities* that demonstrate an ongoing counterintelligence and counterinsurgent logic that uses the specter of international (Muslim) terrorism to expand the counterintelligence of domestic organizations and populations.

This continuity demonstrates the intricacies of how surveillance and infiltration are exercises of sovereign power, governed by white supremacist and (Christian) secularist logics that determine what forms of political and religious thought and practice can flourish and survive (Johnson and Weitzman 2017). As Mahmood astutely observes, it is the remaking of subjectivities and "approved" spiritualities and relationships to history that are the targets of a liberal state's distinctions between religious freedom and state sovereignty. This "modality of political rule that is itself retrospectively called 'a religiously neutral political ethic'" aims to produce *politically* neutral religious ethics (Mahmood 2006, 328). At the same time, leftists, progressives, and interfaith communities similarly seek to exert a *religiously* neutral political ethic via a normative secularity in which Muslims are worked with and for only insofar as they leave their Islam as a theology and theory of the world off the table. "Progressive" Muslims are viewed as sites of radical potentiality should they "free" themselves from their irrational religiosity and "backward" or "traditional" social mores and values, while Muslim anti-imperialists and "extremists" are criminalized and feared, justifying bombing, sanctions, drone warfare, surveillance, entrapment, imprisonment, and solitary confinement.

Tracing the continuities enables us to see how the state perpetually needs to demonstrate its legitimacy, and how Islamic ways of knowing and being have consistently tested that legitimacy on ethical and (extra)legal grounds. That those fighting for Black liberation in the 1960s and 1970s heard the blues adhan speaks to the specificity of how Islam in this place and time has been oriented within the Black Radical tradition and how we may or may not carry that legacy forward. This is the ongoing struggle for abolition, from the seventh century or the fifteenth century onward, sometimes prayed for in the middle of the night but also enacted in other ways. The struggle for abolition has coexisted with (Muslim) theories and practices of enslavement, incarceration, and punishment; how Muslims understand their histories, relations, and accountabilities says much about how they respond to the call of the blues adhan. As I discuss later, how "we suffer and love" indexes our political positions—what we allow in our names, for what sake, and our complicated, possible, and impossible options for survival (Abbas

2014, 503). In the case of the Domain Awareness Center and other Homeland Security–funded programs, the specter of terrorism enables an expansion of policing and surveillance generally, while gang injunctions facilitate the further gentrification of Oakland neighborhoods (Arnold 2011).

Because the connections between Black radicalism and Islam are so little talked about, young Muslims and many of their elders have learned little from these histories and the extent to which the American government and local police will go to root out "terror." Palestinian activist communities have experienced these continuities and the critical shifts that the Patriot Act enabled for law enforcement agencies after 9/11 through the cases of Sami Al-Arian (from the early 1990s to 2015), the Los Angeles 8 (1987–2007), and many others (Pennock 2017; Bazian 2018).[5] In other cases, however, the communal isolation of un-mosqued Muslims or an assumption that justice prevails in American democracy has meant that when a member of their family comes under suspicion, they underestimate the impact, intention, and response of federal authorities. Similarly, "new" Muslims who have recently converted or reinvigorated their Islamic commitments are particularly susceptible to entrapment.

By focusing on Bay Area Muslims and the Islam that they practice as the pressure points of power's effects, I demonstrate how the mechanisms of exclusion and apparatuses of state surveillance cohere and become the processes that manage populations (Foucault 1978; Foucault and Gordon 1980). Much of the literature on surveillance and the security state focuses on generalizable populations without addressing the unevenness of application and the pointedness of the lenses and mechanisms of repression and control (Balkin and Levinson 2006; Price 1998; Borneman and Masco 2015).[6] While the "geographic spread" of Muslim populations impacted their "poor position to defend themselves" (Barkun 2017, 246), I believe that other factors were more significant, including: the dynamics of Muslim communities themselves, racialized and gendered discourses of who Muslims in the United States were, and a prehistory of FBI surveillance.

The FBI's COINTELPRO ravaged the Black Panther Party for Self-Defense and other radical groups of the 1960s and 1970s; many former Black Panthers became Muslim, some via the Nation of Islam, also heavily surveilled, but most through other spiritual genealogies. The ethnic, racial, and class segregation of Muslim communities prevented a distribution of knowledge about COINTELPRO and ongoing FBI surveillance and policing that had predominantly impacted Black Muslim and Palestinian communities and activists pre-9/11. Japanese Americans, mostly on the West

Coast, were quick to respond to anti-Muslim sentiments and policies, remembering their own communities' experiences of incarceration during
World War II. Yet, many predominantly working-class and migrant Muslim communities who were hardest hit by the National Security Entry-Exit
Registration System (NSEERS) program and the Patriot Act, especially on
the East Coast, were not as aware of these histories.

In the years after 9/11, despite more media representation, Muslim activism, and (mis)education about Islam and Muslims, animosity toward
and suspicion of Muslims accelerated and grew (Kishi 2017; Kumar 2021;
Sheehi 2011). As media discourses and the visibility of Islam and Muslims
has increased, so has the proliferation of fearmongering and the practice of
actually banning Muslims and others from entering the country. We can
also place responsibility on the FBI's post-9/11 mission, "the prevention of
terrorist acts," and the discourses of terror and American foreign policies
themselves (Barkun 2017, 247).

American foreign policy continues to dictate a military presence in the
Middle East and other Muslim-majority lands in Asia and Africa (financially,
militarily, or diplomatically) that has contributed to, if not conjured, more
than a million innocent civilian deaths, tens of millions of refugees, and an
unraveling of civil societies and social structures (Watson Institute 2021). It is
difficult to disaggregate American foreign policy from domestic Muslim life
because the neo-imperial and racial logics that inform and enable state action likewise contribute to how Western Muslims and adjacent communities
like non-Muslim Arabs and South Asians are viewed and view themselves in
civil society and how they (and "we") affectively experience perpetual war
(Naber 2014). Muslim communities in the United States are simultaneously
represented as shining examples of American multiculturalism and freedom
of religion while also inhabiting a critical front of the war on terror.[7]

The concept of "terrorism" masks the violence committed by states
(T. Asad 2007) while likewise providing the grounds for popular consent
and the expansion of state power by way of an existential emergency: curb-
ing civil rights, expanding security and surveillance, increasing military
and homeland security spending, and sanctioning "state-organized kill-
ings of 'Islamic militants,' 'radical extremists,' 'terrorists,' 'jihadis,' and any
other number of conjurings of the Muslim in the racialized imagination"
(Daulatzai and Rana 2018, xi). It is these thing that we live with, that shape
the contours of our lives, that produce us as complicit subjects of terror,
from taking our shoes and jackets off at the airport and "see something, say
something," to wishing for or paying taxes toward death and destruction

"at home" and abroad. Asma Abbas suggests that we need "acts of abundance," acts of love and suffering that defy the imposed logic of "a liberal utilitarian calculus" (2014, 511), a "queer calculus" (Kapadia 2019) as opposed to a military-grade one.

In the halls of a nascent Zaytuna College, founder Shaykh Hamza Yusuf complained because a guest speaker at a large public event spoke of Zaytuna College as a rejoinder to discourses of Islamic terrorism. Yusuf was troubled by this ever-present figuring of Muslims—whether good or bad—in relation to terrorism. I did my best throughout the course of my research to honor that concern. At some point it became disingenuous to do so because despite Muslim efforts to remain distinct from, as well as contradict and disprove those discourses, they impact everyday Muslim life—from how people think about and express their Muslimness to how they are perceived or treated by others. That Yusuf himself, Zaytuna students, and other Muslim figures and organizations (including scholars like myself) have received multiple invitations to the White House, public and private philanthropic funding, and other forms of (positive) attention speaks to this impact (and its impending wane as other "issues" or "problems" come to the fore). It is a privilege and choice, or a cultivated sense of Allah-conscious detachment, of some Muslims to walk in the world without this double and triple consciousness, while others are confronted by it every day on multiple levels, whether they experience it themselves or witness it in their Muslim kin (Auston 2017; Abdul Khabeer 2017b).

Kameelah, another student from Zaytuna College, also addressed the Oakland City Council: "I stand before you tonight, a twenty-three-year-old Muslim, Blackamerican woman, member of Masjid Al-Ansar, born, raised, and educated here in this country . . . these streets are our homes and we need to be cognizant that this spy center will only further dismantle our communities. It is harmful to our mental health, it is harmful to our spiritual health. *The people in this community are tense.*" Kameelah brings her embodied experiences as a Black Muslim woman from the East Coast to bear on her experiences and observation of the Bay, diagnosing the effects of prolonged surveillance.

While many community members came to the city council meeting, others were made present through their absence; Hussein, a Yemeni activist, connected the fears and violence his community faced in Yemen due to US-backed drone strikes to the fears and violence they face throughout the Bay Area, as well as at borders and government buildings, stating, "I represent thousands of people in this city who are afraid to come to these places." The scenes above narrate the "tensions produced by holding a complex set of forces in suspension" and how that "tense suspension" (Campt 2017, 51) is carried across a multiracial, multiethnic, and multiclassed Muslim community.

While the FBI quietly retired the recent (2017–2019) designation of "black identity extremist" groups, there have been ongoing discussions in Congress and among security agencies toward creating a domestic terrorism statute that would expand the purview of the FBI and other policing agencies against domestic terrorism (Allam 2019). The history of COINTELPRO and recent cases I discuss below demonstrate the potential of what this would mean; expanding the application of terrorism, even if applied to white nationalists, would greatly threaten any semblance of privacy, free speech, and dissent remaining in the United States.[8]

The executive branch and law enforcement agencies have increasingly applied the terror designation to an ever-expanding category of politically motivated activities; legislation since the country's founding has been experimented with by different administrations "almost always at the expense of constitutional protections and civil liberties" (Center for Constitutional Rights 2008, 2). The expansion of surveillance infrastructures is often seen as a "no-brainer" by city officials, especially when presented with federal funding. Citizen responses become an important intervention to surveillance as "spatial fix" (Gilmore 2007). Gilmore discusses the "prison fix" as a spatial fix in California that provided a solution to surplus funding and land that then bound cities to rural areas in prison and transportation infrastructures. Similarly, the growth of surveillance infrastructures is enabled by Silicon Valley developments, Homeland Security funding, actual reductions in crime and emergent critiques of the prison industrial complex, and anxieties regarding terrorism. The nanotechnologies that enable video and audio data to be stored indefinitely and the ubiquity of mobile phone and GPS technologies combined with private capital and state partnerships, punitive legislation, and the perceived need to police and surveil people and places enable the expansion of who should be surveilled and how (Sojoyner 2021). Here and now, commensurate with the "extraction of time" (Gilmore 2017) and relations of those imprisoned and unfree, the extraction is data, the extraction is the image—the face, the identity, the social activity, the biometric (Browne 2015).

The uneasiness with which I conducted research and with which I write is a further surveillance effect of conducting research within a community whose "right to opacity" and "shared obscurity" are contested (Glissant

1997). As I studied and discussed the video footage of the Oakland City Council meeting with other members of the community, we wondered which Muslim speakers were agent provocateurs. That we assumed that there were agents and informants among us, and that there indeed are, situates this research in a difficult position between ethnographic refusal, care, and description (A. Simpson 2007; 2014; Reese 2019; Shange 2019a).

ALL EYEZ ON ME OR THE BLIND STARES OF A MILLION
PAIRS OF EYEZ, LOOKIN' HARD . . . YOU CAN'T C ME

Twentieth-century Muslim histories of surveillance and counterintelligence chart the processes of Muslim racialization and its entanglement with leftist politics and discursive challenges to state formations. For Muslim communities that have former Black Panthers and other Black, leftist, anti-imperial, and antiwar activists within them, the lessons of COINTELPRO, which targeted Black "radical" groups from the 1950s onward, are a reminder that surveillance, infiltration, and entrapment have been long applied to citizens deemed politically threatening *prior* to breaking any law by virtue of their political beliefs.

Rather than being seen as criminals, African Americans who identified as Moors in the Moorish Science Temple were often viewed by the FBI as "political enemies of the state. . . . In a political sense, they were racial enemies and not criminals. The Islamic, Asiatic nature of the diaspora that Moorish Americans signified was inevitably in conflict with the imperatives of racial Whiteness . . . with the symbolic and material realities of the United States as a racial state" (Johnson 2017, 66; Weisenfeld 2016). While there has been Moorish Science Temple influence in the Bay Area in the form of the Shehada Moors (Moors who had taken the Islamic *shahada*), the Nation of Islam (NOI) and the Black Panther Party (BPP) were the primary enemies of the state in the 1950s and 1960s. Later communities of Black Muslims who overlapped with these earlier formations or who emerged independently were likewise categorized as the "enemy within" and "homegrown terrorist" (Daulatzai 2012, 172; Husain 2020). In the late 1990s, multiple Black Muslim imams and teachers were being surveilled, imprisoned, and exiled throughout the country, and there were tangible fears about the United States government. These histories demonstrate a continuity that did not make headlines, but that can be traced in the radical histories of the Bay Area that also crossed racial lines. Early members of the NOI and BPP included Latinx and Indigenous Muslims like Imam Benjamin Perez and Asian American Black Panthers like Richard Aoki (referred to by one of the Muslim brothers who had been a Panther as "the Asian guy") and a myriad of leftist and internationalist organizations that were in solidarity with the Black Panthers. Seeing the Black Panthers as a political vanguard, multiple groups situated their struggles in relation to the plight of Black people and vice versa. This legacy still lingers, but the demographic shifts, perils of time, and struggles for survival obscured the history and impact of state oppression.

"The San Francisco 8 was probably my biggest wake-up call to the depths of which the involvement in the BPP could affect lives," Hajja Rasheeda's daughter, Kiilu, told me about how in 2007, the San Francisco Police Department arrested her family members and friends for the 1971 murder of a San Francisco police officer.[10] The FBI came knocking on her mother's door in Oakland, and she warned Kiilu that they would always track her, a Panther baby born in the early 1970s, because of her family.

On August 29, 1971, Sergeant John V. Young was killed by shotgun at the front desk of the Ingleside Police Station in San Francisco; a civilian clerk was also injured. In 1973, Black Panthers John Bowman, Harold Taylor, and Ruben Scott were arrested in New Orleans and subjected to multiple days of torture until they signed a confession to the murder. San Francisco police officers Frank McCoy and Ed Erdelatz, who investigated the case, traveled to New Orleans for the interrogation and after asking questions would leave the room intermittently so that New Orleans police officers could proceed with torturing the Panthers.[11] The torture over several days led to confessions, but Bowman, Taylor, and Scott continued to maintain their innocence and the coerced nature of the confession. The case was reopened in 2003, despite the fact that the original case was dropped in 1975 after the statements were deemed inadmissible because they were obtained by torture.

On May 30, 2002, Attorney General John Ashcroft produced new guidelines that announced the FBI's reoriented mission: "The war against terrorism is the central mission and highest priority of the FBI," and "terrorism prevention is the key objective under the revised guidelines" (Ashcroft 2002). San Francisco police officers were deputized as federal agents in 2003 under the auspices of the Joint Terrorism Task Force, a program in which local officers are lent to and deputized as federal agents. The San Francisco Police Department pulled out of the task force in 2017, though the FBI has tried to rekindle this relationship. The task force is still based in San Francisco, however, and has members from police departments throughout the East and South Bay. While the Phoenix Task Force was formed a few years earlier to reinvestigate unsolved police murders, the Department of Homeland Security provided the funds in a new political landscape to revisit the radical history of the 1960s and 1970s uprisings as forms of terror. The history of COINTELPRO, which officially ended with the Church Committee Hearings in 1971, was, like our contemporary moment, profoundly preemptive: to prevent a Black-led revolution, prevent the rise of a Black messiah figure, prevent the growth of Black nationalist organizations, and prevent the potential disruption of the status quo. In this way we see Ashcroft's guidelines from May 30, 2002, as well as 2019–2023 funding and direction toward hate crimes and domestic terrorism, not as a reorientation of the FBI's mission, but rather as an expansion of counterintelligence of domestic organizations and populations.

In 2003, McCoy and Erdelatz, who originally investigated the 1971 case, were brought out of retirement and began visiting and interviewing Panthers more than thirty years later, reminding COINTELPRO survivors of the ongoing reach and memory of government forces. The police themselves said that these arrests and ongoing investigations underscore "the fact that the law enforcement community is never going to forget" (McKinley 2007). On January 23, 2007, eight men ranging in age from fifty-five to seventy-one were arrested in early morning raids in California, Florida, and New York. Two of the men, Herman Bell, fifty-nine (at the time of arrest), and Jalil Muntaqim (Anthony Bottom), fifty-five, were already serving time for the alleged murders of two NYC police officers in May 1971. Police charged that seven of the eight men were members of the Black Liberation Army (BLA) and were part of a "conspiracy to kill law enforcement officers" from 1968 to 1973 (McKinley 2007). The other men included Francisco "Cisco" Torres, fifty-eight, in Jamaica, New York, who with Bell was accused of being a gunman. In San Francisco, Richard Brown, sixty-five, and Richard O'Neal, fifty-seven, were arrested and held on three-million-dollar bail. In Altadena, Los Angeles County, Ray Michael Boudreaux, sixty-four, and Henry Watson "Hank" Jones, seventy-one, and in Panama City, Florida, Harold Taylor, fifty-eight, were arrested. Authorities were unable to locate Ronald Stanley Bridgeforth, sixty-two, who is assumed to be living abroad.

After four and a half years of community activism and legal defense, charges were finally dropped for all the men except Bell and Muntaqim for insufficient evidence. Bell and Muntaqim plead guilty to reduced charges with no additional time served (they had already been serving thirty-plus years), leading to the exoneration of the others. During those four and a half years, family, friends, activists, and legal advocates rallied around the San Francisco 8, putting pressure on journalists, politicians, and the legal system. The state's attempt to diminish the radical legacy of the Black Power and Black Freedom movements largely failed, but it also made its point regarding the ability to maintain pressure through lawfare—taking *time* and other resources away from other forms of community-building and politics these men and their supporters were involved in.

For Kiilu, this was the "first time in my life, I realized why Mother had stayed both militant and active. That there was an ongoing cause for concern about the [lives] of [her] and her comrades. To see men in their seventies rounded up and taken to jail was mind-blowing to me. To hear the stories of torture some of the members of the Party had suffered at the hands of the police through the years was also mind-blowing. It was clear to me that activism was not for the weak at heart and Party members put their lives and freedom on the line for the belief in our people. It's both admirable and frightening the way in which the government interpreted their action." Kiilu's mother Hajja Rasheeda had been a Black Panther and supporter of the BLA before she converted to Islam in the mid-1970s. After her passing in 2017, Rasheeda's family and friends told numerous stories about how she continued to live with the specter of COINTELPRO and how this informed her understanding of American imperialism and the implications of the war on terror. Despite the many hours I spent with Rasheeda as friend and kin, and in the short interviews I was able to conduct with her before her passing, she only alluded to this part of her life history. Speaking of the brutality and uncertainty of the 1970s and their aftermath, she remarked that she was "so grateful that I was able to come out of that with my right mind. And . . . there were some questions about whether I am in my right mind to a certain degree [because] some of that stuff was pretty brutal."

Rasheeda had been exposed to different forms of Islam through her work in the movement and the people she was meeting throughout the 1960s. After she left the Black Panthers in the early 1970s, she returned to Islam via the Nation of Islam, first, as a site where people were "doing something for Black people" in the Bay Area. When the community transitioned to (Sunni) Islam in the mid-1970s, Rasheeda transitioned with them. As her friend, writer Asha Bandele, states, Rasheeda "was deeply rooted in her own spiritual traditions, deep in practice. You have to remember that this was a woman who has seen so many of her comrades, her peers and contemporaries, devastated by the FBI's war on the Black Panther Party. And she woke up one day to stories of her friends dead or imprisoned and alone with a small child. And she went further and further into the regions of her own spirit and soul to strengthen herself."

For Rasheeda and others who first experienced COINTELPRO in the 1960s and 1970s and then the San Francisco 8 case from 2007 to 2011, the continuities between then and now in the contemporary war on terror are plain to see. One of the San Francisco 8, Ray Michael Boudreaux, wasn't surprised when investigators showed up at his house in 2005. "When I watched on TV the Twin Towers come down, deep in my heart I knew that someone will come by and visit me as soon as they can get it organized, and they did. . . . Once upon a time, they called me a terrorist too. To expedite something in the system, they put the 'terror' tag on it, and it gets done" (Glionna and Chawkins 2007).

The Obama administration continued what the Bush administration started by redirecting attention to Assata Shakur (Joanne Chesimard), when it put her at the top of the FBI's "Most Wanted Terrorist List" in 2013. For much of the twentieth century (as well as before and after), "abolition *was* terrorism in the eyes of the state" (Husain 2020). The criminalization of Blackness was "a counter-insurgency strategy against black communities in the shadow of Black Power" (Daulatzai 2013). Labeling Shakur a terrorist now opens not only herself and Cuba, but all her supporters in the United States and struggles against "police brutality, militarism, imperial war, economic exploitation, and racist state practices" to drone strikes, targeted assassinations, and being charged with "'material support for terrorism,'" laws that have been used against Arab and Muslim charity organizations for decades (Daulatzai 2013).

Between COINTELPRO and the war on terror, from the late-1970s onward, Hajja Rasheeda, her family, and her home were a critical part of Medina by the Bay's infrastructure of feeling. She facilitated connections and spread influence throughout Muslim communities across the Bay. She and her husband became close friends with Black Muslim scholar Muhammad Shareef, who represented the *Jama'at* of Shehu Uthman Dan Fodio until Shareef's exile in 2005, and credits Hajja Rasheeda with introducing him to political prisoners Sekou Odinga (released in 2014, incarcerated thirty-three years), and Jihad Abdulmumit (released in 2000, incarcerated twenty-three years) who had been members of the Black Panther Party and Black Liberation Army and were both Muslim.

While he was a prison chaplain, Shareef was accused by prison warden Anthony C. Newland of being a "radical Muslim cleric" who was instigating Muslim inmates in the California Department of Corrections at CDC Solano. In reality, he was doing his job, "which was to inform the CDC and the inmate Muslim population about the fundamental rules of Islam" (Shareef 2015, 163). He was assisting inmates in ongoing litigation regarding their rights to halal food and other rights specific to the Islamic faith that were fundamental to the rehabilitation of inmates. FBI agents began interviewing inmates about him, and his community nationwide became subject to surveillance, infiltration, and FBI raids.[12] For Shareef, "It was not until then that I had a glimpse of the extent of FBI surveillance and the nature of their interdiction into people's lives; and for the first time in my life I became truly frightened" (167).

In the summer of 1999, more than twelve African American imams came together in Atlanta and discussed creating a national confederation of Muslim organizations and communities.[13] Later that month another meeting of prominent Muslim leaders occurred in Leicester, England, which included two of the founders of Zaytuna College. The confederation that eventually formed as a result of the Atlanta meeting was MANA, the Muslim Alliance of North America. Of the more radical (not in the Muslim "extremist" sense) and internationally minded imams from the Atlanta meeting, Muhammad Shareef has chosen exile since 2005 after being heavily surveilled by the FBI; another, Imam Jamil Al-Amin, formerly H. Rap Brown, was convicted of murder in 2002, is currently in an appeals process for a retrial, and suffers from medical neglect while incarcerated; and Imam Luqman Abdullah of Detroit was killed in an FBI raid in 2009. Shareef and others believe that it was the national confederation that Al-Amin was coordinating at that meeting in Atlanta and over the past few decades that led to the events of his arrest in the alleged killing of two police officers, in combination with his history as H. Rap Brown, chairman of SNCC (the Student Nonviolent Coordinating Committee), minister of justice of the Black Panther Party, and being on the FBI's Most Wanted list.[14] Both Imam Luqman and Muhammad Shareef's communities discovered that they were being surveilled and infiltrated, and Luqman's son referred to his father's murder by the FBI as "'unfinished business from COINTELPRO'" (Hussain 2015). Muslims around the country and in the Bay Area often say that Imam Jamil carried forward the work of El-Hajj Malik El-Shabazz, that he was waging a spiritually based movement based on the Qur'anic principle that "verily never will Allah change the condition of a people until they change what is in themselves" (13:11).

For many former Panthers, BLA, Republic of New Africa, and Revolutionary Action Movement members, Islam became a spiritual and programmatic home for enacting sociopolitical, epistemological, and spiritual transformation, counterpolitics, and ontological totality (what Robinson [2000] calls the Black Radical tradition and Wynter (n.d.) and McKittrick [2021] call "indigenous rebellion") that motivated their initial participation in these revolutionary formations. As Imam Jamil describes Islam: "It is the organized program Allah has given whereby you organize yourselves. 'By those who arrange themselves in ranks and thereby are strong in repelling evil.' These are the ranks of *salaat*, prayer" (Al-Amin 1994, 25, quotes a translation of Qur'an 37:1–2). Islam provided discipline, critique, and spiritual grounding, while also providing an ethical-political reasoning for self-defense, struggle against tyranny and oppression, and connection to millions of people and places beyond the boundaries of the nation-state. Despite its long historical presence in the United States as a form of Black religion, Islam is continually narrated as a foreign threat that is racialized as something distinct from Blackness (Abdul Khabeer 2016; Daulatzai 2012; S. A. Jackson 2009); maintaining this distinction and the definitions of what Islam is remains an ongoing state and colonial racial capitalist project.

TERRORIST, GANG MEMBER, PROVOCATEUR

From Hajja Rasheeda to Shaykh Muhammad Shareef's community, (Black) Muslim movements bridge the surveillance regimes of the 1960s to the contemporary era of expanded surveillance. This is not an Allah who sees everything, everything is recorded, Final Judgement consciousness, but rather an infrastructure of "racializing surveillance," what Simone Browne calls "a technology of social control where surveillance practices, policies, and performances concern the production of norms pertaining to race and exercise a 'power to define what is in or out of place'" (2015, 16). Racialized Muslims encounter surveillance at different levels, and while Islam is not a racial category, scholars and activists argue that the discursive, carceral, civilizational, and necropolitical approaches to the "Muslim problem" are better described as anti-Muslim racism rather than Islamophobia (Rana et al. 2020).

An ambiance of surveillance and suspicion profoundly impacts forms of Islamic knowledge and practice and the sociocultural formations of Muslim communities in the United States at the most intimate levels (A. I. Ali 2016; Maira 2014, 2016; Nasir, 2022). The impact of these surveillance effects is measured in the subtleties of modulating one's political views or volume to the open acknowledgment of Muslims who constantly allude to or directly address those "recording," "visiting," "reporting," or "informing" "among us," whether in the mosque, the home, on the internet, or on the phone. A generalized "uncertainty over whether or not surveillance is present" that characterized an era of "new" surveillance in the 1980s (which was not new for Black communities and other racial and political enemies of the state) is in Muslim communities, a certainty that it is indeed present (Marx 1989, 219). This certainty has among Muslims in the United States become a laughable anecdote, amid real material consequences that are exceedingly unfunny.

During the Oakland City Council meeting, Alejandro responds to his mother's concern with an assurance that she need not worry because he already knows "I'm a Muslim. I know my government is watching me." While those in the city government hall chuckled, Alejandro went on to give an account of how the government had "tried to break the bonds of friendship" by threatening his friend with information collected from surveillance of Alejandro's phones, internet use, and activities. For Alejandro, the certainty of surveillance was well-founded and affirmed by his own experiences with it. And though he told his story with eloquence, his voice trembled and his body shook.

The structures and tactics of counterinsurgency, developed in the FBI's counterintelligence programs and used in the Bay Area against groups like the Black Panthers, are being recycled and updated with contemporary technologies and logics to suppress practices of dissent. While in recent years the Department of Homeland Security's Countering Violent Extremism program, renamed "Targeted Violence and Terrorism Prevention," has tried to develop community partnerships with Muslim organizations, its assumptions about and solutions for radicalization have been met with criticism because they put the onus on Muslim beliefs, practices, and states of mental health (Department of Homeland Security 2020).

At the same time, policing techniques and technologies are being implemented in global counterinsurgencies as well (Schrader 2019). The war on terror and the attendant surveillance and security structures it authorizes reorder military and domestic logics toward preemption and anticipation (Kundnani 2015; Rana 2017b). The discursive shift from punishment to the administration of security enables an ever-expanding "set of administrative procedures for managing high-security populations," which has been a part of governing Black people from the era of slavery onward and has in the post-9/11 era expanded exponentially (A. Gordon 2006).

I had recently left the Bay Area when the Oakland City Council meetings about the expansion of the Domain Awareness Center began. One of my interlocutors, Ahmad, told me about these hearings and mentioned that many of the community members from Zaytuna College and Masjid Al-Ansar participated in them. While I followed Ahmad's online reporting of these events and eventually interviewed some of the participants, I also studied the Oakland City Council's video documentation of the hearings. I found myself deciphering blurry CCTV footage, shot from above and at a distance; I had also started requesting the FBI records of a recently deceased friend from the community. While the video data was publicly available and the speakers knew they were being recorded, I felt ethically suspicious, like a discomfited spy, a disembodied observer attempting to glean meaning, expanding my ethnographic object by following my ethnographic subjects beyond the frame of what my eyes witnessed, what my camera recorded.[15] And as I discussed the public footage with Ahmad, we were at the same time wondering which of these Muslim speakers were confidential informants or agent provocateurs?

I still wonder, and I likewise consider how cautious I need to be about drawing attention to these statements and stories, especially in light of Sakina's comments at the city council meeting. Sakina introduced herself as the mother of a son who was "up late past his bedtime in his interest of democracy." A few minutes before, her son told the city council that the Domain Awareness System's acronym "DAC stands for Destroy All Coolness" (followed by enthusiastic applause). Citing the council's intention to "improve safety," Sakina discussed how more surveillance did not increase her family's safety, "rather, it increases our vulnerability to a suspicious and hostile state with a reputation for entrapment and torture of Muslims." She requested that local authorities "not record data on my family and I as we go about the mundane daily activities of our lives, so you can protect us from those hostile forces." For Sakina becoming visible, to be figured in an overdetermined field of representation that surveillance produces was the opposite of safety. Yet, she appealed to the council as a neighbor and constituent, offering an intimacy through her motherhood and the "mundane daily activities" of her family's life in which their presence was not overdetermined. What is troubling about her statement, though, is that in the request not to "record data on my family and I as we go about the mundane daily activities of our lives," her description is uncomfortably close to a description of ethnography. What I wish to do here is refract from the mundanity of Sakina's everyday life to the mundanity with which in the name of safety and security, surveillance and carcerality are seen as solutions.

Saba, Sakina, Alejandro, Kameelah, Ahmad, and Hussein were six of many Bay Area residents who attended and spoke at the hours-long city council meetings in Oakland's City Hall in the winter of 2013–2014. The council was discussing their potential approval of Phase II of the Domain Awareness Center, a city and portwide surveillance system. The Department of Homeland Security had provided the initial funding for the first phase, which was directed toward securing the Oakland Port from potential "terrorist" threats and was implemented in 2008. The second phase was to activate and integrate surveillance cameras and shot-spotter microphones throughout the city and centralize all the potential accompanying data—both public and private—throughout the City of Oakland and the port, including data from license plate recognition, gunshot detectors, neighborhood and freeway surveillance cameras, and GIS tracking that the Oakland Police Department already owned but could not get to function at that point in March 2014.

In the introduction, Saba draws connections between the "terrorist, gang member, provocateur," that "these are all codewords for a person that's in the way of profit and power, both in Oakland and internationally." These codewords figure "Muslims, Black and brown communities, and protestors" as communities to be monitored for their potential criminal activity. "These communities are all monitored in different ways, but all of these ways overlap in our Muslim community," meaning that Muslims belong to Black and brown communities that are already criminalized and that Muslims also use their freedom of speech and assembly to engage in acts of protest in order to raise awareness and engender social critique and transformation. The figures of the terrorist, gang member, and provocateur are produced through surveillance regimes that further displace Muslims, Black and brown communities, and political activists from the rapidly gentrifying and resegregating Bay Area (E. K. Arnold 2011).

Like their non-Muslim ethnic, racial, and class counterparts, Muslim migration to and movement within the Bay Area contribute to its demographic shifts. Some Muslim students move to the Bay for education and often stay in the region, becoming part of the college-educated and upwardly mobile population; while others have moved to the outskirts of the Bay or stayed in place, often because they own their homes, are in rent-controlled apartments, or are in public housing. Former Zaytuna students and scholars who grew up in the Bay have left both individually and en masse in the last decade, for individual reasons or to (re)create communities where they can more comfortably raise their families and transform their relations.

Muslims, Black and brown communities, and protestors, figured as terrorists, gang members, and provocateurs, need to be documented, disciplined, and (dis)placed.[16] The figure of the Muslim and the "preemptive logic of the war on terror" become alibis and rationales for continuing and extending domains of surveillance through the criminalization, racialization, and policing of Black and brown bodies, and, in the Bay Area, the racially and religiously agnostic figure of the protestor as well (Rana 2017b, 122). Such material power and discursive misrecognition is what enabled then mayor of Oakland, Jean Quan, to express surprise at the opposition to the Domain Awareness Center, stating that "I wish I had paid attention to it a little earlier. . . . I really thought it was a no-brainer" (Winston 2014). Quan's mystified response—whether feigned or sincere—to her constituents signaled her lack of technical know-how, her political priorities, and her belief in a surveillance regime that would make people safer. Her thinking echoed the 2004 Intelligence Reform and Terrorism Prevention Act passed in Congress that "required Homeland Security and various other agencies to create what was called an 'Information Sharing Environment,' meaning that local, state, and federal law enforcement agencies would file Suspicious Activity Reports (SARs) on observed and reported activities that can be shared amongst these agencies and private contractors" (Camp and Heatherton 2016). Better information flow between agencies at the federal level was now being brought to the local level to fight local crime, "terrorism," and natural disasters, despite communities' insistence that better organization and more resources at the neighborhood level was what was needed. Rather, citing past earthquakes and fires, Mayor Quan foregrounded Oakland residents' vulnerabilities to natural disasters and the ability to respond to them. Other city officials both publicly and privately discussed how DAC would assist in crime prevention, terrorism, and controlling protestors.

Despite public claims that it would be used to "combat violent crime," the proposed Domain Awareness Center's collection and centralization of data was actually discussed among city staffers as a way to "track political protesters and monitor large demonstrations" (BondGraham and Winston 2013). In a government trade publication, Renee Domingo, the director of Oakland's Emergency Management Services Division and the head of the DAC project team, justified Oakland's need for this centralized surveil-

FIGURE 3.1 This slide was shown at the Oakland City Council meeting by staffers who were justifying the Domain Awareness Center program. Note that the more than seven hundred cameras in Oakland schools were also listed in part of the eventual network of cameras. City of Oakland.

lance system: "'Oakland's long history of civil discourse and protest adds to the need [for the Domain Awareness Center]. . . . The Oakland Emergency Operations Center has been partially or fully activated more than 30 times in the past three years to respond to large demonstrations and protests'" (Bond-Graham and Winston 2013). Other records echo this political mission.

In a January 2012 meeting of the Northern California Area Maritime Security Committee, the director of the port's security explained how "the port's Emergency Operations Center (which now feeds into the DAC) 'made use of seventy new security cameras' to track the protesters, and added that the system will ensure that 'future actions [do] not scare labor away'" (BondGraham and Winston 2013). The security director's concern over "scaring labor" actually obscures the fears of neoliberal corporate and government interests, not the laborers who have historically relied upon and supported community-led protests. As a speaker from the Transport Workers Solidarity Committee stated during the city council meetings, cameras at the Oakland Port were actually "being put in rest areas where longshoremen are taking their breaks; they're being directed against mainly port truckers from Africa, Asia, and Latin America that

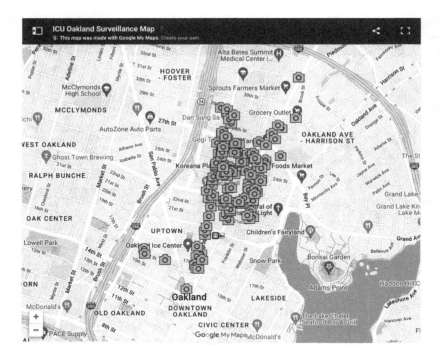

FIGURE 3.2 This map was created by two UC Berkeley students working with ICU Oakland in the early 2010s. They took photographs of every camera visible within a few-block radius to demonstrate the ubiquity of surveillance and the potential for targeted mass surveillance should all these cameras be networked in a program like DAC. icuoakland.wordpress.com/mapping/.

don't have a union. And what they want to do is have a union, have decent wages, but if they have picket lines? Guess what? The police come out there and attack these minority workers who are trying to organize union." The International Longshore and Warehouse Union (ILWU) and, increasingly, the Port Trucker's Association have a long history of aligning themselves with progressive causes. Work slowdowns, refusals to unload, strikes, and protests have been used throughout the port's history to, for example, raise wages and benefits, improve work and safety conditions, and protest wars, dictators, apartheid, and the Israeli occupation in Palestine.

The 2011 Occupy Oakland "shutdown" of the port, which began as a march from the encampment in downtown Oakland's (renamed) Oscar Grant Plaza, was a critical incentive for the Domain Awareness Center's Phase II advancements as a tool that would help control labor strikes and community protests that threaten to slow business at the port. Saba and others at the city council meetings understood that "what is in or out of place" was determined by where cameras were positioned, in what direction, and why (Fiske 1998, 81). Saba drew attention to the significance of the port as "a powerful tool of the people, to slow down your machine. . . . For example, when the U.S. attacked Afghanistan, or when your transportation goons murdered Oscar Grant." Saba references protests against the 2002 invasion of Afghanistan and against both Iraq wars (1991, 2003), as well as protests following the death by BART police of then twenty-two-year-old Oscar Grant on New Year's Eve at the Fruitvale BART station in 2009. More recently, the Arab Resource and Organizing Center (AROC) successfully led #BlocktheBoat, "the longest blockade of Israeli ZIM ships in history," motivated by appeals of the Workers Unions in Palestine. With ILWU Local 10, AROC initiated the blockade at Oakland's port in 2014 and then reactivated the campaign in May 2021, when ZIM, Israel's largest and oldest shipping line that often carries military weapons, tried to dock and unload their shipments again (Arab Resource and Organizing Center 2021). What Saba also makes clear is that the profile of Oakland was changing as ever-increasing rents and property prices in San Francisco were pushing people and capital into the East Bay: "You are trying to develop Oakland into a playground and bedroom community for SF professionals. These efforts require you to make Oakland quieter, whiter, and 'less scary' and wealthier. That means getting rid of Muslims, black and brown people, and protestors."

While the city council eventually voted to limit the surveillance network to the port, Mayor Quan hoped that the City of Oakland would eventually distribute and consolidate the surveillance throughout the city.[17] The normalization of securitization and the better networked images are the key to mobilize "a representational mistake based in the fearmongering of Islam and Muslims" that facilitates "unprecedented flexibility in the workings of social domination and capital accumulation" (Rana 2017b, 114). The economic significance of the Oakland Port and the Bay Area's transforming economies and demographics structure a desire for city officials to facilitate the flexible expansion and interlocking of the terror industrial complex to the prison industrial complex. A banality of surveillance built upon a faith in cameras and public exposure ("because innocent people have nothing to hide") contributes to Quan's assessment of the DAC extension being a "no-brainer." Such comments articulate a desire for transparency, for more cameras, for more governing, and for more funding to tame, or manage and repress "unruly forms of life" (Dillon 2018, 131)—the "terrorist, gang member, provocateur" and nature itself. Such desire is exercised within "a structural relation generated by and productive of policing and the racial state" (Dillon 2018, 124), as well as by the digital forms of life through which we offer and produce our subjectivities for public consumption. The ubiquity of cameras in our "private lives" works with the anticipatory logic and fearmongering of racialized discourses of terrorism, violent crime, and political anarchy to authorize violent repression and uneven rights to opacity and relations of obscurity.

Throughout the City of Oakland, 2016 was celebrated as the fiftieth anniversary of the Black Panther Party's founding. There was an extensive exhibit at the Oakland Museum, and exhibitions and events happened all over the country. While the City of Oakland attempted to capitalize on this history, police and the federal government continue in their efforts to negate this legacy, arresting the San Francisco 8 in 2007, adding Assata Shakur to the FBI's Most Wanted List in 2013, and refusing the paroles and compassionate releases of still-incarcerated and aging Black Panthers and other Black activists (Kitwana 2016; Pilkington and Silverstone 2018). Saba connects and anticipates these events in her city council testimony in 2013–2014: "You want to make Oakland's history fade away, even while you sanitize it and use it to sell the city. You can pave over the blood of the martyrs, but you can't fossilize the spirit of resistance." Martyrs like Black Panther Bobby Hutton are connected to contemporary martyrs like Oscar Grant and lesser-known victims of state violence. As developers attempt to reinvent Oakland, the designation of Uptown being one example amid the ever-increasing tent towns that line major roads, they specifically target those who embody the "spirit of resistance," an essential part of a Bay Area identity that always struggled in proximity to colonial racial capitalist systems in a jostling for local and regional power.

Former Los Angeles Police Chief Bratton (of the broken windows policy in New York) compared counterinsurgency in Iraq to gang warfare in the United States, "referring to gang activity as 'homeland terrorism' and lamenting that the federal government 'needs to get preoccupied with the internal war on terrorism as well'" (Daulatzai 2012, 181).[18] Saba articulates a collective "we" of "terrorist, gang member, provocateur . . . codewords for a person that's in the way of profit and power"; this "we" is incidentally constituted and contingent, but its points of friction and contradiction offer a way to think about how political movements come to fruition and are maintained or disassembled.

In figure 3. 3, I juxtapose Saba and another speaker at the Oakland City Council meetings who introduced himself as "Incognito." Saba is figured

FIGURE 3.3 Saba and Incognito at the Oakland City Council meetings (author).

as "terrorist" whose veil or face mask extends across her face, and Incognito as "provocateur" who also masks his face to index the potentiality of biometric transparency and identification.[19] The niqab or face mask is one way that Saba and her "accomplice" Incognito, who are both perceived as white, get undersight, a kind of "dark sousveillance," while still occupying a frame, not necessarily a frame of surveillance, but that of and for public access in the documentation of these meetings.[20] Others, especially non-white Muslims, avoided entering such a space entirely, relinquishing their ability to appear to a fear of being seen, surveilled, and recorded. A visual similarity undermines the differences in what Saba's veiling is and does, and what her fellow activist's masking is and does. To appear is to resist both disappearance and displacement, but likewise a pronouncement that we the citizens are watching you, our representatives, and appealing to you in the "space of appearance" (Mirzoeff 2017). Saba appears with a sense of refusal, to refuse the "trap of citizenship," claiming her and her community's "right to a shared obscurity" (Glissant 1996, 161). The juxtaposition with Incognito the activist, who likewise refuses, but who revels in obfuscation rather than opacity, enables us to conceptualize visibility and see something of the way that particular positions are negotiated within a visual economy (Poole 2005).

To obfuscate is to render obscure, unclear, or unintelligible; while the young activist has nothing to hide, his masking foregrounds his politics rather than social identity. His rendering himself unintelligible is understood as a political act about privacy and the surveillance state. Saba's veiling, whether or not she usually wears niqab, actually renders her intelligible as a Muslim woman. She becomes *more* visible as an object and target of surveillance, while she also recognizes that she is rarely intelligible beyond the discursive categories through which she is understood ("good" or "bad," threat or victim, radical or moderate). Saba articulates safety and community against the cartographies of capital, redlining, inequality, and diminished life chances, creating an alternative Muslim geography: "We don't find justice in your courts, we don't find education in your schools; we don't find nourishment in your social programs. We find these things in our mosques, our churches, our gatherings, our dinners, our rallies, and our neighborhood corners."

As other Muslim men and women appeared at the hearings, they asserted their presence as Muslim citizens, a significant voting bloc, as Muslims make up 10 percent of Alameda County, and they are concentrated in Oakland. Though visible in the public spaces of Oakland, where they live, work, and play, they were not seen as a part of the population to be secured. While Saba's language tends to distinguish the populations of Muslims, brown and Black communities, and protestors from those on the city council, other Muslim speakers like Sakina and Alejandro appealed to them as members and representatives of the community responsible for protecting their fellow citizens from encroachments on privacy, right to assemble, and dissent. Unlike Saba and Incognito, they presented their names and faces before the council, identifying themselves and requesting recognition of their presence and concerns, while also requesting opacity and shielding from a carceral local and federal gaze.

Imam Zaid Shakir accompanied his students and community members from Masjid Al-Ansar and appealed to the council in terms of their responsibility as local representatives vis-à-vis the federal government and corporations: "Are you going to facilitate the continued dominance of corporations over our lives, our property, our honor, our government, or are you going to serve as the firewall between the corporations, between very, very pernicious forces. . . . You have been elected by the people, and you have a lofty calling because our country is increasingly seeing the evisceration of our constitution, the evisceration of rule for, by, and of the people." It is important to not assume that all Muslims, Black and brown communities, and activists share the same vision to interrupt capital and empire. On the contrary. It is precisely because there are profound differences *within* communities regarding narratives of terror, criminality, and political subversion that radical and transformative change is so challenging to bring about. Contrary to both racist fearmongering and liberal approaches to Muslim "radicalization," belief and Islam are not politically prescriptive.

"WE DON'T HAVE CRIMINAL MINDS"

On June 30, 2015, Adam Shafi, (twenty-two), a young Bay Area man, attempted to board a plane to Turkey at the San Francisco International Airport. FBI and Homeland Security agents met him at the gate and sent him
home. Days later, he was charged with attempting to support a terrorist
organization, Nusra Front in Syria, which has ties to Al-Qaeda, but was
at the time fighting on the same side against Bashar al-Assad as rebels that
the United States—via the CIA—was supplying weapons and training to
(Mazzetti, Goldman, and Schmidt 2017). Shafi spent forty months in the
Alameda County Jail and was eventually freed in March of 2019 after a
mistrial because prosecutors failed to convince a jury and judge of his in-
tent and guilt of providing "material support" to a terrorist organization.
He later accepted a guilty plea of using a fraudulent check to avoid a retrial
but never accepted a terrorism charge, and U.S. District Judge William
Orrick determined that Shafi's time served (three years and four months),
six months of house arrest, and five years of federal probation would be
sufficient, rather than the ten years prosecutors requested.

Shafi's case is one of five recent terrorism cases involving young Bay
Area Muslim men in which a violent crime had not been committed but
in which each young man was vulnerable to entrapment. In three of these
cases, the accused was "heavily assisted by undercover FBI agents posing as
terrorists," and in all cases, they were charged with "*attempted* crimes—four
with attempting to provide 'material support' to a terrorist organization
and one with attempted use of a weapon of mass destruction" (BondGraham 2018). Fighting a federal case takes money and resources, and Shafi, the
son of a Silicon Valley executive, was one of the few who was able to fight his
case and avoid a terrorism charge. His father harbored regret and guilt—"I
just destroyed Adam"—because he had one year earlier brought Adam to the
government's attention when he called on them, concerned that his son had
left a family vacation in Egypt to go to Turkey "to protect Muslims" (Apuzzo
2016). In addition, against their lawyers' advice, Mr. Shafi and Adam spoke
to FBI agents on multiple occasions prior to Adam's arrest in 2015 because
as Adam's father stated in an interview with the *New York Times*, "We don't

have criminal minds. . . . Maybe I'm naïve. I've never dealt with the authorities before. I wanted to cooperate" (Apuzzo 2016).[21]

When I first read about the Shafi case, I was struck by how Adam's father reached out to the American Embassy using the rhetoric of terrorism, stating that his son may have joined a terrorist organization to get their attention so that they would act and look for his son. This triggered a host of state responses that included the FBI's obtaining a Foreign Intelligence Surveillance Act (FISA) warrant, which enabled the FBI to "intercept phone calls and search through text and email messages sent and received by Shafi" (BondGraham 2018). A FISA warrant is not meant for investigating criminal acts by American citizens but rather was "created by Congress to provide the FBI with a means of obtaining foreign intelligence that can't reasonably be obtained by normal investigative techniques" (BondGraham 2018). The treatment of American terror suspects as foreign is enabled by the sense that Islam itself is something foreign and existentially threatening to the United States, which leads to the exceptional status of terror investigations and cases as preemptive and anticipatory through discourses of administration rather than punishment.

Second, what did it mean that there were numerous cases of "radicalization" in the Bay Area, where there was now a Muslim college, more than one hundred mosques, and many schools, community organizations, and programs? Were these institutions even equipped to respond in ways that would be effective, considering these young mens' appropriately empathetic responses (anger, sadness, guilt) to the suffering of Muslims in Iraq, Afghanistan, Syria, Yemen, and elsewhere? This plethora of Muslim resources about "correct" Islam suggests that these cases were less about how to properly interpret and apply Islam and more about sociopolitical life and mental health in the United States.

Third, the politically motivated nature of these speech acts and online activities is often overshadowed by the specter of terrorism and violence. It remains important to hold these motivations in view as particular ethical and political responses to perceived injustices in the world and a sense of responsibility and connectedness to them. For Adam, it was his privilege and guilt that he was *not suffering* what his fellow religionists were going through which motivated his need to respond. This is in direct contrast to multiple theories of radicalism that cite dissatisfaction, criminal tendencies, sexual frustration, and other forms of social failure as reasons people "radicalize." Adam's response of witnessing Syrian suffering from afar was wanting to help those who were suffering; this was a legitimate and ethical response, not a self-serving one.

Muslim scholars and leadership in the Bay Area have focused much of their attention both locally and globally on dispelling discourses of jihad that authorize preemptive attacks on noncombatants. However, the ways young Muslim men (in particular) figure out how to be proper Muslim subjects emerge from their experiences of living in the Bay Area, as much as any propaganda they may read or watch online.[22]

I discuss Shafi's case to challenge the commonsense logics of innocence and criminalization that cohere around Islam and terrorism. We often take for granted how laws meant to protect property and power determine who gets criminalized in what contexts and how out of fear, disagreement, and shame Muslim communities have distanced themselves from those criminalized in the war on terror at the same time that they themselves have been terrorized by it. It is a difficult situation and asks us to think about how safe and secure, how free—to worship, to speak, to assemble, to think, to care—we actually feel.

Abolitionists believe that nobody belongs in a cage, and that cages neither repair nor transform individuals and the circumstances that landed them in the cages to begin with (Kaba 2021). The time extracted from Adam Shafi's forty months to former BPP and BLA member Jalil Al-Muntaqim's forty-plus years (he was finally released in 2020) to Imam Jamil Al-Amin's twenty years thus far, map onto the space-time of Medina by the Bay as relations taken, as well as relations that must actively be worked with and for, to bring close to rather than to distance from. The incarcerated Al-Muntaqim and Al-Amin, the murdered El-Hajj Malik El-Shabazz, his grandson Malcolm Latif, Imam Luqman, the exiled Shaykh Muhammad Shareef, and so many others signify the impossible figures of time, labor, care, and knowledge lost in umma relations. Yet, we also figure the time, energy, care, and knowledge that has gone into repairing and maintaining those relations in the ongoing fights to get our incarcerated kin and other political prisoners free and enacting the legacies of our liberatory lineages. These are the parameters of possible political life and what thinking about Islam as abolition, repair, and transformative justice offers.

DIFFICULT WORK

When the FBI responded to "Allegations of Mosque Surveillance and Monitoring the Muslim Community" in 2008, they stated that "the FBI does not monitor the lawful activities of individuals in the United States, nor does the FBI have a surveillance program to monitor the constitutionally protected activities of houses of worship. We do not target or monitor legal activity of Muslim groups anywhere in the nation" (FBI 2008). But it is only by monitoring legal activity that the FBI can possibly preempt alleged illegal activity, its "new" mission. The difference between "surveillance" and "intelligence gathering" is significant here. Rather than traditional surveillance, informants are placed in mosques, houses of worship, to gather intelligence. It is another form of subcontracting labor that lets government agents say they are not doing anything illegal, while then also fulfilling quotas toward a "productivity baseline" of intelligence gathering related to how many Muslims are within a field office's jurisdiction (Barkun 2017, 249).

While the SFPD officially left the Joint Terrorism Task Force in 2017, a recently revealed white paper has shown that the collaboration violated city ordinances designed to protect the civil liberties of residents (Devereaux 2019). The FBI's Joint Terrorism Task Force continues to be based in San Francisco and includes police officers from throughout the Bay Area. They are involved in "assessments" (a form of intelligence gathering), which have much lower thresholds than investigations, the latter requiring "reasonable suspicion of criminal activity" (Devereaux 2019). The white paper reveals that SF police officers were involved in producing assessments in which no paper trails were created regarding the examination of activities protected by the First Amendment; this suggests that there was a disconnect between what the FBI and SFPD were supposed to do, what they said they were doing, and what they actually did.

Political outrage and activism have been tempered by anti-Muslim racism, Islamophobia, secularism, suspicion, and fear; the discourse of terror and Muslim otherness "keeps it distant and us uninvolved and non-complicit" (Abbas 2014, 505). Muslims themselves have rendered Muslims suspected of terrorism as untouchable and "not Muslim." ISIS members and the Taliban (despite US cooperation with them) are viewed as utterly ungrievable and irredeemable, and the manufactured threat of terror has enabled law enforcement to encroach upon the civil liberties of most of us at staggering levels. We *can* hold a critique and expect accountability of those who cause harm while still remembering that they are human (even when they do not give their victims that same regard); to forget that is to succumb to one of the worst features of a coloniality of thought and being. "Innocence" as a discourse enables progressive activists to organize around Muslim victims, but Muslims who make ethical-political choices to act against the state or American Empire (often on behalf of others) are

more difficult to defend, especially when "violent" methods are deployed
or even thought.

While holding a critique of criminalization and incarceration, it is also important to consider the role Islam has played in prisons as a geography of spiritual redemption, consciousness-building, and organizing. To take the views of incarcerated and caged Muslims, in camps, prisons, and under surveillance, is to see "the world as a prison, with national boundaries, global capital, slavery, and wars of colonization as part of an earthly inheritance" (Daulatzai 2012, 175). In a recent report, the East Bay's Tayba Foundation (Tayba was also another name for the holy city of Medina), which has been providing long-distance education to incarcerated Muslims since 2008, revealed the growth of support for their work. From 2008 when they worked out of the founders' homes with a small budget to now raising much more annually with more than ten staff, Tayba has expanded its work to include life skills and reentry programs. Increasingly, Muslim communities are recognizing the Islamic tenets to feed the prisoner and assist and ideally free those in bondage, as well as extend mercy and compassion. Meanwhile, Muslim kin like Adam Shafi and the hundreds of Muslims who are incarcerated as terrorism suspects (regardless of what they were finally charged with) are being released after having served long sentences. As of September 2019, "there were 421 inmates with a history of, or nexus to, international terrorism, in the federal prison system, according to the Bureau of Prisons" (Shortell 2019). Around sixty to one hundred of those prisoners, many of them Muslim, may be released in the next five to ten years. A number of NGOs have been established to "rehabilitate radicalized individuals" (Shortell 2019) with an emphasis "on the space between cognitive radicalization and the mobilization to violence" (Morton and Silber 2019; see also Morton and Silber 2018). These rehabilitation programs misdiagnose the problem by not acknowledging that the world is upside down. As non-Muslim organizations determine the limits of appropriate religious and political thoughts, federal and local authorities are likewise increasing their capacities to monitor and shape the contours of a politically neutral religious ethic.

In the last year of her life in which she battled with terminal cancer, one phone conversation I had with Hajja Rasheeda stood out. She asked what was being done to support the Muslim sister who had been imprisoned by the US government, the Pakistani scientist. Was there a committee organized to support her; how could we be in touch with them to support their work? Rasheeda considered Aafia Siddiqui a political prisoner and a sister worthy of our support, this at a time when she was also dealing with the everyday struggles associated with her diagnosis.[21] This concern for Siddiqui exemplified Rasheeda's expansive commitment to political prisoners, from Jalil Al-Muntaqim and Marilyn Buck to someone like Siddiqui. It also demonstrates that Rasheeda held a firm and uncompromising position when it came to how the United States treated people based on their beliefs, rather than their alleged crimes. While most Muslims steer clear of Siddiqui and her case for fear of appearing sympathetic toward terrorism and a suspected Al-Qaeda operative, Rasheeda's inquiries into providing support for Siddiqui testified to her understanding of how the US government treated its "enemies" and how she saw Siddiqui as a sister in Islam. Rasheeda recognized the global racialization of Muslims through her studies of and struggles against white supremacy and racial subjugation, relating the effects of systemic racism in schools, prisons, and policing to the effects of American foreign policy and militarization that created and maintained systems of global hierarchy and oppression.

Our fear and love are intimately linked—the ways "we suffer and love index our political locations" and the way our space and time are shaped indexes our relations to states, societies, and ideologies within which we live (Abbas 2014, 503). Abbas asks, "How have we loved in order to suffer this way?" (Abbas 2014, 503). What have we loved in order to suffer this way? For Rasheeda, "the cultural revolution has to be first, you got to disassociate from what you are fighting." This disassociation is the difficult work of addressing "what we have loved" that had made us complicit in settler colonialisms, racial capitalism, and American Empire. As Rasheeda's Panther comrade and sister in Islam, the late Safiya Bukhari, states, the difficult work is the "day-to-day organizing, educating, and showing the people by example what needs to be done to create a new society. The hard, painstaking work of changing ourselves into new beings, of loving ourselves and our people, and working with them daily to create a new reality—this is the first revolution, that internal revolution" (Bukhari 2010, 13).

CHAPTER 4
OUT OF BOUNDS

———

Only when you describe something can you start speculating about it. If something hasn't been described and a record of it doesn't exist—it doesn't matter what form the description takes: a film, a sociological study, a book, or even just a verbal account—then you can't refer to it. You have to describe the thing or situation before you can deal with it. —KRZYSZTOF KIEŚLOWSKI

Not everything can be described. That's the documentary's great problem. It catches itself as if in its own trap. . . . I'm frightened of those real tears. In fact, I don't know whether I've got the right to photograph them. At such times I feel like somebody who's found himself in a realm which is, in fact, out of bounds. That's the main reason why I escaped from documentaries. —KRZYSZTOF KIEŚLOWSKI

ON DESCRIPTION

The above epigraphs by the Polish filmmaker Krzysztof Kieślowski were written within the same text, *Kieślowski on Kieślowski* (1993), which details his transition from documentary to fiction filmmaker. He wavers between the need to describe as an imperative for critique and the impossibility and "out of bounds" nature of description. It is an ethical quandary that marks much documentary and ethnographic work. For anthropologists, understanding bounds are particularly important as we often conduct research across and against bounds; the very idea that there is a boundary enables us to define our field sites. These boundaries are often slippery and ill-defined, and it is the definition and articulation of such boundaries—

marking difference and commonality, geography, or tradition—that become useful, if sometimes violent, analytics.

Kieślowski, however, refers more to ethical-political boundaries, some notion of when our good intentions, alliances, and aims may not be well-served by our works of description. Kieślowski asks whether he has *the right* to film real tears. In addition, on several occasions, images or audio that Kieślowski had recorded were confiscated by officials for purposes with which he was neither aligned nor involved. This manipulation of his footage and the potential impact it could have on people's lives made him feel like "a small cog . . . in a wheel which is being turned by somebody else for reasons unknown to me" (Kieślowski and Stok 1993, 86).

When conducting research with Muslim communities in the United States, I am conscious of the possibility—despite my best efforts—that my work might echo, complement, and serve the work of law enforcement and the racialized control of Muslims (Apuzzo and Sullivan, 2012; ACLU 2010; 2012a; 2012b;). My work may contribute to a contentious state and media landscape in which Muslims are already written within particular frames. These representational modes, from government documents to journalism to Hollywood, increasingly produce more "simplified complex" characterizations and "sympathetic portrayals" of Muslims in a moralistic projection of American benevolence and postracial equality, while simultaneously producing "the logics and affects necessary to legitimize racist policies and practices" (Alsultany 2013, 162).

While I was given authorization (in the form of letters, IRB forms and signatures, and verbal acknowledgment), what right did I really have, except that systemic and self-appointed right within the context of the discipline of anthropology? While my academic credentials and even my cultural credentials (being Muslim and from the Bay Area) may lend some authority and sincerity to my research, it does not give me any right. Through the process of conducting and writing up my research, the terms of arrival mattered less than what I did once I got there and once I physically left; ethical, spiritual, and political responsibility and relation became the more relevant issues. An ethics of knowledge and survival applies not only to what happens in Medina by the Bay, but also to other spaces of study and struggle, other discursive traditions with which I engage within the academy and elsewhere—anthropology, film, Islamic studies, ethnic and race studies, and gender studies.

In this chapter, I step out of the ethnocinematic form to reflect upon producing Islamic and ethnographic knowledge as embodied and relational practice. For Muslims, tears can be a sign of God-consciousness, of an embodied faith and intimacy with the Prophet Muhammad and his family; they are also signs of an intensity of feeling that can feel out of bounds, whether in the context of a documentary or a spiritual and pedagogic relationship. While tears index intimate forms of knowing and affective intensity, they can also signify distance. Tears of an intimate distance lead me to a discussion of gendered geographies and pedagogies. I extend the conversation from chapter 2 to consider what it is to experience learning and devotional activities and ethnography from women's spaces and what that kind of "distance" and gender specificity inhibits and enables. Embodied practices of looking, being seen, intimate distance, and refusing particular forms of visibility and representation reconfigure the ethical and political terms of how we produce and receive knowledge. I follow the flow of tears and embodied, ethnocinematic relations to produce ethically and politically intentioned multimodal ethnographic description and representation.

OUT OF BOUNDS

In chapter 2, I write Imam Zaid Shakir's introduction of Habib 'Umar as an ethnocinematic scene with an omniscient point of view, traversing past ethnographic time and place. In this section I revisit the ethnographic event, a cool and still early April evening in Fremont from the anthropologist-filmmaker's point of view. The room was split in half—men on the left side, women on the right side. There were cushions along the outer edges of each section, reserved for the elders among us, while the rest of us sat on the carpeted floor in haphazard shoulder-to-shoulder, knee-to-knee rows. In the front of the women's section was a crescent-shaped row of black floor seats, reserved for the VIP women in the congregation, mostly elder honored guests of the Bay Area and the Ta'leef Collective. Hadiya, a Yemeni American Ta'leef volunteer, was standing in front in a vibrant and brightly colored blue and green kaftan and emerald-green headscarf.[1] She helped escort women to this section and generally managed seating in the area. I was sitting in the women's section toward the front of the room but several rows back from where the shuyukh were sitting on an elevated and cushioned platform. Much of my view of the male speakers was blocked by an ornate floral arrangement of white Casablanca lilies, orange birds of paradise, white dahlias, white tuberoses, and gold leaves, designed by Sister Khadijah, the beautification matriarch of the Zaytuna community.

Zaid Shakir and Habib ʿUmar were introduced by their student and host Usama Canon, wearing a 1960s–1970s–style safari suit, bowtie, and fez/tarboosh (connoting an homage to Black internationalism, Arab nationalism, and Sukarno and Nehru of the Bandung conference moment, as well as to the Nation of Islam). As a prologue to Habib ʿUmar's lecture, Shakir situated the historical, spiritual, and political significance of the gathering. As I held my camera up to capture some of Shakir's introduction, my arms beginning to shake from the weight of the camera, there ascended in the room an intensity of feeling and spiritual presencing, an electric energy, a heat. As Shakir spoke the following words relayed in the earlier chapter, he began to cry, becoming momentarily overwhelmed as he recalled, experienced, embodied, transmitted, and heard, heard, heard those prayers of his racial and spiritual ancestors, African Muslims kidnapped and enslaved in the Americas:

> And they prayed for this day. They prayed for one day, one day. They prayed [that] one day there would be free men and free women in this land that say "*La ilaha illa Allah, Muhammadun rasul Allah*" (There is no god but God, and Muhammad is the messenger of God).

By "heard" I mean heard that spiritual fortitude forged in the Islamic civilizations of West Africa, disrupted by the Middle Passage, endured through generations of enslavement, centuries of racism; his own family's experiences in the migration from the Jim Crow South to the cold, industrial, and racially structured North; his own conversion to Islam and sitting with scholars and everyday Muslims from Morocco to Iran; and the continued spiritual *samad* (steadfastness), suffering, struggle, seeking, creation, and celebration that characterized so much of Black life in America.[2] Those who had been in the classroom earlier that day or knew the work of Shakir as an imam, scholar, student, husband, father, teacher, gardener, and activist were likewise privy to the possible torrent of words and images that seemed to rush through him. In a previously recorded lecture, "The Unfulfilled Legacy," Shakir (2007) discusses how the historical experiences of African Americans and the early history of Islam in the Americas made them particularly receptive to the message of Islam; he felt that this window of receptivity was not going to last into the next generation, however, and he conveyed a sense of urgency in trying to mobilize Muslims toward directing their daʿwa to this population.

Canon was sitting directly in front of Shakir. He suddenly flinched back, lowering his head and closing his eyes tightly, seemingly struck by the force of Shakir's words and perhaps also by the physical and emotional state of his teacher, his own flood of images, ancestral histories, and accountabilities. Many said they had never seen Shakir like that. Other men around him were beginning to tear up and quietly weep; others watched Shakir intensely, trying to understand what was happening and to not miss a moment of instruction. In the women's section—equally rapt—I heard sniffling and saw wetness on the cheeks.

And as quick as it (whatever "it" was) came, it moved on, and Shakir continued with a passion and force in his words, strengthened by the proof of revelations, the proof of centuries-past visions, and the proof of historical research in the form of Sylviane Diouf's and others' texts about African Muslims enslaved in the Americas, as he recited Allah's revealed text and Allah's creative "work" in these turbulent times of global Islam:

> They prayed that one day there would be people who would come here, and they would bring the light into this darkness, and they would touch the hearts of people, and they would do it at a time when Islam is besieged—when the Prophet of Islam is ridiculed, when the religion of Islam is defamed, and they would be living proof of the power that Allah subhanahu wa-taʻala says, when He says, "*Yuriduna li-yutfiʼu nur Allahi bi-afwahihim wa-Allahu mutimmu nurihi wa-law kariha al-kafirun, wa-law kariha al-kafirun, wa-law kariha al-kafirun*" [Qurʼan 61:8, Shakir repeats the last phrase three times for emphasis]. That Allah would complete His light even though those who reject this religion—who fight this religion, who hate this religion—even though they despise it.

A pause. A catching of breath. I had the hungry gratefulness of a videographer who had captured that incredible moment of truth, mentally congratulating myself on pressing record and positioning my camera just in time. But within seconds I self-admonishingly told myself that I would never show this footage. Though this room was full of hundreds of people, and there was another camera filming, streaming directly in front of Shakir, it felt like a private moment, as Kieślowski says, "out of bounds." Regardless of whether or not he would be okay with it, for me inserting it into a documentary seemed like a violation, whether it be of the imam, the gathering, the ancestors, or that particular moment in time. This brief audiovisual clip could not convey the intensity of that moment; it would feel like yet another historical betrayal.

The video image yields little of the backstory and shows a man with a microphone in one hand, pointing with the other, choking on his words;

moved, surrounded by other men. To represent the multiple histories and presences of this moment would require a centuries-long and globally expansive montage of images, voices, smells, and landscapes. It would also need to convey the continuities and ruptures between the performative labor of Black men and women within Islam in the United States and the forced material and affective labor of African-descended people in the United States more generally. Living and deceased Black Muslims were *still working*, still without compensation in contemporary efforts to locate and historicize Islam in the Americas (Abdul Khabeer 2016). In addition to all this work, the images must also convey the transmitted visions of Arab scholars who foresaw Islam in the West and the work such visions did in constituting Shakir's faith.

The audience consisted of those who were devoted students of Shakir's, those who were more ambivalent about his role in the community, and those who did not know who he was and had come to see and hear Habib 'Umar. To have two Muslim scholars, one from Tarim, Yemen, and one from New Haven, Connecticut, who had established a mosque in Oakland (though had recently moved to a Bay Area suburb), together in the same room and on the same stage, brought together critical influences for the direction of Muslim institutions such as Ta'leef and Zaytuna. For Shakir, the circumstances of this gathering were part of Allah's completing Their light—Habib 'Umar's tour, this multiracial congregation, and the establishment of a Muslim college—they are all signs of Allah's eternal work marked in the vicissitudes of human life.[3]

When Kieślowski refers to the filming of real tears, he refers to those tears that fall as a camera observes life as it happens. Although interviews are also "real life," interview tears conjured by the telling of a memory or a present situation are ontologically different. These tears, though "frightening," register less as out of bounds because they are tied up in the performance of a structured sit-down interview. The interviewee has agreed to enter into this reflective space of the interview, where one is asked questions, and one is already, in a way, out of bounds, in a space exterior to and contemplative of the normal utterances of their everyday lives. The vulnerability marked by real tears and the hush that can accompany them can potentially be a space of reflectivity, but when represented out of lived time and space, put on display, they participate in a regime of visual pleasure that posits power in the spectator.

Slavoj Žižek describes the filming of tears, this encroachment "upon the Other's intimacy," as a "function of *shame* at its purest," not necessarily for oneself but more likely for "what *another* did" (Žižek 2001, 73). For me, there is less a sense of shame, but more a sense of what is necessary, what is not necessary, and what purpose does its representation hold. For Kieślowski, his shift to fiction film was also out of a concern that he not become an informer or police collaborator by virtue of unintentionally documenting something that could be used by the state. It is not a matter of shame but a matter of ethics and politics. Shakir and others' tears compel me to consider tears beyond shame, as ethical, visceral, and intellectual indices of particular experiences and relationships.

While one could attempt a filmic description in order to claim space in a politics of visibility, perhaps a description that leaves more to the imagination elicits more radical possibility and wonder. Recognizing that there is an out-of-bounds is a mystical, critical, and ethical submission to the potential and limits of the image, something akin to *al-ghayb*, the unseen or unknown in Islamic theology (Mittermaier 2019; Suhr 2015; Bubandt, Rytter, and Suhr 2019). If "a politics of visibility conducted on the terrain of the cinematic is inevitably reformist" how does one produce an image that "breaks free from this world, the cinematic, itself" (Keeling 2007, 10)? Challenging the voyeuristic and exploring the possibility of "boredom" that elicits a space for a classically open form of "storytelling" becomes one way of breaking free from the ways we are conditioned to consume images of particular types of bodies (Kracauer 1995; Benjamin 1968). In thinking about the radical expression of those tears and my potential purpose in representing them, I can't help but let them remain unseen (but perhaps heard), however briefly described from my historical and embodied position and narrative relationship.

INDEXICAL TEARS

I benefited more from his crying than his simply transmitting the Hadith.
—IBN AL-JAWZI (BROWN Brown 2009)

Tears perform a certain work in Islam. Tears demonstrate sincerity and intensity of feeling that can also be generated as a pious display. Following the Habib 'Umar tour, I heard Zaytuna staff speaking curiously within their office cubicles about the congregation being moved to tears during his supplications. At the final event of the tour, which was being recorded and streamed, Habib 'Umar spoke of future mediated viewings of this event, closing a thirty-minute *du'a'* (supplication) and a three-week North American tour: "I am leaving you in the protection of Allah, what He has granted you from His generosity that some of those who have not yet come into existence are going to receive . . . and then there [are] people hearing you in far off places now [through live streaming] and there [are] people who are going to hear this tape sometime later [via Youtube, community websites, family, and friends], and all of the good in this moment is going to reach them there. This is the gift of Allah."[4]

Habib 'Umar had begun this supplication in remembrance and recognition, "We gather to remember Sayyiduna Muhammad, and that this land has been connected to his land by means of these hearts that are irrigated [by divine grace]." Throughout the du'a', Habib 'Umar used spatial imagery to convey the opening of paths and a proximity that was made manifest through the supplicating gathering. Repeating a phrase from the Qur'an, "*Fa-inni qarib*" (Indeed, I am near), over and over again, the congregation was raised to a fevered pitch, beseeching in screams, whispers, and thoughts for divine grace, mercy, proximity, and connectedness. "And when My servants ask you, [O Muhammad], concerning Me—*indeed, I am near*. I respond to the invocation of the supplicant when he calls upon Me. So, let them respond to Me [by obedience] and believe in Me that they may be [rightly] guided" (Qur'an 2:186). The sublimity of nearness to Allah, being up to the threshold, jostles the self.[5] The physical manifestations of such momentary or sustained encounters may find a place in the outpouring of tears.

The conversations that followed in the Zaytuna College office cubicles signified the rarity of such tears and emotional displays among (Sunni) Muslims in the Bay Area.[6] This was not an ordinary event in communities that were typically gathered around particular texts and lectures. Usually people held pens and notebooks, not tissues and handkerchiefs. Yet in some ways, it was all the knowledge that this community had benefited from that enabled such responses to Habib 'Umar's supplication. As Hirschkind states, "one is capable of hearing the sermon in its full ethical sense only to the extent one has already cultivated the particular modes of sensory responsiveness presupposed in the discourse's gestural vocabulary, a vocabulary rich in affective, kinesthetic, and visceral dimensions" (Hirschkind 2006, 101).

Capacities had been cultivated for decades in the Bay Area. Even in the overflow room at Ta'leef Collective where the speakers kept cutting out and a dark projected image of Habib 'Umar and his student and translator

John Yahya Rhodus covered the wall (figure 4.2), there was a profound swell and approach "toward Allah." The distance and mediated nature of the du'a' did not preclude an experience of nearness with Allah. This nearness, rather than a movement was more a recognition made sensible, an apprehension of Their constant presence. Hirschkind refers to *huzn* (sadness, melancholia, or mourning) and tears in response to sermons as "not simply expressing the spontaneous movements of an autonomous inner self"; rather, the "performance of huzn" is a "response of the heart" as "affective-gestural expression" of the "listener's ethical character" (2006, 100).

Similarly, in Hamza Yusuf's Sira, Prophetic biography classes at Zaytuna, Yusuf's tears indexed not only huzn, but also an intensity of feeling toward and intimacy with his subject matter. These tears signified an embodied and cultivated love for the Prophet and a moving encounter with his image as Yusuf recounted stories from the Prophet's life. Students had different reactions to such moments. Some sat in rapt attention, marveling, tearing up themselves. Others found it unsettling and strange. Side glances were exchanged, occasional smirks or nervous giggles from students who were caught off guard, who did not know how to react or were distrustful of an embodied display of love for the Prophet. For students seeking an intellectual or informative understanding of Islam, such emotional expressions seemed out of place, and perhaps unteacherly, in the classroom. The chasm between students' and Yusuf's experiences with and knowledge of the Sira was conveyed in such moments, and it was this assumed distance from and presumed lack of knowledge of the life of the Prophet that Yusuf seeks to remedy.

While students arrive with a sense of the historical and spiritual significance of the Prophet Muhammad, they do not necessarily have an embodied passionate and intellectually grounded understanding that Yusuf is attempting to model for and impart to the students. Such cultivation distinguishes the Zaytuna approach from the secularist religious studies approach to the pedagogic transmission of the Prophet's Sira. In this class especially, as in the Clara Muhammad and Masjid Al-Islam schools and the Islamic Study School years before, a unity of knowledge was being sutured, connecting a cognitive understanding of the Prophet's life as a historical event and an embodied relationship for Muslims today. Yusuf marked his own attention to physical manifestations of belief, proximity, or presence in class one day during a discussion of the Prophet Muhammad's modesty. He was describing an incident in which a cloth covering the Prophet's body fell off, and he quickly called for cover, anxious. One of the students laughed. Yusuf immediately responded, concerned about stirring a less-than-dignified response to the Prophet's life.

"I have goosebumps," he said, and he left the classroom. The students were left with one another, stunned. The moment marked a spectrum of experience with and assumed appropriate response to the Sira—adolescent reactions to the mention of nakedness or the solemnity with which Yusuf approached the Sira. Similar to a *khatib* (one who performs a sermon), Yusuf's task "includes not just the modulation of emotional intensities but also the orienting of those emotions to their proper objects" (Hirschkind 2006, 100). This is not an instrumental "rhetoric practice of evoking or modulating the passions as a means to sway an audience toward a point of view," but rather an aim of "constructing the passions in accord with a certain model" (Hirschkind 2006, 100). Laughter and goosebumps join tears as embodied physical manifestations, passions to be shaped, indexing an expansive range of feelings, proximities, capacities, and experiences. Such encounters distinguished the Zaytuna classroom, in particular, from other spaces of Medina by the Bay, as a space of negotiation, and at times confusion. While learning the Sira was meant to bring students closer to the Prophet Muhammad, it could also be disorienting as different understandings of what intimacy should elicit in one's body encountered each other. Tears and tension, laughter, and leaving marked contested bounds of proper response and pedagogy.

INTIMATE DISTANCE

While intimacy was being shaped across centuries, spiritual intimacy across gendered geography was also being cultivated. During one of our one-on-one interviews, sitting opposite each other on the floor of her dorm apartment, Zahrah began to tear up when she spoke of her love for her teacher Imam Zaid Shakir. While reiterating her love and admiration for her parents, she spoke about Shakir's special guidance. He was like a father, a spiritual model, and teacher—one who would help her achieve a desired spiritual and intellectual state while also embodying a form of spiritual and racial kinship they shared as Black Muslims. All this was achieved from a physical distance dictated by particular notions of gendered formality that the female students noticed early on in their academic careers. As Zahrah said, "I'd like to hug Imam Zaid, but I can't do that."

Upon entering a space, Shakir shared high fives with the brothers and gave them strong, loving hugs of support, encouragement, and spiritual vigor, while the sisters stood awkwardly, almost despondent, yearning as he greeted them, "Sisters!" with a grand sweep of his hand to his chest and a slight bow. While they all do not want to necessarily hug Imam Zaid—the thought both mortifies and intrigues—the female students recognize that they are situated differently in relation to their teachers than the male students, and that they are in a gendered space with gendered practices, which they both recognize and desire, but which also proscribe certain intimacies and relationships with their beloved teachers.

At Zaytuna College, the female students were in more proximate and intimate relation to Imam Zaid than most women would be, though his reputation for being an accessible scholar often preceded the arrival of him and his wife, Umm Hasan. When Shakir addresses the audience at Ta'leef, he mostly addresses the men's side of the room.[7] The women watch, listen, and witness this exchange and experience it from what I call an *intimate distance*. Intimate distance refers to a sense of and desire for closeness and proximity typically felt across distances of gender, geography, and time that encompasses a constantly shifting myriad of feelings. In my videos and photographs, I emphasize this distance and spatialization by showing the backs of both men's and women's heads, and the often-mediated forms in which these spaces are negotiated. To compensate for distance or separate spaces, there are often live video or audio feeds to women's sections (figure 4.1). Showing how women experience these spaces draws attention to ways that intimate distance marks their experiences with male leadership and scholarship.

Because women were often farther away from the imam or teacher, they had to engage in *intense listening* to maintain focus on and attention to their words and gestures. This type of hearing and seeing was cultivated and shaped not only by a "shared disciplinary context" but also by the distances and intimacies through which texts and sermons are experienced; these sensibilities "are not something purely cognitive but are rooted in the experience of the body in its entirety, as a complex of culturally and historically honed sensory modalities" (Hirschkind 2006, 101). The spatial dimensions of one's experiences thus affect how cognitive and bodily capacities are mutually developed and engaged. While intense listening across distance was easier in smaller spaces like Zaytuna College's library or Masjid Al-Ansar, in other Muslim spaces this could be quite difficult. As Zahrah reflects: "I wouldn't say the barrier is necessarily that great between women and male scholars, but there definitely is that room where,

FIGURE 4.1 From the back of the women's section during Jumu'a (Friday) prayer service at a mosque in the suburbs of the East Bay. The image of the khatib and the first rows of men is projected on a large screen so that women can see and hear the sermon (author).

FIGURE 4.2 From the women's section in the overflow room at Ta'leef Collective in Fremont during one of Habib 'Umar's final events of the tour. This image was taken during the arousing final du'a' of the tour in which Habib 'Umar's student and, at the time, professor at Zaytuna College Shaykh Yahya Rhodus provided simultaneous translation from Arabic to English (author).

FIGURE 4.3 From the women's section in the Zaytuna library during an optional, informal course offered by Shaykh Yahya Rhodus in the mornings. The course followed the fajr prayers and the recitation of a litany (a long prayer that consists of Qur'anic verses and invocations modeled from the actual prayers of the Prophet Muhammad), the "Wird Al-Latif" by Imam Al-Haddad (d. 1720), which Rhodus had learned in Tarim, Yemen. The library was a space of shifting gendered geographies, in which classes and public events were less formerly designated, as opposed to when the space became a *musalah*, a prayer space (author).

you know, you just can't . . . There is a line that you can't cross, which I think can be kind of sad for women if you just really admire the scholar. But, you know, I don't know, I guess it is what it is. But I'm sure there are ways in which women can be able to interact closely with scholars without there being an issue, you know? *We just have to kind of work on it.* I think it's just kind of new for us, here in the States, and *we have to figure out something to have a model for it.*"

Zahrah articulates a possibility of "working on" the gendered aspects of seeking Islamic knowledge and being in relation to male students and scholars in ways that still uphold homosocial norms. She still desires to be within such bounds of pious formality, yet she points to how such bounds may be unnecessarily limiting. Sisters also welcomed the differences they were afforded due to their gender. Aminah often discussed with her older brother his experiences with his teachers, and after one discussion she reflected on their different experiences: "I was happy that I was a lady, because sometimes, you know, when your shaykh is there, he kind of gives you that look, you know, either he's pleased with you or he kind of knows what is going on with you. But a lady, he usually won't look at for long periods of time, so you are kind of spared from that, like, intense glance. So, because my brother was telling me it was really intense. . . . I was like 'thank goodness, I'm a lady.'"

Because there seems to be a dearth of female Islamic scholars in the United States, Zaytuna sees the education of women as paramount in addressing attitudes about gender and the roles of women in both public and private spheres. I say "seems to be" because there actually are many female Islamic scholars in the United States, and there are critiques directed toward institutions like Ta'leef and Zaytuna for not promoting more female scholars (or particular types of female scholars) to positions of power and visibility.[8] Despite this, Zaytuna College in many ways is attempting to be a coeducational model for female and male students "to interact closely with scholars without there being an issue."[9]

While all the female students recognized that they were in a privileged space regarding their proximity to scholars and access to sacred knowledge, they still saw the ways in which they were slightly distanced. Male students received individualized greetings and words of support, while sisters were often grouped together as a single entity. In the classroom, though, the teachers singled out individual female students, addressing them by name. When I asked students if they thought their gender affected their experience at Zaytuna College, in most instances, the sisters were immediately able to articulate the differences, whether it was in terms of not hugging or high fiving their teachers or in terms of the differences in expectations and pressures regarding future roles as imams or community leaders. The younger brothers often neither considered nor recognized the gendered natures of their experiences and were not aware of the subtle differences or did not know how to articulate how difference was experienced. They did comment on how amazing they thought the sisters were (*"masha'Allah"*), and all the students wondered about what their future leadership roles would look like.[10]

The students also challenged these formalities via forms of companionship oriented toward becoming better Muslims. Salman, an Afghan student from the East Coast, told me about how his awakening in Islam was the result of his friendship with two young women at his mosque. They had participated in a youth program together as teenagers, and the girls' interest in sacred knowledge modeled for him a relationship to Islam he did not know was possible and to which he now aspired. He acknowledged that such male and female friendships may be looked upon with concern and suspicion in many Muslim communities, but he could not negate the fact that these friendships brought him closer to his faith.

Similarly, Steve, who was older than many of his classmates and had only recently converted to Islam, told the female students how he often looked to them to understand how to become Muslim in matters of ethical becoming and the technical aspects of prayer, speech, and other everyday ways of being. Upon hearing this, Ruqayya, a third-generation Black Muslim woman, "found that really amazing, because for me, Steve is somebody who . . . he just has everything so together, and he seems to have such an amazing personality, that I feel like it's amazing that he's looking at me to make sure, you know, that he's going about things in the right way, because I look at him to make sure that I'm doing things, and I look at him, and I just know always that I'm falling short because he does things to such completion."

I emphasize the pedagogy and experience of young Muslim women to offer an analysis for how gendered geographies and difference only "work" when accompanied by mutual respect and oriented toward a common goal of becoming better Muslims and seeing one another as means toward such goals, rather than as distractions from them. When Steve and Ruqayya look at each other, they see each other as kin and as ethical models, not wholly determined by sex and sexuality. Their Islamic perspectives revalue gendered difference as something that shapes the parameters of their formal and informal relations. At the same time, they, their classmates, and their teachers articulate how Islamic knowledge moves in (unexpected) directions that are shaped by relations of power (like race, gender, and age) at the same time that they exceed and defy them.

Many of the female students spoke about not feeling the pressure to become leaders or imams as being freeing. At the same time, they also wished they had gotten more guidance on what to do with their knowledge after graduation. The students who had children or began to have children clearly recognized their roles in educating their children and were also clearer on their rights and responsibilities as spouses, parents, and community members because of their Zaytuna educations. This did not mean that their personal lives were without conflict. Rather, they mobilized what they learned to improve, sustain, or depart from relations, with different levels of communal support or lack thereof.

The intimate distance felt in gendered geographies was likewise felt in texts, where the assumed reader was typically male. Female students had to traverse gendered distances when reading texts that were rarely written with them in mind as readers (although their teachers mentioned that pronoun usage in Arabic often implied both sexes in the use of masculine pronouns). In one of my return visits, gathered female students told me about a question that was raised in one of their Islamic law classes. An older male student, a husband and father, asked Professor Abdullah Ali whether he should expose his daughters to Islamic law (especially in regard to marriage and inheritance) when so much of it cast them in an inferior light. Ali stated that he was perhaps not as equipped to answer the question as this student's female classmates. Thurayya explained to me how she and the others answered.[11] They were able to distinguish between what was Allah's revelation, and how everything else in *fiqh* (Islamic jurisprudence) was speculative and contingent, structured and authorized by human fallibility and circumstance.[12] In this way they were able to recognize and articulate such dissonances in which they were made to feel inferior, which was, in their view, antithetical to the message they received from revelation. I in turn wondered what impact such texts and traditions have on men who are exposed to them. Obviously in this case, a young father recognized its potential effect on his daughters, but in asking the question, he also realized a particular discomfort that he himself had with the tradition.

This was similarly or doubly encountered by teachers and students who were similarly "othered" in texts that discussed race and ethnicity. Black students and scholars had to navigate racializing and racist texts written in previous centuries. While Muslims often assert that there is no racism in Islam, this does not discount, as Thurayya mentions above regarding gender, the speculative, contingent, and fallible aspects of human understanding and practice that may incorporate racist attitudes and commentary into the discursive tradition, both past and present.

Abdul Hamid, a Black student from the Midwest, asked Hamza Yusuf, his white American teacher, why such texts continued to be passed on and taught when they contained explicitly racist views. For Abdul Hamid, this was one category by which to judge the validity or legitimacy of a scholar's works and adherence to the deen. His question was a sincere, critical, and potentially complex legal question that was also a challenge to what place the "tradition" should hold. In this particular case, Yusuf stated that the writer was "a man of his time" and that he shared the majority opinions of his time; they needed to contextualize and situate such writings historically.[13] Yusuf thus invites one to consider the rest of the tradition in this way as well; how do we understand the specific historical, geographical, and sociopolitical contexts in which much of the tradition was and continues to be produced? Abdul Hamid respectfully accepted this answer, but his shifted posture and drifted focus conveyed that he remained skeptical and unconvinced, if not injured as well.[14]

There is often a critique of women who whisper and talk in the back of mas-jids or gatherings, understating an assumption that they are not as devout or pious as men or not held to equal responsibilities in terms of Islamic learning. When one cannot hear the teaching or the khutba or when one is not given space to be there, how should one (re)act? By the same token, when women are rarely "seen" as Muslim scholars or leaders, there is per-haps less aspiration, desire, or encouragement of younger women and their families to pursue such roles and training. Throughout my research I met and heard about women scholars who teach in relative anonymity and yet command immense respect and adoration in their female students and male counterparts. They are typically opposed to being audio or video recorded, limiting the potential for their becoming Muslim media personalities. Their preference for relative anonymity marks a particular form of relationality that stands against liberal feminist notions of female scholarship.

As Muslim women seek just relations in Muslim spaces, it is important to consider what it would mean to keep such notions of gender separation, privacy, and intimacy intact. When equality is commonsensically relegated to a visibility politics, what other forms of dignity and egalitarianism are left behind? Is it possible to think through ways to fight domestic abuse, sexual harassment, war, occupation, health disparities, poverty, and mar-ginalization through alternative structures of the political? Must we always relegate gender separation as a backward thinking, conservative space, or can we think about it as a relational right that suggests other possibilities of agency and being with?[15] For example, I spoke with one female Muslim scholar who was uncomfortable with the prospect of teaching men in a time when women's Islamic education was lacking in the American land-scape, let alone a global Islamoscape.

Many Muslim women scholars do not aspire to celebrity-scholar status and are reluctant to be public figures; in other cases, they express a wariness about Muslim institutions that hire women for visibility and representa-tion, but not for experiential and scholarly knowledge. As Black Muslim abolitionist Kamilah Pickett says, "It's always listen to and follow Black women until a Black woman actually says something that challenges you. Story of my life" (Pickett 2021).

In a time when we see everything, all the time, there is a power to the unseen. I do not want to reify notions of public (political) and private (domestic) realms that are distinct and determined. Nor do I want to reify thinking of gender through a man/woman binary, which Afsaneh Najmabadi suggests is a "very modern imperative" (Najmabadi 2005, 3). Rather, I reinvigorate Cynthia Nelson's analysis of the private and public as gendered spaces of reciprocity and negotiation that complicate liberal expectations and understandings of visibility and representation as markers of equality (that do not necessarily translate into equal power, agency, or improved material realities "behind the scenes"). In her analysis, Nelson recognizes "segregated social worlds, but rather than seeing this as a severe limitation on women, the evidence suggests that the segregation of women can alternatively be seen as an exclusion of men from a range of contacts which women have among themselves" (Nelson 1974, 559).

In the classrooms of Zaytuna, I heard the story of Medinan scholar Imam Malik ibn Anas's (d. 795) daughter Fatima on a number of occasions.[16] Unlike her brothers, Fatima demonstrated the capacity to carry on the tradition of Islamic scholarship. She had memorized his great collection of hadith, *al-Muwatta'*, and was a transmitter of the text. As Imam Malik would conduct his lessons, Fatima would listen from behind a door and tap with her nail when his students made errors in their recitation. Imam Malik and his students would understand the tapping and make corrections. This story was told by male scholars at Zaytuna to express their admiration for female scholarship both historically and in the contemporary moment, in which they acknowledged the intelligence and diligence of female students. The story was also told as an expression of Imam Malik's daughter's modesty in that she taught from behind a screen and with the tapping of her finger.

When Ustadha (Professor) Rania, a female scholar, told me this story again, she told it in terms of the sway that scholars have over their students and its potential danger when the teaching was done across gender. In that telling, she draws attention to the vulnerability of male students to the potential power and effect of a female scholar over them. That young women more commonly study with male scholars may speak to an essentialist assessment of young women's abilities to parse out a teacher's sway intellectually from other potential realms of influence, as well as a male scholar's sense of responsibility to share what he knows, a desire to teach students, and his ability (or inability) to be conscious of and responsible to his potential influence; it could also be a matter of supply and demand. Such power relations between student and teacher are not unique to the Islamic tradition, past or present.

Muslima (Muslim women) scholars demonstrate a critical aspect of feminist pedagogy in that they consciously consider how *who* they are affects how and what they teach. That they are engaged in maintaining a tradition of female scholarship speaks to their commitment to creating subjects rather than objects of knowledge that have a transformative impact on the world and the people around them. It is likewise important to distinguish here between forms of knowledge and particular approaches to them. While Ustadha Rania teaches both men and women in her professional life as a psychiatrist at Stanford University, her preference for teaching only women in subjects of sacred knowledge (Shafi'i fiqh and women's fiqh) is significant and speaks to the particularity of the relationships that develop in the transmission of sacred knowledge. Such distances and intimacies indicate that regardless of the sacredness of knowledge, human fallibilities and vulnerabilities were always and continue to be at the forefront of institutionalization and normative practices.

In *Fictions of Feminist Ethnography,* Visweswaran argues that one "cannot assume the willingness of women to talk, and that one avenue open to [feminist ethnography] is an investigation of when and why women do talk—assessing what strictures are placed on their speech, what avenues of creativity they have appropriated, what degrees of freedom they possess" (1994, 30). Mahmood (2005), Rouse (2004), Taylor (2017), and others describe how pious Muslim women's willingness to submit and surrender forces us to rethink the liberal subject and forms of agency. Abu-Lughod (1990) likewise challenges us to think resistance differently, as a diagnostic of power rather than romantic trope. Visweswaran (1994, 51) suggests "a kind of agency in which resistance can be framed by silence, a refusal to speak," a being-represented-as-subject refusal. This space of critique and critical agency forces us to consider our attempts to describe, name, historicize, and locate subjects within particular frames.

Throughout my research I came across men and women who refused to speak and become subject or placed conditions upon the circumstances of their speaking and subject-making. Some because they had bad experiences with journalists and writers, others because they did not yet trust their own abilities to express themselves or my ability to translate them. Still for others, it related to a particular way of being in the world, an increasingly mediated world that beckons (perhaps demands) one to expose and represent oneself in increasingly public ways.

During the "Tranquility amidst Turbulence" tour described in chapter 2, Habib 'Umar did a "women's event" at a mosque in an East Bay suburb. He was introduced by an Arab American female scholar, Ustadha Loni, who had studied with him and other Haba'ib in Tarim.[17] I had observed a group of women in *niqab* (face veil) at many of the events, and she was of the more prominent with chic bejeweled sunglasses perched on her head. I had been audio-recording and taking video and photographs at many of the tour events. I asked one of her students if she would be okay with me audio-recording her introduction. Her student stated that her teacher would not want to be recorded in any way (note-taking was fine), but that she appreciated that I had asked for permission, obliquely implying that people often attempted to record her without asking permission.

Sitting there in the front row, I listened to Ustadha Loni describe her first experiences in Tarim. How her son who had been studying there begged her to wear a niqab while she visited because this was how things were done there. She expressed her initial shock and reticence at such a request. Why should she? She was a pious Muslim woman, a grown woman with adult children! When she arrived in Tarim, however, she became in awe of the women there. "I want to be like these women . . . who is their teacher?" She wanted what these women had, what they expressed in their eyes, their walks, their words, and their ways of being. She veiled her face and began her studies with the Haba'ib.

In her introduction/lesson, after unveiling her face for her female audience, she described how Habib 'Umar's teachings affected and changed her as a woman, how she "tasted things I never tasted in my life before . . . the smell, [the] taste of the Prophet." She beseeched us, her audience of women, to erase our sins and turn our hearts, to recognize the "light in this *majlis* (gathering) . . . not only for you, but for all the women out there. . . . When you look to the face of the wali, they have *iman* (faith) and they have *taqwa* (God-consciousness). . . . Allah chose you from the umma. This is a moment as if you are in heaven. You are sitting in *janna* (heaven) now."

It is striking how Ustadha Loni urges the female students to look to the face of the wali (here she is referring to Habib 'Umar), while she emphasizes what she saw in women whose faces she could not initially see. They were able to express such iman in their eyes, walks, words, and ways of being. She spoke of a legacy of knowledge in which Muslim women were connected to "the mothers of the believers and his [the Prophet's] pure daughters" and Khadija, who held a "most abundant knowledge." A woman "should take her portion by gaining knowledge" and engaging in pious deeds: "through this she is affirming the meanings of love . . . and defending the sacred law." She urged us to consider our intentions as we sat in this majlis, to gain benefit from it and to recognize our privilege in and accountability to being able to experience such a gathering, to be in the proximity of a wali. How I recognize that privilege and accountability is by relaying some of what I learned from Ustadha and how I learned it—in person, face to face, in my notes, and through my memory. Having been through her own transformation, Ustadha wanted to engender the possibility for other women to develop their own Allah-consciousness, which required that they both unlearn and learn. I gained knowledge from Habib 'Umar through my experience of his student, Ustadha Loni; I received my lesson for the day.[18]

For more than twenty years, Ustadha Loni has been teaching classes in the Middle East, the United States, and online. She does not produce videos and audio recordings that would bring her more visibility, wider audiences, and popularity. She has devoted female students and has the respect of male scholars who know of her. In her biographies on websites, she names the men she has studied with as a form of authentification of her scholarly credentials. These are her public teachers. My initial reaction to encountering sisters like her and Ustadha Rania, who taught the female students at Zaytuna for many years, was "why aren't they more public in their teaching?" especially when many people grumble about the lack of female scholars at national events and conferences. They wish there was more equal representation in Islamic leadership. In questioning my own reactions and expectations, I had to take seriously the appraisals of women scholars and their reasons for controlling their mediated and public presences. They were keeping the sacred sacred.[19]

While the female students at Zaytuna did not initially feel impeded by the lack of female scholars, they also agreed that male students would benefit greatly from taking sacred knowledge from women. In a Zaytuna theology class, Hamza Yusuf stated that after centuries of predominantly male stewardship, perhaps it was time for Muslim women to take the mantle of Islamic scholarship.[20] The potential transformation of the discursive tradition, its transmission, and our material conditions that this transfer could yield can be glimpsed in the powerful work Muslim women already do and have done (Wadud 1999; Hidayatullah 2014; Chan-Malik 2018; Karim 2006).

Toward that end, another frame for thinking about the knowledge practices (da'wa, ta'lim, and ta'dib) that Muslim men and women are engaged in is to consider it as movement-building work.[21] For example, at Masjid Al-Ansar in North Oakland, Sister Alice founded and administers a weekly community feeding program in East Oakland in which hot meals and groceries are distributed to a mostly non-Muslim population. She is not necessarily considered a leader of the community, although she has provided consistent long-term leadership in this on-the-ground service program. Similarly, Hajja Rasheeda was not a scholar, but she was a much-respected role model because of her "consistency and her never putting down the flag . . . people who had survived the '60s as political activists were our heroes." For Oscar, whom we met in early chapters, Hajja Rasheeda

> looked like this is the way you're supposed to *carry it* when you reach a certain age. . . . We took [knowledge] from them. You know, Islam came to us through the generation of elder Muslims who came out of the movement. And we honored that. That meant something to us. Like we . . . even if you weren't Muslim, but you were affiliated with the Black Panther Party? Or the Nation of Islam? Or BLA? Or you had that movement history? Man, we honored that . . . we trying to draw from people who had that history and that experience and who put in that kind of work. Because we were trying to pattern, model our community after them, centered around, you know, Islamic knowledge. That being the core, islam (submission), iman (faith), ihsan (excellence). . . . You are supposed to get wiser, more graceful, closer to Allah, and at the same time be able to maintain that, a certain consciousness. And she embodied that for me.

Oscar talked about how Hajja Rasheeda and her husband were part of the community and how their embodied dispositions, as in the accounts of Aminah, Steve, Ruqayya, and Ustadha Loni, were lessons to be observed and inculcated into one's life.

> They were there and on the ground and at the rally and at the food drive and at the prison and at the classes and in the neighborhood and picking up the trash and dropping off the thing and picking up . . . they were moving with the deen, you know, with everybody else. And I remember wanting to . . . praying that Allah allow me to one day be married to someone who had my back like they had each other's back. And then kinda mature in the deen like they did. It was just beautiful to look at. *They* were beautiful to look at together. . . . I used to just like when they were around.

Oscar describes another kind of pedagogical and embodied relationship, in which Hajja Rasheeda and her husband modeled what it meant to live Muslim lives, to move "with the deen . . . with everybody else;" this was a pedagogical relationship structured by everyday presence, and though she was "one of those people" like David Hilliard, Kathleen Cleaver, and Angela Davis who would "come around to give lectures with hundreds,

sometimes thousands, people in the room . . . she belonged to us . . . like
we claimed her because she's Muslim. We have some proximity and some
intimacy with her." Oscar and others above demonstrate the "ongoing dialectical process of social life in which both men and women are involved in
a reciprocity of influence *vis-à-vis* each other" (Nelson 1974, 554), ordered
through an intimate proximity and distance and in-common orientation
toward Islamic seeking and ethical and sociopolitical transformation.

SIGNS OF REMARKABLE HISTORY, PART 1:
REPRESENTATION AND (QUEER) MELANCHOLY

While I had originally intended to create an observational ethnographic
film at Zaytuna College, after spending time with the Zaytuna students
in their classrooms, I decided against adding that kind of pressure to the
intensities they were already feeling as the first classes of students at a new
Muslim college. I was struck by the role that texts played in the discursive
tradition of Islam, as well as in the scholars' and students' everyday lives
as seekers. I decided to ask community members to choose a text that had
meaning for them that they would recite or read at a time and place of their
choosing. These portraits are assembled in the feature-length film *Signs of
Remarkable History* (2016).[22] The title comes from something Imam Zaid
Shakir said to the students on the first day of orientation in 2010—that
he hoped that this endeavor of establishing a Muslim liberal arts college
would be looked upon in years to come as "signs of a remarkable history."

As I mention in the introduction, Fatemeh, a freshman at Zaytuna College, had declined to participate in one-on-one interviews for my research,
but when I approached her about the film portraits, she expressed interest
in participating. In her description of Oscar Wilde and what drew her to
her particular textual choice, she spoke of his manner: "he's a flashy guy,"
as he posed in cape and floppy chapeau on the cover of the used paperback
she picked up at a bookstore. She was drawn to poetry, theater, and performance. For her final project at Zaytuna's Arabic Intensive two years earlier,
she and a classmate donned mustaches and turbans to perform a comedic
dialogue in Arabic.

I realized that for Fatemeh, the prospect of imagining herself through
another person's words, let alone a particularly witty and flamboyant
nineteenth-century Irish writer and poet, was a thrilling prospect. Her desire
to read poetry for her portrait, and her choice of Oscar Wilde's "Tristitiae,"

articulated an ecumenical approach to self-making and self-representation. She articulated her own Allah-consciousness and directionality toward Allah through Wilde, "But well for him whose foot hath trod/ the weary road of toil and strife/ Yet from the sorrows of his life/ builds ladders to be nearer Allah." The poem speaks to the virtues of suffering, striving, and reflecting as a way "to be nearer Allah," in a world where another ". . . lives at ease/ with garnered gold in wide domain/ nor heeds the splashing of the rain/ the crashing down of forest trees." Wilde articulates for Fatemeh a way she desires to be in the world, paying attention to not only the workings of nature by way of the rain and forest trees, but also "the travail of the hungry years/ a father grey with grief and tears/ a mother weeping all alone." To be witness to such vicissitudes of ease and suffering is to make cultivated ethical choices. Both Wilde and Fatemeh's performances within the world simultaneously relate processes of individuation through disposition, affect, and dress and processes of relationality through seeing Allah's natural and human creations in all their glory, suffering, and cycles of life and death.

Fatemeh was not the only student who appreciated Oscar Wilde; his books were present on many shelves in the students' apartments, often discovered in the used bookstores on Telegraph Avenue or on the shelves of older students who had studied English and creative writing before arriving at Zaytuna. Poetry is an especially intimate form that "travels," and its esteemed position as a language art within Islamic tradition is well known.[23] The poetry club at Zaytuna was its most active club among both male and female students during my initial fieldwork. The female students were also attracted to Wilde's wit and humor and his acute attention to the mannerisms of people and social performance. They were able to relate to and admire his classical education, the moral strictures of Victorian life, and also, perhaps, his queer articulations of difference in his everyday ethical practices and observations. In these ways, Wilde's poetics conveyed further strategies for survival.

"Life's ideal is love; its purification is sacrifice"—Oscar Wilde. Zahrah posted this quote on her blog, amid sayings from her teachers, Islamic scholars, poets, writers, and suras from the Qur'an. In these texts Wilde's ethical sensibilities and similar aspirations toward truth and purification found common company in philosophers and jurists of the Islamic tradition. The students' appreciation of and identity through Wilde speak to the (often unspoken) tensions and potential openings regarding gender and gender performance in spaces that are often overdetermined.[24] While the students are not necessarily seeking out such connections, they ecumeni-

FIGURE 4.4 Still from the film *Signs of Remarkable History* (2016). Fatemeh was drawn to the image of a "flashy guy" on the cover of this book. She also found in this poem a kindred spirit striving "to be nearer God" (author).

cally seek out wisdom and models of sacrifice and Allah-consciousness across diverse waters.

SIGNS OF REMARKABLE HISTORY, PART 2:
REPRESENTATION AND QUEER KINO-EYE

Following the Sunna in which the Prophet Muhammad would name inanimate things, I named my DSLR camera "Nur," which means "light" in Arabic. While I did not consider it at the time, naming my camera Nur spoke to the nonbinary-gendered flexibility of Nur, the camera. While "Nur" is considered a masculine word, it is a name often given to women, as well as the more grammatically feminine form "Nura." Nur was a license to traverse spaces, to occupy space differently by virtue of being connected to this apparatus, the Kino-eye, across gender (Vertov and Michelson 1984). Like light itself, Nur was able to travel. During the fajr classes in the library, I sometimes moved behind Nur and my tripod and left the women's space, which was toward the back of the library, and entered the *barzakh* (an intermediary realm) space in between binary genders (Mittermaier 2011). Off to the side, Nur and I would film brothers from next to them or from directly behind them and the sisters from in front of them and to the side

FIGURE 4.5 Nur and I moved forward in the Zaytuna library to film Shaykh Yahya Rhodus as he taught his fajr course, transcending gendered space. This image works in tandem with figure 4.3 from the "women's section" (author).

(figure 4.5). The only time we filmed brothers from in front in such a space was when we filmed a portrait of Abdurrahman, a former seminary student, as he led the tarawih prayers during Ramadan.[25]

When I asked Abdurrahman what he would like to read for his portrait and when we should film it, he suggested that I should film him reciting the Ramadan tarawih prayers at NYU. He thought that the verses of Surah Yusuf (the twelfth sura) would be especially fitting since it was one of his favorite sections of the Qur'an. Since he was a *hafidh* (one who has by way of memorization preserved the Qur'an), he felt that it made sense for him to choose something from the Qur'an.

Abdurrahman grew up in the Bangladeshi community of the Lower East Side of Manhattan and was in high school there when 9/11 happened. He and his siblings had studied Islam and memorized the Qur'an with a teacher in their apartment; after high school, he attended the pilot seminary program at Zaytuna Institute. After graduating, Abdurrahman enrolled as an undergraduate at New York University. He was an active member of the Muslim Student Association (MSA) at NYU, and he returned to the Bay Area every summer to be a teaching assistant in the Summer Arabic Intensive at Zaytuna. He is now a Muslim chaplain at a university on the East Coast.

Abdurrahman and I discussed how we would achieve such a shot while respecting the rules of prayer in such a way that would be acceptable to all

those who would be praying behind him. After receiving approval from
Imam Khalid of NYU's Islamic Center and announcing the recording to
the congregation, Abdurrahman and I figured out the layout of the shot.
In order to pray in the direction of Mecca, Abdurrahman had to lead the
prayer from a dimly lit corner of the room. There wasn't space for me to stand
to the side, and I really wanted a front-facing shot of Abdurrahman and the
congregation, since this would formally resemble other portraits I had done.
While Nur and the tripod were a partial barrier, neither of us was particularly comfortable with me standing in front of Abdurrahman as he led prayer
(even a brother standing in front of him, despite the tripod, would have been
uncomfortable and distracting and would possibly nullify the prayer). We
determined that I would set up the shot, press record, and then move off to
the side. Because the tarawih recitation is longer than a usual prayer, I would
need to restart the recording after Nur automatically shut it off after twelve
minutes. We decided that I would run up between *rak'ats* (units of prayer)
and restart Nur's recording so that I would get all of the prayer. In all of the
excitement of running back and forth, monitoring sound levels, trying to
stay out of the shot, and minimizing the disruption of the prayer, I missed
one of the breaks in the prayer and therefore missed a section of the sura.
During that particular break, Nur films Abdurrahman visibly waiting for
me to run up, while I am trying to decide whether to rise or not, and then
he decides to continue on and Nur shuts down.

When I assembled a trailer for *Signs of Remarkable History*, Ruqayya told
me that this was one of her favorite parts, while a non-Muslim observer wondered if this was too typical a shot to begin the trailer with, a shot of mostly
South Asian, Arab, and Black men praying. While we see many shots of men
praying in the news, and we may see fictionalized stagings of men in prayer,
we do not usually see shots of men praying from the front. When one is
praying in congregation, one never sees others praying from the front. And
women almost never see men praying from the front because they do not
usually occupy the spaces at the front of a prayer space. This shot was enabled
by a disembodied, mechanical eye, Nur—Dziga Vertov's Kino-eye that can
traverse space, gendered space, in ways that people cannot. This shot was also
enabled by Abdurrahman, Imam Khalid, and their mixed congregation who
were open to working *in relation* to Nur and me within the legal rulings of
prayer to be a part of an academic and creative endeavor.

Because that corner of the room was so dimly lit, Abdurrahman and the
first rows of men had to endure a bright light in their faces as they prayed.
Their focus was challenged, but to our collective knowledges, the sanctity of

their prayer remained intact. Prayer requires intention and certainty in addition to following legal conditions and prescribed acts. Because Abdurrahman knows his fiqh, he was able to ascertain what would be legally sound while also being generous in accommodating the project. In his portrait, he shows the significance of a particular text (the Qur'an) in his life, as well as how he applies his knowledge of this text and the legal tradition in his everyday life.

The three seminary graduates I filmed portraits of requested that I film them reciting texts in everyday practice, whether it be in the classroom, an informal gathering of students, or in prayer. Their choices demonstrate one way in which they fulfill the ʿamal (good works) of knowledge, that it be applied to practice, to good work, to service of the community. The portrait choices likewise show how different individuals at different levels of learning envision their roles as students and teachers of sacred knowledge. While current Zaytuna students demonstrate the aspirational aspects of their study, Zaytuna teachers express the more meditative, solitary, and intellectual processes of their continued study. While the seminary students continue in their studies, they are also acutely aware of their current roles as leaders and teachers. Their choices in self-portraiture demonstrate that awareness, as does their openness of allowing me, a young female (Muslim) anthropologist/filmmaker to direct that process.

OUT OF BOUNDS—REVISITED

In my conclusion of this chapter, I think about the ethics and politics of knowledge production within the parameters of al-ghayb—the unknown and the unseen, which entails approaching matters of knowledge with humility (Mittermaier 2019). Sometimes where we are "placed" means that we will have to traverse distances, cultivating our senses of intimacy and engagement. That distance and efforts to traverse it produce forms of knowledge that Muslim women and anyone who doesn't feel addressed by normative discourses, or a majoritarian "we," bring to Islam as a discursive tradition. Woman-centered pedagogies also demonstrate how a politics of visibility does not always serve to sustain knowledge traditions and relations between women. In *Signs of Remarkable History,* we produce portraits of Muslims and their knowledge practices within terms and temporalities that force an audience to contend with what they may or may not know and to perhaps query a knowledge and power nexus that expects particular forms of ethnographic and ethnocinematic description.

The work of tears also tells us something about the ethics and politics of knowledge production, how we know ourselves in relation to others, from the Prophet Muhammad to our ancestors in Islam. Tears also mark moments of breakthrough and release from things our bodies knew that our conscious selves catch up to (L. R. Gordon 2002). In *Black Skin, White Masks,* Frantz Fanon concludes his chapter on "The Lived Experience of the Black" with tears: "I feel my soul as vast as the world, truly a soul as deep as the deepest of rivers; my chest has the power to expand to infinity. I was made to give and they prescribe for me the humility of the cripple. . . . Not responsible for my acts, at the crossroads between Nothingness and Infinity, I began to weep" (Fanon 2008 [1952], 119). Fanon articulates the contradiction of his sense of deep feeling and infinitude with the constraint of a racist image of Blackness as nonhuman nothingness. His weeping indexes his release from that pressure and restraint, enabling him to chart another path forward (to the "open dimension of every consciousness") (Fanon 2008, 206). We travel with Fanon into the following and final chapter, where we consider what happens when Zaytuna students read the book he published next, *The Wretched of the Earth.* The prayer with which he ends *Black Skins* is directed toward his body: "My final prayer: O my body, make of me always a man who questions!" (Fanon 2008, 206). Fanon brings this bodily disposition of seeking to Algeria, where he considers what it means to put one's body in relation to the wretched, on the line in the struggle for our collective liberation.

CHAPTER 5

EPISTEMOLOGIES OF THE OPPRESSOR AND THE OPPRESSED

———

The Prophet Muhammad (peace and blessings be upon him) once said to us, "Help your brother, the oppressor and the oppressed." We asked, "O messenger of Allah, we understand how we can help one oppressed, but how should we help one who is oppressing?" "By stopping him from oppressing others," he replied. —ANAS IBN MALIK (RA),

Guard yourselves against oppression and so protect your souls from the cry of the oppressed; for surely no barrier exists between the cry of the oppressed and Allah—even if that cry should come from an atheist. —THE PROPHET MUHAMMAD (PEACE BE UPON HIM)

Insomuch as secularity is constitutive of the modern condition, its normative assumptions also seed the life world of those who seek to challenge its legitimacy. —SABA MAHMOOD

SCENE 1—*THIS BOOK*

INTERIOR. ISLAMIC HISTORY CLASS, ZAYTUNA COLLEGE, SPRING 2011, DAY.

We see a CLOSE-UP of a hand with a recent edition of Frantz Fanon's *Wretched of the Earth* (2004 [1963]).

So, he indeed walks us through this process of understanding the consciousness of the colonized and the thirst for liberation, the hunger for liberation, but he also situates this colonial struggle in a wider context. . . .

The CAMERA PANS OUT to reveal a YOUNG NORTH AFRICAN WOMAN holding the book, examining its pages while looking forward at her teacher, IMAM ZAID SHAKIR, as he stands at the board where he has drawn a rough map of Europe, Africa, and Asia. As he points to Libya, he explains:

IMAM ZAID SHAKIR

The monolithic nature of political thought in the Muslim world begins to fragment as you move into the latter part of the nineteenth and the first half of the twentieth century. So, you have your traditional sources of resistance—so ʿAbd al-Qadir al-Jazaʾiri, Omar Mukhtar, the Union of Muslim Scholars in Algeria.[1] But now you have new sources of resistance, and you have new ways of looking at the world. And this is what Fanon analyzes. . . . So, this book really gives us insight into the dynamics of Muslim societies and how historically the sort of monolithic political culture and the monolithic political thought that dominates through much of the history of the Muslim peoples begins to fragment and break down as a result of European encroachment and gradually European hegemony throughout the Muslim world. And it's relevant for Africa and Latin America also and Asia. So, you'll see a lot of times Fanon will frame his arguments specifically in the context of Algeria. But other times, he'll frame his arguments in the context of Africa or Asia or Latin America or what generally came to be known around this time as the Third World.

We see some STUDENTS watch their teacher IMAM ZAID SHAKIR with rapt attention, OTHER STUDENTS are looking down at their notebooks, vigorously taking notes.

DISSOLVE

We see the same classroom, mostly empty. A few STUDENTS linger in the classroom, writing or reading. Other STUDENTS leave their books on their desks as they shuffle out of the classroom. A LATINA WOMAN sits in the back of the classroom with the ANTHROPOLOGIST, who is writing in her notebook. Another professor, SHAYKH HAMZA YUSUF, walks in and looks at the books piled on desks. HE notices *The Wretched of the Earth* on a student's desk and starts to get upset.

SHAYKH HAMZA YUSUF
(pointing to the book, asks no one in particular)

What is this book doing here? Why is it here? I don't want people seeing this here.

(continues to grumble about and deprecate the text)

STUDENT

We are reading it in Islamic History.

SHAYKH HAMZA YUSUF

Who is teaching it?

STUDENT

(quietly) Imam Zaid.

YUSUF becomes quiet, but continues to look troubled.

FADE TO BLACK.
FADE IN WHITE TEXT

Whoever finds good, let him praise Allah, and whoever finds other than that, let him only blame himself.
—PROPHET MUHAMMAD (PEACE BE UPON HIM)

FADE OUT

The ethnocinematic sequence above recreates classroom scenes I observed and recorded at Zaytuna College in its first year, when much of the curriculum and direction of the college were in flux. I nest these scenes within epigraphs and a title card that incorporate hadith that speak to the specific sequence, but that also serve as a reminder to those who are portrayed, to myself who thinks and creates with, and to the reader. The hadith that closes the sequence is especially significant as an ethical reminder of how to interpret what one witnesses (and reads) and to be reflexive about how my ethical and political subjectivity impacts my interpretation and critical intervention.[2]

I was surprised when I heard college cofounder Shaykh Hamza Yusuf criticize the teaching and actual presence of Fanon's text in a Zaytuna classroom. He referred to those outside the college who may draw particular conclusions about its curriculum and mission from seeing the Fanon text in the hands of their students. Yusuf's visceral reaction involved both a prior value judgment on Fanon's theoretical contributions and an expression of concern regarding the possible misperception of the college. Despite his disagreements with it, Shakir saw Fanon's text as foundational for understanding a critical part of Islamic history, demonstrating that one cannot imagine a Muslim future without contending with its colonial histories, as well as with its histories of anticolonial resistance, liberation, and Third World politics. He begins to offer a reading of Fanon that takes seriously the Muslim ways of knowing and being of the Indigenous people of Algeria (who include non-Muslims); I extend his lesson with a question of what it means to order our epistemological, ethical, spiritual, and political practices from the position of the wretched.

In this chapter, we return to the blues adhan and an epistemology for what comes next to consider how liberation theories and theologies come together and apart in Medina by the Bay toward (re)constructing Islamic ways of knowing and being oriented toward survival and salvation, at the scales of the heart, material life, and the umma.[3] Zaytuna College's liberal arts identity is grounded "in the intellectual heritage of two major world civilizations: the Islamic and the Western" (Zaytuna College 2014; 2017). The college emphasizes the commonalities of these two intellectual traditions: "These civilizations share not only common roots but also common aims: to think deeply and systematically about the world (creation), to ponder its ultimate source and purpose (Creator), and to live ethically in the course of our individual and collective lives (spirituality and politics)" (Zaytuna College 2014; 2017).

Where each intellectual tradition and civilization begins and ends is a (colonial and Orientalist) boundary-making that obscures more than it reveals about the relationships between knowledge, ethics, geography, and power and how knowledge has been produced and transmitted over time.[4] These grounded relationships and historical encounters shaped discursive

185

EPISTEMOLOGIES OF THE OPPRESSOR AND THE OPPRESSED

traditions, the narratives about them, and the ways people were inducted into them. While the discourse of "common roots" and "common aims" is a move toward charting a course of living together in relation, in this chapter I attend to differentiation—how the survival of some has often been at expense of others, and how Islam charts a course that requires Muslims to situate roots and aims from the perspectives of the oppressed.[5] The blues adhan calls us to attend to the contradictions of the Western intellectual tradition, how the liberation of particular minds was built upon a hardening of hearts: a foundation of enslavement and social (or sociogenic, rather than ethical) hierarchies that manifest in the formation of the race-concept and the dispossessive logics and environmental degradation of colonial racial capitalism. An epistemology for the next takes that critique and (re)builds how and what we know by taking the good and leaving the bad, reminding us that our individual salvations are relational and contingent upon the well-being and survival of the collective (both within the umma and beyond it).

I reconsider what Wynter calls "our present mode of being human," a "now purely biocentric and homo oeconomicus form" with an attention to the distinctions that a Qur'anic figuration of creation, space, and time yields (Wynter 2003, 282). How does a more robust engagement with Islam as distinct from a secularizing or post-fifteenth-century Christian theological frame shift our conclusions of what comes after or already exists in opposition to what Wynter calls "the Coloniality of Being/Power/Truth/Freedom" (Wynter 2003)?[6] What this and other global frameworks take seriously is the profound reordering of the world, including Muslim worlds, according to racial logics and hierarchies, as well as the colonial capitalist transformation of land, flora, fauna, and people into property (Nichols 2018; Byrd et al. 2018; Robinson 2000). As Maldonado-Torres states, "one can see the 'color-line' as the secular myth of origin or fundamental difference within which other inventions such as modern individuality, freedom, and equality were built" (2014, 698). How does the historical emergence of race, the color line as a discursive construct with material ramifications, impact Islamic thought, theology, and practice?[7] What do we learn from Fanon's weeping, his cathartic opening, which anticipates his move toward anticolonial struggle and the expansive possibilities of his deep and complex identification with the struggles and worldviews of Algerian people?

While some of my interlocutors and teachers may characterize my attention to race, colonization, and neo-imperialism as a disempowered and disenchanted "blaming the West," I instead situate these as descriptions or perceptions of *al-waqi'* (reality), which *empower* us to move beyond civilizational and cultural discourses of West and East and good or bad Muslim, toward witnessing our current conditions and our ways of knowing as they are—materially, as experienced by the most vulnerable among us, and metaphysically, as what we learn from reflecting on revelation and tawhid. Our understandings of reality often differ because we have different experiences and analyses of it, which impact how we theorize history and politics and engage in ethical and political practice.

Within anthropology, there has been a decades-long struggle to end "the *trained inability* of many in the discipline to understand—and treat—race and racialization as constitutive of all modern relations. If race and racialization are not considered to be constitutive of the contemporary world, there is bound to be even less agreement on racism" (Jesús and Pierre 2020, 66). There is a similar "trained inability" within the traditional (and often academic) study of Islam, best exemplified by recent attempts to discredit critical race theory and theories of anti-Muslim racism and their increasing impact on young Muslim scholars and activists (e.g., Dagli 2020; Abdullah bin Hamid Ali 2019a). Such critiques disregard that Muslim scholars have always considered, incorporated, and transformed other epistemic modes into the tradition (for example, the common saying, which was once on Zaytuna College's wall, "Go as far as China for knowledge"), whether they were Indigenous traditions as Islam spread, forms of Greek logic, Chinese science and philosophy, or Asian and African technologies and philosophies that accompanied goods on trade routes as texts and forms of embodied knowledge. Whether or not to do so was also always up for debate in the perennial effort to maintain coherence around what Islam is and is not (T. Asad 1986; al-Ghazali 2004). While Zaytuna College attempts to cohere an education around the best of the Islamic and Western intellectual traditions, toward commensurability, I suggest that we must also foreground the incommensurable, the fundamental flaw of Western liberal humanism and its legacy—its culmination in fascism, genocide, and environmental degradation (Césaire 2001; Fanon 2004, Liboiron 2021).

I ask, what happens when we center our understandings of reality from the point of view of the oppressed, the wretched, and the damned, not as victims, but as sources of the truth from metaphysical and material points of view. This understanding of experience draws from both Islamic and feminist understandings of how an Allah-centered metaphysics and the experiential work in tandem rather than at cross purposes. Muslim (and I include both Shakir and Yusuf here) critiques of and apprehensions about critical theory, including theories of race and gender, stem from its seeming nonmetaphysical and deconstructive quality toward godless visions of liberation and justice; this often engenders alliances with other faith-based and nonreligious social conservatives.[8] Yet in Yusuf's own words, "The metaphysician seeks to understand being—or existence—*as being.* . . . Metaphysics aims to understand first principles, including those of causation itself, its nature, scope, and limits. This invariably means it investigates the contents of our minds, including our presuppositions (all that we assume or take for granted), how it is that we perceive the world, and the effects of those presuppositions on our active life, which are left unexamined by most people" (Yusuf 2017, emphasis in original).

Our presuppositions and how we perceive the world were precisely the issues with which Fanon was concerned toward the salvation of hearts, minds, and bodies. Similarly, the Qur'an also calls Muslims to recognize nature—the sun, moon, stars; earthquakes, droughts, rain, land, waters; bees, camels, elephants, spiders—as Allah's signs for humanity, signs of Allah's creation, mercy, wisdom, and justice. Muslims are called upon to learn from the natural world, including our embodied selves (and our tears) as natural beings, to recognize its provisions and rhythms, and to honor it by being responsible to and caring for it.

The rest of this chapter is divided into three sections that serve as portals and starting points to indicate further avenues for research and *ijtihad* (struggle of interpretation and reasoning). The first section, "1441/1492—EUROPEAN HEGEMONY AND EPISTEMIC DISOBEDIENCE," discusses how considering the epistemological shifts that occur in the fifteenth century from the perspective of the historical Muslim world in relation to the Americas brings new understandings to our critiques of coloniality and Muslim futurity. Section two, "LIBERATION THEORIES AND THEOLOGIES," begins with Hajja Rasheeda's reading of Fanon and moves across decades as Zaytuna scholars may or may not consider liberation theories and theologies in relation to each other. Inspired by the hadith that opens this chapter, the final section, "HELP YOUR BROTHER, THE OPPRESSED, AND HELP YOUR BROTHER, THE OPPRESSOR," discusses efforts to help the oppressed and the oppressors within the larger theoretical and theological debates brought forward in this chapter to demonstrate what is at stake in how Muslims exercise power and from what point of view.

When Imam Zaid Shakir teaches Islamic History to the first cohort of Zaytuna College students, the break in the two-semester course is the year 1492.[9] The fifteenth century marks a historical and epistemological break in an expanding global world system. While the practice of slavery preexists the fifteenth century, the Portuguese enslavement of West Africans beginning in 1441 significantly transforms how slavery is then conducted and racialized. In 1453, the Byzantine capital, Constantinople, is conquered by Muslim tribal leaders, solidifying the establishment of the Ottoman Empire, which lasts until the early twentieth century. In 1492, the "discovery" of the Americas coincides with the expulsion of Muslims and Jews from Spain. The influx of wealth into European coffers, and the degradation of the value of silver and gold, significantly diminishes Muslim civilizations from West Africa to East Asia, while the emergence of race and racial thinking brings about a new era of human definition and differentiation that constructs some as subhuman and nonhuman.

At the same time, the transition from theological to secular notions of the political, the juridical, and the social begins to emerge in the European Renaissance, coinciding with the advent of Western colonization and the transatlantic slave trade, and culminates in the seventeenth century as Europe enters the Protestant Reformation, Age of Reason, and Enlightenment. With this shift from the theological to the secular, a universe designed and ordered by God is sublimated to human machinations. Elsewhere in the world, systemic, moralized, and scientifically reasoned "social inferiorization, and dynamically produced material deprivation," serves to both "verify" a definition of "Man" that renders Others nonhuman and "legitimate the subordination of the world and well-being" of those deemed less human than those who signify "Man" (Wynter 2003, 267). In other words, while Europeans pillage and enslave "the darker nations" (Prashad 2007), they also create "enlightened" definitions of personhood and governance that authorize their actions.

Reading 1492 and the longer period between the thirteenth and sixteenth centuries from a Muslim perspective entails a close attention to how Muslim thought and political structures impacted and were impacted by the shifts in a world system. Professor Shakir's focus in the yearlong history course is to develop students' historical consciousness, drawing them close to the events and figures of the first Muslim community in the seventh century, while also imploring them to investigate the specific social, historical, and political contexts in which Islam functions as, in his words, the "monolithic political culture and the monolithic political thought of the Muslim peoples" and the eventual fragmentation of its political, cultural, and spiritual dominance. While Shakir's claim of Islam as a monolithic influence is complicated by the heterogeneity within Islam and the multiple political and cultural influences that Muslims are exposed to and draw from over time, what he speaks to are the distinctly Islamic ways of knowing, being, and governing that inform diverse societies in which all are not Muslim but are influenced by the modalities of Islamic thought, governance, and cultures.

Similarly, Zaytuna students and scholars are interested in what constitutes "the historical expression of an epistemology—a way of conceiving, composing, and constituting knowledge" that is distinct from what would emerge from the thirteenth to fifteenth centuries onward (in the historical Muslim world, these changes intensify in the nineteenth and twentieth centuries especially through changes in schooling) (Ware 2014, 9; Makdisi 1981). For Shakir, it is critical that students learn how Islam as a worldview influences individuals and communities historically and how to apply this history toward Islamic resurgence in the twenty-first century. By understanding how Islam spreads and transforms societies and then how it begins, in Shakir's words, "to fragment and break down as a result of European encroachment and gradually European hegemony," students can imagine and strategize Islam's survival and possible futures.

The class reads excerpts of Janet Abu-Lughod's *Before European Hegemony* in which she argues for extending the timeline of the West's ascendance to an examination of preexisting world systems between the thirteenth and sixteenth centuries through which two major shifts took place: "the reversed positions of east and west, and the changing relationship between church and state in Europe" (20); Europe's rise is actually "facilitated by the preexisting world economy that it restructured" through "trade-cum-plunder" (361). Precapitalist forms and figures like merchant-accumulators and industrial developers exist in these circuits of trade and production, but "what they lacked were free resources," namely "free" labor in the form of enslaved Africans and Indigenous peoples in the Americas and the plunder of their natural resources through theft and conquest (364). By reading Abu-Lughod and Muslim histories with and against theories of (de)coloniality, racial formation, and secularism, we gain critical insights into how new theories and theologies of the world—from what is human or what is property to what is knowledge itself—transform human relations and contribute to the "intimacies of four continents" (Lowe 2015). The "decline" of Islamic civilizations is an essential historical and "theological" occurrence that enables a conjured narrative of European and Christian superiority.

During Professor Enrique Dussel's visit to Zaytuna College, not long after students had finished reading *The Wretched of the Earth*, Zaytuna College professor Hatem Bazian articulated that the key misdiagnosis of many in the historical Muslim and Arab worlds was "that the progress of the West was due to their scientific [superiority] and also their modes of production." Emergent nations "shifted their educational structure and epistemology and borrowed from Europe the structure, thinking that they can compete and keep up." Historian of West African Islam, Rudolph Ware III, similarly argues how Muslims themselves "saw the supposed decline of Islamic civilization and the ascent of the West as rooted in the failure of old-fashioned Islamic education. They suggested—implicitly or explicitly—that to reach (or regain) the heights of progress, Muslims ought to reform or discard their ways of learning and teaching in favor of others" (15). Yusuf agrees with this theory of declination rooted in Islamic education but situates it within an internal shift that occurred post–Ibn Taymiyya (d. 1328): "the primary cause of the decline, it seems, was the drift away from the philosophical method of inquiry in the metaphysical and physical sciences, both of which had flourished in the early period of Muslim dynamism" (2017). He goes on to lament "a fateful turn in the late nineteenth century: Muslim societies became obsessed with mastering material sciences, especially engineering and medicine" (2017). A "myth of intellectual decline" (Mihirig 2017) was both an Orientalist and technocratic state narrative (El-Rouayheb 2015). The educational and cultural changes instituted in reaction may have fulfilled these assessments, though classical Islamic education persisted beyond the end of the nineteenth century from the basics of Qur'an learning to training in logic and philosophy, especially in West African and Shiʻi traditions (Ware 2014; Zaman 2002; Mottahedeh 1985).

By limiting their analyses in the "old world," Muslims (not all, but generally) have failed, then and now, to recognize, as Dussel points out, the hemispheric connections in which the silver "discovered" and mined by Indigenous and enslaved African labor at Potosí (current-day Bolivia) in 1545 and at Zacatecas (a "free and sovereign state" within current-day Mexico) in 1546, "the silver that the Indians produce with their blood . . . destroyed the army of the Ottoman[s]" at the 1571 Battle of Lepanto in the Ionian Sea. This "European progress," when read across the Atlantic, reveals itself to be built on systems of racial exploitation and theft, grounded in new theological and then secularized and socioeconomic ways of articulating human and material relations. The influx into the world system of silver and gold from the Americas also radically devalued the wealth of Muslim societies from Africa to Asia, which were based on the standards of gold and silver.[10]

When African Americans were reacquainted with and renewed Islam in the early twentieth century, they were drawn to a countercosmology, its alternative mode of being and explanation. This resurgence was likewise taking place in Muslim-majority states across North Africa and South, Southeast, and West Asia that had experienced different levels of coloniality and colonization. African Americans mobilized Islam to address the production and "mis-education" of "the Negro" by starting schools and reshaping selves into a new image (Woodson 1992; S. A. Jackson, 2005). The contemporary impulse at Zaytuna College is similarly a resurgence and renewal; the moment of tension about *The Wretched of the Earth* gestures toward the tension of two options: a de-Westernization or Islamization of knowledge that will reform existing modes and reanimate marginalized modes of knowledge formations; or a decolonial or abolitionist option mobilized toward a transformative reordering of knowledge and its attendant systems. Mignolo describes how the "decolonial and de-westernizing options diverge in one crucial and indisputable point": the de-Westernizing option does "not question the 'civilization of death' hidden under the rhetoric of modernization and prosperity, of the improvement of modern institutions (e.g., liberal democracy and an economy propelled by the principle of growth and prosperity)," while the "decolonial options start from the principle that the *regeneration* of life shall prevail over primacy of the *production and reproduction* of goods at the cost of life" (Mignolo 2009, 161, emphasis in original).

The decolonial option is in line with how some Muslim scholars, Fanon, Wynter, and others see the separation of the formal sciences (logic and mathematics), natural (physical and life) sciences, social sciences, and the humanities as the causes of crises and deterioration of our societies, from environmental degradation and war to widening inequality, poverty, and enclosure (Gagne 2007; Fanon 2008; Wynter 2003). The extraction of morality and ethics from scientific inquiry and knowledge practices—and their attendant discourses of modernity, liberal humanism, and progress—led to fascism and death, best epitomized by the histories of chattel slavery,

colonization, nuclear war, and multiple holocausts and genocides often in
the names of democracy, human rights, the nation-state, and capitalism.

From interventions in language to the revision of history, anti- and decolonial movements, blues epistemologies, Islamic resurgences, and Third
Worldisms sought to reshape questions of knowing and being, while also
articulating aspirations for self-determination, sovereignty, and autonomy
(Getachew 2019). Much of this intellectual and political labor resulted in
neocolonial arrangements that pacified rebellion and difference by absorb-
ing some (into schools, governments, and capital relations) and further
subjugating others into greater forms of disenfranchisement, enclosure,
and premature death (Ferguson 2012; Chatterjee and Maira 2014; Gilmore 2007). At the same time, we see the effects of these movements that
sustained peoples and communities in smaller ways, that flourish beyond
these pages. Many students of the Sister Clara Muhammad Schools, the
Masjid Al-Islam School, the Islamic Study School, the Jama'at of Shehu
Uthman dan Fodio, and Zaytuna Institute, Zaytuna Seminary, and Zaytuna College continue this tradition as they pursue their studies, transmit,
and practice what they have learned in multiple forms.

To understand what it means to be human (a metaphysics and ethics of
being) and how race and otherness are configured within that is a critical juncture through which to understand how the Zaytuna project and a
Third World/ethnic studies project come together and apart. Ethnic studies has failed to instantiate a decolonial epistemology beyond metaphor,
partially because it has not undone a coloniality of being that governs the
academic disciplines and because in many places it has become untethered
from the communities to which it was once so intimately attached and
for which it was given meaning (Tuck and Yang 2012; Okihiro 2016; paperson 2017; Wynter 2006). The autonomy was never attained within the
university, and in our calls to "decolonize the university" or "steal from
the university" or redirect its resources, we still maintain them as settler
colonial scaffolding and pillars of the Western liberal notion of the human
and the distinctions between liberal arts and sciences that have been built
upon notions of the subhuman or nonhuman (Kelley 2016; Harney and
Moten 2013). Similarly, while Zaytuna scholars' critiques of higher education resonate with the critiques of decolonial scholars, they also willfully
participate in strategies of Muslim and Islamic survival that inadvertently
further a settler colonial structure through processes of accumulation, in-
clusion, exclusion, and reform, situating white supremacy and capitalism
(their civilizations of death and scarcity) as tests and burdens, rather than

foundational to the structures that enable Zaytuna's material establishment amid attacks on other Muslim strategies for survival.

At the same time, as I stated earlier, the college's current buildings have seen occupants and ideas come and go. The grounds are being prepared toward permaculture and sustainability; and students graduate without debt. Beehives have been established. Seeds and trees are being planted; students are engaged in study and struggle. What may future harvests yield, God willing?

WRETCHED OF THE EARTH AND THEORIES AND THEOLOGIES OF LIBERATION

When I read *The Wretched of the Earth,* it just changed my life. I'm not going to say I understood all of it at the time, but I understood enough to be able to recognize that oppression was universal, and I wanted to be a part of the chapter that struggled to end oppression worldwide. —HAJJA RASHEEDA

Hajja Rasheeda was a sixteen-year-old Catholic school girl in San Francisco when she joined the Black Panthers in 1967 and started reading Fanon. She was an active member until 1971, when she left to focus on her studies and activism at San Francisco State (1968–1972) and to raise her Panther baby girl, Kiilu. Her commitment to "end oppression worldwide" continued in her life as a Black Muslim from the 1970s onward. Fanon, Mao, and other writers introduced an analysis of history that she could recognize in how social worlds were stratified around her:

> We knew that it was going to be a long struggle. We knew it wasn't going to be like a week or a week and a half, or whatever. We had to everyday come to the campus, stand on line, do the picketing, you know, meet with groups, talk to people, sharing with them information. We were tying our struggles in with the struggles around the world, the international struggles, you know, and sharing, seeing ourselves as oppressed people. Seeing the police presence as an occupation. Seeing the need for relevant education as a means for liberation, for freedom . . . the type of scholarship that came out of this era, and it might not be in the form of research, it might not be in the form of making like *Harvard Review,* but this was a very scholarly movement. It [was] committed to reading and studying and being versed in liberation, you know, a scholar-

ship. So, we had to know who Frantz Fanon was, we studied Du Bois, we studied international leaders, their work . . . so that we could be informed of what we were doing.

From this moment onward, Hajja Rasheeda committed to forty years of study and struggle; she was the principal of an elementary school in Oakland for decades, and she helped establish multiple schools, from the Clara Muhammad School to a charter high school. Her life was willfully oriented toward knowledge practices, relating local work in the community to the struggle "to end oppression worldwide." Her reading of *Wretched* anticipates later readings in and beyond the Zaytuna classrooms. Black teenagers in the Black Panther Party reading Chinese Communist Mao and Black Martinican Fanon writing about the Algerian struggle for liberation from French colonialism and seeing the connections to their own struggles as a domestic colony—this epistemological project had deep reverberations (Murch 2010; Rickford 2016).

One reverberation was in the Bay Area itself, where at Masjid Al-Islam in the 1990s, young Muslims like Oscar became attuned to "the global struggle of Muslims, or rather, it was important to them to connect our struggle in the United States with the global struggle of Muslims in Palestine, at the time Chechnya, at the time the Philippines . . . the way that it was talked about was, 'These were oppressed people struggling against a neo-imperialist, neo-colonial regime.' And, you know, making the same connections between poor and oppressed Black folks in inner city Oakland trying to struggle amid oppression and tyranny coming from the police and state and this type of thing."

In the Zaytuna classroom more than a decade later, Fanon offered a historical lens, both as a witness to history and as a historical force. For Shakir:

> Fanon becomes a chronicler of that emerging Third World revolution. And that's why this is an extremely important book—even though we'll try to point out some of its shortcomings—was very important. It also becomes very important, we mentioned, in Iran; it's translated into Farsi by Ali Shariati, one of the principal ideologues of the Iranian Revolution. It becomes very influential here in the United States because as you move into the latter part of the 1960s, early 1970s, you have the Black Power revolution here. You have the Puerto Rican Liberation movement in the United States. You have a number of moments, very radical time in the United States. And a lot of these movements are influenced by this book. . . . You have serious stuff. How many of you have heard of the

Puerto Rican Liberation Front? They actually had a contingent that went into Congress and shot up the Congress. Congress in Washington, DC! People weren't joking.[11] Here in Oakland, you had the Black Panthers. The Black Panthers, one of the books that influenced their thought was this book. So, Fanon's book is, is very, very influential.

Prior to reading *The Wretched of the Earth,* the class screened *The Lion of the Desert* (Moustapha Akkad, 1981) about the Libyan struggle against Italian colonial occupation led by Omar Mukhtar around Jebel Akhdar (Green Mountain) in Cyrenaica. At a world map in the front of the classroom, Shakir described the regional history of Libya that contributed to the Libyan Civil War that was underway at that time in February 2011: from Islam's entry into the region in 643 to the Ottoman ceding of the province to the Italians in 1912 to British control after World War II to the Kingdom of Libya (1951–1969) to al-Gaddafi's Arab Republic (1969–2011); a critical prison massacre in Tripoli in 1995; to the Benghazi uprising that would mushroom into a civil war, al-Gaddafi's capture and gruesome death in October 2011, and ongoing instability to this day. Imam Zaid explains, "So al-Gaddafi in 1969 overthrows the monarchy and establishes what he calls a *jamahiriyya,* the rule of the masses. . . . Gaddafi sets up this socialist, part Islamic, part socialist, part dictatorship, part, as the Egyptians say, '*mish 'arif eh,*' *ya 'ni,* I don't know what it is. [Class laughs.] And rules Libya in a very contradictory way. On the one hand, certain segments of the population benefit from some of his policies and programs. On the other hand, any sort, any vestige, any hint of political opposition is brutally crushed." Shakir goes on to describe how the oil wealth of Libya was distributed in pan-Africanist projects throughout the continent of Africa, as well as across the Atlantic to the Nation of Islam and other groups, but how it was not evenly distributed across Libya to develop and maintain its infrastructure: "This is why the historical roots are important to understand."

Shakir connects the contemporary situation in Libya (and the rest of North Africa and the Levant) to the colonial and postcolonial history of Algeria and the larger Third World project. Shakir focuses on three issues in his lectures on Fanon: first, he emphasizes the role of religious, colonial, and racial consciousness and education in resistance movements; second, he discusses the neocolonialism that emerges in the region through economic exploitation and dependency; and third, he considers the role of violence in resistance as well as at the level of the state. In both his lectures and comments on students' final papers, he urges nuance on the definition and use of violence. When Shakeela, a South Asian student from Northern California, states that "the real means of reform, change, and healing is through love, compassion, and the Divine intervention of Allah," he reminds her that "there was a lot of violence also—Badr, Uhud, Khandaq, etc.," naming significant battles in which the Prophet Muhammad fought.[12] When she argues that "Fanon's assertion of cathartic violence is made in a vacuum . . . by leaving out a key component of consciousness: faith," Shakir agrees. In Shakir's and many of his students' views, Fanon gives the role of Islam as a unifying and mobilizing force short shrift. Interestingly, Shakeela agrees with Fanon that Islam assuages believers "into a complacency of accepting their fate . . . the acceptance of these situations comes through faith, where the poor and mistreated are promised a passage to heaven. With this belief ingrained in the heart, many can survive the worst of circumstances." Shakeela sees faith as a critical component for surviving the traumas and violence of colonization, while Fanon would see such "complacency" as the problem with organized religion and Indigenous traditions that stymie the historical and psychical process of decolonization.

When Fanon speaks of the need to expand Marxist analysis, he argues for an understanding of the role of the lumpenproletariat, the peasant/farmer, and the racialized and colonized subject, beyond the proletariat-bourgeoisie dialectic. Following Fanon, Shakir discusses how nationalist states continued a cycle of violence within their own nations by targeting their own people and religious leaders, driving "a wedge between the people." While many emergent nations became formally politically sovereign, they were economically tethered to the economies of the Soviet Union or to Europe and the United States and thereby politically influenced by and dependent on these neocolonial relations. In Shakir's view the division between state and religion and the often-violent resolution to that conflict contributes to the material, spiritual, and sociopolitical failure of anticolonial liberation struggles. Relatedly, Dussel emphasizes the need to understand Marx, to have an analysis of "what is capitalism, theologically?" Dussel points out that "the poor is an economical question. And the poor is now produced in the capitalist society. That means I need to know what . . . capitalism [is] . . . hunger is material." In the context of revolutionary and anticolonial struggles, "the South can do a revolution against the North. In Iran, or Nasser in Egypt before. But because they don't know what is capital, they fell back in the capitalism always. And that means they cannot be free of exploitation." So, while a nation may have become free of colonialism as a sovereign nation, it likely remains subject to exploitation and may internally reproduce exploitative relations because of a fundamental disregard for or inability to transform how global structures of capitalism function to further neocolonial and unjust relations.

On the scale of local community, a sense of what is capitalism theologically also matters in terms of how Muslims fulfill individual and communal obligations of preserving what al-Ghazali referred to as the five essentials of human well-being: religion, life, intellect, offspring, and property. For example, zakat, one of the primary pillars of Islam in which Muslims purify individual wealth through its annual redistribution throughout the community, was often used to assist people toward being able to sustain themselves. If racial capitalist structures shape the context in which they facilitate such redistribution, then this larger system must become a theological issue, especially if intentions to preserve well-being are thwarted or ineffective.

As Wynter and others argue, the incomplete epistemological project of the 1950s and 1960s failed to fully dismantle a coloniality of being/power/truth/freedom (Wynter 2003). For Shakir and others at Zaytuna College, the building of a Muslim college was an essential practice of epistemic sovereignty (however authorized by state and federal accreditation agencies); what this sovereignty actually meant and would produce, however, was up for debate. Toward the end of the panel discussion, Shakir and Dussel differed on the distinctions between the individual and the communal relationship with Allah at both material and spiritual levels. While the moderators sutured the divide toward presenting a coherent agreement, it is worth discussing this moment of tension because it speaks to what Hajja Rasheeda and others found in Islam in the aftermath of state violence.

Hajja Rasheeda's introduction to Islam was through the radical Muslim brothers she met in the movement. She initially joined the NOI instrumentally, seeing it as a way to work with and for Black people. Part of her survival post-COINTELPRO and the Panther split was to become more spiritually engaged and to continue to provide service to the community at the level of her family and the larger Muslim and political prisoner communities. She and other Panthers who converted to Islam or found other spiritual infrastructures continued to be committed to serving the people but also needed something more for the next (revolution, struggle, world . . .), especially if they were to sustain themselves and their communities as a form of movement-building in the face of state repression. In this case, Islam itself was the means for survival as Rasheeda and others sustained themselves via Muslim study and ongoing struggle.

Decades later, Oscar found something similar in Islam: "That's what I needed. I was looking for a spiritual discipline. Like some kind of spiritual practice to complement my activism because I was feeling like I didn't have any connection to God, really; even though I believed in God, I wasn't doing anything to show it. And, you know, at a certain point the activism wasn't enough. I needed my own spiritual exercise and discipline to complement that work." Oscar's need for a spiritual discipline to complement and sustain his political commitments continues Shakir's and Shakeela's critique of Fanon (and Marx), while also demonstrating how the political analyses of Fanon (and Marx, by way of Mao) that so infused Bay Area Black study and struggle contributed to his and Rasheeda's conversions to Islam.

As I discuss above, Muslim scholars have mostly disregarded how the accumulation of wealth across the Atlantic contributed to the transformation of Muslim-majority societies and how contemporary systems of racial capitalism contradict Islamic ethics and legal principles (most significantly in terms of interest, debt, and the accumulation and hoarding of wealth). While Shakir agrees with this assessment on the macro level, he demonstrates a discomfort in wholly couching an analysis in terms of "epistemology, alienation, and I think the whole theory of value in Marx's sense . . . we have to restructure how we relate to creation and that our value ultimately . . . doesn't come from our relationship with physical things. . . . Our fundamental value is based on our relationship with Allah. And it's in the context of that relationship that we're either liberated or we're oppressed at a personal level. And if we don't liberate ourselves at that level, then we're always . . . open to be exploited at a material level."

For Shakir, conflict arises in struggles for liberation when the focus is on worldly concerns and power; when "the methodologies and philosophies informing that activism do not account for the existence of Allah, who is, after all, the ultimate dispenser of justice, that activism can become the source of despair and frustration," what he calls "spiritual burnout" (Shakir 2018, 14).[13] For Shakir and others, this manifests in hate, atheism, acceptance of un-Islamic (legally impermissible) practices, and violence. "Every activist must be a scholar in the realm of her activism as she must be conversant with the legal rulings associated with a particular action she may be involved with. . . . Such a person combines the 'worldliness' of activism with the 'spirituality' of the scholar" (Shakir 2018, 13).[14] Shakir argues here that spirituality emerges from the position of the scholar, from the knowledge of legal rulings and the ethical practice of living according to these rulings. Shakir emphasizes this point with the film *Lion of the Desert*, which introduces anticolonial freedom fighter and scholar-warrior Omar Mukhtar as he is teaching the Qur'an to an outdoor classroom of young boys.

For Dussel, the community as an ethical relation precedes the individual relation with Allah, "It's not my personal relation with God. It's the community relation with God." Dussel states, "it's the community first" as in the example of the hadith in the epigraph regarding the atheist: "surely no barrier exists between the cry of the oppressed and God—even if that cry should come from an atheist." This point of tension, which may have been magnified or minimized due to issues of language and translation, speaks to the complexity of how ethics and politics manifest in the temporality of everyday life and in the sweep of grand historical events. For Shakir, "If I personally don't understand my relationship with reality, then I can't contribute to lifting someone up from a lower misunderstanding of reality to a realization of what reality is so that we can constitute a community of meaning. Because before we're communities of physical beings, we're communities of meaning." Shakir speaks here of the differences between understanding al-waqi' (reality) as divinely created and as it manifests in human perception and experience. For R. A. Judy, by way of Sayyid Qutb, if one loses sight of *tawhid*—the oneness of God, "the human endeavor to discover and understand the laws of the physical universe flounders . . . resulting in fragmentary and momentary understandings of reality that cannot provide the basis for a universal and sustainable social justice" (Judy 2007, 119). The role of Islamic study and ethical practice is to situate oneself within these two realities, as Bazian states: "You have to rectify the self, but you have to act in the world in a communal way. Otherwise, community has no meaning. And umma has no meaning without that rectification."

The process of self-rectification and Muslim study could itself present challenges for young aspiring scholars. During the 2012 spring semester, several male students came to Matthew, the Zaytuna College student life coordinator, to discuss their relationships with one another. Over the course of a difficult discussion one student broke down and asked, "What are we doing? Like, we're just in our own heads, this isn't the tradition. This isn't what Islam is about." While the sisters had a strong sense of camaraderie, several of the brothers had started to feel isolated. Matthew explained:

> Those who are serious about the community . . . serious about Zaytuna and serious about studying, they are the ones that are serious about isolating themselves, too, [because] they read these quotes from scholars like Imam al-Ghazali, who . . . says things like . . . "People are only de-

stroyed by people," and say, "You have to seclude yourself, and make sure that other people don't distract you from your pursuit of knowledge" and those things.

And then [there is] all the work on the self and developing the self, pursuing all this knowledge, reading the Qur'an regularly, making *dhikr*,[15] making remembrance of Allah. A lot of that isn't really put into context, in terms of, "Okay, when scholars wrote that, what kind of environment were they actually living in?" They were living in an environment, as far as I can understand, in which the community and the family life is just a given, that's established there. But we've been uprooted from that; we've been torn away from that. And we don't have community; that's not a regular feature of our lives anymore. We're just, our lives are just increasingly more individualized.

Matthew instituted weekly gatherings, Jumu'a Muffins, where the brothers and sisters would meet separately and discuss nonacademic issues and get to know one another better.[16] While this was not the most organic means of cultivating a sense of community, it went a long way toward helping the brothers, especially, open up a space of dialogue and reflection toward understanding that becoming scholars and being in community went hand in hand, that roommates (like family members) had a right to each other's time: "You shouldn't do anything on Fridays, except maybe read a bit of Qur'an, but other than that, you shouldn't do anything but spend time with your roommate, spend time with other people, just spend time with people." As Matthew explains:

There is a saying, of the Prophet Muhammad, Peace Be Upon Him, something to the effect that, "The believer is social, and the best people of our community after the Prophet Muhammad. . . . Peace Be Upon Him, their names are, or as a group they are called, the Sahaba or the *Ashab,* the Companions[;] the very definition of who they were, was that they spent time with a certain person, with the Prophet Muhammad, *salla Allahu 'alayhi wa-alihi wa-sallam.*

. . . It just hit me that this was something that we were really missing. We're missing community, and if we don't have community, it doesn't matter how much knowledge we have. It doesn't matter how much piety we have. It's going nowhere, because then we can't learn from each other. We can't really understand what we need to work on in ourselves, because we are mirrors for each other . . . and we can't really implement the tradition, because so much of the tradition is how we deal with people, how we interact with people, how we learn from people, and teach them. And also in terms of Zaytuna's whole vision—Zaytuna's vision is building leaders, and you can't lead if you don't want to spend time with other people. *SubhanAllah* [Glory be to God or Glorious is God].

False dichotomies between activist and scholar and the sacred and profane or worldly are best attenuated by those who attend to the interrelation between the two. For Shakir, this is best articulated in what is one of his favorite verses of the Qur'an, which he recited for his portrait in *Signs of Remarkable History*: "It is not righteousness to orient your faces East or West [in prayer]. Rather righteousness is to believe in God, Doomsday, the Angels, the Scriptures and the Prophets. [It is to] spend wealth, despite the love for it, for the relative, the orphan, the poor, wayfarers, beggars, and for the liberation of slaves. [It is to] establish the regular prayer, pay the poor due and to faithfully fulfill covenants having convened them. . . ." (2:177). This verse, which describes the ideal being or those who are righteous, outlines how prayer alone does not make one righteous; it is through belief, prayer, zakat, and fulfilling covenants and contracts that are often of private concern and practices directed outward first at the level of family and then broadening toward the poor, travelers, and the enslaved. In Shakir's statements during Dussel's visit, he seems to discount material oppression as something that can be assuaged by spiritual liberation, yet in his constant reference to this Qur'anic verse, and in much of his own activist-scholar practice, he acknowledges the inextricable link between personal and communal salvation situated among the most vulnerable. The most vulnerable can also have other than material connotations; one may not seem *miskin* (needy), but can be very much in need of relation, assistance, and compassion.

Zaytuna and other religious scholars likewise situate suffering on earth within a cosmology of redemption, where it has a spiritual meaning and will be accounted for in the afterlife that will reward and punish individuals accordingly. Such redemptive value at the individual level is in tension with responsibility at the communal level, articulated in multiple verses of the Qur'an and traditions of hadith. In Sura Tawba in the Qur'an, Allah refers to Believers as *awliya'*, which has multiple meanings, including protectors, guardians, helpers, friends, supporters, and saints: "The Believers, men and women, are protectors (awliya') one of another: they enjoin what is just, and forbid what is evil: they observe regular prayers, practice regular charity, and obey Allah and His Messenger. On them will Allah pour His mercy: for Allah is Exalted in power, Wise" (9:71).

Throughout her life, Hajja Rasheeda participated in numerous activist movements and campaigns, while also becoming increasingly devoted to her own spiritual maturation. Her despair, regrets, and frustration, the actual danger in which she lived as a foot soldier for Black liberation, were countered by an ever-increasing faith in Allah. In her post-Panther life, she focused her energies on building and being the infrastructure that could sustain a community in ongoing, eternal struggles for justice. At the same time, she would also drop knowledge to the young Muslims who were building community and themselves alongside her. Oscar remembers her dropping "little tidbits" like, "You all have to understand the seriousness of what it is that you're doing and understand that, you know, these are the kind of things that make the government come after you. Like, they're going to put pressure on you. Because you're trying to do something . . . when you do this kind of social political work, they look bad because this is the kinds of things that they are supposed to be doing. And, you know, realize that this is what that means . . . this is not a fad. This is not some kind of style. . . . It's going to take some sacrifice on you all's part. So, get ready." Oscar remembers Hajja Rasheeda speaking to why one's commitment to justice and community cannot be shallow. She conveys the ways that suffering and survival, activism and other forms of community work, as ethical practices themselves produce their own capacities toward an understanding of al-waqiʿ. Her lessons speak to how such work shifts other people's understanding of reality, undermining the legitimacy of a state that does not attend to the material needs of its citizenry.

Similarly, for Oscar, any tension between "the so-called traditional Muslim scholar" and "the so-called Muslim intellectual/activist" is a false dichotomy and speaks more to the particular contexts in which they often work—at universities, nonprofits, mosques, and on social media. "None of my teachers were like that. All of them were concerned about how to get closer to Allah and how to correct wrongs in the society. In fact, Shaykh Muhammad (Abdullah of the Jamaʿat) would suggest that your ability to correct the wrong in the society is connected to your closeness to Allah. So, in other words, if you're really close to Allah, then you're gonna be compelled to do something about what's going on in society. Not the other way around." Oscar like so many others "came to Islam because I was an activist; I was a student activist in high school and a Black nationalist. And the Islam that made, that sustained me is one that, I believe, values who I am as a Black person and encourages me to do something about issues that are affecting people around me, not just me and my community."

The tradition of Islam in Medina by the Bay has been directed toward the damned and wretched of society in the work of teachers, prison chaplains, prison-serving organizations, and those who have run programs for food, housing, and shelter. There was a time when Muslim travelers could sleep on the floor of masjids across the country without the distrust and security concerns of the last two decades. The sense of responsibility to others was and is a fundamental aspect of Muslim life, likewise exemplified by the multiple online fundraisers Zaytuna students and others have sponsored for burned Black churches and murdered Christians and Jews, as well as for incarcerated immigrants and prisoners. This is the call of the blues adhan, with its epistemological and ontological intervention. For many Muslim scholars and laypeople, social and spiritual transformation and the strategies for Islamic and Muslim survival emerge from the condemned, the wretched and damned of society. Scholars of decoloniality draw attention to the cries of the damned: "It is the cry that animates the birth of theory and critical thought. And the cry points to a peculiar existential condition: that of the condemned" (Maldonado-Torres 2013, 256). To hear the blues adhan is to hear the theory and critical thought from this perspective; it is to attend to and be wary of the prayers of the oppressed. Medina by the Bay encompasses all these things while also holding the complexities and contradictions of what it means to help the oppressor as well.

HELP YOUR BROTHER, THE OPPRESSED, AND HELP YOUR BROTHER, THE OPPRESSOR

SCENE 2

MONTAGE

A. INTERIOR. EVENT HALL, IRVINE, CALIFORNIA, SEPTEMBER 9, 2001, EVENING.

We see HAMZA YUSUF giving an impassioned speech about the U.S. criminal punishment system at a fundraiser for the incarcerated Imam Jamil Al-Amin. Members of the audience nod their heads in agreement.

Imam Jamil is a man who by necessity must speak the truth. That is a dangerous man. Within this government are elements who will do anything to silence the truth. They'll assassinate either the person or the character. . . . This country is facing a very terrible fate; the reason for that is that this country stands condemned . . . it has a great, great tribulation coming to it.

B. INTERIOR. WHITE HOUSE OVAL OFFICE, WASHINGTON, DC, SEPTEMBER 11, 2001, NIGHT.

We see President George W. Bush in a television broadcast from the Oval Office.

PRESIDENT GEORGE W. BUSH

Good evening, today our fellow citizens, our way of life, our very freedom came under attack in a series of deliberate and deadly terrorist attacks. . . .

C. EXTERIOR. FRONT DOOR, HOME IN CONTRA COSTA COUNTY, EAST BAY, SEPTEMBER 20, 2001, DAY.

We see a small cadre of FBI agents outside a suburban home, two approach the front door. One knocks on the door, and it is opened by a Latina Muslim woman.

FBI AGENT

We'd like to speak to Hamza Yusuf Hanson.

UMM YAHYA (WIFE OF HAMZA YUSUF)

He is not here . . . he is with the president.

The agents look at her incredulously. One steps away and makes a phone call. He stands there waiting and then listening.

FBI AGENT (INTO THE PHONE)

He has 100 percent security clearance?

D. VHS RECORDING. INTERIOR. BBC TELEVISION STUDIO, WINTER 2001, EVENING.

We see an old recording of BBC's *HARDtalk* from late 2001. HAMZA YUSUF is seated at a round table across from journalist SARAH MONTAGUE.

HAMZA YUSUF

I think that it is legitimate for anybody in America who wants good for that people to remind people of their moral obligation. I think that American people have a moral obligation to understand things at a deeper level. It's a representative government; we pay taxes. We have to realize that many of the weapons that are flooding the world are coming from France, from England, from America, from Israel . . . we need to reflect on what is going on in the world.

FADE TO BLACK.
FADE IN WHITE TEXT:

Do not mix with the princes and sultans and avoid seeing them; for seeing them and sitting with them and mixing with them is great mischief.
—AL-GHAZALI (D. 1111)

CUT TO BLACK.

In the days following the September 11, 2001, attacks, the FBI came to Shaykh Hamza Yusuf's home in the East Bay to question him about his previous statements while he was simultaneously in Washington, DC, at a meeting of religious leaders with then President George W. Bush. He would later confess that "September 11 was a wake-up call to me. . . . I don't want to contribute to the hate in any shape or form. I now regret in the past being silent about what I have heard in the Islamic discourse and being part of that with my own anger" (O'Sullivan 2001). While many of his critiques of the United States and American society persist, he emphasizes that while we acknowledge our complicities as taxpayers, "We also have to get out of pointing our fingers and blaming the West all the time because that is an empty, disempowering road to go down" (Yusuf 2001). He has thus spent the last two decades on interfaith discourse, religious diplomacy, and establishing Zaytuna College as an Islamic classical liberal arts institution. While Scene 2 conveys some of his thinking around the events of September 11, 2001, it is a selective framing of a historical moment in a longer public life that preceded and follows that watershed event.

Yusuf was recommended to President George W. Bush by a Muslim staffer at the White House to "represent the Muslims," and his teacher, Mauritanian scholar Shaykh Abdullah bin Bayyah, told him that it was incumbent upon him to go.[17] While Yusuf was already gaining prominence among Muslims prior to the September 11 attacks for his da'wa and ta'lim, over the next two decades, he would become a Muslim representative in multiple political venues, ranging from White House consultations and presidential breakfasts to state-sponsored and independent NGO organizations, interfaith initiatives, and global assemblies of Muslim scholars.

In this final section, I examine the relationship between those who oppress, are oppressed, and who witness oppression and how such relations are narrated and transformed in contemporary politics. Questions of freedom, from religious freedom to freedom from oppressive systems, and the struggle between preserving the well-being and dignity of a community and the just and ethical exercise of war, protest, self-defense, rebellion, and militancy become critical points of reasoned and affective engagement that consider the redemptive values of suffering, the responsibility of the witness, and a cosmic order of justice. I approach the immensity of those questions by addressing the crux of what differentiated the reactions to *Wretched of the Earth* above and how these differences relate to Muslim study and struggle.

While Muslims are not responsible for any privilege or blessings they receive based on race, ethnicity, gender, wealth, education, or citizenship, they are responsible *to* those conditions and one another as witnesses to injustice toward restoring just relations. To witness, *shahada* in the Arabic language and as an Islamic concept, is not a passive act of seeing. It is active—from the moment of one's testimony of faith (shahada) to becoming a martyr (*shahid*) in the cause of Allah. As the text of al-Ghazali warns in the scene above, Muslim scholars' spending time with princes and politicians threatens their own souls, which suggests that in order to help oppressors stop their oppression, they must tread carefully so as not to aid this oppression in any way, guarding their own souls and reorienting their focus, time, and energy elsewhere.

Having witnessed "how oppressive some Muslim states are—both for men and for women," Yusuf has often distinguished that, "This is a cultural issue, not an Islamic one. I would rather live as a Muslim in the West than in most of the Muslim countries because I think the way Muslims are allowed to live in the West is closer to the Muslim way. A lot of Muslim immigrants feel the same way, which is why they are here" (O'Sullivan 2001). Yusuf draws attention to secular liberal values of religious freedom, free speech, and freedom of assembly that seem to distinguish the United States and the "Muslim world," while not wholly accounting for the contradictions of de jure versus de facto experiences of freedom as embodied and spiritual. "The Muslim way" Yusuf speaks of may not account for the indignity and harm of experiencing directly or being witness to, complicit in, and benefiting from racism, settler colonialism, poverty, undocumented status, war, occupation, and anti-Muslim racism and Islamophobia. Yusuf's critiques of fellow Muslims, Muslim-majority states, Arab publics, and Black families, which I reference below, have raised the ire of Muslims who are injured directly or indirectly by how his comments and practices may further racism and injustice both domestically and globally, though his intention is to hold everyone, including himself, accountable, as when he said in a late 2001 interview with Sarah Montague on the BBC's *HardTalk*, "I stand condemned. In theological terms, we all fall short of the glory of Allah" (HumbleBeliever 2020).

Black and Indigenous history and experience in these lands and waters and elsewhere demonstrate the contradictions and contingencies of freedom, how the foundations of law and order and freedom of religion are often wielded against the state or withheld by the state toward protecting the property and the power of the few. Black communal conversion to Islam was often a practice toward freedom, a disassociation from the unfreedom of American society, its liberal norms, its nation-statism, and racial capitalism. Both the Honorable Elijah Muhammad and El-Hajj Malik El-Shabazz, however fallibly, witnessed injustice and recognized how Islam required the restoration of just relations and how Islamic knowledge and practice provided the means to do so. While both pursued this Islamic knowledge for their communities, they recognized that knowledge also emerged from and was most clearly heard by the most damned and vulnerable of society.

While Black Muslim communities carried forward Islamic knowledge in their contributions to the discursive tradition, they were later perceived as not practicing authentic forms of Islam because they did not mirror cultural norms in Arab and South Asian Muslim-majority countries. The move toward American cultural citizenship through interfaith endeavors, cultural representation, or political participation was present in Black Muslim communities led by Imam Warith Deen Muhammad, for example, but was typically tempered with ongoing critiques regarding a not-yet-realized ideal of freedom and equality and a knowingness that safety and security sometimes meant staying in and with the Black community but leaving the United States, whether physically or spiritually.

In the 1990s, Zaytuna Institute provided an important space for spiritual edification and renewal to the many young activists who were already working on multiple sociopolitical fronts, from engaging in antiwar and anti-imperial activism to fighting police brutality and campus-based issues (Naber 2012). At the same time, however, as the demographics of Medina by the Bay shifted from a more urban geography to a suburban one oriented around Silicon Valley, narratives of Muslim incorporation and assimilation into the mainstream, mostly promoted by professional-class Arabs, South Asians, West Asians, and figures like Shaykh Hamza Yusuf, via the institutional standing of higher education became more prevalent. While Yusuf spent more than a decade studying Islam in Europe, West Africa, and the Arabian Peninsula, many students would return after just a few weeks or months of study at Islamic universities, madrasas, and with private teachers in the historical Muslim world and would find themselves elevated (or would elevate themselves) in their local communities. While this respect for traditional modes of learning has been essential for the resurgence and survival of Muslim ways of knowing and being, it was often wielded against local ways of knowing and being Muslim, often informed by overseas study as well, that had emerged from the reality of life in the United States. Muslim narratives shifted from understanding white supremacy and racism as foundational to American life and mobilizing Islam for spiritual and material survival to a narrative of Muslim incorporation into a progressive and benevolent United States albeit with growing pains like Islamophobic attacks, Muslim bans, permanent war, surveillance, entrapment, and death. Yusuf mobilized a redemption messaging that exculpated Western imperialism and racism by rendering it to the past and shifted focus on the responsibilities of Muslims themselves. While mobilizing Muslims to become better themselves is essential to Islamic tradition, not attending to the dynamics of power and racial capitalist logics at play often situated Muslim becoming as something that was wholly apart from the material conditions in which people lived, how one's survival and sustenance was tethered to the life possibilities of others.

While earlier criticism of Yusuf was centered on his affiliation with President George W. Bush in the days after the September 11 attacks, recent concerns focus not only on his "relatively uncritical" responses to anti-Muslim rhetoric and policies, but more significantly on his contradictory global affiliations with Arab states. Yusuf and his teacher Shaykh Abdullah bin Bayyah of Mauritania have responded to the hadith about helping oppressors by stopping their oppression, by speaking at the Council of Foreign Relations multiple times and at the United States Institute of Peace (USIP), as well as working for the Forum for Peace in Muslim Societies in the United Arab Emirates. Yusuf's participation with government-supported forums and think tanks like USIP has been both supported and critiqued depending on whether Muslims see participation with the US government as a form of multicultural citizenship, harm reduction, or a betrayal with few positive effects.[18] One concern is that Muslim representational participation (the singular Muslim voice and perspective) endangers Muslims who continue to be subject to surveillance and entrapment, and likewise may undermine collective critiques of the violence of American foreign and domestic policies. His and bin Bayyah's work with the Forum for Peace is seen as particularly contradictory because of the UAE's participation in Saudi attacks on Yemen, which have led to immense suffering and starvation of the Yemeni people.[19] In the last few years (perhaps in response to *nasiha* [advice] from critics and friends), Yusuf has retreated from some of these NGO affiliations, focusing more on interfaith educational institutes and partnerships.

Much of Yusuf's work with NGOs and US-based think tanks continues to coalesce around a conservative politics that is critical of citizen-led efforts to transform the politics of particular countries, espousing a discourse of "obedience to authority" and maintenance of a cosmic hierarchy (Quisay and Parker 2019). Yusuf often collapses armed militancy and nonviolent means of social protest and has increasingly advocated, using Islamic theologies and histories as evidence, for the need to maintain political and social stability even in the face of unjust rulers. Farah El-Sharif writes cogently about how Muslim scholars misplace the Sunni legal edict that advises "obedience to the ruler" in the premodern period, which predates the colonial era and its legacies: "It is seen as disingenuous at best and delegitimizes the Islamic fundamental teaching and noble calling of *Ihsan* in making political legal rulings today . . . this edict muddles the Islamic legal respect for authority, not *absolute power* as it exists today in many modern Arab states, whose rulers now get a 'free pass' (stamped by well-meaning Muslim scholars) to do as they please all in the name of 'preserving security and peace'" (El-Sharif 2018). As Kazmi states, "The situation has less to do with classical Islam, or Islam at all, than with the political economy of Western Arabian Gulf relations" (Kazmi 2017).

Yusuf is wary of the politicization of Islam by "Islamists," while maintaining that his version of Islamic advocacy/diplomacy is somehow not political. In recent years, he and other Zaytuna scholars have moved from a critique of how Islam was hijacked by terrorism on 9/11 to a concern over the hijacking of Islam by Islamists, (Muslim) Marxists, leftists, feminists, and scholars of race and gender. All those who want to address material inequality and enact social transformation on earth are drawn into a broad swath that encompasses what Quisay and Parker refer to as a "Islamist = Marxist = Utopian narrative" (2019). From the Muslim Brotherhood to the movement for Black lives, they are perceived by Yusuf and others as wanting "to tear everything down" and will use violence to do so because as Yusuf says, "They want the ideal world; they want to eliminate evil. . . . This is their goal to create paradise on earth. To create the Marxist dream to create paradise on earth" (Quisay and Parker 2019).

While Yusuf has always recognized the historic injustices of slavery and racism and has often cited El-Hajj Malik El-Shabazz and Muhammad Ali as great Muslim figures, his analysis of how Muslims experience difference and subjugation in the United States often follows a liberal discourse of assimilation and bootstrapism. He often cites the text *How the Irish Became White* (Ignatiev 1995) and his own Irish Catholic roots as a lesson in ethnic assimilation and mainstream acceptance, disregarding that, according to Ignatiev, part of Irish whiteness was built upon an embrace of racism and white supremacy (see also Grewal 2013; Knight 2009; 2013; Hanson 2010; Tourage 2013).

In 2016 at the Reviving the Islamic Spirit Conference in Toronto, Yusuf continued on this line of thought. Evoking his own mother's experiences as an activist during the civil rights movement, Yusuf suggested that the United States has overcome much of its racist history, and he stated that "The United States is probably, in terms of its laws, one of the least racist societies in the world. We have some of the best antidiscriminatory laws on the planet." As El-Hajj Malik El-Shabazz stated decades ago, however, "If birth made you an American, you wouldn't need any legislation, you wouldn't need any amendments to the Constitution. . . . They don't have to pass civil-rights legislation to make a Polack an American" (Malcolm X 1990, 32). What is significant here is not only the difference between de jure and de facto effects of American law, but also the colonial and racial logics of the American legal system, including law enforcement, that are built into its structure and modes of rationalization. Whether one understands this foundational history as a tragic past or as an ongoing structure impacts how individuals interpret "what Islam says" about American law, history, and culture, and what proper responses and strategies for Muslims' survival and salvation should be.

Yusuf argues against Muslims seeing themselves as victims; in his words, self-victimization is both "defeatist" and a "mentality of the powerless. . . .

From a metaphysical perspective, which is always the first and primary perspective of a Muslim, there can be no victims. We believe that all suffering has a redemptive value" (Hanson 2006, 32; see also Quisay and Parker 2019). While the redemptive value of suffering cannot be disputed, Yusuf conflates critiques of white supremacy, imperialism, racial capitalism, Islamophobia, heteropatriarchy, and xenophobia with narratives of victimization that are anything but defeatist, because they often arise out of political struggles that are agentive *and* aim to be redemptive for society as a whole. Similar to his critiques of corruption in Muslim-majority countries, he disregards the significance of struggles for dignity that arise from below, often grounded in a Muslim ethics that aims to assist the oppressor by stopping his oppression.

Amina Wadud's gender jihad and Sherman Jackson's understanding of white supremacy as a form of *shirk* (the greatest sin, taking whiteness as Allah-like) are similarly not claims of victimization but rather efforts to identify and stop injustice and *munkar* (evil), not out of a utopic and materialist vision of justice on earth, but for the sake of the umma and its souls (Wadud 1999; 2006; S. A. Jackson 2005; 2009). In a different, but related context, James Baldwin claims responsibility for the effects of white supremacy: "I didn't drop the [atom] bomb, either. And I never lynched anybody. Yet I am responsible not for what has happened but for what can happen" (Mead and Baldwin 1971, 59; see also Rana 2020). Suffering is not only a test with redemptive value for the one who suffers, but it is also a test of redemptive value for the witness of that suffering and their willingness to suffer with.

At the same 2016 conference, upon being asked by British Indian journalist Mehdi Hasan about Muslim participation in movements against police brutality on behalf of Black and Indigenous people, Yusuf instead pivoted to conservative talking points regarding "black on black crime" and a culture of complaint and victimization.: "A lot of the problems in the United States with the black community being shot by the police. . . . Fifty percent are black on black crime, right? Literally, fifty percent. . . . I just feel like we have so little moral capital at pointing our fingers at other people, and it actually makes me a little sick to my stomach when I see all these people rising up about this anti-, you know, anti this, that, and other white privilege and all these things, and it's like our community is rife with these things, and our religion is so profound."

The following day he clarified his words from the day before and apologized for the harm his comments generated.[20] Yusuf's decontextualizing of communal violence, his perceived refusal to acknowledge contemporary injustices and suggesting that one major problem "is our inability to speak to the Right," before redirecting his comments toward Black moral agency, in which he echoed the 1966 Moynihan Report's claims of black pathology and "troubled" nonpatriarchal family structures, upset many in the community. In also bringing up the racism that exists within the Muslim community, Yusuf equates white supremacist racism with the bigotry of people of color and seemed to belittle the suffering of Black and brown people both in the West and abroad by not situating his criticism within a context of US policies of regime change and permanent war that have resulted in the death and displacement of millions of Muslims in Iraq, Afghanistan, Palestine, and elsewhere.[21]

Black Muslim scholar Ubaydullah Evans responded to Yusuf's comments, which "illustrated a great sincerity but also a painful oblivion to the context of race, power, privilege, and subjugation in which he in particular speaks" by calling upon Yusuf to recognize the ontological fact of whiteness, the entrenched reality of white supremacy, and how Yusuf's embodied experience and effect as a white person, whether he claims it or not, impacts what he understands, how he expresses truth, and how he will be heard (Evans 2016; Grewal 2013; Knight 2009). Evans goes on to discuss how to address the systemic, the individual, and the communal from the Qur'anic perspective, which "holds that every act of human-induced suffering involves three parties: God, the Omnipotent, the oppressor, and the oppressed. Interestingly enough, while the Qur'an consistently addresses the oppressor with the tongue of unsparing accountability, the tongue with which it speaks to the afflicted contains more variance. . . . Quranic pedagogy dictates that people experiencing disgrace also turn toward interiorized evil. . . . in contradistinction to fashionable modes of activism, the Qur'anic paradigm always confronts the existence of corruption and evil as opportunities for introspection and repentance" (Evans 2016). Evans enacts the blues adhan, calling for Black people to "rise up": "If we center white racism when addressing the oppression and subjugation of black people without a complementary discourse in which we center God and the moral agency of black people, we give away all of our self-determination. For if the primary cause of my subjugation is only the pernicious evil of white racism, then the primary source of my redemption can only be the repudiation of that racism. Lamentably, that would mean accepting that the cause of my redemption will be White America's *tawba* (repentance) and not my own. As a self-determining, free black man I can't face that" (Evans 2016). For Hind Makki, a Sudanese Muslim educator, the "controversy" and conversation "must cease to be about whether a thing was misinformed and unintended to harm; the conversation must be about centering the aggrieved and repairing the harm" (Makki 2016).

Evans engages a dual critique toward accountability, while Makki asks us to focus on the question of accountability and repair and to take Black Muslims and others at their word when they speak of injury. Makki and Evans draw our attention to acts of witnessing and how it is not enough to speak of oppressive structures; an epistemology for the next means that with description and critique, we must center and practice accountability and redemption at individual, communal, and structural levels. The partial perspectives offered above demonstrate the Islamic discursive tradition in action and how we need to hold our differences in view as we produce and transmit knowledges, to acknowledge the power differentials and the material conditions that impact which knowledges are upheld and which are subjugated.

The online and offline reactions to Yusuf's comments and his active affiliation with Christian conservatives point to the multiple logics and strategies at play in the ethical political landscape that complicate what striving for justice and survival in the here, now, and next means. Religious freedom is a primary concern for Yusuf, and he believes that the United States and other Western countries are exceptionally tolerant of religious diversity.[22] Yet, I again draw attention to how the state shapes what forms of Islam and other faiths flourish and which are subject to precarity. That Trump's administration, as well as George W. Bush's and Barack Obama's, courted Yusuf (and his students) and not another Muslim leader like the incarcerated Imam Jamil Al-Amin for whom Yusuf had been fundraising in 2001 is a case in point.

Yusuf suggests that "Given the vast power for death and destruction that the human hand now wields, our manifold crises demand wise responses rooted in a real understanding of the sources of those crises: their spiritual, moral, and intellectual foundations. Our problems are not material" (Yusuf 2017). Ultimately, he is correct; our problems are not material from the perspective that there is enough wealth and enough resources to provide shelter, housing, medicine, and education to everyone on the planet. Many decolonial scholars would agree with Yusuf's diagnosis of foundations but would cite the material as symptoms, contexts, and means through which "spiritual, moral, and intellectual foundations" may be transformed. Indeed, crises of scarcity and catastrophe are directly and indirectly man-made and serve as ethical tests.

Yusuf conflates many groups without disaggregating their beliefs, concerns, and strategies and negates the structural forces that shape the

contours of spiritual, moral, and intellectual possibility. Study and struggle situated from the position of the oppressed are seen to be too closely
aligned with Marxist materialist analyses that seek justice on earth at the
expense of submitting to Allah's will more broadly. Seeking justice on earth
is viewed as a utopic project that undermines a theology and cosmology
of divine justice and order, while those who respond to the blues adhan
recognize seeking justice on earth as a daily practice that is a necessary part
of submitting to divine justice.

The Prophet Muhammad, as an example for Muslim conceptions of humanity, offers that the oppressed and oppressors are our "brothers," our kin
to whom we have a responsibility. The hadith that binds oppressors, the
oppressed, and those who witness (and thereby become participants in)
the oppression undoes any notion of subhumanness while also indicating
how we are all related and responsible for one another. At the same time,
the Qur'an differentiates between those who believe and those who disbe-
lieve, those whose hearts are hard, and those who cannot see or hear the
truth. Depending on one's station in life, one has a different responsibility
to those who oppress.

In Fanon's conclusion to *The Wretched of the Earth,* he condemns the
hypocrisy of European humanism and its theological foundations:

> Leave this Europe where they are never done talking of Man, yet murder
> men everywhere they find them, at the corner of every one of their own
> streets, in all the corners of the globe. For centuries they have stifled
> almost the whole of humanity in the name of a so-called spiritual expe-
> rience. Look at them today swaying between atomic and spiritual Dis-
> integration. . . . That same Europe where they were never done talking
> of Man, and where they never stopped proclaiming that they were only
> anxious for the welfare of Man: today we know with what sufferings
> humanity has paid for every one of their triumphs of the mind. (310–11)

Rather than imitate or try to "catch up" to Europe, Fanon suggests
that the Third World start "a new history of Man," which will remember
the good that Europe has offered, but also "not forget Europe's crimes, of
which the most horrible was committed in the heart of man, and consisted
of the pathological tearing apart of his functions and the crumbling away
of his unity" (315). Fanon advocates for something new (and ancient) that
he alludes to earlier when he speaks of Algerians in the face of torture and
in the anticolonial struggle: "The fighting Algerian has an unusual manner
of fighting and dying, and no reference to Islam or to Paradise can explain

that generous dedication of self when there is question of defending his people or shielding his brothers . . . here we find again that very ancient law which forbids any element whatsoever to remain unmoved when the nation has begun to march, when man affirms and claims at the same time his limitless humanity" (295–96).

Fanon dismisses Islam and Paradise too quickly, for conversion to Islam was often that very affirmation and claim for a "limitless humanity." Fanon misses the transformative effect Islam had in reshaping and sustaining human relations from the seventh century onward, giving a jihad (struggle) of the self and jihad in defense of the community meaning that we also witness in the rebellions and marronage of enslaved African Muslims in the Americas; the sumud and ongoing struggle of the Palestinians; the love and lives of El-Hajj Malik, Hajja Betty, and their grandson Malik Shabazz; and the survival of hearts in the face of sanctions in Iraq and Iran. In his analysis of the psychiatric effects of colonization on both the colonized and the colonizer, Fanon draws attention not only to the armed struggle but also to acts of suffering and protection (Fanon 2004, 254–60). These acts are instructive for demonstrating the expansive capacity of human nature and the ways that small and large acts offer alternative logics for how to survive and transform unjust conditions. Fanon inadvertently echoes the Qur'an and centuries of Islamic scholarship regarding "the heart of man," how to preserve, protect, and attend to it in the face of man's forgetting, arrogance, and weakness. This "generous dedication of self" and a "limitless humanity" that offers a "new history of Man" may be universal, but in Algeria it is given meaning as an Islamic poetics, a Muslim way of knowing and being through the centuries, even if some of the Algerians were Jewish, Christian, or were now Communists. It is something that emerges in the silence with which Algerians defeat their torturers, and in their defense and shielding of one another—they know there is more to the world than themselves and the power of men.

For Hamza Yusuf, "The loss of state power, military might, sovereignty, and control is not the end of Islam but a new beginning. It may be the end of political Islam, but it surely portends the resurgence of spiritual Islam. The Prophet Muhammad, peace be upon him, said, 'Islam began as an alien thing, and it will return as an alien thing, so blessed are the strangers.' 'Who are the strangers?' he was asked. 'They are those who rectify my path after people have corrupted it'" (Yusuf 2012, 24). For Yusuf, "the Muslim countries that claim to have Islamic governance happen to be the most corrupt countries in the Muslim world" (Yusuf 2012, 24). Corruption is ethical failure of individuals, but also material and structural at the communal level. Yusuf does not specify which countries he means, but it is important to again consider the material realities—the context and process—of how, for example, Saudi Arabia's corruption and proxy war against Iran is enabled by American support; how the Taliban's ascent came through US support for the mujahidin in the 1980s; how ISIS similarly emerged from the conditions created by the 2003 US-led invasion and war in Iraq; and how corruption and political suppression in Iran is likewise impacted by the pressure put on the country by American sanctions and soft power, and a longer history that includes the CIA-led coup that overthrew Iran's democratically elected prime minister Mohammad Mossadegh in 1953.

Evans and Makki draw our attention to the need for dual critique, accountability to harm and injury that Muslims commit among themselves. While we raise issues of ethics and structure at the scales of the heart, local, and world systems, I also understand Yusuf's call for a spiritual resurgence to battle a world of corrupt and corrupting souls. Yusuf learned from the hate in his own heart that to reorient oneself toward tawhid requires a kind of labor that requires a reflection and reorientation of what and whom one loves.

As we consider a resurgence of spiritual Islam, we must consistently account for how theology and spirituality can simultaneously be wielded in white supremacist and "conquistador" ways (in both the "new" and "old" worlds), as well as in liberatory and abolitionist ways (King 2019). When Muslims in Medina by the Bay have felt betrayed or harmed by their teachers and institutions, they have had to remind themselves that their teachers are fallible and it is the knowledge that remains and matters. I witnessed and experienced myself innumerable efforts to protect and help scholars who injured, oppressed, and caused harm to oneself and others, because of the intimate and intimate yet distant relationships that were created through seeking and transmitting Islamic knowledge. Countless Muslims—though not all—who populate these pages would never wish ill upon individuals from whom they had learned something, no matter how something they had said or done later harmed them or others; there are also many whose relationships to Islam or the Muslim community have been diminished and broken because of the moral, physical, and spiritual injuries they have suffered at the hands of religious authorities or their most intimate relations. Transformative and divine justice, as well as the status of and intimacy with the alien, stranger, wretched, and damned may be ways forward that account for our grounded relationalities and responsibilities to one another.

The dynamic tension between respecting those who hold knowledge and not mistaking the teacher for the knowledge itself is often misunderstood. As Haroon, the audiovisual coordinator of Zaytuna College always says, "I'm here for the message, not the personalities," meaning his decades-long commitment to working at Zaytuna Institute and then the college was not about individual scholars but rather about the knowledge they were transmitting and the need for more people to access and gain that knowledge. Adab is not just about showing and treating scholars with respect; it is also about restoring just relations, which can also mean critical engagement and radical forms of love, abundance, and accountability. If mercy and compassion, as well as benefit of doubt, could be extended to the aliens and damned of the community—its margins, its harmed, and beyond—and not just esteemed scholars, that would demonstrate that the community is indeed on the Prophetic path.

> And they said to me, dwell at the doors of the Sultans:
> "You will receive enriching bounties every now and then."
> And I said: Allah alone suffices me and I am content with Him.
> I only covet knowledge and my Deen.
> I plead not nor fear except my King
> Because only He Almighty can enrich me and save me
> I refer my conditions to those who were defenseless
> At the altar of themselves, in the manner of the Wretched Lowly ones.
>
> —SHAYKH AHMADOU BAMBA MBACKE (d. 1927)[23]

IN THE WAY

(Toward a Conclusion/Opening)

Love us when we are lazy, love us when we are poor . . . love us high as kites,
unemployed, joyriding, time-wasting, failing at school, love us filthy . . .
love us silent, unapologizing sometimes violent . . . when we are wretched,
suicidal, naked, and contributing nothing. Love us then. —SUHAIYMAH
MANZOOR-KHAN

Medina by the Bay is written from a wayfaring that is conflicted and hope-
ful. You are invited/called to join. It is difficult because I have placed this
work on a precipice in which multiple visions for spiritual and material
survival come together, but may also diverge as we move forward. Muslims
can be liberated from oppression, but we/they do not often fit into other
people's or one another's visions for liberation. Pious ones get *in the way* of
feeling "free," while "the pious" may police each other out of sacred space.
At the same time that Muslims are viewed as victims, our/their deaths are
neither grievable nor recognized in the calculus of extermination—neither
grievable nor accounted for nor thought of, epistemologically.

In our contemporary context, one in which "terror has come to live with
and in us," we must seek a politics, following Asma Abbas, "premised on
shedding the aesthetic and sensual pathologies that are the gift of colonialism, liberalism, and capitalism" (Abbas 2014, 503–4). For Abbas, there
operate two narratives of our contemporary condition in which there is
much suffering. The first is that people are desensitized to this suffering,
and the second is that "we operate on a declared consensus that we have

nothing to do with it" because we oppose these "bad things" morally, logically, and practically (508). Such framings normalize "the morality and the structures of sensibility and affect that enable this condition" and produce an "*inability* to suffer; we are saturated with terror, which ends up installing itself as a discontinuous emotional form, a reality separate from other pathos, sealed from sentiments that perhaps were once known to us or available to us" (508). To oppose what colonialism, capitalism, and liberalism have done (to us) in not only material terms, but also the sensorial and affective terms of the heart, we must reconstruct our relational logics and forms through "acts of (and in) abundance that defy those in power and do not serve their purposes. These acts of abundance are acts of love and acts of suffering that defy the imposed logics of the kinds of intimacy, knowledge, and premises that the structure wants from us; they are exceptions to the prescribed modes and unfoldings of love and suffering that do not fit within a liberal utilitarian calculus" (Abbas 2014, 511).

How do we love differently and with abundance? What do we need to *stop* loving in order to defy imposed logics, to enhance our ability to suffer with and return to ways of knowing and being that were once known or available to us? This book is written from love, and multiple forms of fear, the greatest being one of God-consciousness or a lack thereof. Fear that my *khushu'* and *taqwa*, let alone *naql* and *'aql*, were not up to the task. The Black blues singer/composer Nina Simone once spoke of what freedom was for her: "it's just a feeling . . . I've had a couple of times on stage when I really felt free, and that's something else, that's really SOMETHING ELSE . . . no fear, I mean really, no fear . . . a new way of seeing" (Gold 1970). That fear and freedom are so intimately tied, that a true fear of Allah makes fear of any earthly calamity evanesce like vapor, while in the act of creativity one reaches toward that sublimity of *al-ghayb*, the unknown. Something like the blues (adhan), the hijra to Medina, these cries of a new society, a new people, being born.

The Bay Area as Medina, a place perhaps more than anywhere else in the United States, where Muslims are free to imagine a new society (assuming they can afford to live there), is the site from which Yusuf, Shakir, and others seek to support "a spiritual and moral renaissance in the Muslim world" (Yusuf 2012). While the religion has been corrupted, there are also aliens and strangers who continue to rectify it in their everyday struggles with Allah, themselves, and one another. Muslims in the Bay Area and beyond draw on multiple subjugated histories and experiences, taking on the task proposed by M. Jacqui Alexander "of configuring new ways of being and knowing and to plot the different metaphysics that are needed to move away from living alterity premised in difference to living intersubjectivity premised in relationality and solidarity" (2005, 7–8). The contingencies of such future possibilities and limits reside in a grounded orientation toward the discursive tradition of Islam and the material realities of everyday life, a multidirectional critique and theoretical inspiration.

What is offered by *Medina by the Bay* is a local specificity, an examination of the interplay between geopolitics, epistemes, and the ethical-political. Particular forms of Islam emerge from this place and the particular bodies that inhabit it, demonstrating the contingencies of how discourse and tradition are enacted and produced. Zaytuna College is free to transmit Islam as a liberal arts college, while other forms of Islamic knowledge transmission are subject to state surveillance and harassment, although Zaytuna Institute was also under surveillance and the college might still be (Reitman 2021). At the same time, Zaytuna is also subject to secular liberal and Muslim expectations of gender parity in its faculty and student body and questioned about its potential acceptance and treatment of LGBTQIA2S+ and other Muslim minority students. While many, including Zaytuna College founders, assume that queer or queering, Shia, Ismaili, Zaidi, or Ahmadi Muslims would not want to attend Zaytuna College, the opposite is actually true. It is the dissonance between and questions about their faith, umma ideals, dispositions, desires, and senses of social justice and orthodoxy that may bring them closer to the formal study of Islam. A nonnormative gender or sexual orientation and an orientation toward Allah and community are not mutually exclusive, and it is often the experience of being marginalized, damned, or harmed that best attunes particular Muslims toward the *masakin* (needy), the wretched of society.

Identity politics is one thing, but there is also a more expansive metaphysics at stake. Saba Mahmood critically reminds us that there are those for whom sexual and gender liberation are not the driving teleologies of their ethical lives (Mahmood 2005). This does not mean that Muslims do not want to live in dignity in the fullest expressions of themselves; and this does not mean that Muslims who cause harm in their own communities can claim theological innocence from that harm. Many religious communities continue to refuse to acknowledge how racism, racism and heterosexism find shelter in religious orthodoxy. Practices of containment and silencing through authoritative and moralizing structures coexist with everyday practices of making difference livable and imagining forms of relationality anew. The Islamic tradition, both textual and lived, has held spaces of possibility for us to imagine gender and sexuality differently from what we've inherited from colonialism (El-Rouayheb 2005; Najmabadi 2005; 2014; Babayan and Najmabadi 2008; Kugle 2010; 2013; Wadud 1999; 2013). I witnessed this in the Bay Area and I hear about it from Muslims in schools, mosques, and prisons who foreground compassion and doubt over punishment, banishment, and certainty of who someone is, what someone has done or will do, and what Allah wants or expects (Rabb 2014). I also see it foregrounded in the ways that individuals submit to Islam as it has been transmitted to them because it literally saved their lives.

While institutional religion contributes to the stabilizing and disciplining of societies, whether through upholding notions of the nuclear family and gender norms or through allegiances with those in political and economic power, these same institutions have also contributed significant modes of rebellion, social transformation, and critique—as sites of organization, infrastructures of feeling, sources of spiritual and material renewal and support, and theorists and theologians of liberation for this life and/or the next.

Muslim presences, poetics, and politics traverse time and space, producing alternative rhythms and geographies; as the blues adhan bends notes so do prayers bend time and moral arcs. The blues adhan requires us to revisit the histories of slavery, colonialism, and the development of "Man" as a biopolitical and socioeconomic figure as it was established in the fifteenth century (Wynter 2003). The blues adhan also recalls histories of marronage and refuge, study and struggle toward ensuring survival and salvation in this world and the next. The prayers and everyday efforts of enslaved African Muslims in the Americas to maintain Muslim practices of fasting, charity, *dhikr* (remembrance of Allah), and Qur'anic recitation constituted a significant mode of struggle and survival under oppressive conditions that were mobilized in conjunction with rebellion, subterfuge, escape, and marronage (Diouf 1998; Gomez 2005). This shared legacy and kinship by faith coheres Muslims whose multiracial histories and strategies converge in and emerge from the Bay.

An Islamic poetics of the everyday provides a "language in which people thought about and fashioned their experience of the self and in which they spoke to each other about the individual and collective self . . . a language that expresses, not merely a theoretical tension between legal and non-legal norms—but the very ethos of a lived reality comprising a plurality of evidently contradictory meanings in life" (Shahab Ahmed 2017, 36). It is this poetics of ambiguity and ambivalence in conjunction with the social foundation of religion that endures despite the colonialities of thought, being,

truth, and freedom that saturate our everyday lives and logics. Similarly,
how do we understand the margins and the outside as spaces of possibility that grow out of the tension and friction with normative orthodoxies whether religious or secular (Trinh 1991; 1989; hooks 2000; Hidayatullah 2014; Wadud 2006), while also reminding ourselves "of the prolific scale and nature of the *contradictory normative claims* . . . about *what is Islam*" that have been made across fourteen hundred years of Muslim history (Shahab Ahmed 2017, 73)? We benefit from, create beauty out of, and find freedom in limits and constraint; we live and (re)produce at points of friction and dialectical contradiction.

To engage Muslims as companions and to accompany them toward liberation involves articulating a relationality and solidarity—a different metaphysics—that incorporates (or not) a myriad of other desires, ethics, beliefs, and relations of power that may envision justice differently. While I see and attempt to locate Medina by the Bay—a mapping, an archaeology, a potentiality—I also recognize the inherent contradiction of seeking autonomy and building a new society on stolen land, literally enriched by the blood of those killed, worked, tortured, diminished, and denied. I am indebted and implicated, struggling to keep my eyes wide open (don't sleep!) against any claim of innocence I and my kin may be tempted to hide behind.

Peter Nelson identifies as "Coast Miwok" to "fit into the anthropological literature on our culture" and cautions me as I finish writing this book (Nelson 2021, 469). He writes of how anthropologists wrote the extinction of his and other Californian Indian peoples once they couldn't "learn" anything from them, but also how California Indian people are "still here" producing scholarship, "recrafting the story and making space for Indigenous futures . . . unnaming and reassigning value to reflect who we are today" (Nelson 2021, 471; Akins and Bauer 2021). His uncle initially responds to his queries about "old times" by presenting him with a published ethnography and saying, "Well, I don't know. Everything you want to know is probably in here already" (Nelson 2021, 472). Nelson sees this as an effect of anthropology, how anthropology has "laid claim to our intellectual territory . . . stolen our authority to tell our own story, even in our most intimate spaces" (Nelson 2021, 472). While this book, this creative event, emerged from my own attempt to ask questions about old times and what is happening right now, I also know that it is not "everything you want to know" or need to know for that matter.

As the first generation of my family from elsewhere ages and the second generation takes on the role of elders, and likewise as our movement elders of the 1960s–1970s pass on, I have been thinking a lot about what will be transmitted, what will be forgotten and lost, and what will need to be (re) invented and retold. I have always been hailed by Black and blues ways of knowing and being because they emerge from ruptures from a geography, its knowledges, and its lifeways. While the violence and conditions of mobility are not the same nor are they to be compared or analogized, I have consistently turned to these histories and cultures, answering their calls as a form of anticipation of and recognition of the ruptures of language and culture, ways of knowing and being of my ancestors on these lands and across waters and continents. I look to and make relation with those violently uprooted and those who were violently removed, who have survived and who have left knowledge or are actively producing knowledge.

Hajja Rasheeda became another mother, and I another daughter in our last shared years in the world. I continue to learn from and act according to her notions of sacrifice and service, discipline and devotion, and how she consistently reevaluated and strove for new strategies for survival, living, and dying with dignity, style, and grace. From the mid-1970s, Islam became an important modality through which she articulated her social, political, and spiritual commitments. The contradictions of political life and the violence of the state in its efforts to quell Black and Third World insurgencies impacted her life deeply. She continued to live with the traumas of the 1970s and the ongoing decades in which many of her Black Panther and other insurgent kin were incarcerated by continuing to support political prisoners and by shoring up her family and faith as a critical part of the infrastructure of feeling of Medina by the Bay.

It was only in reflecting on her passing and deciding to include her life into my ethnography that I came to understand the lessons that she was imparting to me throughout my time with her. She told me stories about her younger brother, whose mental health issues contributed to his bouts with being unhoused, and how his experiences taught her to always have small bills on her to give to anyone who asked. She also took me along to feed the unsheltered and unhoused in Berkeley, simply setting up a table where we created a two-person assembly line for making sandwiches and lunch bags. These were everyday acts of *sadaqa*, which is commonly (and I think mistakenly) translated as charity, but carries the same root as words relating to trust, friendship, compassion, and belief. These quotidian acts were devotional, political, and pedagogical and worked in tandem with the iterative work she also did toward building institutions like schools, mosques, and prisoner support networks. She also reminded, and perhaps admonished, me that she and her comrades made choices about their futures: they could have gone on to get PhDs, becoming part of the academic establishment, but instead they took risks and made sacrifices fighting for and staying in their communities.

Participating in sadaqa, from giving food to risking one's own sense of security in political struggle, exemplifies the work of "shedding the aesthetic and sensual pathologies" that we have inherited from colonialism, liberalism, and capitalism (Abbas 2014, 504). As Abbas states, "it is through loving, desiring, and being attached that one suffers with and for another, becomes available to another as an ethical-political subject, and musters the energy to sustain or interrupt reality" (Abbas 2014, 514). In my time with Hajja Rasheeda, beyond those specific lessons above, she offered me "a different kind of vision of yourself that you experience in a truly ethical encounter, a kind of co-witnessing that enables people not only to mirror back pain but to also implicate one another in our survival" (King 2019, xi). Part of what bound Hajja Rasheeda and me were the ways our lives intertwined decades apart, that we grew up in adjacent neighborhoods in the City and attended San Francisco Catholic schools. Through our common geographies, our common passions, and then our common faith we saw and felt seen by each other, while we also realized, as Tiffany Lethabo King asserts, "that 'innocence' does not exist within the lifeways of this hemisphere or the modern world. The endeavor of surviving under conditions of conquest is never clean" (King 2019, xi). Though I was paying attention, I didn't see things that I would come to see later, and there will also be things I will not know or understand, nor should. And I lament, though I understand, all the private and clandestine things Rasheeda took with her.

In Arabic, there are two verb forms that deal specifically with engaging in action with others; the third form is typically transitive, while the sixth form is intransitive. These forms account for relationality and mutuality, singling out actions that happen mutually between and with people. While I bring multiple ways of knowing and being together, I also consider what it means to claim responsibility, debt, and betrayal, toward an accounting of how we harm one another whether directly or indirectly. I am a different person now. By thinking multiple traditions and genealogies of wisdom, theories, and theologies together, I am traveling on intentionally difficult terrain toward undoing the theoretical and material grounds on which I stand. Everyone in this book, everyone reading this book, is perhaps a different person now. We are tired, and we have perhaps been most unjust to

IN THE WAY (TOWARD A CONCLUSION/OPENING)

ourselves, meaning we cannot offer justice to others. I hope that this book has illuminated some of what we learn when Muslim ways of knowing and being, Muslim suffering and culpability, are read together and sought for lessons and strategies to survive the long end of times. Admitting culpability and responsibility only works toward collective futures when it is accompanied by a radical form of mercy and compassion, mercy and compassion being the guiding principles of Islam and the primary identifiers of Allah, al-Rahman, al-Raheem (the Most Beneficent and Merciful) with whom I begin and end.

NOTES

INTRODUCTION

1 Masoud is named for my paternal uncle Masoud Kashani (1951–1975), who passed away from injuries sustained in a car accident in San Francisco. He was the youngest son in a family of four brothers and two sisters and was the first in my family to be buried in the soil of the Americas. My father told me about the scramble to find a knowledgeable (Iranian/Shia) Muslim who could administer the rites of *janaza* (funeral absolutions and prayers). In a small section of Muslims buried in a cemetery in Colma, California, he lays next to a young Palestinian man who had passed away the year before.

   Most of my Bay Area interlocutors are given pseudonyms, with the exception of public figures like prominent Islamic scholars, leaders, and institutions. The names I give my beloved interlocutors include practices of remembrance, a making present ("co-presence"), a selection of ancestors and lineages that shape the contours of Medina by the Bay (Jesús 2015). In most cases I do not give schools and other Muslim institutions pseudonyms because they are public-facing institutions that are quite distinct and merit a historical account of their significance; in some cases, they have had extensive media coverage, and as many Muslims would tell you, the FBI already knows about them and are probably in attendance.

2 (Allah is Great/er [4 times]/I bear witness that there is no Allah but Allah [2 times], I bear witness that Muhammad is the Messenger of Allah [2 times]/Come to salah (ritual prayer) [2 times]/ Come to success [2 times]/ Allah is Great/er [2 times]/ There is no Allah but Allah [1 time or 2 times]). This is a translation of the traditional Sunni adhan that was recorded and precedes the Friday afternoon congregational prayer, jumuʻa.

3 The Cham are an ethnic group and religious minority of Southeast Asia, predominantly in Vietnam and Cambodia. A large Cham refugee population arrived in the Seattle area in the late 1970s where they established a refugee center, mosque, and neighborhood.

4 The accompanying videos of the first three scenes can be found on www
.maryamkashani.com under the "Medina by the Bay" project. They invite
a "multimodal" engagement with Medina by the Bay (Collins, Durington,
and Gill 2017).

5 Saba is named for Saba Mahmood (1961–2018), the brilliant and generous anthropologist and human being whose queries into and concerns for
how we live with one another deeply inform these pages.

6 Fatemeh is named for my Iranian grandmother whose death during my
father's youth precipitated the movement of my father's family from
Iran to the United States prior to the Islamic Revolution in 1979. United
States influence and interference in Iran throughout the twentieth
century also impacted when and how my family arrived and stayed in the
Bay Area.

7 Fatemeh actively participated in group interviews, however.

8 I discuss my camera—which, following a Prophetic practice of naming
things, I named "Nur"—in more detail in chapter 4.

9 Iranians, Iraqis, and Palestinians include Jews, Christians, Zoroastrians,
atheists, Marxists, and so forth, but the sociocultural influences of Islam
in combination with Indigenous and adopted traditions are important to
consider.

10 I bring Indigenous and Black feminisms, as well as critical theories and
theologies from Islamic studies, Black Radical tradition, anthropology,
decolonial and ethnic studies, and visual studies together in ways that
may make people of faith and people of critical theory (not mutually
exclusive) uncomfortable, but that for me makes for an essential conversation toward our mutual survival, sustenance, and reproduction.

11 I do not offer a comprehensive account of "everything"; I share and
juxtapose scenes of Medina by the Bay as possible portals, while also
lamenting what remains unspoken, but not unthought. I primarily focus
on Sunni communities because my research snowballed from Zaytuna
College as a starting point, though Shi'i and other Muslim spaces and
individuals are made present intermittently.

12 The AH stands for "After Hijra." The Islamic calendar actually begins with
the Prophet Muhammad's hijra to Medina, marking the place and time of
an Islamic society being born.

13 "Din" (pronounced and spelled throughout this text as "deen") is often
translated as religion, so "medina" is a place where din happens. In classical and formal Arabic (Fusha), most words build out from a three- or four-
letter base. There are ten grammatical forms that this base builds off to
convey different meanings and relationships. I refer to these constructions
throughout the text because they demonstrate the paucity of translation as
Arabic words are imbedded in oceanic webs of grammatical meaning. The
Arabic root D-A(y)-n refers to a myriad of words related to obedience,
submission, possession, debt, credit, and requital. Medina thus means

city, a place that is "so called because [it] had, or [is] held, in possession, or under authority" (Lane and Lane-Poole 1968, vol. 3, 942–45).

14 In the eighth and ninth centuries, hadith are collected and evaluated, contributing to the "Islamic tradition" as part of a transmitted corpus and field of knowledge, but initially the Prophet's speech and actions marked a shift from or commentary on established practices (Hodgson 1974; J. A. C. Brown 2009a).

15 I discuss adab in more detail below. In modern usage it refers to good manners, etiquette, comportment, belles-lettres, literature, or culture. For Zahrah and others in the Zaytuna milieu, adab connotes an embodied, cultivated, and cognitive sense of manners and comportment that recognizes and acknowledges forms of authority, hierarchy, capacity, potential, and rank, as well as ethical decency, justice, mutual respect, piety, and God-consciousness. Because of the multifaceted nature of the word both in Arabic and in translation, it is in the discursive utterances and iterations of "adab" in the everyday around which a type of collective meaning is understood and contested.

16 I use "American Muslim" as a term that denotes location, citizenship-status, (English) language, and cultural positioning in the particular geography and cultural milieu of the United States vis-à-vis a global community of Muslims. I qualify the term because it assumes a tacit acceptance of the modifier "American," and makes little space for the ambivalence Muslims may feel toward the sociopolitical construction and contestation of the United States and dominant American cultural myths and values (see also Chan-Malik et al. 2014).

17 Shakir participated in activism against South African apartheid and continues to speak on many social justice issues, and Bazian was well known as a student organizer, especially on issues related to Palestine and American empire. While Shakir and Bazian's political participation has been more grassroots and community-based, Yusuf's recent political interventions have been oriented toward nongovernmental organizations, think tanks, advising presidents and state leaders, and, of course, Zaytuna College and its evolving programs of publications and public events.

18 I spent eighteen months in and around Zaytuna College and Bay Area Muslim communities from 2010 to 2012. I attended classes; faculty, staff, and student meetings; extracurricular and devotional activities; and congregational prayers, classes, and events at mosques and other spaces. I also visited some students and their families at their homes in the Midwest and on the East Coast. I returned to the Bay at least once a year from 2013 to 2021 and was in communication with Zaytuna graduates, faculty, staff, and community members as they moved or traveled in and out of the Bay Area. My dissertation, "Seekers of Sacred Knowledge: Zaytuna College and the Education of American Muslims," is more focused on Zaytuna College (Kashani 2014).

19 Throughout *Medina by the Bay* and following my interlocutors, I use "Muslim," "(Black) Muslim," "Black Muslim," or "African American Muslim" depending on context and meaning to signify a set of individuals interpellated and self-identified as Muslim and Black and/or African diasporic or descended. Racial/ethnic and nation-state descriptors like "Black" or "American" often delimit and oversimplify complex processes of self and communal identification that refuse processes of racialization and the allegiances of citizenship these terms connote. These same terms are also used by Muslims sincerely and strategically to connote expansive affiliations and attachments that comingle with "Muslim" in ways that can be impossible and undesirable to disentangle. My unwieldy uses of Black Muslim or (Black) Muslim draw attention to this complexity and occur in places where Blackness and Muslimness are deeply interconnected as embodied experiences, epistemologies, and ontologies that shape Medina by the Bay. These may be spaces constituted wholly or predominantly by Black Muslims or that are Black-led spaces with multiracial participation. "(Black) Muslim" attends to the ways that non-Black Muslims, scholars of religion, media, and representatives of the US nation-state attempt to discredit and deauthorize Muslim communities that are predominantly Black by labeling them as "Black Muslim" (Lincoln 1961) or by not including Black people and experiences in representations of Islam and Muslims. This continues to be especially relevant in court cases regarding the religious rights of the incarcerated and historically to cases of conscientious objection and citizenship (Felber 2020). A recent reclaiming of the term "Black Muslim" makes visible the particular genealogies of how Blackness and Islam are co-constitutive and productive (Abdul Khabeer 2016). Black Muslims in the United States also include those who have descended, like El-Hajj Malik El-Shabazz, from enslaved Africans in the Caribbean whose descendants immigrated to the United States.

20 El- or Al-Hajj is an honorific title given to Muslims who have performed the obligatory pilgrimage (Hajj) to Mecca at least once in their lifetime. I use El-Hajj for Shabazz because that is what is on his grave, while I use al-Hajj for Muhammad Ali in accordance with the system of transliteration I am using.

21 The anthropology of Islam has been dominated by the study of majority-Muslim settings where relations with the discursive tradition as a textual corpus shape articulations of piety, modernity, ambivalence, failure, genealogy, and the state (Mahmood 2005; Hirschkind 2012; Deeb 2006; Göle 1996; N. A. Khan 2012; Schielke 2015; Ho 2006; Messick 1993; Varzi 2006; Mittermaier 2011; Moll 2010; Agrama 2012; Larkin 2008a; Deeb and Winegar 2012). The study of Islam in Muslim-minority settings, or sectarian settings as in the work of Deeb and Harb (2013), discusses how Muslim subjectivities are likewise shaped by secularisms, Western feminisms, and racialization (Fernando 2014; Fadil 2009; Jouili 2015;

Bowen 2011; 2016; Mir 2016; A. Khan 2004; Rouse 2004; Chan-Malik
et al. 2014). Research on the urban and suburban geographies of California have weighed more heavily on Southern California, where work on regional racialization and multiracial spaces, solidarities, and movements has built upon and complicated earlier research on ethnic enclaves, racialized geographies, urban/suburban divides, and assimilation and aspirational whiteness (Pulido 2006; Pulido, Barraclough, and Cheng 2012; Banks et al. 2012; Davis 2006). Wendy Cheng draws attention to the specificity of place in racial formation processes, "in which locally accepted racial orders and hierarchies complicate and sometimes challenge hegemonic ideologies and facile notions of race" (Cheng 2013, 10).

22 Anthropologists and scholars of education have moved this framework forward over the last two decades, building upon fieldwork that began before 9/11, but that was often informed by the intensification of Muslim and non-Muslim racialization in its aftermath (Mamdani 2004; J. A. Karim 2009; Maira 2009; Abdullah 2010; Rana 2011; N. C. Naber 2012; Z. A. Grewal 2013; Abdul Khabeer 2016; Corbett 2016; Maira 2016; A. I. Ali 2016; Rana 2017b; Auston 2017; Daulatzai and Rana 2018; Kashani 2018a; Li 2020; Perkins 2021). The scaffolding of such arguments also draws upon the interventions of Sherene Razack and Khaled Baydoun in legal studies; Yvonne Haddad, Julianne Hammer, Omid Safi, Faisal Devji, Edward Curtis IV, and Sherman Jackson in religious and Islamic studies; Karen Leonard, Louise Cainker, Sylvia Chan-Malik, Sohail Daulatzai, Hisham Aidi, Jasbir Puar, Evelyn Alsultany, Arun Kundnani, Mustafa Bayoumi, Keith Feldman, Alex Lubin, Ronak Kapadia, and Deepa Kumar; and the scholar-activisms of Rabab Abdulhadi and Hatem Bazian, and the "Islamophobia Is Racism" Syllabus collective.

23 Emblematic of this debate were a set of essays by Nadia Fadil, Mayanthi Fernando, Lara Deeb, and Samuli Schielke in *HAU: Journal of Ethnographic Theory* 5, no. 2 (2015) responding to prepositions of "too much Islam" set forward in Schielke 2010; Schielke and Debevec 2012.

24 I am the daughter of an Iranian father and Japanese mother who was born and raised in the City (San Francisco), who came of age in the East Bay, Berkeley, and the Town (Oakland), and whose kin are dispersed throughout the City, the South, East, and North Bays. Iyko Day describes how the stereotypes of "yellow peril" and the "model minority" complement each other in an ongoing settler colonial capitalism and racialization of Asians "in which economic efficiency is the basis for exclusion or assimilation" (Day 2016, 7), while Dean Saranillio explains from the Hawaiian context that "while migration in and of itself does not equate to colonialism, migration to a settler colonial space, where Native lands and resources are under political, ecological, and spiritual contestation, means the political agency of immigrant communities can bolster a colonial system initiated by White settlers" (Saranillio 2013, 286). When

Savannah Shange writes about the Sucka Free City as a "progressive dystopia," I feel it . . . home is hard, but folks keep striving (Shange 2019b).

25 The founders of Zaytuna College are well-known Muslim figures who arouse both ardent admiration and trenchant critique. For more detailed examination of Shaykh Hamza Yusuf, see Kugle 2006; Knight, 2009; Z. A. Grewal 2013; Quisay and Parker 2019; al-Azami 2019, 2021; forthcoming work from Quisay; and Yusuf's own writings, audiovisual recordings, and interviews. On Hatem Bazian see Naber 2012 and his own writings and videos; Bazian has also been the subject of multiple Islamophobic and Zionist attacks because of his activism and writing on issues related to Palestinian liberation and Islamophobia. Imam Zaid Shakir has published numerous books and articles, and many of his audiovisual recordings are also in circulation.

26 I use the pronoun "we" throughout the text to enact a relationality oriented toward collective survival. It connects the Muslims of the Bay Area to my readers and to myself. The "we" is a point of struggle and contention that implicates us in one another's lives and deaths (and afterlives!).

27 Some who enter Islam call themselves reverts instead of converts in recognition of the Islamic belief that we are all born Muslim. For some Black Muslims, there is also a sense of reverting back to Islam, which was a faith that many Africans practiced prior to their kidnapping to the Americas.

28 The Islamic "discursive tradition" also includes biographies, memoirs, poetry, commentaries, architecture and artworks, and the breadth and diversity of Muslim life from the seventh century onward (T. Asad 1986; Shahab Ahmed 2017).

29 Some state that this disavowal began as early as immediately after the death of the Prophet Muhammad; others would suggest that the murders of the Prophet's family, including of his grandsons Hasan and Husayn at Karbala, mark a critical disruption of the revolutionary impulse of Islam (Madelung 1997). The Qur'an anticipates and warns about the wrongs believers, or those who say they believe, will commit and what they will do in the name of religion. It also offers them redemptive paths forward should they reflect and turn toward Allah seeking forgiveness and mercy.

30 Sherman Jackson's theological writings on Islam and Black suffering speak to how Muslims must respond to racism (S. A. Jackson 2005; 2009; see also Chan-Malik 2011; Karim 2009; Abdullah 2010), while others discuss the effects of colonialism on Islamic education and law (Ware 2014; Agrama 2012; Mitchell 1988). Malcolm X's autobiography situates Islam as an anti-racist faith in the 1960s, but even then El-Shabazz noticed that racial logics of white supremacy had become global (Malcolm X and Haley 1965; Curtis 2015).

31 Muslim leaders in the United States who call for a "return" or "revival" of the Islamic tradition feel that because they are unencumbered by Arab or Desi "culture," for example, they can best articulate and transmit "true"

Islam. They do this while still referring to their "traditional" scholars, "untouched by modernity" in the historical Muslim world (Z. A. Grewal 2013).

32 For Gumbs and Wallace, "unjust death," similar to Gilmore's "vulnerability to premature death," is due to "capitalism, racism, homophobia, and transphobia" (383). I hold the particularity of their invocation of survival in place, while also attending to how critiques of homophobia and transphobia contribute to both the survival and unjust death of Muslims through the mobilization of human rights and liberal discourses that accuse Muslims (and thus authorize violence against them) of being simultaneously illiberal, fundamentalist, sexually deviant, and sexually frustrated (Puar and Rai 2002; Massad 2007; Puar 2007; El-Rouayheb 2005; Gurel 2017).

33 A smaller number of Muslims arrived as sailors, conquistadors (often having been forced to convert to Christianity prior to their departure), and navigators. Researchers also claim that based on old maps of Muslim geographers and traces of Arabic and Muslim practices in some Indigenous languages and cultures, Muslim explorers may have arrived before Columbus's "discovery" in 1492 (Nyang 1999).

34 Thank you to Abdul Salaam Thomas for reminding me of this hadith.

35 Imam Zaid Shakir and other Muslims enacted this grounded relationality by traveling to Standing Rock in 2016 to stand with the Water Protectors against the Energy Transfer Partners' Dakota Access pipeline (Hindtrospectives 2016; Estes 2019; Estes and Dhillon 2019), while Hatem Bazian's popular "Muslims in America" course in Asian American Studies at uc Berkeley begins with the history of Native genocide and European colonialism in the Americas toward a recognition of how racialization, white supremacy, and Orientalism function in relation and how colonialism would impact the historical "Muslim world" (Aydin 2017) and global migrations.

36 Ruth Wilson Gilmore describes "infrastructure of feeling" as "consciousness-foundation, sturdy but not static, that viscerally underlies our capacity . . . to recognize possibility as we select and reselect liberatory lineages" (2017, 237). Gilmore's use of "infrastructure" to describe what underlies a "constantly evolving accumulation of structures of feeling" describes well the Muslim impulse to maintain, evolve, and keep in motion an Islamic discursive tradition across place and time in a narrative arc tending toward salvation, justice, continuity, and individual and communal responsibility; like a material infrastructure, "it speeds some processes and slows down others, setting agendas, producing isolation, enabling cooperation" (Gilmore 2017, 237).

37 Ferguson urges interdisciplinary scholars to turn their attention "to that small and insignificant thing called the body" toward an examination of how "those little acts of production—reading, writing, teaching, and advising . . . such are the little things that we can deploy in order to imagine critical forms of community" that rather than reproduce or become

absorbed by state hegemonies, undermine them (Ferguson 2012, 232). I draw attention to the "body as geographic" and a site of knowledge as Muslims produce and transmit knowledge, exercise power, and make space, ethically and politically (McKittrick 2006).

38 The Confederated Villages of Lisjan belong to the land of the East Bay, and they are one of many Indigenous communities who came together as Ohlone in the 1960s and 1970s, inspired by Black Power and American Indian movement activism. Urban Indigenous women lead the work of the Sogorea Te' Land Trust toward restoring "people to their rightful place in sacred relationship with their ancestral land" in a process of re-matriation, cultural revitalization, and land restoration, and they suggest that non-Indigenous people living on these lands pay a volunteer Shuumi (gift) land tax toward supporting this work and transforming the legacies of colonization (Sogorea Te' Land Trust 2021). The Sogorea Te' Land Trust, the protection of shell mounds, the development of Black and Indigenous farming (Black Earth Farms), and other resurgent practices build upon the ongoing intertribal work of Indigenous peoples in the Bay Area; in the East Bay, this effort has centered around the Intertribal Friendship House, which was established in 1955, and institutions like the Native American Health Center, established in 1972. Similar institutions, as well as political meetings and alliances, Native student associations on high school and college campuses, pow wows, ceremonies, barbecues, fishing trips, dancefloors, and softball games, work as "hubs" and home spaces for Indigenous peoples throughout the Bay Area (Ramirez 2007).

39 Zaytuna's Center for Ethical Living and Learning was established in 2019. They are developing an orchard and permaculture garden on ten acres of their Berkeley Hills campus, the former Pacific Lutheran Theological Seminary. See also Tlili's *Animals in the Qur'an* (2012) for a (re)defini-tion of *khilafa*. Emily Riddle, a Nehiyaw (Plains Cree) and member of Alexander First Nation in Treaty 6 distinguishes between European political traditions, which define and practice sovereignty as "asserting exclusive control over a territory" and "Prairie NDN political traditions," which "teach us that it is through our relationship with others that we are sovereign, that sharing is not a sign of weakness but of ultimate strength and diplomacy" (Riddle 2020).

40 Hajar is named for Muslim ancestor Hagar/Hajar, wife of Abraham/Ibra-him and mother of Ishmael/Ismail, whom Ibrahim leaves in the desert with her nursing baby that "they might devote themselves to prayer" (Qur'an 14:37). Searching for water, she runs back and forth between the two hills, Safa and Marwa. The well of Zamzam miraculously springs forth, nourishing them both. Ibrahim and Ismail later build the Kaaba here, and during the annual pilgrimage to Mecca, Muslims must run back and forth between the same hills seven times, reliving Hajar's harrowing and heroic ordeal (al-Hibri 1997; Kahf 2016).

41 Many African American Muslims refer to themselves as "indigenous"
to distinguish their emergence as a people with shared experiences and
knowledge of the United States who have mobilized Islam from this
specificity. Wynter articulates how Black people resisted dehumanization and created "another structure of values, an alternative and opposed
consciousness . . . through the transplantation [of] their old cultures onto
a strange soil, its reinvention in new and alien conditions. It was in this
transplantation, this metamorphosis of an old culture into a new, that the
blacks made themselves indigenous to their new land" (Wynter n.d., 46–
47). They adapted themselves to this new world land and transformed it
through dual relationships to the land that produced capital but also opposed the plantation "land-labor-capital-relationship" (49). As Katherine
McKittrick elaborates, this form of indigenization "is not bound up in
spatial claims"; rather, "Indigenization is rebellion. Indigenizations are
ongoing rebellions that demand we think outside our normalized order
of consciousness" (McKittrick 2021, 160).

Within Muslim communities there is internal critique of using "indigenous" in ways that do not distinguish between indigenization as spatial
claim versus rebellion and how it contributes to the structure of settler colonialism, as in "Native Americans" or "American Indians" and their struggles
for sovereignty and relationships to land, water, and one another. Shona
Jackson (2014) describes how in the Caribbean context, "anti-blackness
cannot be understood apart from the subordination of Indigenous peoples
in early Empire, under colonialism, and ultimately in postcolonial nationalism." In the United States, references to enslaved African and post-
Emancipation labor "affirm anti-blackness by valorizing blackness as that
which performs labor for European humanity and, thus, for the humanity
of the black self" (2014). This matter of terminology matters to the extent
that it subsumes histories of Black Muslim and Indigenous relationality
and the ways that becoming Muslim was part of a strategy of survival and
rebellion against European humanism, white supremacy, white religion, and
their respective valuations of morality, property, freedom, and labor. The
term "immigrant" likewise obscures forced and willful migrations to North
America and the "racialized vulnerability and disposability" Muslims face in
terms of potential deportation, incarceration, family separation, disappearance, or assassination domestically and abroad (Day 2015, 107).

42 "Oscar" is named for twenty-two-year old Oscar Grant, who was as-
sassinated by Bay Area Rapid Transit (BART) police Officer Johannes
Mehserle on January 1, 2009, at the Fruitvale Station in Oakland. Grant
was living in Hayward and working in both Hayward and Oakland at
the time of his death but had celebrated the new year in San Francisco
and was on his way home when he was pulled out of the train car for
getting into (but actually attempting to stop) a fight on the train. Two
days before, he and his girlfriend Sophina Mesa had discussed moving

out to Dublin or Livermore to raise their daughter Tatiana. Mehserle had grown up in Napa (in the North Bay), lived in the predominantly white suburb of Lafayette, and had been a BART officer since March 2007. The effects of post–World War II redlining are evident in these social geographies and convey the cultural, racial, and socioeconomic dynamics and demographics of the Bay Area (Self 2003). The Frank Ogawa Plaza in Oakland was named for Grant during the Occupy Oakland movement in 2010–2011. In June 2019, the City of Oakland and BART named the short byway where people get picked up and dropped off at Fruitvale Station Oscar Grant III Way. They also unveiled a mural painted by Oakland artist Senay Dennis, aka Refa One, featuring Grant on the side of the station.

43 While many "native" and "activist" anthropologists are able to make claims about their political projects being in line with or improving the life chances of the people with whom they conduct research, because Muslims in the Bay Area encompass multiple political and spiritual aspirations, identities, and worldviews, my alignment and the contours of my research were not always situated comfortably with individual, institutional, and communal goals (Berry et al. 2017; Narayan 1993). Jackson refers to a "commonsensical acceptance of my nativity" based on his embodying a particular racial politic, by way of his Blackness in Harlem, New York, that nevertheless is complicated by class difference and his way of "seeing," an aspired-to double consciousness, and a complicating double vision (Jackson 2004, 34, 38). My "nativity" was more ambiguous in that I did not carry the common "racial" markers of Muslimness. On a number of occasions, I would say something that would "reveal" my identification as Muslim, and the person to whom I had been speaking to for months (and sometimes even prayed with) would respond in surprise, "I didn't know you were Muslim!" In one case, a female student said, "I did think that you seemed like a Muslim though." Other times, people assumed I converted because I did not appear Middle Eastern, South Asian, Southeast Asian, or African American.

44 Maryam, mother of Isa, is a significant figure in the Qur'an (some Muslims consider her the lone female Prophet of the Abrahamic faiths). She is known as Mary, mother of Jesus in Christianity.

45 There existed real fears about how I would represent students in particular, the most vulnerable to my participant-observation, as many of us developed intimate friendships, and I was privy to many personal and often "controversial" conversations and events. Zaytuna staff, students, and teachers used such ethical frameworks to limit my ethnographic inquiries and challenge and shape the parameters of my research (Kondo 1986; Visweswaran 1994; Wolf 1996).

46 By cinematic, I refer to what Kara Keeling calls a "condition of existence, or a reality, produced and reproduced by and within the regimes of the image Deleuze identifies and describes" (Keeling 2007, 3; Deleuze 1986).

47 How the figure of the Muslim is situated historically as the categorical Other has been discussed in terms of literature, photography, and painting (Alloula 1986; Mitchell 1988; Said 1979; 1997); television and film (Alsultany 2012; Morey and Yaqin 2011; Shaheen 2001; Shohat and Stam 1994; Weber 2013; T. Asad et al. 2009); and increasingly as part of an Islamophobia industry that creates lucrative alliances between conservative Christian groups and Zionists (Lean 2012, 11; Kumar 2021; Kundnani 2015; Shryock 2010; Sheehi 2011). Deleuze asserts that these logics and affects, transmitted through film, television, and media, "not only express, but also organize the movement of globalization" (Deleuze in Keeling 2007, 11), presenting the United States as "benevolent" and "post-racial" (Alsultany 2013, 162). In referring to these mediated discourses, Butler suggests that "such visual and conceptual frames are ways of building and destroying populations as objects of knowledge and targets of war, and that such frames are the means through which social norms are relayed and made effective" (Butler 2010, xix).

48 Ethnocinema has been used in reference to the filmic work of Jean Rouch, Trinh T. Minh-ha, and others (Harris 2010). My use of *ethnocinematic* draws attention to image-making as knowledge production produced by ethnographic writing and attempts to disrupt its logics and stability by drawing attention to its narrative production.

49 Since the early twentieth century, "secular" modes of critique have been considered the primary space where learning and "pure knowledge" can truly happen. As Asad notes, "It is not the secular claim to truth that worries me, but what critique may do to relationships with friends and fellow citizens with whom one deeply disagrees. Critique is no less violent than the law—and no more free. In short, I am puzzled as to why one should want to isolate and privilege 'critique' as a way of apprehending truth. What does this do to the way one is asked to—and actually—lives?" (Asad 2009, 140). "Normative secularity" and its attendant modes of critique often posit moral superiority to "secular visions" (or even feminist and other liberatory visions) of the world (Mahmood 2006, 343, 347). Mahmood offers critique of a "particular normative regime" like political secularism, "not to reject or condemn it," but to "[deprive] it of its innocence and neutrality so as to craft, perhaps, a different future" (Mahmood 2016, 21). Critique can also be a form of care, as in the ethnographic, pedagogic, or ethical relation that always hopes for and anticipates, "perhaps, a different future" (Mahmood 2016, 21; Fernando 2019).

50 Gilmore discusses how Woods originally presented his research under the rubric of a "blues ontology," which may have better encapsulated how entire worlds and forms of consciousness (which included Islam) came with captive Africans that enabled them to survive and struggle (Gilmore in Woods 2017, xii).

51 It is estimated that 10–30 percent of Africans who were enslaved in the Americas were Muslims (Diouf 1998; Singleton 2002; Austin 2012).

Qur'anic recitation and the adhan have distinctive aural and sonic qualities of tone, timbre, and time that are not typically examined as music, yet their affective qualities often move and compel people in ways similar to Western definitions of music. "Distinct vocal characteristics such as solo, unaccompanied singing, the use of melismas [extending a single syllable across multiple notes], slurring and gliding into pitches, and a nasal sound" are all attributes of West African music that were audible in recordings of early African Americans settled in the Deep South and that moved gradually further west and north (El Shibli 2007, 163). El Shibli argues that Islamic influences on the blues have been "ignored because of the difference between Western and Islamic perceptions of what constitutes 'music'" (163). Islamic orality and rhythms, like other Islamic modalities and practices, were dynamically brought into relation with pre-existing forms of music, speech, and custom in West Africa as elsewhere.

52 In addition to Islam's contribution to the blues, the "particular epistemological impact of Islam and Muslim practice on hip hop music and culture," "the development of hip hop ethics and activism," and the Black Radical tradition more broadly have been undertheorized and underacknowledged (Abdul Khabeer 2016, 10; Daulatzai 2012; Aidi 2014). Recent scholarship also expands our understandings of the breadth of the Black Radical tradition and the role that Islam, especially the Nation of Islam and El-Hajj Malik El-Shabazz (Malcolm X) played within it (Rickford 2016; Felber 2020; Murch 2010; Taylor 2017).

53 We also hear the blues adhan at the beginning of Julie Dash's *Daughters of the Dust* (1991), called by the character Bilal Muhammad (played by Umar Abdurrahman). This character was likely a reference to Bilali Muhammad (d. 1857) (or one of his descendants), who was part of a community of enslaved Muslims who lived on the Georgia Sea Islands. He penned a short treatise on ablution and prayer based on his memories of the Maliki text al-Risala by Ibn Abi Zayd al-Qayrawani (922–996) (Hilal 2017; R. B. Turner 2003). When I asked the fim's cinematographer and producer Arthur Jafa how that scene came to be, he said that it was "because he was there" (whether Umar Abdurrahman or Bilal Muhammad) in the Gullah community.

54 Within the Sunni tradition, Bilal ibn Rabah is said to have left the Hejaz for Syria after the death of the Prophet Muhammad to join the jihad and spread Islam there. Within the Shi'i tradition, Bilal refused to recognize Abu Bakr as leader of the community and was exiled from the Hejaz or left to avoid being brought into the succession conflict. His refusal is especially significant because Abu Bakr had paid for Bilal's freedom in the early days of the community. To this Bilal responded, "If you have emancipated me for yourself, then make me a captive again; but if you had emancipated me for Allah, then let me go in the way of Allah" (Rizvi 1987, 28).

55 Islamic scholar Sherman Jackson defines Black religion as an "abiding
    commitment to protest, resistance, and liberation . . . committed to a re-
    fusal to be the object of another's will" (S. A. Jackson 2005, 32). Jackson's
    vision for the "Third Resurrection" takes the "orthodox Sunni tradition"
    as a starting point and sees the United States as a "political arrangement"
    within which "Blackamerican Muslims" may move "from a position
    in which they can only be defined and controlled by the state and the
    dominant culture to one where they are self-defined and exercise enough
    influence over social and political institutions to be able to protect their
    interests and self-determination" (S. A. Jackson 2005, 168). This Third
    Resurrection is both resonant and dissonant with Woods's "Third Recon-
    struction." Both articulate Black structures of refusal and articulation in
    the blues and Black religion that offer anti-racist analyses and freedom
    visions and struggle for a participatory democracy (what W. E. B. Du
    Bois and Angela Davis call "abolition democracy") and the role that
    (Black) "indigenous knowledge, of blues epistemology," plays in denying
    "power to another elite-led regime of stagnation" (Woods 2017, 289).
    Martin Luther King Jr.'s own blues transformation from leader of the civil
    rights–based Second Reconstruction to the Third Reconstruction was
    exemplified by his participation in the Poor People's campaign, which
    called for the "reconstruction of the entire society, a revolution of values"
    (Woods 2017, 187). Woods warns, "The 'civilizing' activity of providing
    'nondeviant' role models for the creation of new men and women must
    come to an end" (Woods 2017, 290). Rather, we must "celebrate and valo-
    rize the millions upon millions, living and dead, who met the regimes of
    daily destruction with unshakeable dignity. In the same vein, the lands,
    rivers, streams, air, plants, and animals of the region must be restored to
    their sacred status" (Woods 2017, 290).

56 Travel and knowledge are intimately connected in the Islamic tradition.
    In a well-documented hadith, the Prophet Muhammad states, "Seek
    knowledge all the way to China." China as a site of knowledge, prior to
    the establishment of Islam there, suggests both an imperative to travel
    for knowledge and a catholic approach to seeking knowledge (at that
    time China was known for its developments in medicine, paper, printing,
    trade, seafaring, etc.). Traveling is also an ethical condition in which one
    encounters the unknown, is unsettled and estranged, is vulnerable to the
    generosity of one's hosts, and carries the responsibility of being a good
    guest. In another hadith, Muslims are encouraged to "be in the world as
    if you were a stranger or a traveler along the path."

57 In "Around the Way Girl" (1990), LL Cool J celebrates the street-smart
    girl from the neighborhood who "ain't scared to do her thing, standing at
    the bus stop, sucking on a lollipop." There is resonance between boroughs
    and bays as I felt hailed by LL as a Japanese-Iranian girl from the city who

was "real independent so your parents be bugging" and who aspired to be that girl who "always know what to say and do." The Around the Way Girl builds communities of care and relative security by loving her girls, code-switching, and learning how to handle the boys and the businessmen who sweat. The song was a rare ode that recognized the bus stop point of view and identified the critical infrastructural role young Black and brown women played and continue to play in the neighborhood, on the dance floor, and in the culture.

1. MEDINA BY THE BAY

1 Steve is named for Stephen Gaines (1971–2021), known around the Bay and beyond as Baba Zumbi of hip-hop crew Zion I. Steve was a seeker and striver; he showed up for people and the movement, and his music and spirit brought joy, hype, and knowledge to the people. For more on his music and contributions see E. K. Arnold (2021) and go listen to his music.

2 Rasmea is named for Rasmea Youssef Odeh (b. 1974), a Palestinian-Jordanian activist who was stripped of her United States citizenship and deported from the United States in 2017. She was targeted for her activism on behalf of Arab Americans and Palestinian liberation and charged with immigration fraud because she had not mentioned a previous conviction (gained through extensive torture) in Israel on her immigration application. She was not allowed to present evidence of her torture by Israeli prison guards nor her post-traumatic stress from this time period (N. Naber 2014; Khader 2017; Ghanayem 2019; Odeh 2019).

3 For those familiar with the US Muslim landscape, to think of Zaytuna College as an assembly of outlaws may seem strange as it represents itself as firmly oriented toward an authoritative and majoritarian Sunni tradition of Islamic theology, law, and other sciences. Yet, as Muslims who prioritize their ethical becomings, their orientations to themselves, Allah, and others through Islamic tradition, they sometimes feel affectively estranged and maligned from what they view as an increasingly atheistic, morally corrupt, aspiritual, and ethically unmoored modern society (even among fellow Muslims).

4 Da'wa has tended to refer to what people do with media or as part of Muslim movements and "revivals" (Mahmood 2005; Rouse 2004; Abd-Allah 2006; Hirschkind 2006; Jouili 2015; Moll 2010; Larkin 2008a; 2008b; L. Abu-Lughod 2005; Kuiper 2021), while ta'lim has been discussed as a form of Muslim schooling that happens at home, in mosques, and in madrasas (schools) (Cook and Malkawi 2011; Hefner and Zaman 2007; Memon 2019; al-Zarnuji, Grunebaum, and Abel 2003). I draw from al-Attas's notion of ta'dib as education (or Islamization of knowledge) because it informs how scholars like Shaykh Hamza Yusuf under-

stand the role and function of Islamic education (F. Ahmed 2018; al-Attas 1985; Daud 2009; MBC 2012).

5 As an umma, Muslims are obligated to know and sustain practices relating to Islamic ritual (prayer, funeral rites, marriage, zakat, hajj, etc.), as well as social structure (caring for orphans and widows; defense of the community and Islam; ensuring the transmission of knowledge; enjoining good and forbidding evil; farming, trade, halal food production and distribution; etc.). Through a combination of individual obligations (fard 'ayn) and communal obligations (fard kifaya), the umma guarantees and reinforces deen (religion) and iman (faith) (Judy 2007, 36–37). It is no coincidence that "din" is in "Medina;" in Arabic, "medina" is the place where din, as submission, obedience, debt, and requital, happens.

6 "Eat to Live" (Sapelo Square 2015).

7 Before Malcolm X established the *Muhammad Speaks* newspaper in 1960, NOI members distributed other Black-owned publications that featured articles written by their membership.

8 Abdul-Malik is named for Malik Amin (1992–2021), a seeker and striver for justice in Chicago, father, and friend. Malik helped create the #BreathingRoom Space in Chicago and was an organizer, creative, and beloved host in multiple spaces. I shared space with him (followed his lead) in the work to end money bail in Illinois. His time in the world was too short, but his legacy lives on in his children and beloveds, his struggle for justice, and the lessons he yielded to so many who knew him.

9 The first part of this dialogue comes from Abdul-Malik's memories; the second is from Maurice Dawson as quoted in Murch (2010, 81).

10 The Fruit of Islam (FOI) and Muslim Girls' Training (MGT) were programs for young Muslim men and women, respectively, that educated them in gendered roles and responsibilities toward the protection, maintenance, care, and uplift of the community.

11 In many (Black) Muslim communities, "pioneers" are elders who trailblazed the path for Islam in the United States. See the song "Grand Ole Pioneer" by Wali Ali produced by Bilalian Cultural Foundation.

12 "Hajja" is an honorific given to a woman who has fulfilled her obligation to make pilgrimage (hajj) to Mecca during the sacred month. Both Hajja Rasheeda and Masjid Al-Ansar (Mosque of the Helpers) are pseudonyms. Although Hajja Rasheeda has passed, for reasons discussed in the third chapter, I have decided to maintain some opacity (if you know you know).

13 The concept of the mujaddid is based on a hadith in which the Prophet Muhammad says, "Allah will send to this umma at the head of each century those who will renew its faith for it" (Voll 2004).

14 In the Sunni tradition, mujaddidun are typically those who return Muslim belief and practice to the ideals and parameters of the Qur'an and Sunna, away from innovations and corruption. In the Shi'i tradition, there is more emphasis on "messianic styles of religious resurgence" (Voll 2004).

In referring to Muhammad and El-Shabazz as renewers, I am working with these multiple definitions of renewal, return, and resurgence, but this is hardly a consensus position, especially in terms of the unorthodox Nation teachings vis-à-vis normative Islam; nevertheless, one cannot discount their important contributions to da'wa, ta'lim, and ta'dib in African American communities and beyond.

15 I thank my cousin Negar and her daughter Shahdi for this phrasing.

16 Murch refers to it as a "flat tongue" (Murch 2010, 44).

17 The Port Chicago munitions explosion occurred on July 17, 1944, at Port Chicago Naval Magazine in Port Chicago, California, which was located on Suisun Bay, the shallow estuary where the Sacramento River and San Joaquin River meet just north of Contra Costa County, named for the Suisun people who lived in the marsh regions farther north and east of Ohlone lands (Solano County). The explosion occurred when munitions being loaded onto cargo vessels bound for the Pacific Theater during World War II exploded, killing 320 sailors, 202 of whom were Black ammunition loaders; in the aftermath, Black soldiers were singled out, charged, and convicted of mutiny when they refused to work under unsafe conditions in the largest mutiny trial in naval history (Allen 1989).

18 In 2020 Oakland's African American population was 99,416 people (23.61 percent), with the majority of loss happening between 2000 and 2010 (Frahm 2020).

19 The earliest mention of Nation of Islam activity in the Bay Area is an FBI record that references an interview with a woman who plans to visit a chapter in Oakland in 1951. In a 1955 memorandum report produced by the FBI for its field offices, Temple 26 in Oakland is included in a map of all of "Muhammad's Temples of Islam," and in a list of other temples or active groups, San Francisco is mentioned as well. In FBI reports informants claim that they do not know where the Oakland temple is. This could be for a number of reasons—a strategy to misinform the FBI or the fact that NOI activities moved around the Bay Area quite a bit.

20 Temple 26A in San Francisco and 26B in Oakland alternated in influence, activity, and population throughout the 1950s–1970s. Rifts developed in the NOI community in regard to the selling of *Muhammad Speaks* newspapers and differences among leadership, many of whom were not from the Bay. Billy and Joseph Stephen, brothers who arrived from Southern California, eventually lead 26B as minister and captain of the Fruit of Islam, respectively. Joseph would as Yusuf Bey get himself and his community caught up in alleged illegal dealings (including the murder of Oakland journalist Chauncey Bailey), leading to the closings of the locally infamous Your Black Muslim bakery in the 2000s (Peele 2012).

21 These texts are read today as foundations for studies of African American, Black, and African Diaspora studies including: W. E. B. Du Bois's *The Souls of Black Folk* (1903), Carter G. Woodson's *The Miseducation*

of the Negro (1933), Ralph Ellison's *The Invisible Man* (1952), E. David Cronon's *Black Moses: The Story of Marcus Garvey* (1955), Melville J. Herscovits's *The Myth of the Negro Past* (1941), and E. Franklin Frazier's *Black Bourgeoisie* (1957) (March 2010, 86).

22 The current Gadar Memorial Hall and Library can be visited in San Francisco's Laurel Heights. https://www.cgisf.gov.in/page/gadar-memorial-hall/.

23 Some sources state that this mosque was established in 1965, but the Islamic Center of San Francisco's website and members say 1959 (Islamic Center of San Francisco 2017).

24 *Hijra* literally means migration, but in connotation it refers to the Hijra of the Prophet Muhammad and his community from Mecca to Medina in 622 CE to escape persecution and practice their faith openly.

25 The poet Daniel Abdul Hayy Moore discussing living in Berkeley (a few blocks from the first Zaytuna College campus) in 1969, just before he met Ian Dallas, later known as Shaykh Abdalqadir As-Sufi. Quoted from "In Memorium of Hajj Abdallah Luongo," formerly on "The Muslims of Norwich" website. http://www.muslimsofnorwich.org.uk/. Accessed on October 10, 2012.

26 Mario is named for Mario Woods, who was killed by San Francisco police on December 2, 2016. Mario was from Bayview-Hunter's Point, a historically Black neighborhood in San Francisco, which like the rest of San Francisco has become increasingly gentrified. The police shootings of Woods, as well as the shootings of Luis Góngora Prat (an unsheltered man killed in April 2016 in San Francisco who was building a home in his Mayan village Teabo, in Mexico's Yucatan), Amilcar Perez Lopez (a Guatemalan immigrant killed by police in the Mission in February 2015), Jessica Williams (a twenty-nine-year-old mother killed in Bayview in May 2016), and many others inspired a seventeen-day hunger strike by the Frisco Five, long time community members and activists (Wong 2016c; 2016a; 2016b).

27 Dar Ul-Islam emerged in the 1960s in Brooklyn, New York, begun by a group of African American converts to Islam who were interested in an Islam that could be an "uplifting force for the poor and downtrodden within the New York slums and ghettoes" (Mukhtar 1994, 54). The movement would spread not only to major cities throughout the East Coast and Midwest, but also to the South in the Carolinas, Alabama, and Georgia, as well as Colorado, Ontario, Trinidad, the West Indies, and Alaska.

28 The shahada is the testimony of faith, in which a person states in Arabic "I bear witness that there is no god but Allah and Muhammad is the Messenger of Allah." After saying the shahada, a person becomes Muslim. "Ya'ni" can be translated as "like" and serves as a similar colloquial filler word. By this time, Arabic was Mario's primary language of study, teaching, and everyday life in Yemen. "Alhamdulillah" can be translated as "praise be to Allah."

29 Naima is named for my friends' daughter, who passed onto the next life too soon, for the light that she brought and the continued guidance she yields.

30 American Muslims traveled for Islamic knowledge prior to this period, but in the 1990s and 2000s the numbers increased due to the revival of "traditional" learning among American Muslim youth (Z. A. Grewal 2013). In the 1970–1980s, Europeans and European Americans traveled abroad, often to Spain and Morocco, in search of more "spiritual" forms of traditional learning. Since 2010, such travel has been limited due to civil wars, military invasions, political and socioeconomic instability, and the war on terror security infrastructures.

31 Hajar alludes to the deaths of two young men from the Masjid community. Each of the stories told in *Medina by the Bay*, the lives and the deaths, deserves its own book, its own time for remembrance and reflection, a moment of prayer (al-Fatiha). I tell this broader story and history because it matters that we think about what happens to our communities at regional scales to get at how personal agency and choices are always set within larger structures, histories, and relationships. When we make decisions in San Jose, they impact what happens in San Leandro and Antioch; when a county puts more money in policing and prisons than in public schools, it impacts what happens in mosques and churches.

32 This usage of "golden age" is in contrast to what Michael Muhammad Knight critiques as Shaykh Hamza Yusuf's use of Islam's lost "golden age." The 1990s was a golden age for many precisely because of its complexity, "diversity and internal contradictions" (Knight 2013).

33 "Masjidi" is a pseudonym.

34 Zakat and sadaqa are two forms of wealth that are redistributed to those in need to purify the giver's wealth and to gain Allah's favor (see Qur'an 9:103). Zakat is obligatory and given annually, while sadaqa is supererogatory and given at any time. While the root letters of zakat (z-k-w) convey meanings related to purification, the root letters of sadaqa (s-d-q) are related to truth and friendship. Often inadequately translated as "charity," sadaqa is actually a gift and trust that suggests how ethical relations between Muslims reflect their relationships with Allah. Wealth and possessions are themselves placed in particular hands as a trust by Allah, and Muslims must dispense them freely.

35 Ta'leef (to reconcile, "bring hearts together") was initially called the Zawiya and met in a rented space in a strip mall in Fremont. Both founders are no longer with Ta'leef, which has expanded to Chicago as well.

36 The first chapter of CAIR (Council on American-Islamic Relations) was established in San Francisco in 1995; ING (Islamic Networks Group) was founded by Maha Elgenaidi, an Egyptian American, in the South Bay in 1993; the American Muslim Alliance was founded by Agha Saeed, a Pakistani American, in 1994; the Ameen Housing Co-Operative of California

was started in 1996 in Palo Alto; and NISA (North American Islamic
Shelter for the Abused) was established in 2002.

37 Nadine Naber (2012) and Sunaina Maira (2016) articulate some of the
critical political work that young Arab and Afghan Muslims influenced
by the Zaytuna school were engaged in throughout the 1990s. They articulated a holistic approach to spiritual and political striving and action
that was demonstrated in their anti-imperial and local commitments.
Zaytuna College cofounder Hatem Bazian was a significant figure in
articulating this positionality and perspective.

38 While I emphasize the efforts of Bay Area Muslims here, it is important
to understand that Zaytuna College is funded by Muslims from around
the world, although the great majority of funders have been US-based.
Incarcerated Muslims donate money to Zaytuna College as well. Almost
5 percent of California's population is incarcerated, and about 9 percent
of the incarcerated in state prisons nationally are Muslim; in some state
prisons, it is around 20 percent or higher (Muslim Advocates 2019).

2. ROOTS, ROUTES, AND RHYTHMS OF DEVOTIONAL TIME

1 Habib (beloved or dear one) 'Umar is one of many Habibs or *Haba'ib*
(the Arabic plural of "Habib"). Throughout this chapter I refer to Habib
'Umar as either Habib 'Umar or the Habib. His name includes a genealogy of his male ancestors; "bin" means son of, therefore, 'Umar son
of Muhammad son of Salim son of Hafiz. A sayyid (descendant of the
Prophet Muhammad), Habib 'Umar fled Tarim as a young man. Many
believe that his father was disappeared and killed in a political purge
wielded by the Socialist regime in the early 1970s (Knysh 2001). Habib
'Umar completed his education in Saudi Arabia and returned to Hadra-
mawt once Yemen was unified in 1990. He opened Dar al-Mustafa Seminary in 1996 and Dar al-Zahra Seminary for women a year later. He is
consistently ranked highly on a list of the "500 Most Influential Muslims"
in the world based on his scholarly influence and lineage (Esposito and
Kalin 2009; Schleifer and El-Ella 2019). In the 2020 and 2021 listings, he
was ranked as the ninth most influential Muslim in the world.

2 Students travel from all over the world to study with the Habib and his
advanced students. Some current Zaytuna College students have attended
Dar al-Mustafa or Dar al-Zahraa during their summer breaks as well.
Once students reach a certain level in their studies, they are "dispatched
to disseminate 'correct' Islam," whether in the surrounding areas or
abroad (Knysh 2001). This international flow of students is enabled by
the presence and translation of long-term students like Mario who have
popularized the teachings and personalities of the Haba'ib (plural of
Habib) both through their travels and through their returning to their

homes and rising in the ranks of local scholars themselves. These traveling teachers and students produce alternative diasporas constituted by and affectively experienced through knowledge-based genealogies and participation in particular modes of daʿwa and taʿlim. Such traveling affiliations and attachments echo and sustain a tradition of journeying Muslims throughout history, but the specific landscapes, technologies, and connections being made now are definitively twenty-first-century (Eickelman and Piscatori 1990; Cooke and Lawrence 2005; Euben 2006).

3 I use "Muhammadaic" in the way that Zaid Shakir (2010) uses it to describe "breezes," "souls," and "truths" that emerge from the example and force of the Prophet Muhammad. While the Orientalist term "Muhammadan" referred to those who follow Muhammad, Muslims and contemporary scholars reject the term, largely because it suggests the worship of Muhammad rather than the One Allah. Shakir does not suggest the worship of the Prophet Muhammad, but rather his significance as Messenger and human exemplar: "It is time for the souls who have imbibed the fragrance of the Muhammadaic truth . . . to rise. Their uprising will not be one of angry mobs demanding justice at any cost. . . . The uprising of the Muhammadaic souls will not be that of frenzied mobs descending into the streets. It will be the rising up of committed believers from the sweetness of sleep in the privacy of their homes to stand before their Lord in deep devotion. . . . It will begin during the night before the watchful gaze of Allah" (Shakir 2010). It is important to note where Malcolm X's "by any means necessary," on the one hand, and Shakir's distinguishing between "angry mobs demanding justice at any cost" and Muhammadaic souls, on the other, may converge and diverge.

4 The term "umma" itself is related to "umm," which means mother. In the Qur'an, "umma" is mentioned sixty-two times, and while it typically refers to a specific or ideal community, nation, or people, it can also mean all of humankind (Qur'an 2:213) or a sociopolitical community as when Jews, Christians, pagans, and Muslims were referred to as an umma in the Constitution of Medina (Denny 2012).

5 Jackson (2005) argues that Muslims from the Middle East and Asia gain "legal whiteness" and impose an "immigrant hegemony" within Muslim communities. Abdul Khabeer (2016) prefers the term "ethnoreligious hegemony," while Chan-Malik (2011) considers Arab and Asian desires for maintaining cultural traditions and languages "ethnic particularism." They join other scholars in articulating how Arabs, Iranians, and others are "not-quite white" and are impacted by US imperialism in the United States and abroad; the racialization that Muslims experience complicates how intra-Muslim conflict is experienced (Samhan 1999; Gualtieri 2009; Jamal and Naber 2008; K. Silva 2016; Maghbouleh 2017; N. Nguyen 2019; Rastegar 2021).

6 Sahabi (singular of Sahaba) means "one who saw Muhammad, and whose companionship with him was long, even if he [has] not related anything from him; or, as some say, even if his companionship with him was not long" (Lane and Lane-Poole 1968, 1653). The Sahaba are traditionally thought to be Muslims who spent time with the Prophet, but there were also non-Muslims in the community, including those who were Jewish, Christian, or Coptic, with whom Muslims engaged in marriage, trade, and political alliances.

7 For example, see Sahih Muslim, no. 2408 (Book 44, Hadith 55).

8 Gestures of respect and hierarchy are a reflection of adab, which requires "the recognition and acknowledgement of one's proper place in relation to one's physical, intellectual, and spiritual capacities and potentials" (S. M. N. al-Attas 1993, 105–6). In this case, Shakir, Habib 'Umar, and his translators' intellectual and spiritual capacities were held in esteem by others in the room, thereby situating them in places of honor to be learned from that evening. This does not discount the possibility that there were others of higher capacity (recognized or hidden) sitting in the audience.

9 By marking certain deceased figures as characters in the scene through their names being in caps, I narrate "co-presences" and the active roles they play as forces in both the cosmological and historical understandings of Islam in the Americas (Jesús 2015).

10 The term "saint," typically associated with Catholicism, is not a direct translation of "wali" or "shahid" (martyr) or other related terms in Arabic, which also have disputed and multiple meanings. It does convey in English, however, a sense of the spiritual standing that El-Hajj Malik El-Shabazz should, within Islamic creedal beliefs, have with Allah in terms of his martyrdom status and the effect that he and his life story have had in "renewing" Islam. The term also connotes something of his spiritual force, not as an intercessor with Allah, but as a model in terms of one who "embodied the meanings" of Prophetic guidance.

11 Members of the Organization of Afro-American Unity, African American Muslims, and other Muslims and non-Muslims have been making pilgrimage to Malcolm's grave since his death in 1965 (Aidi 2014).

12 See Sahih al-Bukhari, no. 7460 (Book 97, Hadith 86).

13 In November 2008, Ayman al-Zawahiri of Al Qaeda also quotes El-Shabazz and cites him as representative of "honorable Blackamericans" as opposed to "house negroes" like Barack Obama, Colin Powell, and Condoleeza Rice (Marable 2011; Marable and Aidi 2009).

14 Zareena Grewal (2013) discusses the possible disappointments and contradictions that approaching the Middle East as archive engenders for Muslims who initially encounter it uncritically. She likewise discusses how Black Muslim histories offer lessons that many Muslim leaders in the

United States have failed to heed. Edward Curtis's recent work (2015) on El-Shabazz's travel journals discusses his negotiation of what the "Muslim world" offered as he developed his understanding of Islam as liberatory theory and praxis.

15 I reference Ruth Gilmore's (2007) definition of racism: "the state-sanctioned and/or extra-legal production and exploitation of group-differentiated vulnerability to premature death" (28).

16 This "Tarek" is named for Tarek "DJ Dusk" Habib Captan (1974–2006) of Los Angeles (and Lebanon), a friend and "angel of mercy."

17 The ninety-nine names of Allah are attributes that are synonymous with Allah's existence. In Islamic teachings they are often distinguished as either *jalali*, having to do with a commanding Godness, or *jamali*, having to do with a nurturing Lordship. These are often taken to be masculine and feminine, respectively, though not necessarily (Wadud 2013). The students invited African American scholar Muhammad Adeyinka Mendes, who spoke about how the "99 Names" should not be taken as prescriptions for gender norms.

18 This pseudonym is named for Yuri Kochiyama (1921–2014), the Japanese American activist who was a member of the Organization of Afro-American Unity and who spent her final years in Medina by the Bay. She and Hajja Rasheeda were friends and comrades who organized for and supported political prisoners. Her life exemplified multiracial solidarity and social justice work, and her conversion to Islam as an act of solidarity with incarcerated Muslims in New York pushes us to think about companionship in expansive ways (Rana 2017a; Fujino 2005). Her internment during World War II and her work for reparations for Japanese Americans also speak to how American citizenship and civil liberties are conditional and tenuous.

19 A *nashid* is a devotional song, hymn, or anthem written in praise of the Prophet Muhammad. It is similar to a qasida, which is a lyrical poem or ode. The Qasida al-Burda (The Prophet's Mantle), composed by Imam Sharafuddin Muhammad al-Busiri (d. 1296), is among the most well known, and it has been translated by a number of scholars including Hamza Yusuf. A daff is a flat, handheld drum.

20 "Matthew" is named for Matthew Africa (1972–2012), deejay and lawyer who grew up and lived in the East Bay. He was a deep listener and collector of rock, punk and new wave, indie and garage rock, funk and soul, and hip-hop music and was equally deep and generous in his relationships. He was a true seeker. In the words of Oliver Wang, "he was a mentor, a guide, a gentle hand on the shoulder that helped point you in the direction you wanted to go (even if you didn't realize it at the time)"; http://soul-sides.com/2012/09/for-matthew-africa/.

21 See Mishkat al-Masabih, no. 3096 (Book 13, Hadith 17).

22 Of course, one does not have to be married to realize and understand gendered difference. The significance of heterosexual marriage in Muslim social formation is important to Muslim communities, yet other forms of companionship and relationality across gender can be equally or more significant. Parent and sibling relationships, as well as friendships and media discourses, are foundational and critical sources of knowledge or mis-knowledge about gendered difference, rights, and responsibilities.

23 Mary took on the name of one of her female elders. Michael is named for Mike "Dream" Francisco (1969–2000), a Bay Area graffiti legend. Mary's husband was also raised on hip hop, and he is one of many Filipinos who converted to Islam in the 1990s–2000s. In his life, Mike Dream built bridges between Filipino and Black communities and between the street and struggles of social justice. DREAM but don't sleep. https://dreamtdk .com/about-us.

24 Some translations of this hadith (no. 32nd of an-Nawawi's Forty Hadith) say, "No harm, nor reciprocating harm."

25 I draw attention to a sense of bound geographies and identities not to reinforce them, but rather, in Lisa Lowe's words, to "focus on relation across differences rather than equivalence, on the convergence of asymmetries rather than the imperatives of identity" (Lowe 2015, 11).

26 Imam Zaid's translates the Qur'anic verse in the moment. The Abdullah Yusuf Ali translation: "Their intention is to extinguish Allah's Light (by blowing) with their mouths: But Allah will complete (the revelation of) His Light, even though the Unbelievers may detest (it)" (Qur'an 61:8).

27 Zaid Shakir (2006a) wrote of this vision upon the passing of his teacher Shaykh Mustafa al-Turkmani in Damascus. Al-Turkmani, a da'i and a scholar, had, unlike many others, always encouraged Imam Zaid to "return to America to work for Islam." He shared this vision with him. A woman's voice translates the man's Arabic to reflect upon my work in the translation of this mystical vision to a contemporary ethnocinematic event.

28 This statement recalls the words of Gil Scott-Heron in "The Revolution Will Not Be Televised" (1970).

29 Located in downtown Oakland, the ICCNC, a primarily Shi'i mosque founded by Iranians in 1995, serves the larger Bay Area community as well. (Young) Malcolm Shabazz converted to Shi'i Islam and believed that his grandfather would have converted to Shi'i Islam because of what he considered its social justice imperative. Shabazz considered moving to the Bay Area because he was inspired by the radical history of the BPP and was encouraged by Yuri Kochiyama, who had known his grandfather and had written the younger Malcolm letters while he was in prison. Upon his release from prison, he traveled and studied Islam in the Middle East, most significantly for a year in Damascus, Syria.

1 See an-Nawawi's *Forty Hadith*, no. 34.

2 Alejandro is named for twenty-eight-year-old Alejandro "Alex" Nieto, who was killed by San Francisco police officers, gentrification, and racism while eating a burrito and chips in Bernal Heights Park in San Francisco on March 21, 2014. Nieto was born to Mexican immigrants Elvira and Refugio Nieto in San Francisco on March 3, 1986; he was a graduate of San Francisco City College and was an active member of the Mission community. On that evening in 2014, a number of recently arrived to Bernal Heights and since moved to the suburbs, white men with dogs determined that Nieto, who was wearing a red San Francisco 49ers football jacket and carrying a taser (he used it in his work as a bouncer at a club), was a threatening presence. Similar to other incidents throughout the Bay Area, long time Black and brown residents of the Bay Area have been viewed as dangerous and threatening to outsiders in their own neighborhoods by recent gentrifying arrivals, speaking to the proprietary and racialized logics of space and security that render some criminal and out of place (Solnit 2016; LLoveras n.d.).

3 Garrett Felber discusses this training bulletin and the dark sousveillance that El-Shabazz and other Muslims engaged in when they printed excerpts of this text in *Muhammad Speaks* or discussed them at meetings (2020, 47–49). Court documents would include In re Ferguson, 55 Cal.2d 663 (1961) and *Williford v. California*, 217 F. Supp. 245 (1963), for example (Morrison 2013).

4 Sahih Muslim, no. 45 (Book 1, Hadith 77).

5 Community organizations like AROC (Arab Resource and Organizing Center), the Asian American Law Caucus, CAIR (Council of American-Islamic Relations), and other legal organizations have been conducting "know your rights" trainings, providing legal defense, and advising Arab, South Asian, and Muslim communities on how to respond to visits from the FBI (don't talk to them and refer them to a lawyer).

6 Some important exceptions to this are A. I. Ali 2016; Browne 2015; Cainkar 2009; I. Grewal 2017; Kapadia 2019; Kumar 2021; Kundnani 2015; Maira 2009; 2016; Mirzoeff 2017; Singh 2019.

7 While the United States has officially pulled out of Iraq and Afghanistan, suggesting an end to the war on terror, its ongoing militarization and debt imperialism in the form of planetary garrisoning (Kim 2021), its facilitation of weapon sales (especially to the Gulf States of the Arabian Peninsula) produced by US corporations, and its ongoing military, diplomatic, and "peace-keeping" actions throughout Asia and Africa suggest otherwise.

8 We are already seeing the implementation of "domestic terrorism" from designations in investigations and intelligence gathering to charge enhancements in cases of civil disobedience and protest related to the pro-

tection of environmental resources and police reform (Taitz and Rather 2023).

9 This section is named for Tupac Amaru Shakur (1971–1996), aka 2Pac, and his album All Eyez on Me (Death Row and Interscope Records, 2015), which both considers what it is to be hyper-visible as a Black man and celebrity, while also finding ways to be stealthy and invisible (Nielson 2010). Tupac traversed the Bay—from Marin City in the North Bay where his family moved for his final year in high school to his emergent rap career, beginning with the Digital Underground, based in Oakland, to fame as a West Coast rapper. In "California Love," he shouts out Oaktown (Oakland), Frisco (San Francisco), Sactown (Sacramento), and then Los Angeles, Pasadena, and Hollywood, a cartography of Black California, which reached its apex at that time in the mid-1990s; a roll call of Black California today would chart a different geography. Afeni Shakur, Tupac's mother, identified with Islam at different stages in her life, from her introduction to the NOI and the teachings of Brother Malcolm as a teenager to her conversion to Islam when she married Lumumba Shakur, becoming his second wife in a polygynous marriage during her years in the Black Panther Party (Guy 2004). Hajja Rasheeda traveled to New York and befriended many of the New York Panthers in the late 1960s and was heartbroken by the split between the East and West Coast Panthers in the early 1970s.

10 See https://www.freethesf8.org/, accessed September 11, 2020. Kiilu is named for Kiilu Nyasha (1939–2018), Black Panther and revolutionary journalist, activist, and comrade-mentor who continued to work for political prisoners, housing rights, and social justice her entire life. "She lived on her own terms and never compromised her dignity under a system she despised. Kiilu loved the people, believed in the people, and fought tirelessly for our collective liberation" (Bartolome 2020, 61).

11 The use of torture by local police officers throughout this period is not well known; the discussion of torture by the CIA, military, and FBI in the war on terror, as well as the work of local activists and journalists, has brought these domestic histories to light. We can see continuities in the decades of torture committed by the Chicago police under former Police Commander Jon Burge at the "black site" Homan Square and its connections to American imperialism and war-making abroad (Ralph 2020; CTJM 2021; Khwaja, Mendoza, and Khan 2022). The description of torture conducted in 1973 reminds us of the ongoing forms of racial terror that police were authorized with in facing enemies; I do not need to re-present this evidence (Jacobs 2007; McKittrick 2014; 2017). Black Panther Kiilu Nyasha describes how the men continue to live with the effects of the torture: "the prolonged tortures left the brothers with permanent injuries, including damaged ear drums, chronic pain, knee problems, arthritis and Post Traumatic Stress Disorder symptoms such as trouble sleeping and nightmares" (Nyasha 2007).

12 The story of one raid is portrayed in the documentary *New Muslim Cool* (Taylor 2009), which focuses on a Jama'at community in Pittsburgh.

13 Jihad Abdulmumit, who had recently been released from federal prison, attended. Similar meetings occurred throughout the 1970s and 1980s as well, as Black Muslims recognized that the specific issues of their communities were not being addressed at other national gatherings like that of the Muslim Students Association and the Islamic Society of North America.

14 Imam Jamil Al-Amin's family also asserts that there are more than forty thousand pages on him in FBI files that they requested.

15 What disturbed me about this approach to "my archive" was my not "being there" in a way that enabled me to be in relation to everyone filmed. Likewise, the aerial, sterile, CCTV quality of the image was so unlike the intimacy I cultivate in my approach to filming. For a discussion about the uncomfortable relations between anthropological fieldwork and espionage, see Borneman and Masco (2015) and Verdery (2018). On the Human Terrain System, the US Army counterinsurgency program that lasted from 2007 to 2015, which continues to impact ongoing military and intelligence approaches, see González (2020) and Besteman et al. (2009).

16 Implicit in these disciplining structures is the privileging of a "scopic regime" (Jay and Ramaswamy 2014) in which identification, anticipation, and suspicion produce particular racialized and gendered figures, whether via the surfaces of the flesh (Fanon 2008; Spillers 1987; Browne 2015; Weheliye 2014) or fabric (M. T. Nguyen 2015; Abdul Khabeer 2016; Fernando 2014; Mir 2016).

17 Savannah Shange (2019b) asks "what we lose when we win" in progressive battles with the state for autonomy and rights. Put another way, "the worst possible outcome of playing the game of 'respectability politics' and 'double consciousness' is winning" (Evans in Rana 2018, 358). I temper the "success" of this victory amid ongoing dispossession and enclosure, the gnawing of those still locked up and the ever-growing populations of unsheltered and unhoused throughout Medina by the Bay.

18 With the support of former New York City mayor Rudy Giuliani, Bratton implemented broken windows policing, which mandated that police officers target minor crimes, misdemeanors like jumping subway turnstiles, smoking marijuana, selling loose cigarettes, graffiti, and prostitution under the assumption that targeting these crimes (forms of disorder) would lessen the frequency of violent crimes. This policy lead to "stop and frisk," which preempted the breaking of laws via forms of racialized suspicion. Both of these policies led to increases in police misconduct, police violence, and targeted mass incarceration of Black and brown communities.

19 During the COVID-19 pandemic, I have been struck by how I and many others have not minded the anonymity that comes with the ubiquity of

face masks. The inability for law enforcement to register faces during the
summer uprisings of 2020 was also a significant form of sousveillance.

20 Maira and Browne document countersurveillance, self-surveillance, or
"dark sousveillance," ways that surveilled objects become subjects that
move in and out of the "frame," to "resist disappearance" and get "out of
sight" or "under sight" (Browne 2015, 21; Maira 2016, 96).

21 I am interested in the difference between not having a criminal mind,
but being criminal-minded, as in *Criminal Minded* (B-Boy Records, 1987)
by Boogie-Down Productions. Being criminal-minded means understanding racial logics and how the law has traditionally facilitated the protection
of white males and their property at the expense of Indigenous and Black
peoples, as well as the poor and other people of color. Rapper/Teacha KRS-1
discussed how the imagery and concept of the album referred to being
"revolutionary-minded" in reference to groups like the Black Panthers,
not drug dealers: "The idea was revolutionaries. If you look at the cover of
Criminal Minded, that's what we were saying modern-day Black Panthers
are. I had the gun belt going over the shoulder, grenades. That wasn't hood.
It wasn't like [we] had guns on the table like we were drug dealers—we
had grenades. Real paramilitary stuff was on the table. We were showing
ourselves to be revolutionaries. Gangsters are really intelligent. We're Black
Panthers" (Reid 2010). Thank you to M.A.

22 Hamza/John Walker Lindh, who was raised in Marin County, converted
to Islam at sixteen and traveled first to Yemen to study Arabic, then to
Pakistan, and finally to Afghanistan where he engaged in jihad for the sake
of Afghan Muslims on the side of the Taliban prior to September 11, 2001.
Lindh became interested in Islam after watching Malcolm X (Lee 1992)
with his mother and later reading Malcolm X's autobiography. He started
visiting mosques in Marin and later San Francisco and took his shahada at
sixteen. Zakariyya, a white convert to Islam from San Francisco who used
to work at Zaytuna Institute (and who also came to Islam through hip hop
and Malcolm X), said of Lindh, "I think John Walker probably got tripped
out when he was in Yemen. Maybe he linked up with some people who said
'Come to Pakistan,' and maybe those people had a political agenda. But
maybe not. There are good scholars in Pakistan. The media makes it sound
like those schools are just a bunch of jihad training camps. Maybe he ended
up there with good intentions and just got caught up" (York 2001). In the
end, the federal government did not have a case against Lindh because he
had not actually engaged in acts of war or terror against the United States,
and like Shafi, he was never found guilty of terrorism. Although the Justice
Department "dropped all charges against the defendant relating to terrorism, the administration would continue to treat the defendant as a terrorist
through the course of his incarceration by imposing what is known by
statute as special administrative measures and by common parlance simply

as a gag order" (Junod 2010). Lindh recently completed seventeen years of his twenty-year sentence and was released on parole.

23 See Bartosiewicz (2009). More Muslims are now mobilizing around her case (Samra 2021).

4. OUT OF BOUNDS

1 This pseudonym is named for Hadiya Pendleton, a fifteen-year-old girl who was shot and killed in Chicago's South Side on January 29, 2013. Her name means "gift" in both Swahili and Arabic. Her death, among too many, served as a clarion call for more attention to gun violence in Chicago. She is remembered by friends and family for the gift that she was, the stories, joy, and care she offered (Delgado, Doyle, Schmich n.d.; Warner 2022).

2 I'm thinking with the Roy Ayers Ubiquity track "Searching" from the *Vibrations* album (1976, Polydor).

3 Unlike most of my interlocutors, who typically use the pronouns "He/His," I use the pronouns "They/Their" to refer to Allah. This does not ascribe plurality to Allah's Oneness, and it should not be read as such. The Arabic masculine pronoun "huwa/hu" is used in the Qur'an to refer to Allah (God) in ways that do not ascribe a gender to Allah due to its expansive referential qualities (it indexes the masculine but can include the feminine). To directly translate "huwa/hu" as "he/him/his" in English does not necessarily convey that same expansiveness and gender neutrality. I do not use the feminine singular for the same reason. This is one instance in which direct translation gets in the way of getting at the exceptional and transcendent nature of Allah (Wadud 2013).

4 *Taleef Night to Remember: Habib Umars Powerful Dua Part 3* (2011). The translation is from the live simultaneous translation that was provided by Yahya Rhodus.

5 "Sublime" comes from the Latin sub- ("up to") followed by limen ("threshold") or limus ("oblique").

6 As a Shi'a Muslim who has witnessed and experienced tearful congregations, I was less surprised.

7 Women in the Ta'leef community had requested separate seating because it enabled women to sit more comfortably (there is often more space in the women's section); children run back and forth between the two sections as older children and young men and women serve tea and pastries. In the Nation of Islam, men and women also sit in their separate sections in chairs, a transformation of church pew arrangements. Just as Hamza Yusuf and others were aesthetically conscious about the design of spaces and products, as well as their own self-representation, there is also a consciousness of how people experience space in terms of aesthetics, gender, authority, learning, and culture. By bringing Arabic calligraphy and graffiti

together, serving tea and pastries, burning oud (aloeswood), and lining the walls with cushions, spaces like Ta'leef treat their congregations like guests, guests who encounter an Islam that is more than just legal rulings. 255

8 There are many female (and male) scholars situated in American and European (as well as African and Asian) universities who are often considered "outside the fold" of a traditional or orthodox Islam. This includes women like Amina Wadud, Leila Ahmed, and Fatima Mernissi, who received varying amounts of "traditional" versus "secular" training in Islamic scholarship. The dynamics at play in terms of which female scholars are deemed "authentic" and "authoritative" has as much to do with the ways they interpret Islamic texts as their relationships to and comportments within particular Muslim communities. Who authorizes such claims for whom is perhaps the more important line of questioning and speaks to the potential in the politics of citation, invitation, and hiring.

9 Such issues are typically unspoken, alluding to inappropriate gender-mixing, sexual conduct, and influence. Gender mixing in and of itself is a debated issue, yet proscriptions regarding it tend to index the fear of illicit sexual activity and suspicions that can arise, thereby disrupting communal relations. Such gender relations are a critical issue for young Muslims, as they are instructed to negate their sexualities and distance themselves from the opposite sex, but then find a spouse and get married. They avoid gender-mixing to show respect for one another, yet it often amounts to upholding Muslim women's piety and sexuality as especially sacred, vulnerable, and receptive (as opposed to active). As in the wider mainstream American culture, it is often young Muslim women who bear the brunt of societal expectations of maintaining cultural norms of piety and honor. Dating is prohibited at Zaytuna, so instead students propose marriage, enabling courting to begin within strictures mandated by consistently shifting and negotiated social norms. Multiple Zaytuna marriages have occurred, it being an ideal location to find a like-minded spouse, most successfully with the participation and consent of parents, others less so.

10 *Masha'Allah* can be translated as "God has willed it," and it is typically used to express an appreciation or recognition of Allah's work in something good, joyous, or beautiful that has happened.

11 Thurayya was "named" by her fellow student "Zahrah," whom I had "named." Thurayya is the Arabic name of the constellation Pleiades.

12 Such speculation refers to interpretation of legal sources and their evidence or proof (daleel) which can be designated zanni (nondefinitive, thereby requiring human consideration) or qat'i (decisive) in Islamic law. For Fatima Mernissi and others, the discursive tradition since the passing of the Prophet Muhammad in the seventh century has increasingly moved toward the preservation of power in a male elite (Mernissi 2010).

13 Yusuf's primary training was in Mauritania around the time that Mauritania abolished slavery in 1981. Slavery continued into the twen-

tieth century via a complex and racialized caste system that drew from Mauritania's colonial history and the influence of Islam. While 'ulama' supported the freeing of slaves because none were a result of jihad (Mauritania practiced a form of chattel slavery where one was born into it by one's enslaved mother), the practice has continued into the twenty-first century and groups like the Initiative for the Resurgence of the Abolitionist Movement (est. 2008) fight for the end of de facto slavery in Mauritania. Islamic tradition has been mobilized both to maintain slavery in Mauritania and to abolish it in Western Africa during the Atlantic slave trade, once again demonstrating the need to investigate the ethical and political together (Ware 2014; E. A. MacDougall 2005). Situating texts historically is important for giving context, but we should also consider those historical contexts in relation to the consistency of the Islamic tradition in regard to difference and deeds. Being a "man of his time" does not exonerate a Muslim, who should challenge injustices wherever and whenever one sees it, even if that estranges them from their community; this is part of the Prophetic tradition. At the same time, when considering the circumstances of revelation, context provides important lessons regarding when a situation has particular or general applicability.

14. Professor Abdullah Ali, who like Yusuf is a Maliki scholar, recently published his thesis examining notions of race within the Maliki tradition (Abdullah bin Hamid Ali 2019b).

15. Turning notions of relational (sexual) rights (Foucault and Rabinow 1997, 161–3) to gendered space, I suggest a way of thinking about gender-specific spaces and relational forms as a Muslim queering of American gender relations and gendered space. The ways in which liberal, state, and particular feminist discourses often frame appropriate forms of gender relations and sexuality often malign Muslim populations and practices as deviant, illiberal, and unmodern (see Puar 2007; Rana 2011). Queer theory allows for a space to think through other forms of relationality being negotiated within multiple authoritative frameworks (Moussawi 2020; Kapadia 2019).

16. Besides conversations and classrooms, there is a recorded example in a video of Hamza Yusuf, published in 2011 but recorded earlier (*The Daughter of Imam Malik by Sheikh Hamza Yusuf*).

17. Ustadha Loni is named for another teacher of mine, filmmaker, educator, and activist Loni Ding (1931–2010). Her Ethnic Studies documentary course at UC Berkeley was an epic education, which sometimes extended across the Bay Bridge when she would give me rides back to the City. She told me that to succeed as a filmmaker, one had to be "obsessed." I initially worried I wasn't obsessed enough, but I learned years later at the editing table that indeed I was. Loni's films, including *Ancestors in the Americas* (2001) and *Nissei Soldier* (1984), continue to be screened, carrying on her vision and care.

18 One morning during the fajr class in the Zaytuna library, Shaykh Yahya
   Rhodus told a story that he had learned from his teachers about an old
   man who would travel a great distance every day to sit with a scholar. His
   daughter would always accompany him. One day he stopped because he
   needed to relieve himself. His daughter gave him advice about how to position himself to not soil his garments. When he was finished, he turned
   back in the direction of their home. When she asked him why, he told her
   that he already learned something that day. This story was told to express
   how knowledge did not always have to come from some great scholar; it
   could also come from a young girl. This story also spoke to the old man's
   ability to recognize knowledge as knowledge.

19 Annemarie Schimmel writes about how it is through a woman's eyes,
   Khadija's, that revelation and the sacred were recognized. Khadija was
   the one who calmed the Prophet Muhammad when he was unsure of
   the angel Gabriel's visit. She made him "see" (Schimmel 1997; see also
   Power of a Woman Shaykh Hamza Yusuf). The Zaytuna students' blog also
   describes Khadija's role in "Khadija Knew," https://zaytunies-blog-blog
   .tumblr.com/post/6028403521/khadijaknew.

20 At the same time, in the early 2010s, a boycott was instituted against
   Fatima Mojahed, an American Muslim da'iya, in Dewbery, England, where
   she was a featured speaker in a Muslim women's gathering. The critique is
   that she is a woman who does not practice purdah and is seen laughing and
   joking in videos to mixed audiences. Imam Tahir Anwar (a San Jose–based
   imam who teaches at Zaytuna College) posted a reaction from British
   'ulama' in support of Mojahed. This incident demonstrates both the wide
   range of opinions regarding female scholars and the potential critiques
   Zaytuna scholars and students will face based on the coeducation, gender-
   mixing, and promotion of particular forms of female scholarship.

21 Women like Ella Baker worked behind the scenes building movements
   of young people and coordinating the work for which male public figures
   like Martin Luther King Jr., James Farmer, and Stokely Carmichael received much of the credit and glory (Collier-Thomas and Franklin 2001;
   Ransby 2003). The Black Panther Party depended on the work of key
   female figures who did much of the organizing of campaigns and social
   projects (Brown 1992; McGuire 2010). Ethnographies specifically about
   Muslim women (Deeb 2006; Göle 1996; Hafez 2011; Kanaaneh 2002;
   Khalili 2007; Mahmood 2005; Rouse 2004) articulate the way Muslim
   women are active agents in imparting knowledge, organizing for social
   and political justice, cultivating ethical subjectivities, and impacting the
   lives of their respective communities, though they are not well-known
   figures like their male counterparts.

22 The film can be viewed at www.maryamkashani.com.

23 I am reminded here of Ruth Forman's "Poetry Should Ride the Bus" (1993).

24 I do not know if the students were aware of his being a significant historical and literary figure regarding "the love that dare not speak its name,"
although any quick research would soon reveal these associations. The
students were quite conscious of debates about homosexuality both within
the wider American context and within Islam. They raised the issue in their
Islamic law classes, as well as in gatherings with scholars elsewhere.

25 Tarawih prayers are night prayers done during the month of Ramadan,
often during which the entirety of the Qur'an is recited.

5. EPISTEMOLOGIES OF THE OPPRESSOR AND THE OPPRESSED

The first two epigraphs are from Yusuf 2012; the third epigraph is from
Mahmood 2016, 183. While the first hadith stresses assisting the oppressor by preventing his oppression (restraining his hand), the Qur'an also
warns of being in proximity to or in alliance with those who oppress
(*zhalam*): "And incline not to those who do wrong (*zhalamu*), or the Fire
will seize you; and ye have no protectors other than Allah, nor shall ye be
helped" (Qur'an 11:113; al-Dar'i 2012).

1 'Abd al-Qadir al-Jaza'iri (1808–1883) was a Qadiri Islamic scholar who
led a military struggle against the French colonial invasion of Algeria,
was exiled in France, and later settled in Damascus, Syria. Omar Mukhtar
(1858–1931) was a Qur'an teacher who led a guerilla war and resistance
movement against the Italian colonization of Libya. During French rule
in Algeria, the Union (or Association) of Muslim Scholars (Jam'iyat al-
'Ulama', est. 1931) advocated for an Algerian nation grounded in the Arabic language and Islamic traditions (though they were critical of Sufism
and marabouts); during the Algerian War of Independence (1954–1962)
they aligned with the National Liberation Front.

2 The hadith is from Nawawi's *Forty Hadith* 24.

3 This reconstruction is in relation to but distinct from the reconstruction
or Islamization of knowledge put forward by Muhammad Iqbal (d. 1938)
(2013); Seyyed Hossein Nasr (b. 1933) (1981; 1993); Isma'il Al Faruqi (d.
1986) (2018; see also Z. A. Grewal 2013); and Syed Muhammad Naquib
al-Attas (b. 1931) (1980; 1985; see also F. Ahmed 2018). The distinction
is in how I foreground the impact of the race concept and coloniality in
these histories and processes of Islamic knowledge. For a similar discussion in relationship to modernity, see Zaidi (2006; 2011).

4 Zaytuna's liberal arts program focuses on the Hellenic and Christian
aspects (e.g., Aristotle and Aquinas) of the Western tradition prior to
the Age of Reason; the students' philosophy course in their junior year
is a survey of Western thought from antiquity to contemporary critical
theory, and they also consider "Western Enlightenment thought and its

turn away from virtue ethics, specifically in Emmanuel Kant's deontologi-
cal ethics and John Stuart Mill's utilitarianism" in their senior course on
ethics (Zaytuna College 2017, 2023).

5 This is a nuanced point of *ikhtilaf* (difference) in the discursive tradition,
where some view the primary subject of Islamic ethics, law, and theology as those with political, social, religious, and economic authority
and responsibility in this world, whereas others foreground the agentive
potential and responsibility of the oppressed.

6 Similar theorizations of our historical present include Asad's "formations
of the secular (2003); Du Bois's "color line" (1990); Quijano's "racism/
ethnicity complex" (1971); Mignolo's coloniality as modernity (2009);
Winant's "global racial complex" (2001); Lowe's "colonial divisions of
humanity" (2015); Horne's "the apocalypse of settler colonialism" (2018);
and da Silva's "analytics of raciality" (2007).

7 There have been multiple theological challenges to white supremacy
within Islam, from the Nation of Islam's theologies of "white devils" to
the foundational tenets of Islam being an antiracist system in which we
were made "into nations and tribes that ye may know each other. Verily
the most honored of you in the sight of Allah is the most righteous of
you" (Qur'an 49:13).

8 In 2019, Yusuf was appointed to Secretary of State Pompeo's Commission
for Human Rights, which was mandated to redefine human rights law
through a return to "natural law"; the commission largely consisted of
religious conservatives and was seen as a rejoinder to human rights laws
that include rights regarding sexuality, gender identity, and reproductive
rights such as abortion, as well as rights of indigeneity. Some Zaytuna
scholars have also recently aligned themselves with conservative Christians who assert that they are vulnerable to public discourses and federal
and state laws that contradict and malign their religious views regarding
gender and sexuality. LGBTQIA2S+ peoples are viewed sympathetically as
those who must refrain from sin, or that which is considered haram. At
the same time, Zaytuna's location in the San Francisco Bay Area (as well
as Hollywood and mainstream representation) may make it seem that a
(white, homonationalist) "gay agenda" is more powerful and influential
than it actually is. Religious discourses continue to contribute to the
disproportionate violence, estrangement, incarceration, and death of
LGBTQIA2S+ individuals and their communities, while Muslims locally
and beyond seek to live queer lives that exceed normative and inclusive/
exclusive discourses of both Islam and LGBTQIA2S+.

9 Zaytuna College no longer uses this model, nor Shakir's syllabus; my
ethnography of "Zaytuna 1.0" offers a glimpse of one moment in Zaytuna
College's short history toward enabling us to think about its potential
futures. Students now take a one-semester Islamic History course and a

constitutional law course. They also take general courses in politics, economics, philosophy, and contemporary Muslim thought (focused on the late seventeenth century to the present) (Zaytuna College 2017, 20; 2023).

10 During the Q&A session, one Zaytuna student asked about reinstalling the gold standard to restructure economies more equitably. Dussel argued that this would not address the fundamental idolatry toward the market as "the hand of God," which was structured to produce poverty. Bazian asserted that "The Prophet did mandate a particular monetary structure. . . . He specified that it has to be gold and silver and fixed the ratio between them. The Prophet himself was a merchant . . . to rethink prior to the modern capitalist structure in terms of the gold standard, the Bretton Woods agreement 1945, it still does not deal with how to go to prior to 1492 and prior to this capitalist structure and how to rethink if it's possible" (on Bretton Woods and the effects of global financialization, see also Kim 2022). Shakir emphasized that the student's question came from seeking out a starting point, from which to recalibrate finance capital, yet Dussel consistently returned to the problem of the market itself and individualized social reproduction.

11 Shakir is not romanticizing militant uprising, but rather conveying a very different political moment in which members of the Puerto Rican Nationalist Party "fired several shots . . . to free [themselves] of colonial domination" (Ruiz 2019, 35).

12 Shakeela is named for Shakeela Hassan, who immigrated from India in the 1950s to Chicago where she and her husband Mohammad Zia Hassan (1933–2017) were welcomed into the fold of the family of Elijah and Clara Muhammad. She created the iconic caps that Elijah Muhammad would wear, and their ongoing grounded relationality "defied current divisions between 'immigrant and indigenous' Muslims in the United States" (Sapelo Square 2018). Shakeela writes about the making of the fez in *A Starry Crown: Making of a Fez* (Hassan 2020), and I learned from Shakeela and her husband while recording interviews for the Muslims of the Midwest project (https://muslimsofthemidwest.org/).

13 In 2006, Imam Zaid Shakir wrote that one of the ways to preserve and sustain Islam is to distinguish between what it offers in terms of the ethical and the maintenance of our souls and how it may work in relation to particular political analyses and strategies: "Reducing Islam to an ideology threatens to subordinate those laws and principles to political imperatives that have little to do with Islamic teachings. If this happens consistently enough, the social foundation of our religion may be lost. As Muslims we may well continue in our various struggles. However, those struggles would be better informed by the revolutionary teachings of Bakunin, Georges Sorel, Rosa Luxemburg, Lenin, Mao, Che Guevara, and others than by the revelation given to our Prophet Muhammad, Peace and Blessings of Allah upon him" (Shakir 2006b).

14 Ustadha Leenah Safi, a graduate of Zaytuna College, writes in her preface of the same text *Towards Sacred Activism* (Walid 2018) that today "we see Muslims too shallowly engaging Islam to be transformed by it, let alone for them to then transform society through it. Being a Muslim has become an identity marker just like any other, stripping it of its vertical meaning in attachment to the Divine" (L. Safi 2018, 19).

15 Dhikr is the remembrance of Allah, often done through the repetitive recitation of short phrases or words that glorify Allah with the working of beads on a string called *misbah* or *tasbih*. They resemble in both appearance and usage Catholic rosary beads and Buddhist meditation beads.

16 *Jumu'a,* means Friday, and it is the day of the requisite (for men) congregational prayer within the Islamic week, Salat al-Jumu'a. "Jumu'a" comes from the root letters J-M-'A, which mean to gather, to unite, combine, or bring together. *Jami'a,* the Arabic word for "university," also comes from the same root and connotes the bringing together of many subjects in a place of learning, where people gather to transmit knowledge.

17 Yusuf gave President G. W. Bush a copy of the Essential Qur'an, which he had spent the previous night annotating for the most pertinent verses. He also gave him Arabic calligraphy by fellow white Muslim convert Muhammad Zachariyya, whose work is presented on the US postal Eid stamp, and a copy of *Thunder in the Sky: Secrets on the Acquisition and Exercise of Power* (Cleary 1993) translated by Thomas Cleary, which presents classical Chinese Taoist texts that, in Yusuf's words, describe "the humanistic use of power." He then articulated four key points: (1) that Islam had nothing to do with the September 11 attacks, that it "teaches mercy, compassion and when it uses martial force, it uses it with just laws. Noncombatants are never involved"; (2) the danger of polarization: the only people who benefit from a "clash of civilizations" are "warmongers"; (3) the need for consensus (*ijma'*) and a summit meeting with "the most prominent Muslim Ulema [*sic*] (scholars) in the Muslim world to declare terrorism as inconsistent with the teachings of Islam," with an additional interfaith meeting, perhaps in Jerusalem or Rome, rejecting "state terrorism or individual terrorism . . . political means to political ends"; and (4) "that this country had a responsibility in creating just regimes because of the power this country has. That we have to recognize the oppression and extreme circumstances in the Muslim world that breeds the type of extremism that exists in some parts of the Muslim world" (Yusuf 2001).

18 Another way this is articulated is through the metaphoric "seat at the table." If one is not at the table, one may be served on the table. On the other hand, one does not want to get stuck at the table (especially if everything being served contains pork, as it is considered unlawful or unethical to consume it).

19 Zaytuna College scholars' previous relationships with Turkey have also been questioned as Erdogan's government continues to jail and disappear

journalists, intellectuals, and activists (though they soured in 2016 over Zaytuna scholars' treatment of Erdogan at the funeral of Muhammad Ali—they did not allow him to speak).

20 He also apologized directly for slighting Yasir Qadhi, who in the past had been critical of Yusuf. He also clarified comments regarding the use of Islam as a political ideology that leads to groups like Al Qaeda and ISIS. In his comments the day before he seemed to insinuate that groups like the Muslim Brotherhood were responsible for ISIS. For more commentary on risgate, as it came to be called, see https://www .blackmuslimpsychology.org/ris2016controversy.

21 Fifty years earlier, Baldwin noted what Martin Luther King Jr. learned when he went to Chicago in 1966: "That there was a whole generation of black people whom he was completely unable to touch. . . . It was so much more devious to say to one of those kids, 'We shall overcome.' To say that, with patience, time will do this or that was absolutely mean- ingless. . . . What you had to do was deal with him as though he were a valuable human being because no one had ever treated him as though he had any value. Finally they began to do it themselves" (Mead and Bald- win 1971, 58). King's approach to politics changed dramatically after his failed campaign in Chicago, leading to the inception of the Poor People's campaign in 1967.

22 Within weeks of the RIS event, Yusuf was courted by the Trump adminis- tration; he attended the National Prayer Breakfast in February 2017 and in 2019 joined the Human Rights Commission organized by Secretary of State Pompeo.

23 Quoted in El-Sharif 2018.

REFERENCES

Abbas, Asma. 2014. "In Terror, in Love, Out of Time." In *At the Limits of Justice: Women of Colour on Terror*, edited by Suvendrini Perera and Sherene Razack, 503–25. Toronto: University of Toronto Press.

Abd-Allah, Umar F. 2006. *A Muslim in Victorian America: The Life of Alexander Russell Webb*. New York: Oxford University Press.

Abdul Khabeer, Su'ad. 2016. *Muslim Cool: Race, Religion, and Hip Hop in the United States*. New York: New York University Press.

Abdul Khabeer, Su'ad. 2017a. "Africa as Tradition in U.S. African American Muslim Identity." *Journal of Africana Religions* 5, no. 1: 26–49.

Abdul Khabeer, Su'ad. 2017b. "Suad Abdul Khabeer Responds to Amna Akbar and Jeanne Theoharis." *Boston Review*. February 28, 2017. https://www .bostonreview.net/forum_response/suad-abdul-khabeer-suad-abdul -khabeer-responds-amna-akbar-and-jeanne/.

Abdul Khabeer, Su'ad. 2018. "To Be a (Young) Black Muslim Woman Intellectual." In *With Stones in Our Hands: Writings on Muslims, Racism, and Empire*, 287–97. Minneapolis: University of Minnesota Press.

Abdullah, Zain. 2010. *Black Mecca: The African Muslims of Harlem*. New York: Oxford University Press.

Abu-Lughod, Janet L. 1989. *Before European Hegemony: The World System A.D. 1250–1350*. New York: Oxford University Press.

Abu-Lughod, Lila. 1990. "The Romance of Resistance: Tracing Transformations of Power through Bedouin Women." *American Ethnologist* 17, no. 1 (Feb. 1990): 41–55.

Abu-Lughod, Lila. 2005. *Dramas of Nationhood: The Politics of Television in Egypt*. Chicago: University of Chicago Press.

ACLU. 2010. "ACLU and Asian Law Caucus Seek Records on FBI Surveillance of Mosques and Use of Informants in Northern California." American Civil Liberties Union. March 9, 2010. http://www.aclu.org/racial-justice -religion-belief/aclu-and-asian-law-caucus-seek-records-fbi-surveillance -mosques-and-u.

ACLU. 2012a. "Mapping the FBI: Uncovering Abusive Surveillance and Racial Profiling." American Civil Liberties Union. https://www.aclu.org /mapping-fbi-uncovering-abusive-surveillance-and-racial-profiling.

ACLU. 2012b. "ACLU Eye on the FBI Alert—Mosque Outreach for Intelligence Gathering." American Civil Liberties Union. https://www.aclu.org/other /aclu-eye-fbi-alert-mosque-outreach-intelligence-gathering.

Agrama, Hussein Ali. 2012. *Questioning Secularism: Islam, Sovereignty, and the Rule of Law in Modern Egypt*. Chicago: University of Chicago Press.

Ahmed, Farah. 2018. "An Exploration of Naquib Al-Attas' Theory of Islamic Education as *Ta'dīb* as an 'Indigenous' Educational Philosophy." *Educational Philosophy and Theory* 50, no. 8: 786–94.

Ahmed, Sara. 2010. *The Promise of Happiness*. Durham, NC: Duke University Press.

Ahmed, Shahab. 2017. *What Is Islam: The Importance of Being Islamic*. Princeton, NJ: Princeton University Press.

Aidi, Hisham. 2014. *Rebel Music: Race, Empire, and the New Muslim Youth Culture*. New York: Pantheon Books.

Aidi, Hisham. 2016. "The Political Uses of Malcolm X's Image." *The Nation*. July 12. https://www.thenation.com/article/archive/the-political-uses-of -malcolm-x-image/.

Akins, Damon B., and William J. Bauer, Jr. 2021. *We Are the Land: A History of Native California*. Oakland: University of California Press.

Akkad, Moustapha, director. *The Lion of the Desert*. 1980. YouTube video, 02:53. October 13, 2019. https://www.youtube.com/watch?v=3zUBLjAAgWg.

Alcoff, Linda Martín. 2011. "An Epistemology for the Next Revolution." *Transmodernity: Journal of Peripheral Cultural Production of the Luso-Hispanic World* 1, no. 2: 67–78.

Alexander, M. Jacqui. 2005. *Pedagogies of Crossing: Meditations on Feminism, Sexual Politics, Memory, and the Sacred*. Durham, NC: Duke University Press.

Alhassen, Maytha. 2010. "The Liquor Store Wars." CounterPunch.Org. July 23. https://www.counterpunch.org/2010/07/23/the-liquor-store-wars/.

Alhazen, Ibn, and A. I. Sabra. 1989. *The Optics of Ibn Al-Haytham. Books I–III, On Direct Vision*. 2 vols. London: University of London.

Ali, Abdullah bin Hamid. 2019a. "How Islamic Is Critical Race Theory?" *Lamppost Education Initiative* (blog). June 13. https://lamppostedu.org/critical -race-theory.

Ali, Abdullah bin Hamid. 2019b. *The "Negro" in Arab-Muslim Consciousness*. Swansea, UK: Claritas Books.

Ali, Abdullah Yusuf. 2002. *The Meaning of the Holy Qur'an*. Beltsville, MD: Amana Publications.

Ali, Arshad Imtiaz. 2016. "Citizens under Suspicion: Responsive Research with Community under Surveillance." *Anthropology and Education Quarterly* 47, no. 1: 78–95.

Ali, Kecia. 2016. *Sexual Ethics and Islam: Feminist Reflections on Qur'an, Hadith, and Jurisprudence.* London: Oneworld Publications.

Allam, Hannah. 2019. "5 Takeaways about the Trump Administration's Response to Far-Right Extremism." NPR.org. June 7, 2019. https://www.npr.org/2019/06/07/730346019/5-takeaways-about-the-trump-administrations-response-to-far-right-extremism.

Allawi, Ali A. 2009. *The Crisis of Islamic Civilization.* New Haven, CT: Yale University Press.

Allen, Robert L. 1989. *The Port Chicago Mutiny: The Story of the Largest Mass Mutiny Trial in U.S. Naval History.* Oakland, CA: Equal Justice Society.

Alloula, Malek. 1986. *The Colonial Harem.* Theory and History of Literature 21. Minneapolis: University of Minnesota Press.

Alsultany, Evelyn. 2012. *Arabs and Muslims in the Media: Race and Representation after 9/11.* New York: New York University Press.

Alsultany, Evelyn. 2013. "Arabs and Muslims in the Media after 9/11: Representational Strategies for a 'Postrace' Era." *American Quarterly* 65, no. 1: 161–69.

Al-Amin, Imam Jamil. 1994. *Revolution by the Book (The Rap Is Live).* Beltsville, MD: Writers' Inc.

Angail, Nadirah. 2016. "Hamza Yusuf and the Dangers of Black Pathology." Tumblr. *Struggles of a Covered Girl* (blog). December 25. https://strugglinghijabi.tumblr.com/post/154946891650/hamza-yusuf-and-the-dangers-of-black-pathology.

Ansari, Zaynab. 2015. "Blurred Lines: Women, 'Celebrity' Shaykhs, and Spiritual Abuse." *MuslimMatters.Org* (blog). May 27. https://muslimmatters.org/2015/05/27/blurred-lines-women-celebrity-shaykhs-spiritual-abuse/.

Apuzzo, Matt. 2016. "Only Hard Choices for Parents Whose Children Flirt with Terror." *New York Times.* April 9, 2016. https://www.nytimes.com/2016/04/10/us/parents-face-limited-options-to-keep-children-from-terrorism.html.

Apuzzo, Matt, and Eileen Sullivan. 2012. "FBI Muslim Scandal: Documents Show San Francisco FBI Office Illegally Collected Information on Local Muslims." *Huffington Post.* March 28. http://www.huffingtonpost.com/2012/03/28/fbi-muslim-scandal_n_1386482.html. Accessed April 4, 2012.

Arab Resource and Organizing Center. 2021. "Block the Boat: Arab Resource and Organizing Center (AROC)." https://blocktheboat.org/.

Arnold, Eric K. 2011. "Oakland Gang Injunctions: Gentrification or Public Safety?" *Race, Poverty and the Environment* 18, no. 2: 70–74.

Arnold, Eric K. 2021. "From Underground Anonymity to National Acclaim: The Life and Art of Steve 'Zumbi' Gaines." *The Oaklandside.* August 23. https://oaklandside.org/2021/08/23/life-art-steve-zumbi-gaines-zion-i-bay-area-hip-hop/.

Arnold, Thomas Walker. 1896. *The Preaching of Islam: A History of the Propagation of the Muslim Faith.* Westminster: A. Constable.

266   Asad, Muhammad. 2000. *The Road to Mecca*. 4th rev. ed. Louisville, KY: Fons Vitae.

Asad, Muhammad. 2012. *Message of the Qur'an*. London: Book Foundation.

Asad, Talal. 1986. *The Idea of an Anthropology of Islam*. Washington, DC: Center for Contemporary Arab Studies, Georgetown University.

Asad, Talal. 1993. *Genealogies of Religion: Discipline and Reasons of Power in Christianity and Islam*. Baltimore, MD: Johns Hopkins University Press.

Asad, Talal. 2003. *Formations of the Secular: Christianity, Islam, Modernity*. Stanford, CA: Stanford University Press.

Asad, Talal. 2007. *On Suicide Bombing*. New York: Columbia University Press.

Asad, Talal. 2009. "Reply to Judith Butler." In *Is Critique Secular? Blasphemy, Injury, and Free Speech*, edited by Talal Asad, Wendy Brown, Judith Butler, and Saba Mahmood, 137–45. Townsend Papers in the Humanities, no 2. Berkeley: Townsend Center for the Humanities Distributed by University of California Press.

Asad, Talal, Wendy Brown, Judith Butler, and Saba Mahmood. 2009. *Is Critique Secular? Blasphemy, Injury, and Free Speech*. Berkeley: University of California Press.

Ashcroft, John. 2002. "Transcript of Attorney General John Ashcroft, Remarks on FBI Reorganization." U.S. Department of Justice. https://www.justice .gov/archive/ag/speeches/2002/53002agpreparedremarks.htm.

al-Attas, Syed Muhammad Naguib. 1985. *Islam, Secularism, and the Philosophy of the Future*. New York: Mansell Publishing.

al-Attas, Syed Muhammad Naguib. 1993. *Islam and Secularism*. Kuala Lumpur: International Institute of Islamic Thought and Civilization.

al-Attas, Syed Muhammad Naquib. 1980. "The Concept of Education in Islam." Muslim Education Foundation. http://www.mef-ca.org/files/attas-text -final.pdf.

Austin, Allan D. 2012. *African Muslims in Antebellum America: Transatlantic Stories and Spiritual Struggles*. New York: Routledge.

Auston, Donna. 2017. "Prayer, Protest, and Police Brutality: Black Muslim Spiritual Resistance in the Ferguson Era." *Transforming Anthropology* 25, no. 1: 11–22.

Aydin, Cemil. 2017. *The Idea of the Muslim World: A Global Intellectual History*. Cambridge, MA: Harvard University Press.

al-Azami, Dr. Usaama. 2019. "Shaykh Hamza Yusuf and the Question of Rebellion in the Islamic Tradition." *MuslimMatters.Org* (blog). September 15. https://muslimmatters.org/2019/09/15/shaykh-hamza-yusuf-and-the -question-of-rebellion-in-the-islamic-tradition/.

Al-Azami, Usaama. 2021. *Islam and the Arab Revolutions: The Ulama between Democracy and Autocracy*. Oxford: Oxford University Press.

Babayan, Kathryn, and Afsaneh Najmabadi. 2008. *Islamicate Sexualities: Translations across Temporal Geographies of Desire*. Cambridge, MA: Harvard University Press.

Bald, Vivek. 2013. *Bengali Harlem and the Lost Histories of South Asian America.* 267
Cambridge, MA: Harvard University Press.

Balkin, Jack M., and Sanford Levinson. 2006. "The Processes of Constitutional
Change: From Partisan Entrenchment to the National Surveillance State."
Fordham Law Review 75: 489.

Banks, Ingrid, Gaye Johnson, George Lipsitz, Ula Taylor, Daniel Widener, and
Clyde Woods, eds. 2012. *Black California Dreamin': The Crises of Cali-
fornia's African-American Communities.* Santa Barbara: UCSB Center for
Black Studies Research.

Barker, Joanne, ed. 2017. *Critically Sovereign: Indigenous Gender, Sexuality, and
Feminist Studies.* Durham, NC: Duke University Press.

Barker, Joanne. 2018. "Territory as Analytic: The Dispossession of Lenapehok-
ing and the Subprime Crisis." *Social Text* 36, no. 2 (135): 19–39.

Barkun, Michael. 2017. "The FBI and American Muslims after September 11."
In *The FBI and Religion: Faith and National Security before and after 9/11,*
edited by Sylvester A. Johnson and Steven Weitzman, 1st ed., 244–55.
Berkeley: University of California Press.

Bartolome, Tina. 2020. "Kiilu Taught Me: Letters to My Comrade." In *Black
Panther Afterlives: The Enduring Significance of the Black Panther Party,*
edited by Diane C. Fujino and Matef Harmachis. Chicago: Haymarket
Books.

Bartosiewicz, Petra. 2009. "The Intelligence Factory: How America Makes Its
Enemies Disappear." *Harpers Magazine.* November. https://harpers.org
/archive/2009/11/the-intelligence-factory/.

Bayoumi, Moustafa. 2008. *How Does It Feel to Be a Problem?: Being Young and
Arab in America.* New York: Penguin.

Bazian, Hatem. 2018. "Sami Al-Arian and Silencing Palestine." In *With Stones in
Our Hands: Writings on Muslims, Racism, and Empire,* 306–25. Minneapolis: University of Minnesota Press.

Bazian, Hatem, and Farid Senzai. 2013. "The Bay Area Muslim Study: Establishing Identity and Community." Washington, DC: Institute for Social
Policy and Understanding.

Bazzano, Elliott, and Marcia K. Hermansen. 2020. *Varieties of American Sufism:
Islam, Sufi Orders, and Authority in a Time of Transition.* Albany: State
University of New York Press.

Beliso-De Jesus, Aisha. 2013. "Religious Cosmopolitanisms: Media, Transnational Santería, and Travel between the United States and Cuba." *American Ethnologist* 40, no. 4: 704–20.

Beliso-De Jesús, Aisha M. 2015. *Electric Santería: Racial and Sexual Assemblages of
Transnational Religion.* New York: Columbia University Press.

Beliso-De Jesús, Aisha M. and Jemima Pierre. 2020. "Special Section:
Anthropology of White Supremacy." *American Anthropologist* 122, no. 1:
65–75.

Bendaoui, Assia. 2018. *The Feeling of Being Watched*. HD. Documentary. Women Make Movies.

Benjamin, Walter. 1968. *Illuminations*. New York: Harcourt.

Berry, Maya J., Claudia Chávez Argüelles, Shanya Cordis, Sarah Ihmoud, and Elizabeth Velásquez Estrada. 2017. "Toward a Fugitive Anthropology: Gender, Race, and Violence in the Field." *Cultural Anthropology* 32, no. 4: 537–65.

Besteman, Catherine Lowe, and Network of Concerned Anthropologists Steering Committee. 2009. *The Counter-Counterinsurgency Manual: Or, Notes on Demilitarizing American Society*. Chicago: Prickly Paradigm Press.

BondGraham, Darwin. 2018. "Terror or Entrapment?" *East Bay Express*. January 3. https://www.eastbayexpress.com/oakland/terror-or-entrapment/Content?oid=12242075.

BondGraham, Darwin, and Ali Winston. 2013. "The Real Purpose of Oakland's Surveillance Center." *East Bay Express*. December. https://www.eastbayexpress.com/oakland/the-real-purpose-of-oaklands-surveillance-center/Content?oid=3789230.

Borneman, John, and Joseph Masco. 2015. "Anthropology and the Security State." *American Anthropologist* 117, no. 4: 781–85.

Bowen, John R. 2011. *Can Islam Be French?: Pluralism and Pragmatism in a Secularist State*. Princeton, NJ: Princeton University Press.

Bowen, John R. 2016. *On British Islam: Religion, Law, and Everyday Practice in Shari'a Councils*. Princeton, NJ: Princeton University Press.

Broussard, Albert S. 2001. "In Search of the Promised Land: African American Migration to San Francisco." In *Seeking El Dorado: African Americans in California*, edited by Lawrence Brooks De Graaf, Kevin Mulroy, Quintard Taylor, and Autry Museum of Western Heritage, 181–209. Los Angeles: Autry Museum of Western Heritage; Seattle: University of Seattle Press.

Brown, Adrienne M. 2017. *Emergent Strategy: Shaping Change, Changing Worlds*. Chico, CA: AK Press.

Brown, Elaine. 1992. *A Taste of Power: A Black Woman's Story*. 1st ed. New York: Pantheon Books.

Brown, Jonathan A. C. 2009a. *Hadith: Muhammad's Legacy in the Medieval and Modern World*. Oxford: Oneworld Publications.

Brown, Jonathan A. C. 2009b. "Maṣlaḥah." In *The Oxford Encyclopedia of the Islamic World*. Oxford Islamic Studies Online. http://www.oxfordislamic-studies.com.proxy2.library.illinois.edu/print/opr/t236/e0514.

Browne, Simone. 2015. *Dark Matters: On the Surveillance of Blackness*. Durham, NC: Duke University Press.

Bubandt, Nils, Mikkel Rytter, and Christian Suhr. 2019. "A Second Look at Invisibility: Al-Ghayb, Islam, Ethnography." *Contemporary Islam* 13, no. 1: 1–16.

Bukhari, Safiya. 2010. *The War Before: The True Life Story of Becoming a Black Panther, Keeping the Faith in Prison, and Fighting for Those Left Behind*. New York: The Feminist Press at City University of New York.

Butler, Judith. 2010. *Frames of War: When Is Life Grievable?* London: Verso. 269

Byrd, Jodi A. 2011. *The Transit of Empire: Indigenous Critiques of Colonialism.* Minneapolis: University of Minnesota Press.

Byrd, Jodi A., Alyosha Goldstein, Jodi Melamed, and Chandan Reddy. 2018. "Predatory Value Economies of Dispossession and Disturbed Relationalities." *Social Text* 36, no. 2 (135): 1–18.

Cainkar, Louise. 2009. *Homeland Insecurity: The Arab American and Muslim American Experience after 9/11.* New York: Russell Sage Foundation.

Camp, Jordan T., and Christina Heatherton. 2016. "Broken Windows, Surveillance, and the New Urban Counterinsurgency: An Interview with Hamid Khan." In *Policing the Planet: Why the Policing Crisis Led to Black Lives Matter.* New York: Verso.

Campt, Tina M. 2017. *Listening to Images.* Durham, NC: Duke University Press.

Center for Constitutional Rights. 2008. "Restore, Protect, Expand: The Right to Dissent." 100 Days to Restore the Constitution series. New York: Center for Constitutional Rights. https://ccrjustice.org/home/get-involved /tools-resources/publications/publication-restore-protect-expand-right -dissent.

Césaire, Aimé. 2001. *Discourse on Colonialism.* Translated by Joan Pinkham. New York: Monthly Review Press.

Chan-Malik, Sylvia. 2011. "'Common Cause': On the Black-Immigrant Debate and Constructing the Muslim American." *Journal of Race, Ethnicity, and Religion* 2, no. 8: (May): 39.

Chan-Malik, Sylvia. 2018. *Being Muslim: A Cultural History of Women of Color in American Islam.* New York: NYU Press.

Chan-Malik, Sylvia, Evelyn Alsultany, Su'ad Abdul Khabeer, and Maryam Kashani. 2014. "'A Space for the Spiritual': A Roundtable on Race, Gender, and Islam in the United States." *Amerasia Journal* 40, no. 1: 17–33.

Chang, Jeff. 2016. *We Gon' Be Alright: Notes on Race and Resegregation.* New York: Picador.

Chatterjee, Piya, and Sunaina Maira, eds. 2014. *The Imperial University: Academic Repression and Scholarly Dissent.* Minneapolis: University of Minnesota Press.

Chen, Nancy N., and Trinh T. Minh-ha. 1992. "'Speaking Nearby:' A Conversation with Trinh T. Minh-ha." *Visual Anthropology Review* 8, no. 1: 82–91.

Cheng, Wendy. 2013. *The Changs Next Door to the Díazes.* Minneapolis: University of Minnesota Press.

Cleary, Thomas, trans. 1993. *Thunder in the Sky: Secrets on the Acquisition and Exercise of Power.* Boston: Shambhala Productions.

Collier-Thomas, Bettye, and V. P. Franklin. 2001. *Sisters in the Struggle: African American Women in the Civil Rights-Black Power Movement.* New York: NYU Press.

Collins, Samuel Gerald, Matthew Durington, and Harjant Gill. 2017. "Multimodality: An Invitation." *American Anthropologist* 119, no. 1: 142–46.

Connolly, William E. 2002. *Neuropolitics: Thinking, Culture, Speed*. Minneapolis: University of Minnesota Press.

Cook, Bradley J., and Fathi H. Malkawi, eds. 2011. *Classical Foundations of Islamic Educational Thought*. Provo, UT: Brigham Young University.

Cooke, Miriam, and Bruce B. Lawrence. 2005. *Muslim Networks from Hajj to Hip Hop*. Islamic Civilization and Muslim Networks. Chapel Hill: University of North Carolina Press.

Cooley, John K. 2002. *Unholy Wars: Afghanistan, America, and International Terrorism*. London: Pluto Press.

Corbett, Rosemary R. 2016. *Making Moderate Islam: Sufism, Service, and the "Ground Zero Mosque" Controversy*. Stanford, CA: Stanford University Press.

Coulthard, Glen Sean. 2014. *Red Skin, White Masks: Rejecting the Colonial Politics of Recognition*. Minneapolis: University of Minnesota Press.

Coulthard, Glen Sean, and Leanne Betasamosake Simpson. 2016. "Grounded Normativity/Place-Based Solidarity." *American Quarterly* 68, no. 2: 249–55.

CTJM. 2021. "The Burge Case." Chicago Torture Justice Memorials. https://chicagotorture.org/reparations/history/.

Curtis, Edward E. 2006. *Black Muslim Religion in the Nation of Islam, 1960–1975*. Chapel Hill: University of North Carolina Press.

Curtis, Edward E. IV. 2002. *Islam in Black America: Identity, Liberation, and Difference in African-American Islamic Thought*. Albany: State University of New York Press.

Curtis, Edward E. IV 2015. "'My Heart Is in Cairo': Malcolm X, the Arab Cold War, and the Making of Islamic Liberation Ethics." *Journal of American History* 102, no. 3: 775–98.

Curtis, Edward E. IV, and Sylvester A. Johnson, eds. 2015. "Special Issue: The Meaning of Malcolm X for Africana Religions: Fifty Years On." *Journal of Africana Religions* 3, no. 1: 1–150.

Dagli, Caner K. 2020. "Muslims Are Not a Race." *Renovatio: The Journal of Zaytuna College*. February 6. https://renovatio.zaytuna.edu/article/muslims-are-not-a-race.

al-Darʿi, Imam Muhammad b. Nasir. 2012. *The Prayer of the Oppressed*. Translated by Hamza Yusuf. Danville, CA: Sandala Press.

Dash, Julie, director. 1991. *Daughters of the Dust*. American Playhouse, Geechee Girls, WMG Film.

Da Silva, Denise Ferreira. 2007. *Toward a Global Idea of Race*. Minneapolis: University of Minnesota Press.

Daud, Wan Mohd Nor Wan. 2009. "Al-Attas' Concept of Taʿdib as True and Comprehensive Education in Islam." *SeekersGuidance* (blog). December 19. https://seekersguidance.org/articles/general-artices/al-attas-concept-of-tadib-as-true-and-comprehensive-education-in-islam-wan-mohd-nor-wan-daud/.

The Daughter of Imam Malik by Sheikh Hamza Yusuf. 2011. http://www.youtube.com/watch?v=pvXlOswmBy4&feature=youtube_gdata_player.

Daulatzai, Sohail. 2012. *Black Star, Crescent Moon: The Muslim International and Black Freedom beyond America*. Minneapolis: University of Minnesota Press.

Daulatzai, Sohail. 2013. "Are We All Muslim Now? Assata Shakur and the Terrordome." *Al Jazeera*. May 9. https://www.aljazeera.com/indepth /opinion/2013/05/20135712155495678.html.

Daulatzai, Sohail, and Junaid Rana, eds. 2018. *With Stones in Our Hands: Writings on Muslims, Racism, and Empire*. Minneapolis: University of Minnesota Press.

Davis, Mike. 2006. *City of Quartz: Excavating the Future in Los Angeles*. London: Verso.

Dawson, Michael C., and Ming Francis. 2016. "Black Politics and the Neoliberal Racial Order." *Public Culture* 28, no. 1 (78): 23–62.

Day, Iyko. 2015. "Being or Nothingness: Indigeneity, Antiblackness, and Settler Colonial Critique." *Critical Ethnic Studies* 1, no. 2: 102–21.

Day, Iyko. 2016. *Alien Capital: Asian Racialization and the Logic of Settler Colonial Capitalism*. Durham, NC: Duke University Press.

Deeb, Lara. 2006. *An Enchanted Modern: Gender and Public Piety in Shi'i Lebanon*. Princeton Studies in Muslim Politics. Princeton, NJ: Princeton University Press.

Deeb, Lara, and Mona Harb. 2013. *Leisurely Islam: Negotiating Geography and Morality in Shi'ite South Beirut*. Princeton, NJ: Princeton University Press.

Deeb, Lara, and Jessica Winegar. 2012. "Anthropologies of Arab-Majority Societies." *Annual Review of Anthropology* 41, no. 1: 537–58.

Deleuze, Gilles. 1986. *Cinema*. 2 vols. Minneapolis: University of Minnesota Press.

Delgado, Jennifer, Bridget Doyle, and Mary Schmich. n.d. "Hadiya's Friends." *Chicago Tribune*. http://graphics.chicagotribune.com/hadiyas-friends/ Accessed on January 4, 2023.

Denny, F. M. 2012. "Umma." In *Encyclopaedia of Islam*. 2nd ed. http:// referenceworks.brillonline.com/entries/encyclopaedia-of-islam-2/umma -COM_1291?s.num=66&s.start=60.

Department of Homeland Security. 2020. "Targeted Violence and Terrorism Prevention Grant Program." February 14. https://www.dhs.gov /tvtpgrants.

Devereaux, Ryan. 2019. "FBI and San Francisco Police Have Been Lying about Scope of Joint Counterterrorism Investigations, Document Suggests." *The Intercept* (blog). November 1. https://theintercept.com/2019/11/01/fbi -joint-terrorism-san-francisco-civil-rights/.

Devji, Faisal, and Zaheer Kazmi, eds. 2017. *Islam after Liberalism*. New York: Oxford University Press.

Dillon, Stephen. 2018. *Fugitive Life: The Queer Politics of the Prison State*. Durham, NC: Duke University Press.

Diouf, Sylviane A. 1998. *Servants of Allah: African Muslims Enslaved in the Americas*. New York: New York University Press.

Diouf, Sylviane A. 2019. "What Islam Gave the Blues." *Renovatio | The Journal of Zaytuna College.* June 17. https://renovatio.zaytuna.edu/article/what-islam-gave-the-blues.

Du Bois, W. E. B. 1990. *The Souls of Black Folk.* New York: Vintage Books/Library of America.

Edwards, Erica R. 2016. "Foreword." In *The Terms of Order: Political Science and the Myth of Leadership.* Chapel Hill: University of North Carolina Press.

Eickelman, Dale F., and James P. Piscatori. 1990. *Muslim Travellers Pilgrimage, Migration, and the Religious Imagination.* Berkeley: University of California Press.

Emmelhainz, Irmgard. 2015. "Conditions of Visuality under the Anthropocene and Images of the Anthropocene to Come." *E-Flux Journal* 63 (March): 13.

Esposito, John L., and Ibrahim Kalin, eds. 2009. *The 500 Most Influential Muslims.* Washington, DC: Georgetown University Press.

Estes, Nick. 2019. *Our History Is the Future: Standing Rock versus the Dakota Access Pipeline, and the Long Tradition of Indigenous Resistance.* London: Verso.

Estes, Nick, and Jaskiran Dhillon. 2019. *Standing with Standing Rock: Voices from the #NoDAPL Movement.* Minneapolis: University of Minnesota Press.

Euben, Roxanne Leslie. 2006. *Journeys to the Other Shore: Muslim and Western Travelers in Search of Knowledge.* Princeton, NJ: Princeton University Press.

Evans, Ubaydullah. 2016. "Discussing Controversy: Hamza Yusuf at RIS Convention-Ustadh Ubaydullah Evans." Lamppost Education Initiative (blog). December 28. https://lamppostedu.org/discussing-controversy-hamza-yusuf-at-ris-convention-ustadh-ubaydullah-evans.

Fadil, Nadia. 2009. "Managing Affects and Sensibilities: The Case of Not-Handshaking and Not-Fasting." *Social Anthropology* 17, no. 4: 439–54.

Fanon, Frantz. [1963] 2004. *The Wretched of the Earth.* Translated by Richard Philcox. New York: Grove.

Fanon, Frantz. [1967] 2008. *Black Skin, White Masks.* London: Pluto Press.

Al Faruqi, Isma'il. 2018. *Isma'il Al Faruqi: Selected Essays.* Herndon, VA: International Institute of Islamic Thought.

FBI. 2008. "FBI Response to Allegations of Mosque Surveillance and Monitoring of the Muslim Community." https://www.fbi.gov/news/pressrel/press-releases/fbi-response-to-allegations-of-mosque-surveillance-and-monitoring-of-the-muslim-community.

Felber, Garrett. 2020. *Those Who Know Don't Say: The Nation of Islam, the Black Freedom Movement, and the Carceral State.* Chapel Hill: University of North Carolina Press.

Ferguson, Roderick A. 2004. *Aberrations in Black: Toward a Queer of Color Critique.* Minneapolis: University of Minnesota Press.

Ferguson, Roderick A. 2012. *The Reorder of Things: The University and Its Pedagogies of Minority Difference.* Minneapolis: University of Minnesota Press.

Fernando, Mayanthi. 2014. *The Republic Unsettled: Muslim French and the Contradictions of Secularism*. Durham, NC: Duke University Press.

Fernando, Mayanthi. 2019. "Critique as Care." *Critical Times* 2, no. 1: 13–22.

Field, Les W., and Alan Leventhal. 2003. "'What Must It Have Been Like!' Critical Considerations of Precontact Ohlone Cosmology as Interpreted through Central California Ethnohistory." *Wičazo Ša Review*, 18, no. 2: 95–126.

Field, Les W., Alan Leventhal, and Rosemary Cambra. 2013. "Mapping Erasure: The Power of Nominative Cartography in the Past and Present of the Muwekma Ohlones of the San Francisco Bay Area." In *Recognition, Sovereignty Struggles, and Indigenous Rights in the United States: A Sourcebook*, edited by Amy E. Den Ouden and Jean M. O'Brien, 287–309. Chapel Hill: University of North Carolina Press.

Fiske, John. 1998. "Surveilling the City: Whiteness, the Black Man and Democratic Totalitarianism." *Theory, Culture and Society* 15, no. 2: 67–88.

Forman, Ruth. 1993. "Poetry Should Ride the Bus." In *We Are the Young Magicians*. Boston: Beacon Press.

Foucault, Michel. 1978. *The History of Sexuality*. New York: Pantheon Books.

Foucault, Michel, and Colin Gordon. 1980. *Power/Knowledge: Selected Interviews and Other Writings, 1972–1977*. New York: Pantheon Books.

Foucault, Michel, and Paul Rabinow. 1997. *Ethics: Subjectivity and Truth*. New York: New Press.

Frahm, Casey. 2020. "Oakland, California Population 2020 (Demographics, Maps, Graphs)." https://laney.edu/college-accreditation/wp-content/uploads/sites/482/Introduction_A-C_Evidence/INT-1_OAK_Pop_Review.pdf.

Fuentes, Carlos. 1992. *The Buried Mirror: Reflections on Spain and the New World*. New York: Houghton Mifflin Company.

Fujino, Diane Carol. 2005. *Heartbeat of Struggle: The Revolutionary Life of Yuri Kochiyama*. Minneapolis: University of Minnesota Press.

Gagne, Karen M. 2007. "On the Obsolescence of the Disciplines: Frantz Fanon and Sylvia Wynter Propose a New Mode of Being Human." *Human Architecture: Journal of the Sociology of Self-Knowledge* 5 (2007): 251–63.

Galvan, Juan, ed. 2017. *Latino Muslims: Our Journeys to Islam*. Scotts Valley, CA: CreateSpace. latinomuslims.net.

Getachew, Adom. 2019. *Worldmaking after Empire: The Rise and Fall of Self-Determination*. Princeton, NJ: Princeton University Press.

Ghanayem, Eman. 2019. "Colonial Loops of Displacement in the United States and Israel: The Case of Rasmea Odeh." *Women's Studies Quarterly* 47, nos. 3–4: 71–91.

GhaneaBassiri, Kambiz. 2010. *A History of Islam in America: From the New World to the New World Order*. New York: Cambridge University Press.

al-Ghazali, Abu Hamid Muhammad. 2004. *Deliverance from Error: Five Key Texts Including His Spiritual Autobiography, al-Munqidh Min al-Dalal*, edited by Ilse Lichtenstadter. Translated by R. J. McCarthy. Louisville, KY: Fons Vitae.

274

al-Ghazali, Abu-Hamid Muhammad. 2010. *The Marvels of the Heart: Science of the Spirit*. Louisville, KY: Fons Vitae.

Gibson, Dawn-Marie, and Jamillah Karim. 2014. *Women of the Nation: Between Black Protest and Sunni Islam*. New York: NYU Press.

Gilmore, Ruth Wilson. 2002. "Race and Globalization." In *Geographies of Global Change: Remapping the World*, 2nd ed., edited by R. J. Johnston, Peter J. Taylor, and Michael J. Watts, 261–74. Malden, MA: Blackwell.

Gilmore, Ruth Wilson. 2007. *Golden Gulag: Prisons, Surplus, Crisis, and Opposition in Globalizing California*. Berkeley: University of California Press.

Gilmore, Ruth Wilson. 2017. "Abolition Geography and the Problem of Innocence." In *Futures of Black Radicalism*, edited by Gaye Theresa Johnson and Alex Lubin, 225–40. Brooklyn, NY: Verso.

Glionna, John M., and Steve Chawkins. 2007. "8 Ex-Radicals Arrested in '71 Police Slaying." *Los Angeles Times*. January 24. https://www.latimes.com /archives/la-xpm-2007-jan-24-me-panthers24-story.html.

Glissant, Édouard. 1996. *Caribbean Discourse*, 2nd ed. Translated by J. Michael Dash. Charlottesville: University Press of Virginia.

Glissant, Édouard. 1997. *Poetics of Relation*. Translated by Betsy Wing. Ann Arbor: University of Michigan Press.

Goeman, Mishuana. 2013. *Mark My Words: Native Women Mapping Our Nations*. Minneapolis: University of Minnesota Press.

Gold, Joel, director. *Nina: A Historical Perspective*. Vimeo video, 22:57. January 21, 2012. https://vimeo.com/35413162.

Göle, Nilüfer. 1996. *The Forbidden Modern: Civilization and Veiling*. Ann Arbor: University of Michigan Press.

Gomez, Michael A. 2005. *Black Crescent: The Experience and Legacy of African Muslims in the Americas*. London: Cambridge University Press.

González, Roberto J. 2020. "Beyond the Human Terrain System: A Brief Critical History (and a Look Ahead)." *Contemporary Social Science* 15, no. 2: 227–40.

Goodstein, Laurie. 2006. "U.S. Muslim Clerics Seek a Modern Middle Ground." *New York Times*. June 18. http://www.nytimes.com/2006/06/18/us /18imams.html.

Gordon, Avery. 2006. "US: Supermax Lockdown." *Le Monde diplomatique*. November 2006. https://mondediplo.com/2006/11/09usprisons.

Gordon, Lewis R. 2002. "A Questioning Body of Laughter and Tears: Reading *Black Skin, White Masks* through the Cat and Mouse of Reason and a Misguided Theodicy." *Parallax* 8, no. 2 (23): 10–29.

Grewal, Inderpal. 2017. *Saving the Security State: Exceptional Citizens in Twenty-First-Century America*. Durham, NC: Duke University Press.

Grewal, Zareena A. 2009. "Marriage in Colour: Race, Religion, and Spouse Selection in Four American Mosques." *Ethnic and Racial Studies* 32, no. 2: 323–45.

Grewal, Zareena A. 2013. *Islam Is a Foreign Country: American Muslims and the Global Crisis of Authority*. New York: New York University Press.

Gualtieri, Sarah M. A. 2009. *Between Arab and White: Race and Ethnicity in the Early Syrian American Diaspora*. Berkeley: University of California Press.

Gumbs, Alexis Pauline, and Julia Roxanne Wallace. 2016. "Something Else to Be: Generations of Black Queer Brilliance and the Mobile Homecoming Experiential Archive." In *No Tea, No Shade: New Writings in Black Queer Studies*, 380–94. Durham, NC: Duke University Press.

Gurel, Perin. 2017. *The Limits of Westernization: A Cultural History of America in Turkey*. New York: Columbia University Press.

Guy, Jasmine. 2004. *Afeni Shakur: Evolution of a Revolutionary*. New York: Atria Books.

al-Haddad, Imam Habib Abdullah. 2011. "Ad-Dawah At-Tammah Wa-Tadzkirah Al-Amamah (The Perfect Summons and a General Admonition)." Pamphlet.

Haddad, Yvonne Yazbeck, Farid Senzai, and Jane I. Smith, eds. 2009. *Educating the Muslims of America*. New York: Oxford University Press.

Hafez, Sherine. 2011. *An Islam of Her Own: Reconsidering Religion and Secularism in Women's Islamic Movements*. New York: NYU Press.

Hallaq, Wael B. 2013. *The Impossible State: Islam, Politics, and Modernity's Moral Predicament*. New York: Columbia University Press.

Hammer, Juliane. 2012. *American Muslim Women, Religious Authority, and Activism: More Than a Prayer*. Austin: University of Texas Press.

al-Hanbali, Ibn Rajab. 2001. *The Heirs of the Prophets*. Translated by Zaid Shakir. Chicago: Starlatch.

Hanson, Hamza Yusuf. 2006. "Tribulation, Patience and Prayer." In *The State We Are In: Identity, Terror and the Law of Jihad*, edited by Aftab Ahmad Malik, 32–40. Bristol: Amal Press.

Hanson, Hamza Yusuf. 2010. "Amid Mosque Dispute, Muslims Can Look to Irish-Catholics for Hope." *The Christian Science Monitor*. September 16. https://www.csmonitor.com/Commentary/Opinion/2010/0916/Amid-mosque-dispute-Muslims-can-look-to-Irish-Catholics-for-hope.

Harney, Stefano, and Fred Moten. 2013. *The Undercommons: Fugitive Planning & Black Study*. Brooklyn, NY: Minor Compositions.

Harris, Anne. 2010. "Race and Refugeity: Ethnocinema as Radical Pedagogy." *Qualitative Inquiry* 16, no. 9: 768–77.

Harrison, Faye V., ed. 1997. *Decolonizing Anthropology: Moving Further toward an Anthropology for Liberation*. Arlington, VA: American Anthropological Association.

Hassan, Shakeela Zia. 2020. *A Starry Crown: Making of a Fez*. Independently published.

Hefner, Robert W., and Muhammad Qasim Zaman. 2007. *Schooling Islam: The Culture and Politics of Modern Muslim Education*. Princeton, NJ: Princeton University Press.

Hermansen, Marcia. 2000. "Hybrid Identity Formations in Muslim America: The Case of American Sufi Movements." *The Muslim World* 90 (Spring): 158–97.

al-Hibri, Azizah. 1997. "My Muslim Ancestor Hagar." *Lilith*. March 31.

Hidayatullah, Aysha A. 2014. *Feminist Edges of the Qur'an*. New York: Oxford University Press.

Hilal, Reem M. 2017. "Marking the American Landscape: African Muslim Slave Writings and the Place of Islam." *Journal of the African Literature Association* 11, no. 2: 135–48.

Hindtrospectives. 2016. "Why I Stand with Standing Rock #NoDAPL." *Hindtrospectives* (blog). September 14. http://www.patheos.com/blogs /hindtrospectives/2016/09/why-i-stand-with-standing-rock-nodapl/.

Hirschkind, Charles. 2006. *The Ethical Soundscape: Cassette Sermons and Islamic Counterpublics*. New York: Columbia University Press.

Hirschkind, Charles. 2012. "Beyond Secular and Religious: An Intellectual Genealogy of Tahrir Square." *American Ethnologist* 39, no. 1: 49–53.

Hirschkind, Charles, and Brian Larkin. 2008. "Introduction: Media and the Political Forms of Religion." *Social Text* 26, no. 3 (96): 1–9.

Ho, Engseng. 2006. *The Graves of Tarim: Genealogy and Mobility across the Indian Ocean*. Berkeley: University of California Press.

Hobson, Emily K. 2016. *Lavender and Red*. Oakland: University of California Press.

Hodgson, Marshall G. S. 1974. *The Classical Age of Islam*. Vol. 1: *The Venture of Islam*. Chicago: University of Chicago Press.

hooks, bell. 2000. *Feminist Theory: From Margin to Center*. Cambridge, MA: South End Press.

Horne, Gerald. 2018. *The Apocalypse of Settler Colonialism: The Roots of Slavery, White Supremacy, and Capitalism in Seventeenth-Century North America and the Caribbean*. New York: Monthly Review Press.

Howell, Sally. 2014. *Old Islam in Detroit: Rediscovering the Muslim American Past*. New York: Oxford University Press.

HumbleBeliever. 2020. "Shaykh Hamza Yusuf on the State of America & the World after Sept. 11 (2001 Interview)." YouTube video. August 6, 2020. 23:25. https://www.youtube.com/watch?v=W6XfkjxldDI.

Husain, Atiya. 2020. "Terror and Abolition." *Boston Review*. June 11. https:// bostonreview.net/race/atiya-husain-terror-and-abolition.

Hussain, Murtaza. 2015. "Killing of Detroit Imam in 2009 Described as 'Nothing Less Than a Cover-Up.'" *The Intercept* (blog). August 9. https:// theintercept.com/2015/08/09/family-detroit-imam-killed-police-files -lawsuit-supreme-court/.

Ibn Hisham, 'Abd al-Malik, Muhammad Ibn Ishaq, and Alfred Guillaume. 2001. *The Life of Muhammad: A Translation of Isḥāq's Sīrat Rasūl Allāh*. New York: Oxford University Press.

Ibn Kathir. 2003. *Tafsir Ibn Kathir*. London: Darussalam.

Ignatiev, Noel. 1995. *How the Irish Became White*. New York: Routledge.

INCITE! 2006. *Color of Violence: The Incite! Anthology*. Cambridge, MA: South End Press.

Iqbal, Muhammad. 2013. *The Reconstruction of Religious Thought in Islam*. Stanford, CA: Stanford University Press.

Islamic Center of San Francisco. 2017. "About Us." https://www.icofsf.org /about-us.

Izutsu, Toshihiko. 2002. *Ethico-Religious Concepts in the Qur'ān*. Montreal: McGill-Queen's University Press.

Jackson, John L., Jr. 2004. "An Ethnographic Filmflam: Giving Gifts, Doing Research, and Videotaping the Native Subject/Object." *American Anthropologist* 106, no. 1: 32–42.

Jackson, Sherman A. 2005. *Islam and the Blackamerican: Looking toward the Third Resurrection*. New York: Oxford University Press.

Jackson, Sherman A. 2009. *Islam and the Problem of Black Suffering*. New York: Oxford University Press.

Jackson, Sherman A. 2011. "Convocation Address." Zaytuna College. September 7.

Jackson, Sherman A. n.d. "The Impact of Liberalism, Secularism and Atheism on the American Mosque." https://www.alimprogram.org/uploads/1/2/5 /5/125574672/the-affects-of-liberalism-secularism-and-atheism-on-the -american-mosque.pdf. Accessed November 14, 2021.

Jackson, Shona. 2014. "Humanity beyond the Regime of Labor: Antiblackness, Indigeneity, and the Legacies of Colonialism in the Caribbean." *Decolonization* (blog). June 6. https://decolonization.wordpress.com/2014/06 /06/humanity-beyond-the-regime-of-labor-antiblackness-indigeneity -and-the-legacies-of-colonialism-in-the-caribbean/.

Jackson, Shona. 2019. "Movement and Time: A Diasporic Response to Grounded Light." *American Quarterly* 71, no. 2: 343–52.

Jacobs, Ron. 2007. "MR Online | A Legacy of Torture: From Cointelpro to the Patriot Act." *MR Online* (blog). January 5. https://mronline.org/2007/01 /05/a-legacy-of-torture-from-cointelpro-to-the-patriot-act/.

Jamal, Amaney A., and Nadine Christine Naber. 2008. *Race and Arab Americans before and after 9/11: From Invisible Citizens to Visible Subjects*. Syracuse, NY: Syracuse University Press.

Jay, Martin, and Sumathi Ramaswamy, eds. 2014. *Empires of Vision: A Reader*. Durham, NC: Duke University Press.

Jobson, Ryan Cecil. 2020. "The Case for Letting Anthropology Burn: Sociocultural Anthropology in 2019." *American Anthropologist* 122, no. 2: 259–71.

Johnson, Sylvester A. 2017. "The FBI and the Moorish Science Temple of America, 1926–1960." In *The FBI and Religion: Faith and National Security before and after 9/11*, edited by Sylvester A. Johnson and Steven Weitzman, 1st ed., 55–66. Oakland: University of California Press.

Johnson, Sylvester A., and Steven Weitzman, eds. 2017. *The FBI and Religion: Faith and National Security before and after 9/11*. Oakland: University of California Press.

Jordan, June. 1977. *Things That I Do in the Dark: Selected Poetry*. New York: Random House.

Jouili, Jeanette S. 2015. *Pious Practice and Secular Constraints: Women in the Islamic Revival in Europe*. Stanford, CA: Stanford University Press.

Judy, Ronald A. T. 2007. "Some Thoughts on Naguib Mahfouz in the Spirit of Secular Criticism." *Boundary 2* 34, no. 2: 21–54.

Junod, Tom. 2010. "Innocent." *Esquire*. February 15. https://www.esquire.com /features/the-state-of-the-american-man/ESQ0706JLINDH_106.

Kaba, Mariame. 2021. *We Do This 'til We Free Us: Abolitionist Organizing and Transforming Justice*. Chicago: Haymarket Books.

Kahf, Mohja. 2016. *Hagar Poems*. Fayetteville: University of Arkansas Press.

Kanaaneh, Rhoda Ann. 2002. *Birthing the Nation: Strategies of Palestinian Women in Israel*. California Series in Public Anthropology 2. Berkeley: University of California Press.

Kapadia, Ronak K. 2019. *Insurgent Aesthetics: Security and the Queer Life of the Forever War*. Durham, NC: Duke University Press.

Karim, Jamillah. 2006. "Through Sunni Women's Eyes: Black Feminism and the Nation of Islam." *Souls* 8, no. 4: 19–30.

Karim, Jamillah Ashira. 2009. *American Muslim Women: Negotiating Race, Class, and Gender within the Ummah*. New York: New York University Press.

Kashani, Maryam. 2014. "Seekers of Sacred Knowledge: Zaytuna College and the Education of American Muslims." PhD diss., University of Texas, Austin.

Kashani, Maryam. 2018a. "Habib in the Hood: Mobilizing History and Prayer towards Anti-Racist Praxis." *Amerasia Journal* 44, no. 1: 61–84.

Kashani, Maryam. 2018b. "The Audience Is Still Present: Invocations of El-Hajj Malik El-Shabazz by Muslims in the United States." In *With Stones in Our Hands: Writings on Muslims, Racism, and Empire*, edited by Sohail Daulatzai and Junaid Rana, 336–53. Minneapolis: University of Minnesota Press.

Kazmi, Zaheer. 2017. "Beyond Liberal Islam." *Aeon*. December 21. https://aeon .co/essays/is-it-time-to-look-beyond-the-idea-of-liberal-islam.

Keeling, Kara. 2003. "'In the Interval': Frantz Fanon and the 'Problems' of Visual Representation." *Qui Parle* 13, no. 2: 91–117.

Keeling, Kara. 2007. *The Witch's Flight: The Cinematic, the Black Femme, and the Image of Common Sense*. Durham, NC: Duke University Press.

Keeling, Kara. 2011. "I = Another: Digital Identity Politics." In *Strange Affinities: The Gender and Sexual Politics of Comparative Racialization*, edited by Grace Kyungwon Hong and Roderick A. Ferguson, 53–75. Durham, NC: Duke University Press.

Kelley, Robin D. G. 2016. "Black Study, Black Struggle." *Boston Review*. March 1. https://www.bostonreview.net/forum/robin-kelley-black-struggle -campus-protest/.

Kelley, Robin D. G. 2021. "Why Black Marxism, Why Now?" *Boston Review*. January 25. https://bostonreview.net/race-philosophy-religion/robin-d-g -kelley-why-black-marxism-why-now.

Khader, Nehad. 2017. "Rasmea Odeh: The Case of an Indomitable Woman." *Journal of Palestine Studies* 46, no. 4: 62–74.

Khalili, Laleh. 2007. *Heroes and Martyrs of Palestine: The Politics of National Commemoration*. Cambridge Middle East Studies 27. Cambridge, UK: Cambridge University Press.

Khan, Aisha. 2004. *Callaloo Nation: Metaphors of Race and Religious Identity among South Asians in Trinidad*. Durham, NC: Duke University Press.

Khan, Naveeda Ahmed. 2012. *Muslim Becoming: Aspiration and Skepticism in Pakistan*. Durham, NC: Duke University Press.

Khwaja, Maira, Marie Mendoza, and Maheen Khan. 2022. "Chicago to Guantá-namo: Connections in an Ecosystem of Violence." Mapbox Storytelling, Invisible Institute. Chicagopolicetorturearchive.com. 2022. https:// invinst.github.io/.

Kieślowski, Krzysztof, and Danusia Stok. 1993. *Kieślowski on Kieślowski*. Boston: Faber and Faber.

Kim, Jodi. 2022. *Settler Garrison: Debt Imperialism, Militarism, and Transpacific Imaginaries*. Durham, NC: Duke University Press.

King, Tiffany Lethabo. 2019. *The Black Shoals: Offshore Formations of Black and Native Studies*. Durham, NC: Duke University Press.

Kishi, Katayoun. 2017. "Assaults against Muslims in U.S. Surpass 2001 Level." *Pew Research Center* (blog). November 15. https://www.pewresearch.org /fact-tank/2017/11/15/assaults-against-muslims-in-u-s-surpass-2001 -level/.

Kitwana, Bakari. 2016. "The 16 Black Panthers Still behind Bars." *Colorlines*. December 31. https://www.colorlines.com/articles/16-black-panthers -still-behind-bars.

Knight, Michael Muhammad. 2009. *Blue-Eyed Devil: A Road Odyssey through Islamic America*. New York: Soft Skull Press.

Knight, Michael Muhammad. 2013. "Michael Muhammad Knight vs. Hamza Yusuf." March 19. https://www.vice.com/en/article/7be3y4/michael -muhammad-knight-vs-hamza-yusuf.

Knight, Nsenga. 2015. *(X) Speaks*. Performance-based social practice project. https://nsengaknight.com/xspeaks/.

Knysh, Alexander. 2001. "The 'Tariqa' on a Landcruiser: The Resurgence of Sufism in Yemen." *The Middle East Journal* 55, no. 3: 399–414.

Kondo, D. K. 1986. "Dissolution and Reconstitution of the Self: Implications for Anthropological Epistemology." *Cultural Anthropology* 1, no. 1: 74–88.

Koshy, Susan, Lisa Marie Cacho, Jodi A. Byrd, and Brian Jordan Jefferson. 2022. *Colonial Racial Capitalism*. Durham, NC: Duke University Press.

Kracauer, Siegfried. 1995. *The Mass Ornament: Weimer Essays*. Cambridge, MA: Harvard University Press.

Kugle, Scott Alan. 2006. *Rebel between Spirit and Law: Ahmad Zarruq, Saint-hood, and Authority in Islam.* Bloomington: Indiana University Press.

Kugle, Scott Alan. 2010. *Homosexuality in Islam: Critical Reflection on Gay, Lesbian, and Transgender Muslims.* Oxford: Oneworld.

Kugle, Scott Alan. 2013. *Living out Islam: Voices of Gay, Lesbian, and Transgender Muslims.* New York: NYU Press.

Kuiper, Matthew J. 2021. *Da'wa.* Edinburgh: Edinburgh University Press.

Kumar, Deepa. 2021. *Islamophobia and the Politics of Empire: Twenty Years after 9/11.* Brooklyn, NY: Verso.

Kundnani, Arun. 2015. *The Muslims Are Coming! Islamophobia, Extremism, and the Domestic War on Terror.* Brooklyn, NY: Verso.

Lane, Edward William, and Stanley Lane-Poole. 1968. *An Arabic-English Lexicon.* 8 vols. Beirut: Librairie du Liban.

Larkin, Brian. 2008a. "Ahmed Deedat and the Form of Islamic Evangelism." *Social Text* 26, no. 3 (96): 101–21.

Larkin, Brian. 2008b. *Signal and Noise: Media, Infrastructure, and Urban Culture in Nigeria.* Durham, NC: Duke University Press.

Lean, Nathan Chapman. 2012. *The Islamophobia Industry: How the Right Manufactures Fear of Muslims.* London: Pluto Press.

Lee, Spike, director". 1992. *Malcolm X.* United States: Warner Bros. 202 minutes.

Leonard, Karen Isaksen. 1992. *Making Ethnic Choices: California's Punjabi Mexican Americans.* Philadelphia: Temple University Press.

Li, Darryl. 2020. *The Universal Enemy: Jihad, Empire, and the Challenge of Solidarity.* Stanford, CA: Stanford University Press.

Lincoln, C. Eric. 1961. *The Black Muslims in America.* Boston: Beacon Press.

Lings, Martin. 1983. *Muhammad: His Life Based on the Earliest Sources.* London: Islamic Texts Society.

LLoveras, Walter Martínez. n.d. "Justice for Alex Nieto." Justice 4 Alex Nieto. http://justice4alexnieto.org/. Accessed February 17, 2020.

Lorde, Audre. 1984. *Sister Outsider: Essays and Speeches.* Trumansburg, NY: Crossing Press.

Lorde, Audre. 1988. "Equal Opportunity." *Feminist Studies* 14, no. 3: 440–42.

Lovejoy, P. E. 1994. "Background to Rebellion: The Origins of Muslim Slaves in Bahia." *Slavery and Abolition* 15, no. 2 (January): 151–80.

Lowe, Lisa. 2015. *The Intimacies of Four Continents.* Durham, NC: Duke University Press.

Liboiron, Max. 2021. *Pollution Is Colonialism.* Durham, NC: Duke University Press.

Lugones, María. 2006. "On Complex Communication." *Hypatia* 21, no. 3: 75–85.

MacDougall, David. 2006. *The Corporeal Image: Film, Ethnography, and the Senses.* Princeton, NJ: Princeton University Press.

MacDougall, E. Ann. 2005. "Living the Legacy of Slavery: Between Discourse and Reality (Les ayants droit de l'esclavage. Entre discours et réalité)" *Cahiers d'Etudes Africaines* 45, nos. 179–80): 957–86.

Madelung, Wilferd. 1997. *The Succession to Muḥammad: A Study of the Early Caliphate.* Cambridge: Cambridge University Press.

Maghbouleh, Neda. 2017. *The Limits of Whiteness: Iranian Americans and the Everyday Politics of Race.* Stanford, CA: Stanford University Press.

Maharawal, Manissa M., and Erin McElroy. 2018. "The Anti-Eviction Mapping Project: Counter Mapping and Oral History toward Bay Area Housing Justice." *Annals of the American Association of Geographers* 108, no. 2: 380–89.

Mahmood, Saba. 2005. *Politics of Piety: The Islamic Revival and the Feminist Subject.* Princeton, NJ: Princeton University Press.

Mahmood, Saba. 2006. "Secularism, Hermeneutics, and Empire: The Politics of Islamic Reformation." *Public Culture* 18, no. 2: 323–47.

Mahmood, Saba. 2016. *Religious Difference in a Secular Age: A Minority Report.* Princeton, NJ: Princeton University Press.

Maira, Sunaina. 2009. *Missing: Youth, Citizenship, and Empire after 9/11.* Durham, NC: Duke University Press.

Maira, Sunaina. 2014. "Surveillance Effects: South Asian, Arab, and Afghan American Youth in the War on Terror." In *At the Limits of Justice: Women of Colour on Terror.* Toronto: University of Toronto Press.

Maira, Sunaina. 2016. *The 9/11 Generation: Youth, Rights, and Solidarity in the War on Terror.* New York: NYU Press.

Makdisi, George. 1981. *The Rise of Colleges: Institutions of Learning in Islam and the West.* Edinburgh: Edinburgh University Press.

Makki, Hind. 2016. "Facebook Post." December 25. https://www.facebook.com/HindMakkiPublic/posts/10101266786197111.

Malcolm, X. [1965] 1990. *Malcolm X Speaks: Selected Speeches and Statements,* edited by George Breitman. New York: Grove Weidenfeld.

Malcolm, X, and Alex Haley. 1965. *The Autobiography of Malcolm X.* New York: Grove Press.

Maldonado-Torres, Nelson. 2013. "On the Coloniality of Being: Contributions to the Development of a Concept." In *Globalization and the Decolonial Option,* edited by Walter D. Mignolo and Arturo Escobar. New York: Routledge.

Maldonado-Torres, Nelson. 2014. "Race, Religion, and Ethics in the Modern/Colonial World." *Journal of Religious Ethics* 42, no. 4: 691–711.

Mamdani, Mahmood. 2001. "Beyond Settler and Native as Political Identities: Overcoming the Political Legacy of Colonialism." *Comparative Studies in Society and History* 43, no. 4: 651–64.

Mamdani, Mahmood. 2004. *Good Muslim, Bad Muslim: America, the Cold War, and the Roots of Terror.* New York: Pantheon Books.

Manzoor-Khan, Suhaiymah. 2019. "This is Not a Humanizing Poem." Postcolonial Banter. Birmingham: Verve Poetry Press.

Marable, Manning. 2011. *Malcolm X: A Life of Reinvention.* New York: Viking.

Marable, Manning, and Hisham Aidi. 2009. *Black Routes to Islam.* New York: Palgrave Macmillan.

Marx, Gary T. 1989. *Undercover: Police Surveillance in America*. Berkeley: University of California Press.

Marx, Karl, and Friedrich Engels. 1978. *The Marx-Engels Reader*. 2nd ed., edited by Robert C. Tucker. New York: W. W. Norton.

Masjidul Waritheen. 2021. "An Nas Program | Masjidul Waritheen." https://www.masjidulwaritheen.org/an-nas-program/.

Massad, Joseph Andoni. 2007. *Desiring Arabs*. Chicago: University of Chicago Press.

Massey, Doreen. 1994. *Space, Place, and Gender*. Minneapolis: University of Minnesota Press.

Mazzetti, Mark, Adam Goldman, and Michael S. Schmidt. 2017. "Behind the Sudden Death of a $1 Billion Secret C.I.A. War in Syria." *New York Times*. August 2. https://www.nytimes.com/2017/08/02/world/middleeast/cia-syria-rebel-arm-train-trump.html.

MBC. 2012. Interview of Syed Muhammad Naquib Al-Attas with Hamza Yusuf. Rihla with Hamza Yusuf. http://www.youtube.com/watch?v=3F600ME7mM8&feature=youtube_gdata_player.

McCloud, Aminah Beverly. 1995. *African American Islam*. New York: Routledge.

McGuire, Danielle L. 2010. *At the Dark End of the Street: Black Women, Rape, and Resistance—A New History of the Civil Rights Movement from Rosa Parks to the Rise of Black Power*. 1st ed. New York: Knopf.

McKinley, Jesse. 2007. "8 Arrested in 1971 Killing of San Francisco Police Officer." *New York Times*. January 24. https://www.nytimes.com/2007/01/24/us/24frisco.html.

McKittrick, Katherine. 2006. *Demonic Grounds: Black Women and the Cartographies of Struggle*. Minneapolis: University of Minnesota Press.

McKittrick, Katherine. 2014. "Mathematics Black Life." *The Black Scholar* 44, no. 2: 16–28.

McKittrick, Katherine. 2017. "Commentary: Worn Out." *Southeastern Geographer* 57, no. 1: 96–100.

McKittrick, Katherine. 2021. *Dear Science and Other Stories*. Durham, NC: Duke University Press.

Mead, Margaret, and James Baldwin. 1971. *A Rap on Race*. Philadelphia: Lippincott.

Melamed, Jodi. 2015. "Racial Capitalism." *Critical Ethnic Studies* 1, no. 1: 76–85.

Memon, Nadeem Ahmed. 2019. *A History of Islamic Schooling in North America: Mapping Growth and Evolution*. Routledge Research in Religion and Education. New York: Routledge.

Menendian, Stephen, and Samir Gambhir. 2019. "Racial Segregation in the San Francisco Bay Area, Part 2." Berkeley, CA: Hass Institute. https://haasinstitute.berkeley.edu/racial-segregation-san-francisco-bay-area-part-2.

Mernissi, Fatima. 1991. *The Veil and the Male Elite: A Feminist's Interpretation of Women's Rights in Islam*. Translated by Mary Jo Lakeland. Cambridge, MA: Perseus Books.

Messick, Brinkley Morris. 1993. *The Calligraphic State: Textual Domination and History in a Muslim Society*. Berkeley: University of California Press.

Mignolo, Walter D. 2009. "Epistemic Disobedience, Independent Thought and Decolonial Freedom." *Theory, Culture and Society* 26, nos. 7–8: 159–81.

Mihirig, Abdurrahman. 2017. "The Myth of Intellectual Decline: A Response to Shaykh Hamza Yusuf." *Maydan* (blog). November 27. https://themaydan.com/2017/11/myth-intellectual-decline-response-shaykh-hamza-yusuf/.

Mir, Shabana. 2016. *Muslim American Women on Campus: Undergraduate Social Life and Identity*. Chapel Hill: University of North Carolina Press.

Mirzoeff, Nicholas. 2017. *The Appearance of Black Lives Matter | NAME*. Ebook. https://namepublications.org/item/2017/the-appearance-of-black-lives-matter/.

Mitchell, Timothy. 1988. *Colonising Egypt*. Berkeley: University of California Press.

Mittermaier, Amira. 2011. *Dreams That Matter: Egyptian Landscapes of the Imagination*. Berkeley: University of California Press.

Mittermaier, Amira. 2019. "The Unknown in the Egyptian Uprising: Towards an Anthropology of al-Ghayb." *Contemporary Islam* 13, no. 1: 17–31.

Moll, Yasmin. 2010. "Islamic Televangelism: Religion, Media and Visuality in Contemporary Egypt." *Arab Media and Society*, no. 10: 1–27.

Morey, Peter, and Amina Yaqin. 2011. *Framing Muslims: Stereotyping and Representation after 9/11*. Cambridge, MA: Harvard University Press.

Morrison, Adam Daniel. 2013. "Religious Legitimacy and the Nation of Islam: In Re Ferguson and Muslim Inmates' Religious Rights in the 1950s and 1960s." MA thesis, University of California, Santa Barbara. http://www.proquest.com/pqdtglobal/docview/1505378392/abstract/A9A6AD6D9BCF42C7PQ/1.

Morton, Jesse, and Mitchell D. Silber. 2018. "When Terrorists Come Home: The Need for Rehabilitating and Reintegrating America's Convicted Jihadists." Counter Extremism Project. https://www.counterextremism.com/sites/default/files/CEP%20Report_When%20Terrorists%20Come%20Home_120618.pdf.

Morton, Jesse, and Mitchell D. Silber. 2019. "Lessons from a Year in the CVE Trenches." *Lawfare*. June 23. https://www.lawfareblog.com/lessons-year-cve-trenches.

Mottahedeh, Roy P. 1985. *The Mantle of the Prophet: Religion and Politics in Iran*. New York: Simon and Schuster.

Moussawi, Ghassan. 2020. *Disruptive Situations: Fractal Orientalism and Queer Strategies in Beirut*. Philadelphia: Temple University Press.

Muhammad, Precious Rasheeda, and Mahasin Abu Aleem. 2014. "Make It Plain: The Truth about the Muslims Called Bilalians." *Muslim History Detective* (blog). March 4. https://www.patheos.com/blogs/preciousmuhammad/2014/03/make-it-plain-the-truth-about-the-muslims-called-bilalians/.

Mukhtar, Curtis R. M. 1994. "Urban Muslims: The Formation of the Dar Ul-Islam Movement." In *Muslim Communities in North America*, 51–74. Albany: State University of New York Press.

Murch, Donna Jean. 2010. *Living for the City: Migration, Education, and the Rise of the Black Panther Party in Oakland, California.* Chapel Hill: University of North Carolina Press.

Muslim Advocates. 2019. "Fulfilling the Promise of Free Exercise for All: Muslim Prisoner Accommodation in State Prisons." Free Exercise Report. Washington, DC: Muslim Advocates. https://muslimadvocates.org/wp-content /uploads/2019/07/Fulfilling-the-Promise-of-Free-Exercise-for-All-Muslim -Prisoner-Accommodation-In-State-Prisons-for-distribution-7_23–1.pdf.

Naber, Nadine. 2012. *Arab America: Gender, Cultural Politics, and Activism.* New York: New York University Press.

Naber, Nadine. 2014. "Imperial Whiteness and the Diasporas of Empire." *American Quarterly* 66, no. 4: 1107–15.

Najmabadi, Afsaneh. 2005. *Women with Mustaches and Men without Beards: Gender and Sexual Anxieties of Iranian Modernity.* Berkeley: University of California Press.

Najmabadi, Afsaneh. 2014. *Professing Selves: Transsexuality and Same-Sex Desire in Contemporary Iran.* Durham, NC: Duke University Press.

Narayan, Kirin. 1993. "How Native Is a 'Native' Anthropologist?" *American Anthropologist,* New Series 95, no. 3 (September): 671–86.

Nasir, M. Bilal. 2022. "Conjuring the Caliphate: Race, Muslim Politics, and the Tribulation of Surveillance." *Political Theology* 23, no. 6: 560–75.

Nasr, Seyyed Hossein. 1981. *Knowledge and the Sacred.* Edinburgh: Edinburgh University Press.

Nasr, Seyyed Hossein. 1993. *The Need for a Sacred Science.* Albany: State University of New York Press.

Nasrabadi, Manijeh, and Afshin Matin-Asgari. 2018. "The Iranian Student Movement and the Making of Global 1968." In *The Routledge Handbook of the Global Sixties: Between Protest and Nation-Building*, 443–56. New York: Routledge.

Nawawi, 1233–1277. 1999. *Commentary on the Riyâd-Us-Sâliheen.* Riyadh: Dārussalām Publishers & Distributors.

an-Nawawi, 1233–1277. 1979. *an-Nawawi's Forty Hadith.* Lahore, Pakistan: Ahbab Publications.

Nelson, Cynthia. 1974. "Public and Private Politics: Women in the Middle Eastern World." *American Ethnologist* 1, no. 3: 551–63.

Nelson, Peter. 2021. "Where Have All the Anthros Gone? The Shift in California Indian Studies from Research 'on' to Research 'with, for, and by' Indigenous Peoples." *American Anthropologist* 123, no. 3: 469–73.

Nguyen, Mimi Thi. 2015. "The Hoodie as Sign, Screen, Expectation, and Force." *Signs: A Journal of Women in Culture and Society* 40, no. 4: 791–816.

Nguyen, Nicole. 2019. *Suspect Communities*. Minneapolis: University of Minnesota Press.

Nichols, Robert. 2018. "Theft Is Property! The Recursive Logic of Dispossession." *Political Theory* 46, no. 1: 3–28.

Nielson, Erik. 2010. "'Can't C Me': Surveillance and Rap Music." *Journal of Black Studies* 40, no. 6: 1254–74.

Njoroge, Njoroge, ed. 2013. "He the One We All Knew." *Biography* 36, no. 3: 485–93.

Nyang, Sulayman S. 1999. *Islam in the United States of America*. Chicago: ABC International Group.

Nyasha, Kiilu. 2007. "Persecuting Panthers: The San Francisco 8 and the Ongoing War against the Black Panther Party." Indybay.Org. www.indybay.org /newsitems/2007/04/21/18403248.php.

Oakland Planning History. 2013. "The Changing Face of Oakland." The Planning History of Oakland, CA. http://oaklandplanninghistory.weebly .com/the-changing-face-of-oakland.html.

Odeh, Rasmea. 2019. "Empowering Arab Immigrant Women in Chicago: The Arab Women's Committee." *Journal of Middle East Women's Studies* 15, no. 1: 117–24.

Okihiro, Gary Y. 2016. *Third World Studies: Theorizing Liberation*. Durham, NC: Duke University Press.

O'Sullivan, Jack. 2001. "'If You Hate the West, Emigrate to a Muslim Country.'" *The Guardian*. October 7. http://www.guardian.co.uk/world/2001/oct /08/religion.uk.

paperson, la. 2017. *A Third University Is Possible*. Minneapolis: University of Minnesota Press.

Peele, Thomas. 2012. *Killing the Messenger: A Story of Radical Faith, Racism's Backlash, and the Assassination of a Journalist*. New York: Crown.

Pellow, David N., and Lisa Sun-Hee Park. 2002. *The Silicon Valley of Dreams: Environmental Injustice, Immigrant Workers, and the High-Tech Global Economy*. New York: New York University Press.

Pennock, Pamela E. 2017. *The Rise of the Arab American Left: Activists, Allies, and Their Fight against Imperialism and Racism, 1960s–1980s*. Chapel Hill: University of North Carolina Press.

Perkins, Alisa. 2021. *Muslim American City: Gender and Religion in Metro Detroit*. New York: NYU Press.

Pickett, Kamilah. 2021, August 13, 2021. Personal communication.

Pickthall, Marmaduke William. 1976. *The Meaning of the Glorious Qur'an*. New York: NYU Press.

Pilkington, Ed, and Tom Silverstone. 2018. "The Black Panthers Still in Prison: After 46 Years, Will They Ever Be Set Free?" *The Guardian*. July 30. https://www.theguardian.com/us-news/2018/jul/30/black-panthers -prison-interviews-african-american-activism.

Poole, Deborah. 2005. "An Excess of Description: Ethnography, Race, and Visual Technologies." *Annual Review of Anthropology* 34, no. 1: 159–79.

Power of a Woman Shaykh Hamza Yusuf. 2011. http://www.youtube.com/watch?v=sUPRQbPnymo&feature=youtube_gdata_player. Accessed September 1, 2013.

Prashad, Vijay. 2007. *The Darker Nations: A People's History of the Third World.* New York: New Press.

Price, David H. 1998. "Cold War Anthropology: Collaborators and Victims of the National Security State." *Identities Global Studies in Culture and Power* 4, nos. 3–4: 389–430.

Puar, Jasbir K. 2007. *Terrorist Assemblages: Homonationalism in Queer Times.* Durham, NC: Duke University Press.

Puar, Jasbir K., and Amit Rai. 2002. "Monster, Terrorist, Fag: The War on Terrorism and the Production of Docile Patriots." *Social Text* 20, no. 3: 117–48.

Pulido, Laura. 2006. *Black, Brown, Yellow, and Left: Radical Activism in Los Angeles.* Oakland: University of California Press.

Pulido, Laura, Laura Barraclough, and Wendy Cheng. 2012. *A People's Guide to Los Angeles.* Berkeley: University of California Press.

Quijano, Aníbal. 1971. *Nationalism & Capitalism in Peru: A Study in Neo-Imperialism.* New York: Monthly Review Press.

Quisay, Walaa, and Thomas Parker. 2019. "On the Theology of Obedience: An Analysis of Shaykh Bin Bayyah and Shaykh Hamza Yusuf's Political Thought." *Maydan* (blog). January 8. https://www.themaydan.com/2019/01/theology-obedience-analysis-shaykh-bin-bayyah-shaykh-hamza-yusufs-political-thought/.

Rabb, Intisar A. 2014. *Doubt in Islamic Law: A History of Legal Maxims, Interpretation, and Islamic Criminal Law.* New York: Cambridge University Press.

Rahemtulla, Shadaab. 2020. "The Qur'an, the Bible, and the Indigenous People of Canaan: An Anti-Colonial Muslim Reading." In *Resistance to Empire and Militarization: Reclaiming the Sacred,* edited by Jude Lal Fernando, 213–32. Sheffield: Equinox Publishing.

Ralph, Laurance. 2020. *The Torture Letters: Reckoning with Police Violence.* Chicago: University of Chicago Press.

Ramirez, Renya K. 2007. *Native Hubs: Culture, Community, and Belonging in Silicon Valley and Beyond.* Durham, NC: Duke University Press.

Ramnath, Maia. 2011. *Haj to Utopia.* Berkeley: University of California Press.

Rana, Junaid. 2011. *Terrifying Muslims: Race and Labor in the South Asian Diaspora.* Durham, NC: Duke University Press.

Rana, Junaid. 2017a. "No Muslims Involved: Letter to Ethnic Studies Comrades." In *Flashpoints for Asian American Studies,* edited by Viet Thanh Nguyen and Cathy Schlund-Vials, 101–14. New York: Fordham University Press.

Rana, Junaid. 2017b. "The Racial Infrastructure of the Terror-Industrial Complex." *Social Text* 34, no. 4 (129): 111–38.

Rana, Junaid. 2018. "'Make a Way Out of No Way': An Interview with Ustadh Ubaydullah Evans on the Islamic Tradition and Social Justice Activism." In *With Stones in Our Hands: Writings on Muslims, Racism, and Empire*, edited by Sohail Daulatzai and Junaid Rana, 354–64. Minneapolis: University of Minnesota Press.

Rana, Junaid. 2020. "Anthropology and the Riddle of White Supremacy." *American Anthropologist* 122, no. 1: 99–111.

Rana, Junaid, Evelyn Alsultany, Lara Deeb, Carol Fadda, Su'ad Abdul Khabeer, Arshad Ali, Sohail Daulatzai, Zareena Grewal, Juliane Hammer, and Nadine Naber. 2020. "Pedagogies of Resistance: Why Anti-Muslim Racism Matters." *Amerasia Journal* 46, no. 1: 57–62.

Ransby, Barbara. 2003. *Ella Baker and the Black Freedom Movement: A Radical Democratic Vision*. Chapel Hill: University of North Carolina Press.

Al Rashid, Sundiata. 2014. "From Bean Pie to Baklava: Islam in the San Francisco Bay Area." Master's thesis, Graduate Theological Union, Berkeley.

Rastegar, Mitra. 2021. *Tolerance and Risk*. Minneapolis: University of Minnesota Press.

Razack, Sherene. 2008. *Casting Out: The Eviction of Muslims from Western Law and Politics*. Toronto: University of Toronto Press.

reelblack. 2020. *Minister Louis Farrakhan on Donahue (1990) #ADOS #InstitutionalizedRacism*. https://www.youtube.com/watch?v=wwbRugNYcVk.

Reese, Ashanté. 2019. "Refusal as Care." *Anthropology News* 60, no. 3: e135–38. https://doi-org.proxy2.library.illinois.edu/10.1111/AN.1181.

Reid, Shaheem. 2010. "KRS-One Recalls Making of Criminal Minded." MTV News. August 27. http://www.mtv.com/news/1646650/krs-one-recalls-making-of-criminal-minded/.

Reis, João José, and A. Brakel. 1993. *Slave Rebellion in Brazil: The Muslim Uprising of 1835 in Bahia*. Baltimore, MD: Johns Hopkins University Press.

Reitman, Janet. 2021. "'I Helped Destroy People.'" *New York Times*. September 1. https://www.nytimes.com/2021/09/01/magazine/fbi-terrorism-terry-albury.html.

Rickford, Russell John. 2016. *We Are an African People: Independent Education, Black Power, and the Radical Imagination*. New York: Oxford University Press.

Riddle, Emily. 2020. "Mâmawiwikowin." *Briarpatch Magazine*. September 10. https://briarpatchmagazine.com/articles/view/mamawiwikowin.

Riguer, Leah Wright. 2017. "Neoliberal Social Justice: From Ed Brooke to Barack Obama." https://items.ssrc.org/reading-racial-conflict/neoliberal-social-justice-from-ed-brooke-to-barack-obama/.

Rizvi, Sayyid Sa'eed Akhtar. 1987. *Slavery from Islamic and Christian Perspectives*. Vancouver: Vancouver Islamic Educational Foundation.

Robinson, Cedric J. 2000. *Black Marxism: The Making of the Black Radical Tradition*. Chapel Hill: University of North Carolina Press.

Rosemont, Franklin. 1975. "Preface." In *Blues and the Poetic Spirit*, by Paul Garon. London: Eddison.

El-Rouayheb, Khaled. 2005. *Before Homosexuality in the Arab-Islamic World, 1500–1800: Khaled El-Rouayheb.* Chicago: University of Chicago Press.

El-Rouayheb, Khaled. 2015. *Islamic Intellectual History in the Seventeenth Century: Scholarly Currents in the Ottoman Empire and the Maghreb.* Cambridge: Cambridge University Press.

Rouse, Carolyn Moxley. 2004. *Engaged Surrender: African American Women and Islam.* Berkeley: University of California Press.

Ruiz, Sandra. 2019. *Ricanness: Enduring Time in Anticolonial Performance.* New York: NYU Press.

Safi, Leenah. 2018. "Preface." In *Towards Sacred Activism*, 19–21. Baltimore, MD: Al-Madina Institute.

Safi, Omid, and Juliane Hammer eds. 2013. *The Cambridge Companion to American Islam.* New York: Cambridge University Press.

Said, Edward W. 1979. *Orientalism.* New York: Vintage Books.

Said, Edward W. 1997. *Covering Islam: How the Media and the Experts Determine How We See the Rest of the World.* Rev. ed. New York: Vintage Books.

Samhan, Helen Hatab. 1999. "Not Quite White: Racial Classification and the Arab American Experience." In *Arabs in America: Building a New Future*, edited by Michael Suleiman. Philadelphia: Temple University Press.

Samra, Jummanah Abu. 2021. "Free Aafia Siddiqui: The Most Wronged Woman in the World—MG." *Muslim Girl.* October 1. https://muslimgirl.com/save-dr-aafia-siddiqui/.

Sapelo Square. 2015. "Black Muslim Politics: A Journey with Food after Embracing Islam." Sapelo Square. October 6. https://sapelosquare.com/2015/10/06/a-journey-with-food-after-embracing-islam/.

Sapelo Square. 2018. "Dr. Shakeela Hassan and the Making of an American Muslim Icon—Sapelo Square." November 14. https://sapelosquare.com/2018/11/14/dr-shakeela-hassan-and-the-making-of-a-american-muslim-icon/.

Saranillio, Dean Itsuji. 2013. "Why Asian Settler Colonialism Matters: A Thought Piece on Critiques, Debates, and Indigenous Difference." *Settler Colonial Studies* 3, nos. 3–4: 280–94.

Sarwar, Ghulam. 1982. *Islam: Beliefs and Teachings.* London: Muslim Educational Trust.

Schielke, Joska Samuli. 2010. "Second Thoughts about the Anthropology of Islam, or How to Make Sense of Grand Schemes in Everyday Life." *ZMO Working Papers* 2: 16.

Schielke, Joska Samuli. 2015. *Egypt in the Future Tense: Hope, Frustration, and Ambivalence before and after 2011.* Bloomington: Indiana University Press.

Schielke, Joska Samuli, and Liza Debevec. 2012. *Ordinary Lives and Grand Schemes: An Anthropology of Everyday Religion.* New York: Berghahn Books.

Schimmel, Annemarie. 1997. *My Soul Is a Woman: The Feminine in Islam*. New York: Continuum.

Schleifer, S. Abdullah, and Omayma El-Ella, eds. 2019. *The Muslim 500: The World's 500 Most Influential Muslims, 2020*. Amman: The Royal Islamic Strategic Studies Centre.

Schrader, Stuart. 2019. *Badges without Borders: How Global Counterinsurgency Transformed American Policing*. Berkeley: University of California Press.

Scott-Heron, Gil. 1971. "The Revolution Will Not Be Televised." Track 1 of *Pieces of a Man*. Flying Dutchman. Album.

Self, Robert O. 2003. *American Babylon: Race and the Struggle for Postwar Oakland*. Princeton, NJ: Princeton University Press.

Shaheen, Jack G. 2001. *Reel Bad Arabs: How Hollywood Vilifies a People*. New York: Olive Branch Press.

Shakir, Zaid. 2006a. "The Passing of Shaykh Mustafa Al Turkmani (May Allah Be Well-Pleased with Him)." *Contemplating Chishti* 2013. September 5. http://alchishti.wordpress.com/2006/10/05/the-passing-of-shaykh -mustafa-al-turkmani-may-allah-be-well-pleased-with-him/.

Shakir, Zaid. 2006b. "Islam: Religion or Ideology?" *New Islamic Directions*. July 26. https://www.newislamicdirections.com/new_nid/article/islam _religion_or_ideology.

Shakir, Zaid. 2007. *The Unfulfilled Legacy*. CD. Sandala.

Shakir, Zaid. 2010. "Rallying of the Muhammadaic Forces." *Emel—The Muslim Lifestyle Magazine* 71. August. http://www.emel.com/article?id=75&a_id =2086.

Shakir, Zaid. 2018. "Foreword." In *Towards Sacred Activism*, 11–17. Baltimore, MD: Al-Madina Institute.

Shange, Savannah. 2019a. "Black Girl Ordinary: Flesh, Carcerality, and the Refusal of Ethnography." *Transforming Anthropology* 27, no. 1: 3–21.

Shange, Savannah. 2019b. *Progressive Dystopia: Abolition, Anthropology, and Race in the New San Francisco*. Durham, NC: Duke University Press.

Shareef, Muhammad. 2015. "The Decisive Solution." Maiurno, Sennar, Sudan: Sankore' Institute of Islamic-African Studies International. http://siiasi .org/wp-content/uploads/2015/06/the_decisive_solution-updated.pdf.

El-Sharif, Farah. 2018. "The Problem of 'Political Sufism.'" *Maydan* (blog). December 15. https://www.themaydan.com/2018/12/problem-political -sufism/.

Sheehi, Stephen. 2011. *Islamophobia: The Ideological Campaign against Muslims*. Atlanta, GA: Clarity Press.

El Shibli, Fatima. 2007. "Islam and the Blues." *Souls* 9, no. 2: 162–70.

Shohat, Ella, and Robert Stam. 1994. *Unthinking Eurocentrism: Multiculturalism and the Media*. New York: Routledge.

Shortell, David. 2019. "'American Taliban' Released from Prison, a Key Case for Questions about Radicals Re-Entering Society." CNN. September 27.

https://www.cnn.com/2019/05/22/politics/john-walker-lindh-american
-taliban/index.html.

Shryock, Andrew. 2010. *Islamophobia/Islamophilia: Beyond the Politics of Enemy and Friend*. Bloomington: Indiana University Press.

Silva, Kumarini. 2016. *Brown Threat*. Minneapolis: University of Minnesota Press.

Simpson, Audra. 2007. "On Ethnographic Refusal: Indigeneity, 'Voice' and Colonial Citizenship." *Junctures: The Journal for Thematic Dialogue*, no. 9 (December): 67–80.

Simpson, Audra. 2014. *Mohawk Interruptus: Political Life across the Borders of Settler States*. Durham, NC: Duke University Press.

Simpson, Leanne Betasamosake. 2017. *As We Have Always Done: Indigenous Freedom through Radical Resistance*. Minneapolis: University of Minnesota Press.

Singh, Nikhil Pal. 2019. *Race and America's Long War*. Oakland: University of California Press.

Singleton, Brent. 2002. "The Ummah Slowly Bled: A Select Bibliography of Enslaved African Muslims in the Americas and the Caribbean." *Journal of Muslim Minority Affairs* 22, no 2: 401–12.

Slahi, Mohamedou Ould. 2017. *The Mauritanian*. Originally published as *Guantánamo Diary* (2015). New York: Little, Brown and Company.

Smith, Huston. 1991. *The World's Religions: Our Great Wisdom Traditions*. New York: HarperCollins.

Smith, Linda Tuhiwai. 2012. *Decolonizing Methodologies: Research and Indigenous Peoples*. London: Zed Books.

Sogorea Te' Land Trust. 2021. "Purpose and Vision." The Sogorea Te' Land Trust. https://sogoreate-landtrust.org/purpose-and-vision/.

Sohi, Seema. 2014. *Echoes of Mutiny: Race, Surveillance, and Indian Anticolonialism in North America*. Oxford: Oxford University Press.

Sojoyner, Damien M. 2013. "Black Radicals Make for Bad Citizens: Undoing the Myth of the School to Prison Pipeline." *Berkeley Review of Education* 4, no 2: 241–63.

Sojoyner, Damien M. 2021. "You Are Going to Get Us Killed: Fugitive Archival Practice and the Carceral State." *American Anthropologist* 123, no 3: 658–70.

Solnit, Rebecca. 2000. *Hollow City: The Siege of San Francisco and the Crisis of American Urbanism*. New York: Verso.

Solnit, Rebecca. 2016. "Death by Gentrification: The Killing That Shamed San Francisco." *The Guardian*. March 21. https://www.theguardian.com/us -news/2016/mar/21/death-by-gentrification-the-killing-that-shamed-san -francisco.

Spillers, Hortense J. 1987. "Mama's Baby, Papa's Maybe: An American Grammar Book." *Diacritics* 17, no. 2: 65–81.

Stacey, Judith. 1988. "Can There Be a Feminist Ethnography?" *Women's Studies International Forum* 11, no. 1: 21–27.

Starrett, Gregory. 1998. *Putting Islam to Work: Education, Politics, and Religious Transformation in Egypt*. Berkeley: University of California Press.

Suhr, Christian. 2015. "The Failed Image and the Possessed: Examples of Invisibility in Visual Anthropology and Islam." *Journal of the Royal Anthropological Institute* 21 (S1): 96–112.

Taitz, Sarah and Shaiba Rather. 2023. "How Officials in Georgia are Suppressing Political Protest as 'Domestic Terrorism.'" American Civil Liberties Union. March 24, 2023. https://www.aclu.org/news/national-security/how-officials-in-georgia-are-suppressing-political-protest-as-dometic-terrorism.

Taleef Night to Remember: Habib Umars Powerful Dua Part 3. 2011. https://www.youtube.com/watch?v=cZiURqV2cVM.

Taylor, Jennifer Maytorena, director. 2009. *New Muslim Cool*. Specific Pictures video. 01:23. https://specificpictures.com/work/new-muslim-cool/.

Taylor, Ula Yvette. 2017. *The Promise of Patriarchy: Women and the Nation of Islam*. Chapel Hill: University of North Carolina Press.

T'lili, Sarra. 2012. *Animals in the Qur'an*. Cambridge: Cambridge University Press.

Tourage, Mahdi. 2013. "Performing Belief and Reviving Islam: Prominent (White Male) Converts in Muslim Revival Conventions." *Performing Islam* 1, no. 2: 207–26.

Trinh, T. Minh-Ha. 1989. *Woman, Native, Other: Writing Postcoloniality and Feminism*. Bloomington: Indiana University Press.

Trinh, T. Minh-Ha. 1991. *When the Moon Waxes Red: Representation, Gender, and Cultural Politics*. New York: Routledge.

Trinh, T. Minh-Ha. 1999. *Cinema Interval*. New York: Routledge.

Tuck, Eve, and K. Wang Yang. 2012. "Decolonization Is Not a Metaphor." *Decolonization: Indigeneity, Education & Society* 1, no. 1: 1–40.

Turner, Richard Brent. 2003. *Islam in the African-American Experience*. Bloomington: Indiana University Press.

Turner, Richard Brent. 2021. *Soundtrack to a Movement: African American Islam, Jazz, and Black Internationalism*. New York: New York University Press.

Turner, Wallace. 1982. "Oldest Pakistani Community in U.S. Draws Zia to Sacramento." *New York Times*. December 12. http://www.nytimes.com/1982/12/12/us/oldest-pakistani-community-in-us-draws-zia-to-sacramento.html.

Valrey, J. R. 2013. "Malcolm's 29th Birthday Commemorated: An Interview wit' Shaykh Hashim Alauddeen." *San Francisco Bay View*. September 20. http://sfbayview.com/2013/09/malcolms-29th-birthday-commemorated-an-interview-wit-shaykh-hashim-alauddeen/.

Varzi, Roxanne. 2006. *Warring Souls: Youth, Media, and Martyrdom in Post-Revolution Iran*. Durham, NC: Duke University Press.

Verdery, Katherine. 2018. *My Life as a Spy: Investigations in a Secret Police File*. Durham, NC: Duke University Press.

Vertov, Dziga, and Annette Michelson. 1984. *Kino-Eye: The Writings of Dziga Vertov*. Berkeley: University of California Press.

Visweswaran, Kamala. 1994. *Fictions of Feminist Ethnography*. Minneapolis: University of Minnesota Press.

Visweswaran, Kamala. 1998. "Race and the Culture of Anthropology." *American Anthropologist* 100, no. 1: 70–83.

Voll, John O. 2004. "Tajdid." In *Encyclopedia of Islam and the Muslim World*, edited by Richard C. Martin, 2:675–76. New York: Macmillan Reference USA. https://link.gale.com/apps/doc/CX3403500483/GVRL?u=uiuc _uc&sid=bookmark-GVRL&xid=59407bfa.

Vries, Hent de, and Samuel Weber. 2001. *Religion and Media*. Stanford, CA: Stanford University Press.

Waajid, Khalid. 2021a. Interview with a Pioneer of the Nation of Islam, Benjamin _Perez. Posted by waajidsvideo. https://www.youtube.com/watch?v =PCGj8fGVIlI.

Waajid, Khalid, 2021b. *An Nas Graduation Celebration 2021*. Posted by waajidsvideo. https://www.youtube.com/watch?v=GA3QwCEsHng.

Wadud, Amina. 1999. *Qur'an and Woman: Rereading the Sacred Text from a Woman's Perspective*. New York: Oxford University Press.

Wadud, Amina. 2006. *Inside the Gender Jihad: Women's Reform in Islam*. Oxford: Oneworld Academic.

Wadud, Amina. 2013. "The 99 Names: Allah Is Not He or She." *Religion Dispatches*. September. http://www.religiondispatches.org/dispatches/guest _bloggers/3269/the_99_names__allah_is_not_he_or_she/.

Walid, Dawud. 2018. *Towards Sacred Activism*. Baltimore, MD: Al-Madina Institute.

Ware, Rudolph T. III. 2014. *The Walking Qur'an: Islamic Education, Embodied Knowledge, and History in West Africa*. Chapel Hill: University of North Carolina Press.

Warner, Val. 2022. "Mother of Hadiya Pendleton Talks on Coping 10 Years after Losing Daughter in Kenwood Park Shooting." *ABC 7 Chicago*. August 12. https://abc7chicago.com/chicago-gun-violence-kenwood-shooting -hadiya-pendleton-park/12119707/.

Warrior, Robert Allen. 2005. "Canaanites, Cowboys, and Indians." *Union Seminary Quarterly Review* 59, nos. 1–2: 1–8.

Watson Institute. 2021. "Human Costs." Costs of War. August. https://watson .brown.edu/costsofwar/costs/human.

Webb, Gary. 1998. *Dark Alliance: The CIA, the Contras, and the Crack Cocaine Explosion*. New York: Seven Stories Press.

Weber, Cynthia. 2013. *"I Am an American": Filming the Fear of Difference*. Chicago: University of Chicago Press.

Weheliye, Alexander G. 2014. *Habeas Viscus: Racializing Assemblages, Biopolitics, and Black Feminist Theories of the Human*. Durham, NC: Duke University Press.

Wehr, Hans. 1979. *A Dictionary of Modern Written Arabic (Arabic-English).*　293
Weisbaden: Otto Harrassowitz Verlag.

Weisenfeld, Judith. 2016. *New World A-Coming: Black Religion and Racial Identity during the Great Migration.* New York: New York University Press.

Winant, Howard. 2001. *The World Is a Ghetto: Race and Democracy since World War II.* New York: Basic Books.

Winston, Ali. 2014. "Oakland City Council Rolls Back the Domain Awareness Center." *East Bay Express.* March 5. https://www.eastbayexpress.com /SevenDays/archives/2014/03/05/oakland-city-council-rolls-back-the-dac.

Wolf, Diane L., ed. 1996. *Feminist Dilemmas in Fieldwork.* Boulder, CO: Westview.

Wong, Julia Carrie. 2016a. "Mario Woods, Black Man Killed by Police, 'Had 20 Gunshot Wounds.'" *The Guardian,* February 12, sec. US news. https:// www.theguardian.com/uk-news/2016/feb/12/mario-woods-autopsy-san -francisco-police-fatal-shooting.

Wong, Julia Carrie. 2016b. "The Life and Death of Luis Góngora: The Police Killing Nobody Noticed." *The Guardian.* August 12. https://www .theguardian.com/society/2016/aug/12/luis-gongora-san-francisco -police-shooting-homelessness.

Wong, Julia Carrie. 2016c. "DoJ Review of San Francisco Police Finds 'Institutional Bias' against Minorities." *The Guardian,* October 12. https://www .theguardian.com/us-news/2016/oct/12/san-francisco-police-justice -department-report-bias.

Woods, Clyde Adrian. 2017. *Development Arrested: The Blues and Plantation Power in the Mississippi Delta.* New York: Verso.

Woodson, Carter Godwin. 1992. *The Mis-Education of the Negro.* Hampton, VA: UB & US Communication Systems.

Wynter, Sylvia. 2003. "Unsettling the Coloniality of Being/Power/Truth/ Freedom: Towards the Human, after Man, Its Overrepresentation—An Argument." *CR: The New Centennial Review* 3, no. 3: 257–337.

Wynter, Sylvia. 2006. "On How We Mistook the Map for the Territory, and Re-Imprisoned Ourselves in Our Unbearable Wrongness of Being, of Désêtre: Black Studies toward the Human Project." In *Not Only the Master's Tools: African-American Studies in Theory and Practice,* edited by Lewis R. Gordon and Jane Anna Gordon, 107–69. Boulder, CO: Paradigm Publishers.

Wynter, Sylvia. n.d. "Black Metamorphosis: New Natives in a New World." https://monoskop.org/images/6/69/Wynter_Sylvia_Black _Metamorphosis_New_Natives_in_a_New_World_1970s.pdf.

Yazzie, Melanie K., and Cutcha Risling Baldy. 2018. "Introduction: Indigenous Peoples and the Politics of Water." *Decolonization: Indigeneity, Education, Society* 7, no. 1, 1–18.

York, Anthony. 2001. "John Walker's Brothers and Sisters." *Salon.* December 21. http://www.salon.com/2001/12/22/converts/.

Yusuf, Hamza. 2001. *America's Tragedy: An Islamic Perspective*. Audio cassette. Alhambra Productions.

Yusuf, Hamza. 2012. "Introduction." In *The Prayer of the Oppressed*, Imam Muhammad b. Nasir al-Darʿi. Translated by Hamza Yusuf, 1–32. Danville, CA: Sandala Press.

Yusuf, Hamza. 2017. "Is the Matter of Metaphysics Immaterial? Yes and No." *Renovatio: The Journal of Zaytuna College*. https://renovatio.zaytuna.edu /article/the-matter-of-metaphysics.

Zaidi, Ali Hassan. 2006. "Muslim Reconstructions of Knowledge and the Re-Enchantment of Modernity." *Theory, Culture and Society* 23, no. 5: 69–91.

Zaidi, Ali Hassan. 2011. *Islam, Modernity, and the Human Sciences*. New York: Palgrave Macmillan.

Zaman, Muhammad Qasim. 2002. *The Ulama in Contemporary Islam: Custodians of Change*. Princeton, NJ: Princeton University Press.

al-Zarnuji, Burhan al-Din, Gustave E. von Grunebaum, and Theodora Mead Abel. 2003. *Instruction of the Student: The Method of Learning*. Chicago: Starlatch Press.

Zaytuna College. 2014. "College Catalog 2014–2015."

Zaytuna College. 2017. "College Catalog Academic Year 2017–2018."

Zaytuna College. 2018. "Permaculture Design Certificate." Zaytuna College. 2018. https://zaytuna.edu/extendedlearning/permaculture-design -certificate. Accessed March 22, 2018.

Zaytuna College. 2020. "In Medina: Building a Just Society." November 1, 2020. YouTube video. 1:12:59. https://www.youtube.com/ watch?v=w6AhFRNlqjg&ab_channel=ZaytunaCollege.

Zaytuna College. 2023. "College Catalog 2022–2023." https://zaytuna.edu /college-catalog-2022-2023.

Žižek, Slavoj. 2001. *The Fright of Real Tears: Krzysztof Kieślowski between Theory and Post-Theory*. London: British Film Institute.

INDEX